REGULATING MARRIAGE MIGRATION INTO THE UK

Law and Migration

Series Editor
Satvinder S. Juss, King's College London, UK

Migration and its subsets of refugee and asylum policy are rising up the policy agenda at national and international level. Current controversies underline the need for rational and informed debate of this widely misrepresented and little understood area.

Law and Migration contributes to this debate by establishing a monograph series to encourage discussion and help to inform policy in this area. The series provides a forum for leading new research principally from the Law and Legal Studies area but also from related social sciences. The series is broad in scope, covering a wide range of subjects and perspectives.

Other titles in this series:

Chinese Immigration Law
Guofu Liu
978-1-4094-0940-3

The Control of People Smuggling and Trafficking in the EU Experiences from the UK and Italy
Matilde Ventrella
978-0-7546-7466-5

Gender and Migration in 21st Century Europe
Edited by Helen Stalford, Samantha Currie and Samantha Velluti
978-0-7546-7450-4

Migration, Work and Citizenship in the Enlarged European Union
Samantha Currie
978-0-7546-7351-4

Refugee Law and Practice in Japan
Osamu Arakaki
978-0-7546-7009-4

Regulating Marriage Migration into the UK

A Stranger in the Home

HELENA WRAY
Middlesex University, London, UK

Routledge
Taylor & Francis Group
LONDON AND NEW YORK

First published 2011 by Ashgate Publishing

2 Park Square, Milton Park, Abingdon, Oxon OX14 4RN
711 Third Avenue, New York, NY 10017, USA

Routledge is an imprint of the Taylor & Francis Group, an informa business

First issued in paperback 2016

British Library Cataloguing in Publication Data
Wray, Helena.
Regulating marriage migration into the UK : a stranger in the home. -- (Law and migration)
1. Emigration and immigration law--Great Britain--History--20th century. 2. Emigration and immigration law--Great Britain--History--21st century. 3. Foreign spouses--Legal status, laws, etc.--Great Britain. 4. Domestic relations--Great Britain--History--20th century. 5. Domestic relations--Great Britain--History--21st century.
I. Title II. Series
342.4'1082'0865-dc22

Library of Congress Cataloging-in-Publication Data
Wray, Helena, 1960-
Regulating marriage migration into the UK : a stranger in the home / by Helena Wray.
p. cm. -- (Law and migration)
Includes bibliographical references and index.
ISBN 978-1-4094-0338-8 (hardback : alk. paper)
1. Emigration and immigration law--England. 2. Intercountry marriage--England.
I. Title.

KD4134.W73 2011
342.4108'2--dc22

2011015948

ISBN 978-1-4094-0338-8 (hbk)
ISBN 978-1-138-25584-5 (pbk)

For Jem, Hannah, Isabel and Louis

Contents

Table of Cases

A (Pakistan) [2004] UKIAT 00034
AB (Bangladesh) [2004] UKIAT 00314
AB (Democratic Republic of Congo) v SSHD [2007] EWCA Civ 1422
AB (Jamaica) v SSHD [2007] EWCA Civ 1302
Abdulaziz, Cabales and Balkandali v United Kingdom, ECtHR, Series A, no. 94
Ahmet v SSHD, 27 June 1972, Imm AR TH/3018/71(24)
AK and others (Long term third party support) Bangladesh [2006] UKIAT 00069
Alexander v Immigration Appeal Tribunal [1982] WLR 1076
AM (Ethiopia) v Entry Clearance Officer [2008] EWCA Civ 1082
AM (Inability to make entry clearance application) Somalia [2004] UKIAT 00276
AM (Third party support not permitted R281(v)) [2007] UKAIT 00058
Amjad Mahmood v ECO Islamabad [2002] UKIAT 01819
Anseereeganoo v SSHD [1981] Imm AR 30
AS (Somalia) v SSHD [2009] UKHL 32
AT v Hoque and Singh [1988] Imm AR 216

B v SSHD [2000] Imm AR 478
Baig v ECO Islamabad [2002] UKIAT 04229
Beoku-Betts v SSHD [2008] UKHL 39
Bibi Barkat, TH/36849/78 (1761)
BK and others v ECO Ankara [2005] UKAIT 00174
Blessing Edore v SSHD [2003] EWCA Civ 736
BS India v SSHD [2002] UKIAT 00660 (check)
Buckland v Buckland [1968] P 296

Carpenter v SSHD [2003] QB 416 C-60/00
CB (Validity of marriage: proxy marriage) Brazil [2008] UKAIT 00080
CH (Jamaica) v SSHD [2007] EWCA Civ 792
Cheema v SSHD [1982] Imm AR 124
Chikwamba v SSHD [2005] EWCA Civ 1779
Chikwamba v SSHD [2008] UKHL 40
Constantinides v SSHD, 21 June 1973, Imm AR 30 TH/3043/72 (160)
Countess de Conway's Case (1834) 2 Knapp 364
CS (Race discrimination: Proper approach) Jamaica [2006] UKAIT 00004

DR Morocco [2005] UKIAT 00038

EB Kosovo v SSHD [2008] UKHL 41

ECO (Dhaka) v AA [2005] UKIAT 00105
ECO, Islamabad v Mohammad Jahangir Hussain [1991] Imm AR 476
EH (Palestinian – entry clearance – proportionality) Iraq [2005] UKIAT 00062
Ex p. Arman Ali v SSHD [1999] EWHC Admin 830

F (Jamaica) [2003] UKIAT 00152
Fasbender v Attorney General [1921] F 1082

GA ('Subsisting' marriage) Ghana [2006] UKAIT 00046
GX v SSHD (Kosovo) [2002] UKIAT 03352

H v H [1953] 2 All ER 1228
Hashim v ECO Karachi [2002] UKIAT 00928
HB and others v SSHD [2006] EWCA Civ 1713
HC (Availability of Entry Clearance Facilities) Iraq [2004] UKIAT 00154
Hector v SSHD [1972] Imm AR 41
Hirani v Hirani (1982) 4 FLR 232
Huang (FC) v SSHD [2007] UKHL 11
Huang and others v SSHD [2005] EWCA Civ 105

IN (Domestic violence – IDI policy) Pakistan [2007] UKAIT 00024
Ishiodu v ECO, Lagos, 29 August 1974 (Imm AR 56)
Ishtiaq v SSHD [2007] EWCA Civ 386

J (Serbia and Montenegro) [2003] UKIAT 00151
J (Uganda) v SSHD [2007] EWCA Civ 802
Jaha v SSHD [205] EWCA Civ 968
JF (Article 8: inconsistency, family members) Angola [2005] UKIAT 00173
JL (Domestic violence: evidence and procedure) India [2006] UKAIT 00058

K (Russia) [2003] UKIAT 00082
KA and others (Adequacy of maintenance) Pakistan [2006] UKAIT 00065
KC v City of Westminster Social and Community Services Department [2008] EWCA Civ 198
Khawaja v SSHD [1983] 2 WLR 321
KJ (Entry clearance proportionality) Iraq CG [2005] UKIAT 00066

LA (Pakistan) v SSHD [2009] UKAIT 00019
LH (Truly exceptional – Ekinci applied) Jamaica [2006] UKIAT 00019
LK (Serbia) v SSHD [2007] EWCA, 3 December
LM (Democratic Republic of Congo) v SSHD [2008] EWCA Civ 325

M (Croatia) [2004] UKIAT 00024
Mahad (Ethiopia) v ECO [2009] UKSC 16

Malik v SSHD [1981] Imm AR 134 (check)
MD (14 years not disproportionate) Bangladesh [2004] UKIAT 00208
Metock v Minister for Justice, Equality and Law Reform [2009] QB 318
MH v SSHD (Pakistan) [2002] UKIAT 04685
MK (Adequacy of maintenance-disabled sponsor) Somalia [2007] UKIAT 00028
MK (Somalia) v Entry Clearance Officer [2008] EWCA Civ 1521
Mohamed Numanul Islam Choudhury v IAT [1990] Imm AR 211
Mohammed Afzal v Visa Officer, Islamabad [1986] Imm AR 474
Mohammed Saftar v SSHD [1995] AR 1
Mohd Meharban v Entry Clearance Officer, Islamabad [1989] Imm AR 57
Mussarat v SSHD, 12 January 1971, Imm AR 45
MW (Liberia) v SSHD [2007] EWCA Civ 1376

N (Kenya) [2003] UKIAT 00102
NA (Customary marriage and divorce – evidence) [2009] UKAIT 00009
NC (Bare talaq – Indian Muslims recognition) Pakistan [2009] UKAIT 00016
NG (Pakistan) v SSHD [2007] EWCA Civ 1543
Noruwa (Proportionality appeal: assessment, not discretion) Nigeria [2001] UKIAT 00016

OA and OA (Intention to co-habit 'intervening devotion') Nigeria [2005] UKIAT 00026

Papadopoulos v SSHD [1974] Imm AR 46
Papayianni v SSHD [1974] Imm AR 1
Pervez Iqbal v Immigration Appeal Tribunal [1988] Imm AR 469
PK (Article 8, Return, Marriage-Refugee) Democratic Republic of Congo [2002] UKIAT 05220
PM (Jamaica) v SSHD [2007] EWCA Civ 937
Puttick v Attorney General [1980] Fam 1

Quila v SSHD [2010] EWCA Civ 1482
Qureshi v Qureshi [1972] Fam 173

R (on the application of B) v SSHD [2002] EWCA Civ 1797
R (on the application of Baiai and another) v SSHD [2006] EWHC 1454 (Admin)
R (on the application of Baiai and others) v SSHD [2006] EWHC 823 (Admin)
R (on the application of Baiai and others) v SSHD [2006] EWHC 1035 (Admin)
R (on the application of Baiai and others) v SSHD [2008] UKHL 53
R (on the application of Bujar Semanaj) v SSHD [2007] EWHC 1704 (Admin)
R (on the application of Ekinci) v SSHD [2003] EWCA Civ 765
R (on the application of Manpreet Kaur) v SSHD [2004 EWCA Civ 818
R (on the application of Olofinusi) v IAT [2002] EWHC 2106
R (on the application of Parven Begum) [2010] EWHC 1897 (Admin)

R (on the application of Surinder Singh) v IAT and SSHD [2003] EWHC 248
R (on the application of Tamil Information Centre) v SSHD [2002] EWHC 2155 (Admin)
R (Serbia and Montenegro) [2003] UKIAT 00187
R (Sri Lanka) [2003] UKIAT 00093
R v Chief Immigration Officer ex p. Gbadegesin [1998] EWHC Admin 408
R v Chief National Insurance Commissioner ex p. Connor [1981] QB 758
R v Home Secretary ex p. Hussain (1972) unreported
R v Home Secretary ex p. Rajput, The Independent, 8 February 1989
R v IAT and Seada Bi and others [1983] Imm AR 82
R v IAT and Surinder Singh ex p. SSHD [1992] ECR I-4265, Case C-370/90
R v IAT ex p. Aftab Hussain [1992] Imm AR 212
R v IAT ex p. Arun Kumar [1986] Imm AR 446
R v IAT ex p. Aurangzeb Khan [1989] Imm AR 524
R v IAT ex p. Bashir (DC), 15 March 1988
R v IAT ex p. Girishkumar Somabhai Patel [1990] Imm AR 153
R v IAT ex p. Iram Iqbal [1993] Imm AR 270
R v IAT ex p. Jarnail Singh Sandal [1981] Imm AR 95
R v IAT ex p. Kandiya and Khan [1990] Imm AR 377
R v IAT ex p. Khan [1983] Imm AR 32
R v IAT ex p. Kotecha [1982] Imm AR 88
R v IAT ex p. Kulbander Kaur [1991] Imm AR 107
R v IAT ex p. Manjula Jethva [1990] Imm AR 450
R v IAT ex p. Matwinder Singh, The Times, 15 April 1987
R v IAT ex p. Mohammed Khatab [1989] Imm AR 313
R v IAT ex p. Naushad Amad Kandiya [1989] Imm AR 491
R v IAT ex p. Rafika Bibi [1989] Imm AR 1
R v IAT ex p. Shameem Wali [1989] Imm AR 86
R v IAT ex p. Shivprasad Bhagwandas Gondalia [1991] Imm AR 519
R v IAT ex p. Sukhivan Singh [1988] Imm AR 527
R v IAT ex p. Syed Akhtar Hussain [1989] Imm AR 382
R v IAT ex p. Vinod Bhatia [1985] Imm AR 39 (Queen's Bench Division of the High Court)
R v IAT ex p. Vinod Bhatia [1985] Imm AR 50 (Court of Appeal)
R v Immigration Officer at Prague Airport ex p. ERRC [2004] UKHL 55
R v *Ministry of Defence ex p. Smith* [1996] 1 All ER 257
R v Secretary of State ex p. Brind [1991] 1 AC 696
R v Secretary of State for the Home Office ex p. Puttick [1981] 1 QB 767
R v SSHD ex p. Ahmed and Patel [1998] EWHC Admin 453
R v SSHD ex p. Daly [2001] UKHL 26
R v SSHD ex p. Gangadeen and another [1997] EWCA 2799
R v SSHD ex p. Ghulam Fatima [1985] QB 190
R v SSHD ex p. Ghulam Fatima [1986] AC 527
R v SSHD ex p. Isiko [2000] EWCA Civ 346

R v SSHD ex p. Jagdishchandra Jinabhai Prajapati [1990] Imm AR 513
R v SSHD ex p. Khaira [1998] EWHC Admin 355
R v SSHD ex p. Mahmood [2000] EWCA Civ 315
R v SSHD ex p. Otusi [1997] EWHC Admin 1165
R v SSHD ex p. Phansopkar [1975] 3 All ER 497
R v SSHD ex p. Singh [1997] EWHC Admin 59
R(A) v SSHD [2007] EWCA Civ 655
R(S) v SSHD [2007] EWHC 51 (Admin)
Radwan v Radwan (No. 2) [1973] Fam 35
Raja Zafar Zia v SSHD [1993] Imm AR 405
Rewal Raj v Entry Clearance Officer, New Delhi [1985] Imm AR 151
RH (Para 289A/HC395 – no discretion) Bangladesh [2006] UKAIT 00043
Rokeya and Rably Begum v Entry Clearance Officer, Dhaka [1983] Imm AR 631
RS (Spouse's pending claim: removal bar?) Sri Lanka [2004] UKIAT 00195

S (India) [2003] UKIAT 00162
SA (Entry clearance in Jordan – proportionality) Iraq CG [2006] UKAIT 00011
Sadhu Singh v SSHD, 19 March 1973, Imm AR 67 TH/581/72(126)
Samaroo and another v SSHD [2001] EWCA Civ 1139.
SB v Entry Clearance Officer, Islamabad [2002] UKIAT 06623
Scott and Sebright (1886) 12 PD 21, 56 LJP 11
Shala v SSHD [2003] EWCA Civ 233
Silver v Silver [1955] 1 WLR 728
Singh v Singh [1971] P 226
SK (India) [2006] UKAIT 00067
SM (Entry clearance application in Jordan, proportionality) Iraq CG [2007] UKAIT 00077
SM and others (Entry clearance, proportionality) Afghanistan GC [2007] UKAIT 00010
SS (ILR, Article 8 return) Sri Lanka [2004] UKIAT 00126
SSHD v Abbas [2005] EWCA Civ 992
SSHD v Akaeke [2005] EWCA Civ 947
SSHD v Akrich [2004] QB 756
SSHD v Baiai and others [2007] EWCA Civ 478
Strbac v SSHD [2005] EWCA Civ 848
Subhash v SSHD [1979-1980] Imm AR 9
Sumeina Masood v IAT [1992] Imm AR 69
Szechter v Szechter [1971] P 286

TM (views of ECO – weight attached) Pakistan [2005] UKAIT 00044

Udny v Udny (1869) LRI Sc & Dir 441

V (Democratic Republic of Congo) [2003] UKIAT 00131

Vervaeke v Smith [1983] AC 145
VW and MO (Article 8 – insurmountable obstacles) Uganda [2008] UKAIT 00021

Yunying Jia v Migrationsverket, Case C-1/05

Zahra v Visa Officer, Islamabad [1979-1980] Imm AR 48
ZB and HB (Validity and recognition of marriage) [2009] UKAIT 00040

Acknowledgements

Many people helped me do the work that became this book. My thanks go to them all including Mahmud Quayum of Camden Community Law Centre whose anger at the injustice of the primary purpose rule first made me think about marriage migration; Professor Werner Menski of the School of Oriental and African Studies, University of London for guidance and encouragement throughout; Middlesex University who gave me time and financial support; Mandy Ivemy and other visa staff who made the field visit possible; and Judy Vaknin, Middlesex University archivist, who helped me locate invaluable historical resources. Finally, loving thanks to my husband, Jem, whose humour and kindness has been remarkable except to those who know him.

Chapter 1
Introduction: The 'Problem' of Marriage Migration

This book is concerned with the regulation of marriage migration by the British state from 1962 until 2010.[1] It analyses decisions made by three institutions: the legislature, the judiciary and the entry clearance service (later the visa service). It identifies the assumptions and beliefs upon which decisions were predicated and which, it is argued, combined to create an informal and unarticulated hierarchy of acceptable marriages for the purposes of regulation. This volume finds that these assumptions and beliefs were, in the main, consistently held across all three institutions for much of the period between 1962 and 1997. After 1997, decisions showed more fluidity and ambivalence.

Marriage migration invokes numerous anxieties, strategies and ambitions and has been seen as problematic and controversial in the UK as elsewhere in Europe.[2] From a government perspective, marriage migration (and family migration in general) permits the entry of migrants who would not otherwise be admitted and may even be primary targets for refusal. It directly engages the interests of UK residents in ways that may conflict with broader political priorities. Such conflicts are not unusual, but the critical factor here is that intimate and defining relationships are pitched against macro policy decisions. The outcome is that, faced with undesired marriage migration, governments must make a stark choice: to accept the unwanted stranger or to reject the UK-resident spouse, making him or her into a stranger unable to enjoy his or her most intimate relationship in their own home. Regulating marriage migration therefore involves weighing up the claims of the UK resident and the desirability or otherwise of the migrant. The result is that marriage migrants are implicitly ranked hierarchically, with their status decided according to a range of fluctuating characteristics. Charting these fluctuations over time is a major theme of this book and provides insight into

---

1 The analysis ends with the change of government following the May 2010 General Election. The term 'marriage migration', as used here, means migration where the UK-based partner is a national or long-term resident and includes cohabiting couples and civil partners where the relationship is the basis of the entry rights. It does not include, except incidentally, partners who accompany or join migrants entering on work or other visas.

2 For a discussion of the position in some other European countries, see De Hart 2006, Digruber and Messinger 2006, Foblets and Vanheule 2006, Roggeband and Verloo 2007, Van Walsum 2008, Block 2010, Bonjour 2010 and Schmidt 2011.

the changing ways in which difference was conceptualised and how some UK residents might more easily be designated as 'outsiders'.

Who is a Marriage Migrant?

In 1962, when the main part of this book begins, those applying to enter were usually seeking family reunification, to bring together families that had already been established. They were typically the spouses of recent immigrants from New Commonwealth countries. As labour migration diminished and the families of migrants matured, there was a switch to family formation, the creation of a new family unit. Applicants were more often men and women engaged or married to those who had travelled to the UK as children or who had been born there. The overwhelming focus was on applicants from the Indian sub-continent entering arranged marriages, although other nationalities, including those from the Caribbean, also featured.

In the post-1997 period, immigration to the UK increased and diversified. Marriage migration to the UK remained an important source of migrants, reflecting the position of family migration as the dominant mode of legal entry into Europe (Kofman 2004: 243). However, it declined proportionately as a source of long-term entry over the period, presumably due to increases elsewhere (see Charsley 2011). It increased numerically until 2006, after which it declined sharply. Between 1999 and 2002, it hovered around 30,000 per year, climbing to just 47,500 in 2006, before falling back to just over 31,000 in 2009.[3]

Some change in the composition of marriage migrants is observable. In 1999, 38.45 per cent of all marriage-related visas were issued on the Indian sub-continent. In 2004, it was still 38.41 per cent, but by 2009, it had fallen to 32.31 per cent. Other regions showed little change. For example, the figures for the Americas in the same years were 14.20 per cent in 1999, 11.04 per cent in 2004 and 13.64 per cent in 2009. However, there was a large increase in the proportion of migrants entering from the rest of Asia and the Middle East (14.07 per cent in 1999, 19.42 per cent in 2004 and 24.78 per cent in 2009) and, to a lesser extent, Africa (13.79 per cent in 1999, 15.04 per cent in 2004 and 17.85 per cent in 2009).[4] The Indian sub-continent has declined, relatively speaking, as a source of marriage migration, although it remains the single largest group.

---

3 Calculations drawn from Home Office 2004: Table 1.6 and 2010a: 62. However, Home Office 2010a: 54 shows higher global totals, although with the same pattern of decline.

4 Percentages rounded to two decimal places and calculated by the author using statistics in Home Office 2004: Table 1.6 and 2010a: 62. Calculations for 2004 and 2009 include civil and unmarried partners, which were not counted in 1999. These accounted for 0.25 per cent of visa issues in 2004 and 8.19 per cent in 2009.

These figures are only a very approximate guide. They cannot capture many important permutations, for example, changes in the composition and numbers of migrants already in the UK who remain after marriage. The immigration statistics (Home Office 2010a: 87-9) suggest that significant numbers of marriage migrants who achieve settlement did not enter in that capacity. In 2008, for example, 57,390 spouses obtained settlement, although only 41,330 of these had entered on the basis of marriage to a British national or resident. A significant proportion of those settling therefore entered as spouses of workers or students and gained settlement with their spouse or in an unrelated capacity and switched. Other spouses will have entered outside the main immigration system, for example, as the family member of a European Economic Area (EEA) national or through human rights or refugee claims. EEA family members (including spouses but also children and other relatives) in particular became an important source of non-European migrants. In 2002/3, 20,000 family permits were issued by entry clearance posts (excluding those issued within the UK). By 2004/5, this had increased to nearly 25,000.[5] The 2009 immigration statistics (Home Office 2010b: Table 4b) show that 25,015 non-EEA nationals were recognised as having the right to reside in the UK in 2009. In 2007, 22,730 family permits were issued, falling to just under 19,000 by 2009 (Home Office 2010a: 54). Not all entrants will have been spouses, but the number is likely to be a significant proportion. The distribution of these EEA family members is quite different from those entering under domestic law, perhaps reflecting migratory patterns elsewhere in Europe. The largest single national group, comprising more than 4,000 entrants, was from Brazil. While India, Pakistan and Bangladesh had 3,880 issues between them, 15.51 per cent of the total number, this was a smaller proportion than under national law, although it was still significant.

Thus, while a complete picture is not available, it seems that South Asia remained an important source of marriage migrants. The persistence of South Asian marriage migration, which is reflected in the continuing academic interest in that area (for example, Charsley 2006, Ballard 2008 and Shah 2011), may explain why, while attention partially switched post-1997 to short-term entrants and irregular migrants who marry in the UK, towards the end of the period discussed in this book there was a renewed focus on cultural practice and international South Asian arranged marriages. However, there are significant numbers of marriage migrants who are not easily detected through a focus on those who enter because of their relationship with a British resident or national and who are arguably under-researched. The Philippines, for example, are now the third largest national group obtaining marriage-related settlement, behind only India and Pakistan (Charsley 2011). Much of this is male, suggesting a link with the recruitment of female Philippine nurses and domestic labour. Marriage migration from developed countries and which is mainly white has always existed but is rarely discussed, let alone problematised. South Africans (believed to be mainly white) were the fifth

5 Dr Kim Howells MP, HC Hansard, 31 January 2006, col. 355W.

largest and US citizens the seventh largest group of nationals acquiring settlement through marriage (Charsley 2011).

In the main, marriage migrants appear to be female. In 1999, 66.54 per cent, in 2004, 66.82 per cent and, in 2009, 68.01 per cent of those granted entry for marriage were women, so this trend does not appear to be changing.[6] Detailed breakdown is available only pre-2003 in South Asia, but these show that fewer men applied and more men proportionately were refused (Home Office 2003: 42). These gender ratios may not reflect the entire picture, as the observation above about the Philippines suggests. While the global figures suggest that female marriage migrants from the Indian sub-continent still outnumber males by a significant margin, Charsley (2011), looking at the wider category of marriage-related settlement, found a much more evenly balanced gender distribution from the region. It seems likely that more men than women entered through non-marriage routes and then gained leave to remain or entered as the spouses of workers or students (see Chapters 7 and 8 for a discussion of attempts to control switching).

Marriage migrants are well represented among those who settle long term in the UK. While they only represented 12 per cent of non-visit visas granted in 2004, 34 per cent of those who achieved settlement in 2009 had entered as family members.[7] However, a substantial proportion of marriage migrants either leave the UK or remain without leave. Of family migrants who entered in 2004, only 55 per cent had achieved settlement after five years, while 63 per cent were still lawfully present (Achato, Eaton and Jones 2010: 5-6).

It therefore seems that there is not much known about marriage migrants and that headline figures and common conceptions may be misleading. Very poor migrants and sponsors are likely to be under-represented as they will be unable to meet economic criteria, although some may enter through the spouse reunification provisions for refugees or, more rarely, through an Article 8 claim. Similarly, those originating from regions where record keeping is poor may find it difficult to meet the necessary formalities (see Chapters 5 and 9). Some bias towards the more prosperous and educated may therefore be expected.

Marriage Migrants and the Law

The analyses employed in this book focus on that part of UK immigration law which, from 1962 until 2010, controlled the admission of the spouses of British

6 Percentages calculated by author from Home Office 2004: Table 1.6 and 2010a: 62. Figures for 2004 and 2009 do not include civil and unmarried partners, even though they were counted, as these were not differentiated by gender.

7 The term 'family migrant' may also include children and dependent relatives, but it seems that only spouses, civil partners, same-sex partners, civil partners, unmarried partners and fiancé(e)s were included in this category (Achato, Eaton and Jones 2010: 3).

nationals or permanent UK residents. In these cases, the entering spouse usually becomes a permanent resident and it is this feature that has particularly provoked anxiety and stringent regulation.

Marriage migration has often been seen as problematic and different means have been used to control it. Those specific to marriage are analysed in detail in later chapters. Others, such as financial criteria, which apply to many types of immigrant, are considered only so far as they specifically affect marriage migration. Common reasons for refusal have evolved alongside the circumstances of applicants. The absence of formal documentation rationalised the rejection of many claims for reunification of families originating from the Indian sub-continent. The primary purpose rule (see Sachdeva 1993 and Chapters 4 and 5 for a full account) was used mainly against male applicants seeking to join the daughters of first-generation immigrants. Following abolition of that rule in 1997, there were fewer refusals, although some applicants were denied entry on the grounds that the parties did not intend to live together or could not establish a valid marriage. After 2003, and before being severely frustrated by the courts, the requirement to leave the UK and obtain entry clearance became a major way to control short-term and irregular migrants who relied on marriage to found a claim to remain (see Chapters 7 and 8). Most recently, measures aimed at preventing forced marriages have reduced some forms of culturally unacceptable immigration (see Chapter 7). These methods of control have been enabled, executed and supported or, more rarely, challenged by the institutions examined here: Parliament, the judiciary and the entry clearance or visa service.

Modern regulation of immigration is to be found primarily in the Immigration Rules made by the Home Secretary under s. 3(2) Immigration Act 1971. Prior to this Act, entry was regulated either under the Aliens Restrictions Acts 1914 and 1919 (and prior to that the Aliens Act 1905) or under the Commonwealth Immigrants Acts 1962 and 1968. These statutes were supplemented by Aliens Act Orders or instructions to officials. The characteristics of the regime prior to the 1971 Act are discussed in Chapter 2.

Revisions to the Immigration Rules are laid before Parliament and become law unless they are subject to negative resolution of either Chamber, a very rare occurrence. The current provisions affecting marriage are found in Part 8 (paras 277-95) of the current Immigration Rules (HC 395). These regulate the admission (or extension of leave) of spouses and civil partners (who are now treated identically), unmarried partners and fiancé(e)s. There are a number of requirements that applicants must meet, including the following:

1. The UK sponsor must be present and settled in the UK or admitted for settlement on the same occasion (para. 281).[8] Non-national residents have, since 1985, been treated identically to British nationals.

---

8 Under HC 395, para. 6, 'settled' means (i) free from restrictions as to the period in which the person may remain and (ii) ordinarily resident in the UK, without having entered

2. In marriage applications, the applicant must be 'married to' or the 'civil partner' of the sponsor (para. 281(i)(a)). For those educated in European bureaucratic norms, proving this through the presentation of a marriage certificate is usually relatively straightforward. However, those who marry using non-formal or customary ceremonies, which are common in many regions, must use evidence of a different kind and may find that the validity of the marriage is not accepted. These issues are discussed further in Chapters 5 and 9.
3. Since 1988, only one spouse to a polygamous marriage has been permitted to enter (para. 278). An application will be refused if the other spouse has ever been in the UK, has a certificate of entitlement to the right of abode or has entry clearance as a spouse. The Rules do not specify that the previous entry must have been as a spouse, although the Immigration Directorate Instructions state that presence as a visitor, illegal entrant or on temporary admission does not count for these purposes.[9]
4. Applicants for entry must obtain entry clearance before arrival under paras 281, 290 and 295. Entry clearance for Commonwealth nationals seeking admission as family members effectively became compulsory in 1979 and its effects are examined in Chapters 5 and 9. Those seeking leave to remain in the UK without entry clearance for marriage must now have been given prior leave to enter as a fiancé(e) or for a period of more than six months. The prohibition on 'switching' is a recent development that is discussed in Chapters 7 and 8.
5. The parties must have met (para. 281), excluding those who marry by proxy and have not met subsequently. This requirement also applies to fiancé(e)s (para. 290) and this has proved problematic in some arranged marriages. The judicial interpretation of the requirement is discussed in Chapter 4.
6. The marriage must be subsisting and the parties intend to live together (after marriage, in the case of fiancés): paras 281, 290 and 295A. Following the abolition of the primary purpose rule in 1997, this rule, along with the probationary period of two years before indefinite leave is granted, is now the primary means of testing that a marriage is genuine. From 1983 until 1997, parties also had to establish that it was not the primary purpose of the marriage to obtain admission to the UK.[10] The primary purpose rule was the principal means of preventing non-white, particularly male, marriage immigration and is discussed at length in Chapters 2, 3 and 4. The role played by the 'intention to live together' is discussed mainly in Chapter 4.

---

or remained in breach of the immigration laws or, if so, having subsequently been given leave to remain.

9 Annex C, para. 6.1.

10 The final version of the rule was in HC 251, paras 47 and 50.

7. There will be adequate accommodation for the parties and any dependants without recourse to public funds in accommodation which they own or occupy exclusively and the parties will be able to maintain themselves and any dependants adequately without recourse to public funds (paras 281, 290 and 295A). 'Maintenance and accommodation' requirements apply throughout the Immigration Rules. A specific issue, discussed in Chapter 8, is government attempts to restrict third-party assistance to couples (and families), undermining traditions of extended family support. A more general point is that, while a policy of protecting the public purse may be relatively uncontroversial, the requirements have the effect of excluding some of the poorest UK residents from participation in international family reunion or formation.
8. Both parties must be aged at least 21 at the time of their arrival in the UK or of their grant or variation of leave (para. 277), with an exception for spouses of members of the armed forces. The minimum age has been raised progressively in the recent period and contrasts with a minimum age for marriage in the UK of 16 (with parental consent). Questions about the minimum age of marriage, forced marriage and the acceptability of very young marriages are considered later in this chapter and also in Chapters 6 and 7.

In recent years, in addition to the Immigration Rules, immigration has been increasingly controlled by frequently changing statutes. Statutory measures relevant to marriage applications include s. 24 Immigration and Asylum Act 1999 and ss. 19-25 Asylum and Immigration (Treatment of Claimants, etc.) Act 2004. These govern the conduct of marriages involving non-EEA nationals and are discussed in Chapters 7 and 8.

The International Legal Context

The UK operates within the framework of international law, although individuals may rely on this only as provided for under UK domestic law and, in determining individual claims, most international legal conventions function only as a support for claims made under domestic law and as an aid to interpretation. The exceptions are EU law and the main provisions of the ECHR.[11]

International law recognises the right to marry and found a family.[12] There is also a prohibition on arbitrary interference with, and a right to respect for, family

---

11 EU law, formerly called European Community law, is part of the UK legal system by virtue of the European Communities Act 1972. The ECHR refers to the European Convention for the Protection of Human Rights and Fundamental Freedoms.

12 For example, the Universal Declaration of Human Rights (UDHR), Article 16(1); ECHR, Article 12; the International Covenant on Civil and Political Rights (ICCPR),

life and a right for children to live with their parents.[13] There may be a right to family reunification across borders, but not in all cases. Such a right is specifically granted to children (see Article 10 UN Convention on the Rights of the Child and the discussion in Jastram 2003: 186-7), but it is more inchoate when married couples are involved. However, some protection from expulsion and, more rarely, a right to admission is implied by the terms of several international instruments (see Jastram 2003: 191-7). In practice, almost all states make provision for family reunification and formation, although these are often subject to conditions and limitations.

For UK nationals, residents and their spouses, both EU law and the ECHR provide enforceable rights that may sometimes reinterpret or supersede domestic law. Since the implementation of the European Communities Act 1972 and the UK's entry into what was then the EEC on 1 January 1973, EU law has been a consistently challenging backdrop to the domestic regime, providing a contrast to and often an implicit criticism of more restrictive domestic laws, as well as a practical solution for some caught by its limitations. EU law, which aims to remove obstacles from the exercise by EEA nationals of free movement rights, has consistently provided more liberally for family reunion than domestic law. Many British nationals, frustrated in their efforts to have a non-EEA spouse live with them under the domestic regime, have used EU provisions, which are available to British nationals who work or otherwise exercise relevant free movement rights in another member state.[14] In recent years, there has also been growing concern about non-British EEA nationals who move to the UK, marry third-country nationals and secure their entry, an issue discussed further in Chapter 7. Significant measures, such as concessions introduced to the primary purpose rule in 1992 (see Chapter 3) or the introduction of the certificates of approval scheme in 2005 (Chapter 7), were arguably driven by the presence of alternative routes of entry under EU law.

While the UK ratified the ECHR in 1951 and provided a right of direct petition in 1966, it is only since implementation of the Human Rights Act 1998 that rights under the ECHR have had a significant impact on the daily adjudication of immigration control. The Human Rights Act does not permit primary legislation to be displaced where it is incompatible with the ECHR, but there is a strong interpretive duty, and secondary legislation and administrative practices must be compliant with Convention rights, as defined in the Act.[15] Article 8, the right to respect for family and private life, has been particularly important in recent domestic case law on marriage migration (see Chapter 8). Here the discussion

Article 17(2).

13 UDHR, Article 12; ECHR, Article 8; ICCPR, Article 17; UN Convention on the Rights of the Child (CRC), Articles 9, 10 and 16.

14 Case C-370/90, *R v IAT and Surinder Singh ex p. SSHD* [1992] ECR I-4265; Case C-60/00, *Carpenter v SSHD* [2003] QB 416.

15 Convention rights are Articles 2-12 and 14 of the Convention, Articles 1-3 of the First Protocol and Article 1 of the Thirteenth Protocol (s. 1).

will focus on the application of human rights principles by the UK courts and the reader is referred to other texts for a detailed consideration of the Convention itself or of the Human Rights Act. In brief, however, while Article 8 ECHR requires respect for existing family life, which includes the life of married couples, this does not necessarily require admission or even non-expulsion of a non-national spouse if family life can be enjoyed elsewhere, a point pursued further in Chapter 8. Nonetheless, despite its limitations (as Chapter 8 demonstrates), Article 8 can be a powerful tool in checking unbridled government enthusiasm for disrupting migration through marriage.

Perspectives on Marriage Migration

Marriage migration is a prism through which many other concerns and anxieties are filtered. It is also a subject that may be viewed in many different lights. There are several strands that are relevant here. Firstly, to regard marriage migration purely as a problem of 'immigration' adopts too parochial a perspective. Cross-border movement is a continuous global phenomenon that has only been recently and partially disrupted by modern immigration controls. It is also necessary to acknowledge migrants' own agency, avoiding an idealised perspective whereby migrants become the passive victims of government machinations instead of individuals and even communities who strategise around and respond to policy according to their own priorities and norms. Another issue is the problematic nature of categorisations; the meaning of a 'genuine', 'bogus' or 'sham' marriage, a 'forced marriage' or of even more imprecise concepts such as 'love', 'purpose' or 'intention' have all, at various times, been critical to applications and yet resist the type of binary interpretation that is central to such decision-making. A further question is that of stereotyping and discrimination. Assumptions about marriage are closely linked to assumptions about gender, while beliefs about race, class and belonging have long influenced immigration control. At the same time, the presence of different cultures and marriage practices, some of which are regarded as incompatible with values of equality and personal autonomy, raise difficult questions of management and regulation for the state. Finally, policy on marriage migration may be represented from two contrasting viewpoints: as an attempt to prevent the entry of unwanted migrants or as efforts to restrict and control the aspirations of UK residents to live their family life as they choose – either the resident or the migrant may be foregrounded. All these strands feed into assumptions, represented in policy, law and decision-making, about what represents a legitimate claim in immigration terms.

These strands are not only multiple in themselves but intersect and interact in multiple ways so that a unitary perspective fails to convey the shifting, multi-dimensional nature of regulation and its perception. It is frequently the case that, from one perspective, a policy may look like a rational response to a challenge to legitimate state authority while, from another, it resembles an attempt to frustrate the essential rights of UK residents. Equally, the claims of migrants may be seen as a reasonable attempt to establish their married life in optimal conditions or as an opportunistic effort to circumnavigate immigration controls. This book therefore does not adopt a single perspective but analyses policy in the light of these multiple points of view. However, the unifying feature is that, taken together, they permit the analysis of changing conceptions of the lineaments of legitimate state power, of who does and does not belong in the UK, the shifting and contingent nature of that belonging, particularly for some populations, and how, particularly for women, marriage represents a public declaration of allegiance as well as a private commitment. In summary, they permit the identification of an implicit hierarchy of acceptable marriages. This hierarchy, composed of both official and unofficial elements, adjusts and evolves over time, while the place that a particular marriage occupies within it depends upon the characteristics of both parties and the circumstances of the marriage.

The Transnational Perspective

Transnationalism recognises that migration is 'a long-term process … a trajectory' (Grillo 2007: 200), which results in 'sustained linkages and ongoing exchanges among non-state actors based across national borders' (Vertovec 2008: 3). Transnationalism challenges a state-centred perspective on migration, viewing it as a dynamic and multi-stranded process whereby individuals forge and sustain connections in both the new and the old state (Levitt 2004: 2). It enriches the understanding of family migration (see Kofman 2004, Smith 2004 and Kofman and Meetoo 2008 for a discussion), offering a less parochial and more theoretical analysis than the conventional government framework and seeing family migration as more than a single discrete act whereby an entire family either relocates to or is created in a new location. These connections affect more than the migrant individual and have an impact upon family members, as well as the wider community in both the country of origin and the country of destination. Transnational families, according to Bryceson and Vuerola (quoted in Kofman and Meetoo 2008: 3), 'live some or most of their time separated from each other, yet hold together, managing to maintain a feeling of unity and collective welfare, despite geographical distance'. These links may be sustained into the second generation and children of migrants often demonstrate an acute if sometimes problematic transnational consciousness (Levitt 2009). Transnational activity may take place in a number of social arenas, including the community or family, and may also take the form of a set of attitudes, values and competences (Koehn and Rosenau 2002 and Mau, Mewes and Zimmerman 2008). According to Vertovec (2008: 3), it is not a new phenomenon, but it has been accelerated and expanded by global forces and new forms of communication.

Transnationalism's embrace of the continuing nature of cross-border exchange, as opposed to older notions of a single migratory crossing, makes it a useful instrument for analysing the persistence of international marriages, despite sometimes draconian government controls. However, there is the danger of overstating its extent (Castles and Miller 2009: 32) and, in the context of this book, care is needed in defining what is meant by a transnational marriage. A marriage might be described as transnational if, amongst its purposes, there is the maintenance or promotion of transnational ties. The paradigmatic example is the international arranged marriage (see Ballard 2008), particularly where these involve, for example, members of the same family, caste or other group. In the UK, these marriages are associated primarily with families originating from the Indian sub-continent, but they may occur in a range of ethnic and national groups (see the discussion in Ballard 2008: 49 and Palriwala and Uberoi 2008a: 32). The motives for such a marriage include family solidarity and aspirations for social improvement, and their negotiation, although apparently traditional in form, often reflects calculations of the relative value of each spouse according to a more modern set of values than might be expected (Palriwala and Uberoi 2008a: 31-3).

However, the transnational environment within which such marriages take place should not cause the personal aspirations of the individual to be neglected. Transnationalism creates new motivations, hopes and pressures affecting marriage decisions, but these do not necessarily promote transnationalism as such. Reasons for entering an international arranged marriage can include a desire to respect tradition but may also encompass more forward-looking objectives, including the cementing of international family relationships, a renegotiation (not always successful) of 'traditional' gender relations and the possibility of trading the chance of migration for a higher status spouse than would otherwise be expected (Beck-Gernsheim 2007: 279-85). Family members who arrange international marriages may also have reasons that are connected to but are not synonymous with the transnational aspects of their family lives, for example, disciplining a wayward child or protecting cultural values (Ballard 2005: 61). There is the risk of a potentially misleading form of synecdoche. The marriage is an international marriage arranged in a transnational context, but the marriage itself may not be motivated entirely or at all by the aim of promoting that transnational context. The distinction is important because, as will be seen, international arranged marriages have often been treated as cynical vehicles for immigration or, more recently, as obstacles to integration. Designating international arranged marriages as entirely or even primarily transnational makes an over-categorical designation easier to sustain.

By contrast, international marriages contracted according to European norms and apparently based purely on the relationship between the couple do not, at first glance, fit so easily within a transnational paradigm. However, some non-arranged international marriages between individuals with a common cultural or ethnic background may be partly motivated, explicitly or otherwise, by the desire to strengthen continuing links. Where this is not the case, the marriage will often have arisen in the context of transnational social networks, resulting, for example, from global business, work or education or through the internet. Even if more concrete transnational ties do not already exist at the start of such a marriage, given the facility with which they may now be established, the likelihood is that they will exist in future. Transnationalism is also partly a state of mind and cosmopolitan individuals may see international marriage as an alliance with someone who shares more of their outlook, experience and values than many of their compatriots. Affinities may arise between groups of different origins because of a shared 'internationalist' outlook within a privileged environment or a shared experience of marginalisation in a less privileged one (see Beck-Gernsheim 2007: 274). Acknowledging the differences within cosmopolitanism is critical. As Grillo (2007: 212-13) points out, it is not a single transcendent perspective but a range of perspectives determined by culture, nation, ethnicity and class. What distinguishes the international marriages of Pakistani cousins, of a Latvian cleaner and an Afghan asylum seeker who meet in the UK, and of academics who meet at a conference in Australia may not be that one marriage is more or less transnational than the other, but the acceptability of the transnationalism in question. This analysis suggests that transnationalism is, in itself, not a problem but that particular manifestations of it may be. Recent discourse, discussed in Chapters 6 and 7, has assumed an opposition between integration and transnational marriages within minority communities. Yet close examination suggests that the actual position is less clear-cut than may be supposed and not all transnational marriages receive the same degree of attention (Beck-Gernsheim 2007: 271-2). The literature on transnationalism suggests that it is not, in itself, an obstacle to integration; in fact, the reverse may be the case (Vertovec 2009: 77-84 and Castles and Miller 2009: 32). If that is so, where marriages have a transnational flavour but are perceived as problematic, it may not be the transnationalism that is to blame but some other factor.

Subject to this definitional clarity, transnationalism is a useful tool for analysing some of the apparently puzzling aspects of marriage migration. The existence of transnational social spaces helps to explain why international marriages have persisted amongst minority communities, despite frequent predictions of their demise, a phenomenon not confined to the UK (Beck-Gernsheim 2007: 275-6). Marriage provides a way to meet family obligations and cement important transnational kinship links. Much contemporary discourse focuses on the problematic aspects of continuing international arranged marriages which exist and are discussed at various points in this book. The result is that such marriages are often seen purely as attempts by the elder generation to impose their will on the younger and there have been calls for restraint to be shown in this context. However, as suggested, the picture is more complex and many young people, while having reservations in some cases, are often willing participants for their own reasons that are connected to their transnational identity.

Transnationalism also acknowledges migrants' own agency in the face of restrictive immigration controls. This book is primarily a study of regulation and its implementation by state institutions. There is a danger that the migrant becomes a bit player, a passive victim of government power. In reality, migrants have been active and strategic in negotiating state controls to further their own interests.

Transnational networks within migrant communities often provide the practical tools by which migrants can negotiate multiple obstacles of discrimination, immigration control and global inequality. In that context, there is no binary divide between migration for work and other purposes and migration for marriage. Each may facilitate the other (Palriwala and Uberoi 2008a: 26). Marriage can assist in sustaining and even advancing transnational exchanges, while transnational connections may be used to promote a desired marriage, for example, through provision of a job or accommodation for the couple.

An awareness of the complexity of transnational lives and the multiple and competing systems of law and morality by which these are lived provides valuable insight in another way. Transnationalism may result in adherence to multiple legal and normative systems. This can cause difficulties relating to the recognition of marriages and divorces where these do not comply with dominant UK norms. The technical legal arguments that surround these cases are symptomatic of a deeper tension between some forms of transnational family life and the claim of the state to centralised authority. This becomes particularly acute when these tangle with immigration control, commonly regarded as an issue of sovereign state power. The reliance by migrants on what are seen as archaic or oppressive legal norms or informal arrangements can easily become characterised as insubordination. The matter may, in fact, be more one of mutual incomprehension. As Cotterell (2009: 493) points out, legal norms and moral values are not fixed but bear different meanings in different places and contexts. From the majority British perspective, polygamous marriages, marriages involving mentally disabled partners or *talaq* divorces are discrete phenomena that are in profound conflict with norms of equality and should not be granted legitimacy. From the perspective of the protagonists, they represent long-standing practices exercised within a complex context and offer a socially acceptable means of regulating the complicated problems that so frequently beset family life. Their derecognition can feel like a broader slight on the values and norms by which they live (see Cotterell 2009: 496-7). This does not mean that the state has no right of intervention, but it does explain why these conflicts are not susceptible to easy resolution. It must also be acknowledged that, in the immigration field at least, concern over oppressive family relations is capable of manipulation, as occurred, it has been argued, in relation to forced marriage (Wray 2009a and Chapters 6 and 7).

Culture, Oppression and Marriage Migration

The previous section alluded to marriage practices that conflict with majority values within the UK but which are sanctioned within some legal systems and cultures. These include *talaq* divorce, particularly bare *talaq*, child marriages, marriages involving disabled partners who cannot give meaningful consent, marriages involving parties who do not meet until or even after the wedding (if it is conducted by proxy) and polygamy. Forced marriage, an issue of current contemporary concern, might be included in a list of such practices. Although it is not endorsed by any culture or religion, forced marriage is nonetheless closely connected to the arranged marriage system in which parents and other family members claim the right to choose a marriage partner; in addition, as numerous commentators have observed, there is not a clear demarcation between arranged and forced marriage but a spectrum of conduct (Bhabha 2007: 24-5).

These practices are often regarded as incompatible with values of gender equality, protection of the vulnerable and individual autonomy. These issues have surfaced at various times and in various guises throughout the period discussed in this book and have been the subject of different forms of regulation, including the requirement for the parties to have met in both fiancé and spouse applications, the progressive raising of the minimum age for entry and sponsorship and the prohibition on the entry of more than one spouse in polygamous marriages. While each of these measures is discussed in its context later in the book, the underlying issue in all cases is complex to resolve and is, briefly and necessarily inadequately, discussed here.

Advocates of pluralistic approaches to culture and law argue that it is both wrong and unrealistic to expect migrants and communities of migrant origin to accept the authority of a single, centralised legal system in relation to their personal and cultural life. The argument has both a normative and a pragmatic basis. The normative argument relates to the critical importance that one's own culture plays in identity and the hardship involved in its loss or non-recognition (Bhamra 2007). The pragmatic argument notes that minorities will find ways to express their cultural norms regardless of official disapproval and the state does best to recognise and negotiate around that fact, 'to manage them [i.e. conflicts] wisely' (Chiba, quoted in Shah 2005: 8). These are powerful arguments. The degree of affective attachment to one's own cultural norms should not be under-estimated and many people feel bereft if they are unable to operate within them. Legal and normative systems, either official or unofficial, draw their coherence and authority from a set of shared cultural values and ideals. Understanding these is necessary in order to understand the place and value of a particular practice, and the state should not intervene heavy-handedly. The state may thus have difficulty 'managing wisely', showing a poor understanding of apparently objectionable practices, taking them out of their context and failing to see how they fit within a complex system of cultural and legal norms. There is also the danger of essentialism, of ignoring or even unintentionally stifling internal challenge and debate. At the same time, majority discourse often presupposes a position of cultural superiority, wherein the values of the dominant group are seen as universal and culture-free. In the case of migrants, this may be compounded by a strong sense that it is appropriate for relative newcomers to adapt their ways to those of longer resident majority groups (see Ballard 2008 and Enright 2009: 338). In this way, a highly exclusionary 'politics of belonging' may be established which legitimises the marginalisation or worse of 'outsider' groups based on the assumed backwardness of their norms (Yuval-Davis 2006).

However, the pluralist perspective has drawn some well-rehearsed criticisms. The literature is wide but the main reference point is arguably Okin 1999 and the subsequent debate (see Okin 2005: 67-9 for an overview). In essence, the argument is that permitting minorities to have autonomy in personal laws ignores or even entrenches oppression and inequalities of power within groups or, by prioritising plural values over those of equality, postpones their resolution to some indefinite future date. These inequalities are often presented primarily on a gender axis and much of the debate has been conducted by feminists, but they may also turn on age, social status, sexuality and so on. There is an extensive literature debating how to reconcile respect for group autonomy with respect for individual rights. Rights of exit as a solution are problematic, particularly if they entail high emotional costs and the loss of cultural identity (Reitmann 2005: 193-6). Victims of a forced marriage, for example, may find that escape means isolation from their family and community, and results in distress that they find intolerable (Phillips and Dustin 2004: 541-3). However, in the words of Okin (2005), there are 'no simple answers' and attempts at external regulation risk re-invoking the original objections as well as being potentially counter-productive (Phillips and Dustin 2004: 545), while measures based on dialogue or consultation alone may be excessively compromised or weak (Okin 2005). There are many different nuanced positions (for a sample, see Eisenberg and Spinner-Halev 2005), but none that entirely resolves the tensions.

In this book, the question arises largely in the context of immigration control measures which claim to protect the position of the vulnerable. As a purely pragmatic question, their effectiveness is doubtful. Banning the entry of second wives in a polygamous marriage, for example, may lead to a life of isolation in the country of origin. Raising the age of entry and sponsorship may cause young spouses to be abandoned overseas in a forced marriage until of age to sponsor, without the resources and support networks on which they might otherwise call. In general, using immigration control to inhibit practices regarded as undesirable can increase hostility and suspicion and impede long-term resolution (see Chapter 6 and Wray 2009a).

However, the pragmatic arguments are insufficient on their own or the question would simply be one of designing more efficient forms of regulation wherever a minority engages in practices viewed by the majority as unjust. This point is particularly important in immigration, where other competing interests can easily be downplayed. The prohibition on entry and sponsorship of spouses under 21 may, overall, reduce the number of forced marriages, but it also interferes with other rights, including the preference for young marriage within some groups, a preference that is not widely shared by the majority and can therefore easily be dismissed. In such instances, a principled basis for resolving such conflicts is needed, but it is not easy or even possible to determine what this should be. It is perhaps easier to argue how such decisions should not be made. Bhamra (2007: 27-9), for example, points to the limitations of human rights norms, which have not been constructed on the basis of concern for specific cultural diversity. Yet there is no culturally and ethically neutral space in which such decisions can be reached. They will inevitably involve the legislator, judge or other decision-maker drawing on his or her own value system, a system which will include the weight given to respect for cultural diversity and to other competing values. A conscious and culturally sensitive process of decision-making, in which all perspectives (include those of the differentiated groups within the minority) are given equal respect and consideration, is arguably the best that can be hoped for and it is according to this criterion, as well as the pragmatic one, that immigration control measures that regulate cultural practices will be assessed in this book.

In making or evaluating such decisions, a firm grip has to be kept on the actualities of the problem in question. What is the harm done by the disapproved practice? Is the proposed measure the most effective and least intrusive possible? To what extent does its implementation interfere with other rights and how critical are these? These types of evaluation, familiar from proportionality exercises in human rights law even if human rights law is not itself the solution, can never take place in a cultural vacuum, but nor can they be avoided.

Gender, Race and Class

Marriage migrants have often suffered discrimination attributable to gender and racial stereotypes, and the analysis of these forms a major part of this book. Race and gender have frequently intersected, creating particular forms of discrimination against certain groups. Intersectional discrimination is now widely recognised as creating problems for the most marginalised or oppressed groups, and this has been the case in immigration as elsewhere.

Gender itself is a contested and unstable concept (see Calavita 2006: 105-9 for a discussion) and has often been overlooked as a factor in migration (Palriwala and Uberoi 2008a: 8). The meaning and significance of gender have changed over the decades discussed in this book and, although some themes have persisted, its visibility as a factor in policy-making has varied even while it has never been entirely absent. Gender assumptions have shaped UK immigration control since its inception or even before, as the rules on married women's nationality discussed in Chapter 2 demonstrate. In later years, as overt sex discrimination became legally and politically unacceptable, more concealed gender-related control strategies evolved, such as the primary purpose rule. In the recent past, claims to promote gender equality have sometimes been deployed in aid of measures that are argued here to have the opposite effect, such as the prohibition on the entry of a second wife to a polygamous marriage or measures against forced marriage (see Chapters 6 and 7).

Marriage migration may offer opportunities of personal advancement for migrants of either gender, but official treatment and public perception have been and remain strongly gender-specific, even if the law is now formally neutral. However, 'gender disadvantage' should not be taken as being synonymous with 'female disadvantage'. Men, particularly non-white men, have frequently been the victims of gender-based beliefs about marriage migration. In fact, women may be able to turn excessive state focus on male marriage migrants to their advantage and use marriage migration to compensate for their lack of leverage at home or in other more male-dominated areas of migration. Women's marriage migration 'may often be the most efficient and socially acceptable means to disadvantaged women to achieve a measure of social and economic mobility' (Palriwala and Uberoi 2008b: 23-4). Even where women do not themselves migrate for marriage, they may use their economic power and the relative vulnerability of a migrant husband to seek a renegotiation of traditional gender relations. While this may result in more freedom for the individual, it can also create new wider forms of gender disadvantage in terms of expectations of women on marriage (Palriwala and Uberoi 2008b: 39-40). UK-based husbands, on the other hand, may prefer an overseas spouse in order to re-engineer local gender norms in the opposing direction and obtain a more compliant, 'traditional' wife. Overseas spouses of both genders may be seen by diasporic communities as a means of reinforcing and transmitting cultural or religious values (Palriwala and Uberoi 2008b: 41). The relationship between gender and marriage migration is thus mutually interactive and fluid: gender assumptions have shaped marriage migration and its regulation while these, in turn, may disrupt traditional gender relations.

The history of immigration control has been suffused with assumptions about the significance of race (see, for example, Layton-Henry 1992 and Paul 1997 for a detailed account). This has been as much the case in marriage migration as elsewhere. As Chapters 3, 4 and 5 demonstrate, at least until the recent period, the control of marriage migration has always been primarily aimed at particular ethnic or national groups. As a concept, race is even more imprecise than gender. While it is now widely accepted that there is no scientific evidence to support a biological notion of race or of a hierarchy of races, people often behave as if these exist. Race is a social contruct that can be used to justify differences in treatment and its representation changes over time. Since the Second World War, an accusation of racism has been seen as a serious moral challenge and the existence of racism is often strenuously denied. Race discrimination may therefore be disguised by use of terms of social, cultural or religious difference (Howard 2008: 10-12).

It follows that, while immigration policy may have had racially based aims, these had, of necessity, to be disguised. This was achieved by the use of apparently neutral terminology within complex legislative provisions, of concealed administrative practice and of proxies. The complicated terms of the Commonwealth Immigrants Act 1962, for instance, appear to be neutrally drawn, but its effects were highly discriminatory. The discrimination endured by thousands of South Asians under the entry clearance system, described in Chapter 5, was largely concealed from public scrutiny. Gender was used as a proxy for race during the period (discussed in Chapter 3) when the entry of most Commonwealth husbands was banned. However, it was a crude weapon, affecting white women, and became socially and legally unacceptable. It was replaced by the primary purpose rule, which, from a government perspective, had more acceptable gender and race dimensions as it could be deployed selectively. More recent manifestations have been different again, focusing on cultural rather than physical markers. Race is thus a protean social construct and is adept at finding new guises. However, not all discussion of difference is merely a new manifestation of an old evil. Legitimate policy issues are engaged by some culturally specific phenomena (for example, forced marriage or polygamy), but, as discussed, the boundaries between justified intervention and disguised discrimination are difficult to determine. Given the history of cultural discrimination in the control of marriage migration, that there is often a sceptical attitude is unsurprising.

Race and gender have also arguably been somewhat displaced in the recent period. In Chapter 6, it is observed that immigration policy in the post-1997 period has been characterised by new priorities and that these have, to an extent, disrupted former markers of difference (Sales 2005). In particular, skills, language and education have become more prominent determinants, leading to large numbers of entrants from the expanding middle classes in formerly stigmatised ex-colonies such as India. Social class or, perhaps more accurately, human and cultural capital have always been factors in determining who is an undesirable marriage migrant. However, in the past, these were more closely aligned with race and nationality. This has now at least partially changed and nationality alone is a less reliable indicator of acceptability. It is arguable that recent discourse around aspects of cultural practice and norms reflects disguised fears about the entry of poorly educated migrants, lacking linguistic skills and adaptability, as well as attempts to find markers of difference that are more nuanced than race or nationality (see Chapters 6 and 9 and Wray 2009a for more information).

Gender, race and class (in the sense used here) are thus inseparably intertwined as determining factors in the hierarchy of acceptable marriages. All three are social constructs whose meaning changes over time and which may, at various moments, stand as proxies for each other or be represented in different ways. They may also intersect with each other or with other characteristics such as age or immigration status to create particular sites of disadvantage where extreme negative stereotyping may be applied. Chapter 5 describes the treatment of poor, often rural South Asian marriage migrants by the entry clearance service. Both men and women were subjected to different but equally damaging forms of discrimination, culminating in 'virginity tests' on some women and the dismissal *en masse* of husbands as liars and opportunists. Their humiliation and refusal were made possible by the unique combination of their gender, race and class. More recently, male asylum seekers who married in the UK were stigmatised by the combination of their gender, nationality and lack of immigration status.

Bogus, Sham and Genuine Marriages

The control of marriage migration has often relied on the designation of some marriages as 'sham' or 'bogus' or as 'marriages of convenience'. Marriages entered solely for immigration purposes exist and, if immigration control is accepted as legitimate, so must at least some efforts to prevent them. However, regulation has generally been over-inclusive, an argument that is pursued in various chapters of this book. This has often represented an opportunistic government strategy. An over-broad designation allows unwanted marriage migrants to be held responsible for their own refusal and permits both the public and government to avoid confronting the consequences of an unjust or discriminatory policy. Such sleights of hand are common in immigration law (see Wray 2006d for a discussion) and are facilitated in marriage migration by the problematic nature of the presumed opposition between 'bogus' and 'genuine' marriages.

Conventional discourse in the West would posit the paradigmatic 'genuine' marriage as one where the parties are motivated primarily by romantic love. While many marriages involve a degree of pragmatism, the closer that a marriage comes to this romantic ideal, the more likely it is to be genuine. Such a view is an obvious over-simplification and not only because a significant minority of British nationals enter arranged marriages in accordance with their cultural norms, in which affection is seen as following rather than pre-dating the marriage. The marriage market is a universal phenomenon (see Grossbard-Shechtman 2003: 3) and its workings are arguably disguised rather than displaced by romantic expectations. The opportunity for material or social advancement, including through migration, is a major advantage in this market and may result in matches between apparently ill-matched partners. The process is not necessarily cynical. While a party may sometimes consent to marriage only because there are so few other opportunities for social mobility, in other instances, what has been called the 'cultural logic of desire' means that prospective spouses who are otherwise considered unappealing are enhanced, even glamourised, by their association with the more powerful or prestigious nation or culture (Del Rosario 2008). In such circumstances, it is impossible to disentangle the 'good' motivation of romance from the 'bad' motivation of social advancement through migration.

If looking at motivation is unreliable, there are also dangers in using the content of the marriage to judge whether it is genuine. Most marriages, even those entered for entirely pragmatic reasons, share some common characteristics: cohabitation, sexual relations, mutual care, sharing of resources and so on. However, in all cultures, there are atypical marriages where one or more of these are absent. In some transnational families, for example, it is common for spouses to spend lengthy periods apart as one or both parties pursue their interests in the other country. While most spouses also have some shared elements in their background, couples who apparently do not share age, education or language may nonetheless have a common experience of marginalisation that has brought them together.

Conversely, the presence of particular characteristics may indicate a bogus marriage or may be explicable in other ways. Monetary exchange is a recognised aspect of some marriage rituals. There is also the danger of 'reading back'; hindsight may tell us that a marriage which fails may have been unwise, but it should not be used to decide, in the absence of other evidence, that it was bogus. Hurt or resentful spouses may also not be entirely truthful, whether with themselves or with others, when it comes to assessing retrospectively the other party's intentions on entering into a marriage.

There is thus a substantial area of uncertainty which is liable to manipulation. The current UK law, for instance, requires couples to show an intention to live together permanently. In most cases, the test is well understood and does not give rise to conceptual difficulty, but it has been deployed somewhat arbitrarily where the authorities have regarded a marriage as undesirable according to majority norms (see Chapter 8). However, if cohabitation is not an entirely reliable guide, it is difficult to see what else might be used, given the absence of a single defining feature and the offensiveness of intrusive questioning about marital relations. Perhaps the best test is one where a marriage is considered bogus only where none of the usual observable characteristics is present.

Such is the case in the definition adopted by EU law: a marriage concluded 'with the sole aim of circumventing the rules on entry and residence'.[16] However, as will become apparent from Chapter 7, this definition has been regarded by the UK (and by other member states) as unsatisfactory partly because of evidential issues and partly because there are substantial numbers of marriages where there is evidence of content to the marriage beyond the circumvention of immigration control, but the overseas spouse is nonetheless regarded, at best, as opportunistic. Debating whether such marriages fall within the category of genuine or bogus is somewhat beside the point, which is that, given the impossibility of establishing such binary divisions, what are the justifiable outer limits of state power to determine who may live as married partners within its borders?

Structure, Subject Matter and Research Methods

This book is divided into two parts of unequal length. The first part deals with the period between 1962 and 1997, and the other with the 13 years from 1997 to 2010. Within each part, the activities of the legislature, the judiciary and the entry clearance service are separately examined. This structure implies that the cut-off dates represent pivotal moments of change and this is, subject to reservations expressed here, the argument that is made. The year 1962 represents the moment at which Commonwealth immigration to the UK was first controlled by legislation. While the Commonwealth Immigrants Act 1962 was concerned primarily with the movement of workers rather than family members, its implementation is accepted by most commentators to have caused the stresses that resulted in later controls on Commonwealth spouses. The election of the Labour government in 1997 represented another critical moment when the assumptions that had governed policy for several decades, and which had resulted in policy stasis on family migration over most of the previous decade, were challenged by a new

16 Council Resolution 97/C 382/01 of 4 December 1997 (Official Journal C 382 of 16.12.1997).

government and new problems. The Labour government at least acknowledged the existence of a multicultural and diverse society, even if its policy responses have been controversial. The book concludes with the defeat of the Labour government in May 2010.

Naturally, it is not suggested that changes in approach happened instantaneously on these dates. The Commonwealth Immigrants Act 1962 was the outcome of several years of anxiety over non-white immigration, during which non-legislative measures, such as administrative controls, were pursued (see Chapter 2). Although the Act was passed in 1962, the first attempts to control Commonwealth family migration did not occur until 1965 and major controls began in 1969. The Labour government elected in 1997 acted rapidly by abolishing the primary purpose rule only one month after its election, an important symbolic change that also made a practical difference to affected spouses. However, many of the most significant changes in policy direction occurred over a number of years and took longer to filter through. The Human Rights Act 1998, for example, was not implemented until 2000 and its most significant case law on migrant spouses, in all likelihood an unanticipated side-effect of the Act, did not begin until 2007. Changes to attitudes within the entry clearance system are even harder to trace reliably over time, although it is argued here that there was some evolution in the post-1997 era which started to become evident in 2005.

The dates that separate the different sections of this book can perhaps best be described as representing the moments at which new directions became if not inevitable, then very likely. The 1962 Act was the moment at which particular social issues were definitively attributed to unwanted non-white immigration and subsequent difficulties were inevitably also defined in the same way. The incoming Labour government of 1997 was seen as a fresh, modernising force accountable to non-white urban populations in ways that the previous government had not been. New policy directions were the natural consequence, even if they did not take place immediately. The context of each of these moments is further explored in the introductory chapters to each part (see Chapters 2 and 6).

This book is concerned with the regulation of marriage migration to the UK. It does not aim to provide a comprehensive account of the phenomenon of marriage migration itself. Governments respond to public pressure and their own perception of problems, and the result is that their efforts may focus excessively on particular aspects. These aspects become politicised, are the subject of contestation and come to dominate public debate. This was particularly marked in the case of marriage migration from South Asia which, for a lengthy period, was regarded as synonymous with marriage migration itself. During this time, spouses of other nationalities continued to enter the UK, albeit in smaller numbers, and the occasional newspaper report suggests that some of them, particularly from the Caribbean, encountered difficulties similar to those reported in South Asia while white spouses encountered few obstacles. However, the overwhelming majority of government attention and public critique focused on the Indian sub-continent and the account here reflects that. As an account of the official response, this is appropriate, although disparities between government attention and the proportionate size of the phenomenon are sometimes noted. It is also a methodological issue. This discussion draws heavily on contemporary sources, and information on the treatment of migrants from areas other than the Indian sub-continent is largely absent. This remains a gap in the knowledge, but it is not one that this account, concerned as it is with the priorities of government, can fill.

The book is an account of two periods, one that is now historical and one that is, at least in its latter stages, still almost contemporaneous. It follows that there cannot always be the same degree of critical distance in evaluating policy. There already exists a significant literature offering a critique of policy and its implementation in the post-1962 period. While immigration policy since 1997 as a whole has been evaluated in recent articles and books, marriage migration has not received the close scrutiny of the earlier period. Rectifying that omission is one purpose of this book, but the account that is offered is less mediated than that of the earlier period. The sources available for the two periods also differ. For the earlier period, the author was reliant on documents, in particular, newspaper archives and case reports that had been preserved because others found them significant. For the later period, she conducted her own searches of news reports, official documents and judicial decisions, and was assisted by the greater range and easier availability of much information. She was also able to use her own direct observation and interview.

Other aspects of the sources are problematic. Even where the same document has remained consistently available throughout, its significance may change. Hansard provides a reliable record of parliamentary proceedings, but the significance of such proceedings in determining the shape of legislation has arguably altered over time, given the growth of centralised executive government. Hansard also needs careful interpretation. A controversial statement made by a minister is of more significance than the same words used by a backbencher. All politicians may moderate or exaggerate their true intentions for political effect. Journalistic reports are a valuable means of enriching and humanising what might otherwise be a dry legalistic analysis, but it must also be recalled that journalists and their employers have agendas and prejudices. While there is an effort here to use high-quality reports from across the political spectrum and to place the more polemical reportage in context, determining what is reliable is an inexact and subjective art. It follows that the book is an interpretive account of legal history, which draws on sources that are themselves often interpretations. However, the sources used are multiple and are often consistent with each other. Where there are discrepancies, ambiguities or gaps, these have been pointed out.

Part I of this book opens with a chapter that acts as its introduction, providing the context for the period that is first considered – 1962-1997. It looks at two episodes that pre-dated the control of Commonwealth marriage migration and which, in different ways, prefigured it: the control of families under the Aliens Act 1905 and the rules that, until 1948, governed the nationality of married women. It also looks at the pressures and manoeuvres that eventually resulted in the 1962 Act. Chapter 3 considers decisions made by the legislature from 1962, when immigration from the Commonwealth was first formally regulated, to 1997. It traces the evolution in legislative approach towards marriage emigration from broad permissiveness to severe restriction. In doing so, it identifies beliefs and assumptions about race, immigration, gender and marriage. Chapter 4 examines judicial decision-making during the same period in areas relevant to marriage migration and identifies similar values to those observed in Chapter 3, as well as some specific judicial values. Chapter 5 contains a detailed investigation into the conduct of the entry clearance service until 1997, a period during which it achieved notoriety for its exclusionary decision-making, particularly on the Indian sub-continent. That part of the book draws upon the existing literature and goes beyond it by synthesising information from a wide range of sources including archived and other contemporary material, including newspaper reports.

Part II begins with Chapter 5, which introduces the post-1997 period by outlining changes to immigration policy and to the perception of older immigrant groups, and new fears about immigration, security and social cohesion. The following chapters consider legislative, judicial and administrative decision-making after 1997. They reflect these new emphases and the contradictions contained within them. The conclusion, contained in Chapter 10, draws together the threads of the argument and proposes a principled basis for future policy.

PART I
1962-1997

Chapter 2
Before the 1962 Act

Introduction

This chapter provides a context for the analysis of regulation from 1962 that begins in Chapter 3. It examines three episodes from before 1962, each of which illustrates that the assumptions and beliefs and the consequent practices that became so prominent after 1962 had antecedents. These episodes are the rules obliging married women to adopt their husbands' nationality, the implementation of the Aliens Act 1905 and the government response to non-white post-war immigration. It is not suggested that these were the only occasions on which such assumptions and practices were observable; they are examples selected to illustrate their deep roots prior to the main period under consideration, although it was not until after 1962 that they fatally combined, causing the regulatory regime discussed in later chapters.

Dummett and Nicol (1990: 188) note that alien immigration as a whole remained uncontroversial even after non-white Commonwealth immigration became the focus of scrutiny. The attitudes and practices discussed in this book became visible in response to the perceived threat of mass non-white Commonwealth family immigration. Yet, despite the apparent preceding calm, it is suggested here that they did not emerge at once and fully formed, but were already present. Certainly, the legal regime already embodied sex discrimination. Prior to 1962, Commonwealth nationals had freedom of movement into the UK despite attempts in the 1950s (discussed below) to introduce administrative curbs. The admission of alien spouses, on the other hand, had been regulated since the Aliens Restrictions Acts 1914 and 1919 and implemented through Aliens Orders. Until the British Nationality Act 1948, the alien wives of British men automatically became British nationals on marriage and were free to enter. After the 1948 Act, they were still normally permitted to enter (see the discussion in Bhabha and Shutter 1994: 31-2). Meanwhile, female British residents born in the UK, 'with a substantial connection' to or 'well-established' in the UK were permitted to bring in alien husbands if refusal would result in hardship, a question left to the immigration officer's discretion. The Aliens Orders also provided that the wife and children of alien male workers should be admitted for the same period of time as the worker, provided they could be supported, while female workers had no such corresponding right.

It has been observed that women are seen as reproducers of nationality and ethnicity, literally as mothers and figuratively in terms of embodying and reproducing culture (Yuval-Davis and Anthias 1989: 6-10). In recent times, as

Chapter 6 notes, this has been most visible in the context of minority cultures. However, women in majority British society may also carry this burden, although it is perhaps less noticeable within a dominant culture. In particular, a woman's choice of spouse may be regarded as a statement of allegiance as well as of personal preference. This is apparent historically from the long debate on married women and nationality. Women's role in safeguarding the moral health of the nation was also suggested by aspects of the implementation of the Aliens Act 1905. The Act's implementation also prefigured, in a minor way, the strong unofficial culture in the entry clearance service, which is discussed in Chapter 5. The adoption of administrative means to control immigration as well as complex attitudes towards non-white Commonwealth immigration and race discrimination were apparent in the response to the post-war migratory movements that preceded the Commonwealth Immigrants Act 1962. This chapter thus examines three aspects of the background to the period which began in 1962: the debate about married women's nationality, the implementation of the Aliens Act 1905 and initial responses to post-war non-white Commonwealth migration.

Married Women's Nationality

The rule that a married woman must adopt her husband's nationality upon marriage was founded on the principle of conjugal unity under which a wife's personality was incorporated into that of the husband, although, luckily for her, '(t)he wife was not reduced to the position in law of, say, a dog' (Williams 1947: 18); it was a question of guardianship rather than ownership. Writing in 1947, Glanville Williams cited the Bible as the origin of the common law concept and quoted Shakespeare and Byron to demonstrate its deep roots in our culture. However, conjugal unity did not represent a principled attachment to the family unit for the sake of the pleasures of married life or the security of children. It was concerned primarily with reproducing patriarchy and hierarchy within the family. It applied to areas of law such as taxation and domicile where it reinforced the authority of a male head of household. This was also the case in the nationality of married women where conjugal unity was consistently enforced by law from the mid-1800s until 1948.[1]

Section 16 Naturalisation Act 1844 provided that a foreign-born woman automatically became British upon marriage to a British man and s. 10(1) Naturalisation Act 1870 stated that 'a married woman shall be deemed to

1 As well as provision in the Naturalisation Acts, parliamentary drafters in the period between 1905 and 1948 were meticulous in ensuring that the law reflected the status of wives as sharing the nationality of their husbands. The Aliens Restriction (Change of Name) Order 1914, for example, prohibited aliens from changing their names but provided that nothing shall affect the right of a woman who marries an alien from using her married name. Such a woman, even if of British nationality, would have become an alien on marriage and would otherwise have been affected by the Order.

be a subject of the state of which her husband is for the time being a subject'. Commentators (for example, Jones 1947: 72 and Dummett and Nicol 1990: 87-8) as well as the Select Committee (1923) argued that the prior common law position had been that a woman's nationality did not change upon marriage.[2]

The effects of the rule could be severe. Expatriated women were liable to deportation, lost their voting rights (after enfranchisement in 1928) and, until 1933, had to register with the police. They might become stateless.[3] Women married to Germans were liable to have their property confiscated in the aftermath of the First World War.[4] Access to increasingly important social benefits such as pensions or health insurance was more difficult for these women (Page Baldwin 2001: 533). After the implementation of the Aliens Act in 1905, the rules on nationality interacted with immigration law so that British-born women married to aliens had no absolute right to re-enter their country of birth.[5] Admission would, in law, have depended upon their ability to meet the criteria for entry. Between enactment of the Aliens Act 1905 and its repeal, women had the protection of s. 1(3) of that Act, which provided that an alien should not be refused for want of means if they were born in the UK and their father was a British subject. There was no provision for women who failed on health grounds. The Aliens Restrictions Acts of 1914 and 1919 and the consequent Aliens Order 1920 contained no exceptions. There do not seem to be reports of women being refused entry, although there must have been cases in which they could have failed to qualify for admission. Such women would have been immediately identifiable as aliens after passports became compulsory in 1920. It is possible that the wide discretion given to immigration officers was always exercised in favour of such women. Some support for this may be found in a *Jewish Chronicle* report shortly after commencement of the Aliens Act 1905, which described the surprise of officials when they detained the wife of a Dutchman only to find she was an Englishwoman. While she may have been English-born, she was no longer a British national, although the report suggests ignorance of the point.[6]

However, officials were apparently fully aware of the legal position when 'forces sweetheart' Gracie Fields married an Italian film director and enemy alien in 1940.[7]

2 Baron Parke in *Countess de Conway's Case* (1834) 2 Knapp 364, 368.

3 According to reports in *The Times*, this was regularly the case in the 1930s for women married to American citizens, as America required a residence period of one year before it permitted naturalisation.

4 *Fasbender v Attorney General* [1921] F 1082.

5 The same principle was adopted in other countries. US citizenship was automatically conferred on foreign women who married US citizens from 1855, while in 1907 the Expatriation Act 1907 expatriated American women who married foreigners. Independent citizenship was achieved in 1934 (Calavita 2006: 114). Women automatically adopted their husband's nationality in the Netherlands until 1964 (Van Walsum 2008).

6 21 September 1906.

7 'Our Gracie "lost her nationality"', BBC News, 1 June 2007: http: //news.bbc.co.uk/1/hi/england/manchester/6711189.stm (accessed 10 June 2011).

Her passport was renewed and she returned to the UK during the war to entertain troops and factory workers, but there was official concern that 'by naturalising her we may be naturalising a woman who has practically severed her connection with this country'. However, fear of 'propaganda' by 'Women's Societies' seems to have prevailed. This was probably prudent given the state of public opinion at that time. While in 1914, only one MP had opposed inclusion of the provision for married women in the British Nationality and Status of Aliens Bill, other parliamentarians agreeing that to allow women their own nationality 'would depart from the practice of the civilised world' (Paul 1997: 12), by the 1930s and 1940s, many public figures across the political spectrum expressed sympathy for women forcibly deprived of their nationality. One of the many parliamentary bills to remedy the situation was introduced in 1930 'amid general cheers'.[8]

Yet, notwithstanding apparent popular support, the law did not change until 1948. Although practical problems such as ensuring consular protection to women abroad or statelessness were cited, the critical issue was the maintenance of a uniform imperial identity (Page Baldwin 2001). At the outset, this was linked to the necessity of maintaining good order and the role of the family in maintaining and reproducing imperial hierarchy in miniature (Klug 1989: 22). Writing in the nineteenth century, Cockburn (1869: 216) said:

> By a system of law, founded upon and giving effect to these principles (including the adoption by a wife of her husband's nationality), aliens would be placed on the footing which a generous comity should dictate; the inconvenience of a double nationality would be prevented; everyone would know where his allegiance was due, without being exposed to the danger of having conflicting claims made on it, and if in need of protection, would know where to look for it; governments would not be troubled by claims for protection involving doubtful and embarrassing questions of nationality.

In 1923, the Foreign Office believed that it was 'desirable that the family should be a unit which is all subject to the same administration and control' (Select Committee 1923: 41-2). Baty (1936: 247) found the argument of female subordination so compelling that he could barely comprehend that it might ever have been otherwise:

> When we consider the enormous power with which a husband is invested over his wife by the Common Law, it seems monstrous that she could ever conceivably be thought to be subject to a competing control exercised by an alien power. Her duty to her husband and her Sovereign could never be at variance in so shocking a fashion … These antimonies … are flatly incompatible with the unity of person which is the essential basis of the common law view of marriage.

8 *The Times*, 26 February 1930.

Women who disrupted the normal order by allying themselves with aliens were seen to have excluded themselves from the imperial family. Wyndham Bewes, Secretary of the Nationality Committee of the International Law Association, argued that a woman knew the consequences of marrying an alien and should take them into account when deciding whether to marry (Select Committee 1923: paras 1301-9). At para. 1302, he said: 'If she does not want to change her nationality and must change her nationality on marriage, she will not marry and I think in that case she had better not marry.' A Home Office official is quoted by Page Baldwin (2001: 541) as saying, in 1925, that 'it seems right and reasonable that a British woman who voluntarily throws her lot in with an alien by marrying him, ought to be prepared to assume his nationality as part of the transaction'. The rule was also presented as being for women's own protection, were she tempted to marry a polygamous 'Oriental'. The prospective loss of her nationality was the only disincentive likely to dissuade her. Meanwhile, if women who married aliens were lost to empire, men who married alien wives thereby extended it by maintaining the 'British character' of the family (Page Baldwin 2001: 538-9).

Feminist demands for women to be recognised as independent actors cut across such notions of female subordination but were not a challenge to empire (see Page Baldwin 2001: 523-5 for a discussion of feminist participation in the imperial identity). In fact, it was quite the reverse; feminists saw the opposition as being between enforced obedience and allegiance freely given through personal commitment:

> … a woman is as attached to her nationality as a man is. She considers it quite as important a personal right as does a man, and it is a very serious thing to deprive her of a privilege of this kind without her consent … It is not treating her with due respect and it is not treating nationality with due respect. (Chrystal Macmillan, Select Committee 1923: 127)

However, while there was, latterly, sympathy for women's claims, it was easily subordinated to the more urgent need to maintain legal uniformity within an increasingly restive Commonwealth. Relations with the Commonwealth were seen as critical, as Page Baldwin (2001) and others (for example, Hansen 2000: 43-4) make clear. Women's claims to determine their own nationality were legitimate but relatively unimportant. It was impossible to impose change on the Dominions, there was no agreement on the question and separate legislation would have meant acknowledging the crumbling of the single imperial nationality (Page Baldwin 2001: 544-54). The Second World War provided further reason for delay even while the problem was exacerbated by marriages between British women and allied servicemen.[9] By the end of the war, the necessity for nationality legislation in the light of Canada's intention to act unilaterally provided the opportunity for reform

9 *The Times*, 5 July 1933, 26 July 1938, 25 January 1939, 1 April 1941 and 25 March 1942.

(Paul 1997: 14-15) and the law was finally changed in the British Nationality Act 1948.

The Aliens Act 1905 and the Entry of Spouses

According to Juss (1993: 32), '[t]he modern control of immigration begins with the Aliens Act 1905'. Although it was not the first legislation to control the entry of aliens (see Dummett and Nicol 1990: 83, 106 and Stevens 2004: 19-32), it initiated a permanent system of control, which, although soon repealed, is the ancestor of modern immigration control. The origins, structure and application of the Act have been discussed widely elsewhere (Landa 1911, Gartner 1960, Roche 1969, Garrard 1971, Gainer 1972, Dummett and Nicol 1990, Shah 2000, Stevens 2004, Winder 2004 and Wray 2006d). They are not considered here except insofar as they are relevant to the argument made here that aspects of the application of the Act anticipated attitudes that became far more marked in later eras.

Under s. 1 of the Act, leave to land would be refused if the immigration officer believed the immigrant to be 'undesirable' because he:

- could not show that he had in his possession or was in a position to obtain the means of decently supporting himself and his dependants (if any);
- was a lunatic or idiot, or owing to any disease or infirmity appeared likely to become a charge upon the rates or otherwise a detriment to the public;
- had been convicted of certain crimes; or
- had an expulsion order against him.

Political and religious refugees were not to be refused for want of means or the probability of becoming a charge on the rates. Despite this exemption, most refusals were on the first two grounds. Under s. 2, immigrants who were refused could appeal to the Immigration Board.

Detailed accounts of the Act's implementation appeared in the *Jewish Chronicle* from its commencement in January 1906 until 1914 when war supervened. These reports appear to be comprehensive, also encompassing the minority of cases involving non-Jewish aliens. Refusal rates remained low throughout the period (Wray 2006d: 314) and too much cannot be extrapolated from the relatively few refusals reported. Nonetheless, they suggest the adoption, at least in some cases, of patterns of decision-making that would become familiar in later eras. Although modern standards of administrative legality cannot be applied, there was a drift towards personal judgement and unofficial standards.

The Act's wording assumed that a married male alien's wife and children would accompany him and that the family would be considered as a unit. Yet husbands frequently came in advance and called for their family only when established. These sole applicants were sometimes treated with suspicion. It was feared that they would earn insufficient funds to support the family abroad, who would come to the UK and be a burden. There was however no automatic right of entry for a spouse and children who had, upon arrival, to meet the criteria in their own right. While these refusals were arguably not authorised by the Act, they suggested anxiety about the claims that family migrants might make and which could prove difficult to resist. Wives and children who followed husbands were also sometimes rejected, although, when challenged by immigrants' representatives, initial refusals were occasionally overturned. There were no reported cases of women who had come ahead being joined later by husbands, although one young tailor did try to join his fiancée. Although the man had some funds, these had been provided by his fiancée and he was refused.[10]

Where families came together, the Act required the alien to be able to 'decently support' himself and any dependants. While the reasoning was often absent or sketchy, it seems that officials and the Board sometimes took account of factors unauthorised by the Act or raised the evidential bar. For example, employers who gave evidence of willingness to employ an alien were asked if they could not find an Englishman to do the work, though this was not a criterion under the Act. Officials also insisted that the alien should have a prior job offer in the same trade as he had exercised in his home country. Guidelines suggesting how aliens could establish their means were rapidly transformed into rigid minimum requirements, which were necessary but not sufficient to establish the right to enter.[11]

Some officials showed little compunction in splitting up families in defiance even of the statutory exception for refugees, as some early examples demonstrate. One applicant fleeing the pogroms sent his wife and children ahead but stayed behind for two weeks to sell the family furniture. The wife and children were accepted but the husband was refused, despite having more than the minimum level of funds. A man who arrived with his wife and sister was refused because he had contracted tuberculosis after hiding in damp cellars while the women were admitted. One striking case involved a deaf-mute child of nine who arrived with her parents and five siblings. All except her were accepted and the family had little option but to return her alone to Germany, where the Jewish community took her in. Unusually, her refusal received wider publicity and, following a deputation to Parliament and other adverse publicity, she was permitted to return.[12]

Following this case in early 1906 and other representations, Home Secretary Gladstone sent a letter to the Boards, expressing his view that Parliament had not intended the Act to be applied with a rigidity which excluded consideration of great personal hardship or suffering caused to women and children (Landa 1911: 316). While there were perhaps fewer cases of brutal separation in its immediate aftermath, by August 1906, the *Jewish Chronicle* was reporting that the recent mood of generosity had already receded. Individual family members continued

10 *Jewish Chronicle* (*JC*), 5 January 1906, 5 July 1907, 3 December 1909, 23 August 1912, 30 August 1912 and 26 September 1913.

11 Letter by Joseph Prag, *JC*, 19 September 1913.

12 *JC*, 26 January 1906, 23 February 1906, 2 March 1906, 16 March 1906.

to be refused including, in one case, a girl of six travelling with her mother and five siblings, although she was eventually admitted for treatment at the Jewish Shelter.[13] Occasionally, officials were swayed the other way by an excess of romantic sensibility. A young male refugee was admitted after an initial refusal when he described his bravery in defiance of orders to shoot demonstrators. A young Polish woman who had also been refused was permitted to stay after she announced her intention to marry the young hero. As a 'good-natured' officer explained: 'We must not spoil such a romance.'[14]

Foreshadowing later practice, discrepancies were occasionally used to cast doubt upon parties' credentials, including as to whether they were really married. Under the Act, marriage was not a precondition of dependency, but it is unclear from the reports whether this was understood or whether refusal reflected disapproval of unmarried relationships and fears of prostitution.[15] There was no obligation to give reasons and officials may not have articulated to themselves the grounds of suspicion. Traditional double standards were sometimes observable. A 38-year-old man landed with a young woman described as his domestic servant. The man had considerable funds and explained that he had a wife and family in Russia. When the girl admitted that the pair were living together, she was refused while the man was accepted.[16] The Boards were sometimes active in ensuring that proprieties were observed. In one instance where there was doubt over the marriage, the parties were admitted only after the Board had enquired as to whether the husband would look after his wife 'as a husband should'.[17] Women were admitted on condition that they married within a certain period or were required to live at a separate address pending the marriage.[18]

Throughout the whole period of the operation of the Aliens Act, there was much anxiety about the 'white slave trade'. Women whose situation was irregular or who were assessed to be 'good looking' were subject to closer examination. Comments as to a woman's personal attractiveness regularly featured in deliberations. Single women were routinely detained while the respectability of their connections was verified.[19] As a means to prevent prostitution, these measures were ineffectual. The *Jewish Chronicle* pointed out that traffickers and their victims could evade detection by travelling first or second class.[20] Nor were refusals effective in protecting vulnerable women from exploitation. Lone women without language skills or an obvious source of income might be at risk in London, but returning

13 *JC*, 17 August 1906, 5 February 1907, 23 September 1910, 30 September 1910.
14 *JC*, 19 January 1906.
15 *JC*, 7 September 1906, 8 July 1910, 10 September 1910, 28 July 1911.
16 *JC*, 10 May 1907.
17 *JC*, 7 September 1906.
18 *JC*, 24 March 1911, 8 August 1913.
19 *JC*, 10 January 1912, 10 November 1911, 5 September 1913.
20 *JC*, 29 May 1914, 17 July 1914.

them penniless to a hostile environment was not necessarily safer. Proposed solutions such as hostels did not materialise.

Post-War Commonwealth Migration

Government responses to migration from Commonwealth countries after the Second World War have been well documented (see, for example, Dummett and Nicol 1990: Chapter 9, Paul 1997 and Hansen 2000) and a comprehensive account is not given here. Rather, the aim is to demonstrate that, as argued by these authors amongst others, responses to mass non-white migration were shaped by pre-existing conceptual and legal structures. These, in turn, played a large part in determining the post-1962 legislative and policy response to Commonwealth family migration discussed later in this book.

The legal and institutional narrative of post-war migration began with the British Nationality Act 1948, although the structure of this Act was, in turn, partly determined by earlier laws, in particular the British Nationality and Status of Aliens Act 1914. The 1914 Act defined the common law status of British subject as including (although not limited to) those born within and the children of fathers born within 'His Majesty's dominions and allegiance' (s. 1) and provided common rules for naturalisation within the Empire. Informal local citizenships were nonetheless permitted to accommodate local desires for self-determination (Paul 1997: 11). In the face of unilateral action by Canada in 1946 to define fully the citizenship of its nationals, the 1948 Act was 'an attempt to reconstitute' the notion of subjecthood (Hansen 2000: 35). Under the new Canadian law, Canadian citizens were still British subjects, but their status flowed not from personal allegiance to the Crown but from an entitlement to citizenship determined by the Canadian government, undermining the direct relationship of the Crown with its subjects. That relationship was characterised by the indivisibility of all subjects and free movement between the Commonwealth and the UK, a freedom that had hitherto been used mainly by white Britons and their descendants (Hansen 2000: 39). In responding to Canada's moves, the government's priority was to maintain the unity of the Commonwealth and the UK's pre-eminent role within it, even at the cost of disrupting the previously unmediated relationship of subject and Crown (see the discussion in Dummett and Nicol 1990: 133-42). The outcome was the 1948 Act, under which subjecthood was no longer the consequence merely of residence or birth within the Commonwealth but was attained primarily via nationality. The primary distinction in the Act was between 'citizens of United Kingdom and Colonies' (CUKCs) and 'citizens of Independent Commonwealth Countries' (whose ability to settle their own nationality was acknowledged), all of whom, along with some other smaller groups, remained British subjects. Irish nationals, meanwhile, were acknowledged not to be subjects but retained all the rights and duties of subjecthood (Paul 1997: 98). At the time, it was not foreseen that the non-white citizens of the remaining colonies (including many Caribbean and

African colonies at the time) or of newly independent countries such as India would use their subject status to enter the UK.

Once these latter groups began responding to labour shortages, immigration restrictions elsewhere, particularly in the USA, and cheap transport by moving to the UK, the government was faced with the irreconcilable imperatives of preventing large-scale non-white immigration and avoiding direct race discrimination against Commonwealth nationals. Such immigration was seen as highly problematic and qualitatively different from both movement between white Commonwealth countries and limited non-white migration for study or similar purposes. This reflected what Paul (1997: 22) calls the 'racialized understanding' shared across all parties and which 'reified race as a biological reality instead of recognizing it as a social construct'. This was perhaps hardly surprising given contemporary conceptualisations of race.

The preference was for using European workers, recruited from among the millions of displaced persons and refugees, to fill labour shortages. This was not only for reasons of racial preference. Displaced persons were often already supported by the government through contributions to their camps. Being aliens, they were also liable to selection and control measures that could not be used on Commonwealth citizens. Yet it soon became apparent that such workers could not be directed or deported in the manner first envisaged, whereupon efforts were made to ensure their integration and acceptance (see Paul 1997: Chapter 3). These adaptations and the political invisibility of the movement of white Commonwealth citizens and Irish nationals contrast with the anxiety surrounding the entry of non-white Commonwealth migrants, even though many of them had cultural, educational and linguistic affinities with the UK.

This anxiety was sometimes expressed through crude racial stereotyping. Paul (1997: 114-18) evokes the language of invasion and embattlement that characterised official responses to the arrival of the *Empire Windrush* in 1948. This did not abate with time. A report commissioned by ministers and completed in 1953 claimed that 'coloured' workers were unsuited for employment due to their low output, irresponsibility, quarrelsomeness and lack of discipline. They were also more easily provoked into violence and were lacking in stamina. Women were reported as being 'slow mentally' (Dummett and Nicol 1990: 179 and Paul 1997: 134). However, for the most part, such beliefs were not publicly expressed. In the aftermath of Jewish genocide in Europe, overt racial discrimination was unacceptable, while the need to foster Commonwealth relations made all the legislative alternatives practically impossible. But official consternation is well documented (see, for example, Paul 1997: Chapter 6). As various accounts make clear (Paul 1997: Chapters 5 and 6, and Hansen 2000: Chapters 3 and 4), governments were preoccupied with the issue long before action was taken through the Commonwealth Immigrants Act 1962. Policy stasis was the result of indecision and fluctuating and different priorities amongst the elite rather than acceptance of such non-white immigration.

Formal legislation being regarded as unachievable, there were attempts to fix the problem through administrative measures promoted, Dummett and Nicol (1990: 177-8) suggest, by officials rather than politicians, although the accounts of Layton-Henry (1992: 29-30) and Paul (1997: 153) suggest high-level political involvement. Means such as language tests and taxes had previously been used to control intra-imperial non-white migration and the entry of non-white seamen into the UK (Dummett and Nicol 1990: 115-21, Paul 1997: 13 and Shah 2000: 70-71). In the post-war period, new techniques were adopted specifically for use against non-white subjects. The term 'British subject' was omitted from travel certificates commonly used to procure entry to French colonial Africa in order to prevent their use for entering the UK (Dummett and Nicol 1990: 177). At the instigation of the British, the governments of Pakistan and India discouraged the emigration of illiterate and unskilled persons in a variety of ways, including refusal of passports, increased costs and additional administrative hurdles. Governors of West Indian territories also refused to issue passports to some individuals, although attempts to secure more rigorous controls foundered after the 'race riots' of 1958. High Commissions publicised the difficult conditions allegedly awaiting would-be migrants (Paul 1997: 152-3).

The extent to which the government's preoccupation with non-white immigration followed, colluded in or manipulated public opinion (see, for example, Dummett and Nicol 1990: Chapter 10, Layton-Henry 1992: 28-41, Paul 1997: Chapter 6 and Hansen 2000: 118-19) is not a question that can be determined here. It is clear that, whatever the motivation and howsoever it was disguised, limiting non-white immigration was the indubitable purpose of policy. Eventually, however, administrative measures were found to be insufficient or ineffective. Rising immigration, fuelled partly by fears of impending controls, riots in 1958 and renewed pressure following the re-election of the Conservative Party in 1959 created sufficient impetus for change. Even so, legislation was still not passed until 1962.

The Commonwealth Immigrants Act 1962 reflected and failed to resolve the tensions that had been caused by the 1948 Act. While some preferential arrangements with former colonies are understandable, it is logical that countries should distinguish, in granting rights of entry, between nationals and non-nationals. Under the 1948 Act, rights of entry extended far beyond those who remained British citizens. If that had become untenable, the most consistent path was to use nationality law to determine those subject to immigration control. However, by the early 1960s, many colonies had still to achieve independence, so that retaining free movement for CUKCs and not for independent Commonwealth nationals would have left large non-white populations still able to enter, while controls on non-nationals would have affected the white population of the independent Old Commonwealth. As Hansen (2000: 102-6) explains, further nationality reform was viewed as problematic for various reasons, including the implication of a second-class citizenship for colonial citizens. The end result was the creation of controls that depended less on nationality than on racial difference, creating problems that remained unresolved for decades.

However, these discriminatory aspects were not evident on the face of the legislation. The 1962 Act applied to all Commonwealth citizens with an exception for those born in the UK or whose passports had been issued by the UK government, including in Ireland. This innocuous-seeming exemption meant that controls still applied to 'citizens of United Kingdom and Colonies' whose passports had been issued by colonial authorities (i.e. not the government) and who were predominantly non-white. Meanwhile, Commonwealth citizens living in independent countries and who claimed citizenship in other ways, for example, by descent, were exempt because their passports were issued by British High Commissions, i.e. directly by the government.

Controls applied to all other Commonwealth entrants, whether or not they were Citizens of the United Kingdom and Colonies (CUKCs), and took the form of a work voucher system, supplemented by provisions for examination of documents, immigration offences, detention, deportation and the imposition of conditions of entry. While the Act applied in theory to all citizens of independent Commonwealth countries, its broad terms and its permissive formulae (for example, under s. 2 an immigration officer 'may' but was not obliged to refuse entry to those affected by the Act), supplemented by both published and secret instructions to immigration officers authorised by s. 16, ensured that white Commonwealth nationals who were not British citizens also continued to enter unhindered.

The work voucher scheme did not apply to groups such as returning residents, students, the independently wealthy and, critically for this book, the wife or child under 16 of those who entered or were already present in the UK. It is this aspect of the Act that is the starting point for the discussion in the next chapter. The argument made here is that the provisions of the Act and the circumstances which led to its implementation created a particular legal context for the control of Commonwealth family migration in the following period. Particular issues had been determined to be critical and legislative structures had been designed to accommodate them. Even if priorities and policy objectives changed over time, legislators had to work from these pre-existing structures or undertake the difficult task of creating new ones. Creating these structures had involved the adoption of strategies and techniques, which were then an obvious resource to fall back on in dealing with future dilemmas.

Discussion

This book argues that a hierarchy of acceptable marriages emerges from an overview of decision-making. The location of a marriage in the hierarchy depends upon the weight attached at a particular moment to factors such as gender, race and compliance with legal and social norms, the precise nature and relative priority of these shifting throughout the period under discussion. The three episodes discussed in this chapter were selected because they demonstrate that the attitudes which informed decision-making and determined the hierarchy were not new but were already present, while the practices and strategies adopted to implement these also had antecedents.

Later in this book, it is argued that, where British women married in unapproved ways, not only did their husbands face rejection but they themselves were also perceived to have excluded themselves from national membership. As already observed, women commonly carry a particular burden in terms of maintaining and reproducing the nation state. A perceived ambiguity in a woman's loyalties tends to create hostility and a drive to fix her within binary categories. This tendency was given concrete form by the uncompromising legal rule on the adoption of a husband's nationality. While the rule did not seem, in practice, to be used to prevent affected women's admission to the UK, it did cause them other substantial difficulties. Such women's personal interests were subordinated to the perceived need, initially, to keep clear the boundaries of membership and ensure the reproduction of social and gender-based hierarchies within the family and, later, to preserve Commonwealth unity. Somewhat paradoxically, while such women were regarded as lacking sufficient autonomy to serve two masters (husband and Empire), women who transgressed by marrying an alien had to accept the consequences of their own folly. While, in the period discussed in the succeeding chapters, women slowly gained formal equality under the law as regards the admission of their spouses, the tendency to regard women more than men as acting disloyally or foolishly in marrying outside the nation state has persisted, particularly where certain nationalities and certain types of migrant have been involved.

Only a relatively small number of refusals were made under the Aliens Act 1905, but those that did occur suggested that commitment to the unity of the migrant family seems to have been shallow, easily displaced and dependent upon the family replicating and preserving in miniature wider social values. Those perceived as being deviant in some respect did not receive the same acknowledgement of their family life. Decision-making under the Aliens Act suggests that those who failed to conform to contemporary standards of morality were regarded less favourably, even though this involved the importation of standards not sanctioned by law. Fears about family immigration similar to those which dominated immigration policy from the 1960s onwards were also observable. As in later eras, the entry of spouses and children may be perceived as an insidious form of immigration in which humanitarian claims are pitched against anxieties about labour displacement and numerical domination. This type of unofficial 'moral gatekeeping' is characteristic of immigration control through marriage, although its actual nature and extent have varied and should be carefully delineated (see also Wray 2006a).

The pattern of refusal under the Aliens Act also suggests an incipient unofficial culture. The development of such unofficial cultures in decision-making has been widely observed in the modern literature (see, for example, Hawkins 1984, Loveland 1994 and Halliday 2000). No argument is made here as to whether immigration control is more or less prone to such tendencies, nor is it suggested that officials implementing the Aliens Act were acting according to any official or semi-official policy. Rather, they operated in an environment in which there was little external oversight or accountability and developed their own *ad hoc* unofficial standards in order to reach decisions which they regarded as fair. Such unofficial standards are also observable in the later practices of the entry clearance service.

It may also be the case that governments or senior officials knowingly engage in unofficial policy measures to further ends that cannot be publicly acknowledged. Such policies, which often cannot be discerned by a perusal of public materials, became a common recourse, as demonstrated by the measures taken in the post-war period to minimise non-white immigration control through control of passports and other administrative tools, and by the use of instructions and discretion under the Commonwealth Immigrants Act 1962, the meaning of which was barely apparent on its face. As discussed later in this book, there is evidence that the conduct of entry clearance officials for many years was not just a case of individual or collective deviancy but represented an official policy disguised by apparently neutral regulation and which aimed to minimise numbers.

The post-war period was the first time that the government had to confront large-scale non-white immigration. Such immigration was seen as entirely different from the movement of white Commonwealth nationals. The 1962 Act imposed controls on the UK's own nationals, creating divisions based mostly on skin colour and imposing a major incongruity with the normal functions of nationality that persisted for decades. It attempted to do this in ways that were not immediately plain, even if few people were actually deceived. The Act, and the administrative measures that preceded it, were premised on the assumption that race mattered and that non-white immigration posed a particular threat, even if racism itself was regarded as an evil and its appearance was to be avoided.

Several major themes explored in succeeding chapters were thus present in the legal structures and institutional practices that existed before Commonwealth marriage migration became a crucial issue. The critical role of race and gender in assessing marriages, the tendency to exclude those who do not conform to majority norms and anxiety about the implications of family migration were all visible in the earlier periods discussed here and played a major part in determining the unofficial hierarchy of marriages that became apparent in later years. Also present were the strategy and tactics used to implement the hierarchy, including the adoption of unofficial standards in decision-making and recourse to administrative measures and obscure legislation to achieve ends that could not be publicly admitted.

However, the major difference with the earlier period is that, in confronting non-white Commonwealth marriage migration, all the beliefs and practices mentioned here were brought into play at once, creating a perfect regulatory storm that hindered the entry of many thousands of particularly male spouses from the Indian sub-continent. How that storm developed and played out between 1962 and 1997 in the legislature, the judiciary and the entry clearance service is the subject of the next three chapters.

Chapter 3

Inclusion to Exclusion: Marriage Migration, Commonwealth Citizens and the Legislature 1962-1997

The Commonwealth Immigrants Act 1962

The previous chapter showed that the Commonwealth Immigrants Act 1962 placed immigration restrictions for the first time upon citizens of the United Kingdom and Colonies (CUKCs). The 1962 Act provided that only those whose CUKC passports had been issued by the British government or by a representative of the government were free from controls. In essence, this meant those who had been born in the UK or who had obtained their passport from the High Commissioner of an independent state. Those whose passports were issued by a colonial authority, i.e. those who lived in remaining colonies, were now subject to the same controls as nationals of independent Commonwealth countries. The racial bias of the statute was not evident on its surface but was nonetheless present. Those whose passports were issued by the High Commissioner of an independent state were largely the white descendants of British emigrants living in the 'Old Commonwealth' countries such as Australia or Canada and who had citizenship through descent. They retained their right of entry, unlike not just nationals of the 'New Commonwealth' such as India, who were no longer CUKCs, but also CUKCs living in the remaining (predominantly non-white) colonies. These latter individuals could no longer freely circulate within the territory of the country of which they were citizens. The provisions of the Act were supplemented by instructions to Immigration Officers (Cmnd 1716) and secret instructions, and gave officials sufficient discretion to ensure discrimination between white and non-white Commonwealth citizens (Dummett and Nicol 1990: 183-4). The Act required Commonwealth citizens subject to control to satisfy an immigration officer that they were entitled to enter on one of a number of grounds: that they were a returning resident or the wife or child under 16 of a returning resident, that they were in possession of an employment voucher, intended to study or had enough funds to support themselves and any dependants without working (for a more detailed discussion of the Act's provisions, see Dummett and Nicol 1990: 183-5).

Many concerns were expressed during parliamentary debate, including the need to avoid (open) race discrimination and the maintenance of Commonwealth ties. Fears about family immigration were only occasionally expressed and even then indirectly and by well-known anti-immigration figures. Sir Cyril Osborne, for example, made reference to the supposed high birth rate amongst immigrants and to Indian citizens who arrived without proper documentation and, after regularisation, sent for their families.[1] Within the mainstream of political debate, there seems at first to have been a strong presumption in favour of married relationships. Initially, the right of wives and children of those permitted entry under the Act was considered so self-evident that it was omitted from the Bill and was dealt with through instructions to immigration officers. It was argued, presciently, in debate that Commonwealth immigrants' rights needed firm protection.[2] R.A.B. Butler, the Home Secretary, moved amendments in Committee to put the right of wives and children on a statutory basis, saying: 'There has never been any doubt in our minds that returning residents, wives and dependent children ought to be admitted.'[3] Such a matter was so important that 'it should not be left to be framed in administrative instructions'.[4] Refusal on medical grounds or because of a criminal record also did not apply to wives or to children under 16.

There was also a strong commitment to ensuring the admission of unmarried women living in 'permanent association' with a man, so that 'the rights of these women should be respected in the same way as if they were already married under our system', a sentiment expressed by an opposition MP but assented to by the government side.[5] However, the provisions were only to be found in instructions to immigration officers, which provided that a woman 'living in permanent association with a man, even if not married to him, should be treated for this purpose as a wife' and that the immigration officer 'should bear in mind any local custom or tradition tending to establish the permanence of the association'.[6] Although this provision seems to have been conceived with Caribbean families in minds, Sachdeva (1993: 48) points out that it had the potential to benefit South Asian families where reliable marriage records were often absent and this may help explain why such a stance did not last.[7] There was some opposition on the grounds of principle, particularly in the Lords, Lord Milverton asking: 'Are we trying to turn this Bill into a kind of legitimisation of concubinage?'[8] For the most part, however, the view was, as Lord Silkin put it, that it was a question of recognising the existence of 'the unmarried wife'.[9] This permissive treatment of Commonwealth immigrants' families was not based primarily upon a commitment to family life; it was predicated on the close

1 HC Hansard, 22 June 1961, col. 1657; HC Hansard, Written Answers, 11 July 1961, col. 35.

2 HC Hansard, 5 December 1961, col. 1293.

3 Ibid., 6 February 1962, col. 318.

4 Ibid.

5 Ibid., col. 322.

6 Cmnd 1716, May 1965, para. 25.

7 See the remarks of George Brown, HC Hansard, 1 November 1961, col. 169 and *Zahra v Visa Officer, Islamabad* [1979-1980] Imm AR 48, discussed in Chapter 4.

8 HL Hansard, 20 March 1962, col. 484.

9 Ibid., col. 488.

relationship between Commonwealth immigrants and the UK, while the presence of large numbers of unaccompanied males was seen as problematic for social reasons.[10] The presumption in favour of marriage in immigration was therefore, even in its moment of maximum impact, contingent.

There were also suggestions in the debate of a hierarchy of acceptable relationships, a recurrent theme of this book. It was implicitly expected that unmarried women should regularise their position as soon as possible once they were in the UK, as the extract quoted above ('as if they were *already* married' – emphasis added) suggests. Married Commonwealth women were immune from deportation, but an unmarried woman living in permanent association was not. The Lord Chancellor emphasised that while he expected discretion to be frequently exercised in favour of such women, they were not to be accepted unconditionally:

> ... it is not right to separate people living a family life together. But it is different when an immigrant has been proved to have abused the hospitality of this country by committing a serious offence. Any such person is *prima facie* suitable for deportation, and exemptions must be narrowly and precisely drawn.[11]

The 1962 Act also assumed that only men were primary migrants. This did not accord with reality, as Bhabha and Shutter (1994: 37-9) point out, and women MPs moved an amendment to replace the word 'wife' with 'spouse'. This was not selected for debate but was briefly discussed in Committee.[12] It was acknowledged that a husband might sometimes wish to follow a 'career wife', but the matter should be dealt with through instructions to immigration officers and such husbands would normally be admitted. However, the Minister, Mr Renton, argued that:

> ... we have strong reasons for not treating husbands and wives in exactly the same way in the granting of unrestricted right of entry. In the Bill, as in our nationality law, we have assumed that the husband is the head of the family and that the wife acquires his domicile.[13]

He also maintained that a wife who had been ill-treated and deserted might obtain a voucher, come to the UK and obtain a good job. The husband, hearing of this, might 'follow her to batten onto her'. The comment anticipated later arguments that immigration restrictions are in the interests of vulnerable women.

In the event, instructions to immigration officers provided that the normal rule was to admit a husband coming to join a Commonwealth wife ordinarily resident in

---

10 For example, single male immigrants were explicitly linked with rising rates of sexually transmitted disease: HC Hansard, 5 December 1961, col. 1224.

11 Ibid., col. 493.

12 HC Hansard, 6 February 1962, cols 326-33.

13 Ibid., col. 330.

the UK even without an employment voucher, unless there were reasons to refuse on the grounds of health, criminality, likely recourse to public funds or because the wife did not wish the husband to join her. In doubtful cases, the strength of the wife's connections with the UK should be taken into account.[14]

The reservations about unmarried women and the husbands of women migrant workers illustrate a recurring aspect of the hierarchy of marriages. People must accept the adverse consequences of their failure to conform to dominant values. However, these consequences were often quite nuanced. Unmarried women living in 'permanent association' were not refused entry, but their continued presence was more conditional than that of married women. Marriages that did not conform to the norm of the male breadwinner and head of household were also less favourably viewed but were not entirely excluded, while those where the wife had a strong connection with the UK stood higher. The implicit hierarchy depended not just on the conformity of the marriage but on the position of the UK-based party, a theme that was to become increasingly prominent.

The 1965 Changes

The Commonwealth Immigrants Act 1962 had been presented as an emergency measure and was opposed by Labour. Its effects were not entirely as anticipated. Immigration from India and Pakistan increased as a result of the employment voucher system. New Commonwealth family immigration also increased rapidly. Many commentators see the restrictions in the 1962 Act as the cause of this rise, as it encouraged migrants to bring over their families and entrench their position (see, for example, Holmes 1988: 26). Hansen (2000: 20, n. 60) disputes this, arguing that immigrants will always be disinclined to leave and that family migration is an inevitable consequence of work migration. Regardless of cause and effect, the rising numbers of dependants soon became a major source of debate.

Parliamentary discussion over the period in which the first controls on Commonwealth family migration were put into place reveals a familiar pattern. Marginal figures strongly opposed to immigration persistently alluded to the 'problem' of excessive New Commonwealth immigration. This took various forms, including reference to immigrants' birth rate, incidence of sexually transmitted disease, polygamous marriage habits, inhumane and unsafe child care practices, and the sheer number of dependants either already present or waiting to come over, described by one peer as a 'frightful shadow'.[15] More moderate politicians

14 Cmnd 1716, May 1962, para. 29.

15 See, for example, Sir C. Osborne, HC Hansard, Written Answers, 1 April 1965, col. 268 or 31 May 1965, cols 141-2; Lord Elton, HL Hansard, 6 July 1965, col. 1163; Sir C. Osborne, HL Hansard, Written Answers, 18 February 1963, col. 4; Miss Quennell, HC Hansard, Written Answers, 16 April 1964, col. 82; Mr N. Pannell, HC Hansard, Oral Answers, 9 July 1964, col. 617; Captain Kerby, HC Hansard, 9 December 1963, col. 40;

sought to resist these insinuations but with increasing difficulty. While the virtues of immigration and immigrants were still defended, debate had shifted towards terms set by those opposed to further immigration: numbers, overcrowding and abuse. By the time that a Labour government returned to power in 1964, further control of immigration was a prominent issue following the unexpected return of a Conservative MP in Smethwick after a racially charged local campaign (Bevan 1986: 79). By this time, the necessity of immigration control was taken for granted and immigration had become synonymous with New Commonwealth immigration. Alien immigration remained subject to a more restrictive regime and was uncontroversial, while immigration from the Old Commonwealth was barely mentioned. When it was discussed, it was seen as unproblematic, even where there was abuse of the rules.[16] On the other hand, there was resistance to acknowledging the racial aspects of policy. There were occasional overt references to 'coloured' or 'Afro-Asian' immigration, but use of such terms was avoided by mainstream politicians, who emphasised that the policy was not intended to operate on colour or racial lines, even though that is what happened.[17]

In this period, there seemed to be little appetite for the draconian restrictions of later years. Nonetheless, commitment to the reunion of Commonwealth families had to compete with unceasing arguments in favour of further controls based on premises that almost all politicians now accepted. The way out of the impasse, adopted then as in later eras, was to crystallise discontent around the undeserving case of the fraudulent applicant. Abuse had been regularly raised by those promoting further controls in the period leading up to 1965, particularly around dependants, including the apparent ease with which the admission of polygamous or common law wives could be abused.[18] In February 1965, Sir Frank Soskice, the Home Secretary, agreed that there was 'evidence that under the existing control evasion on a considerable scale is taking place', including among dependants, and announced that fresh instructions would be given to immigration officers.[19] These would include greater scrutiny of dependants' claims, the start of an administrative process discussed further in Chapter 5, which had catastrophic consequences for immigrants but from which politicians could distance themselves.

Early in 1965, monthly statistics started to be kept, detailing the country of origin, the category and the numbers of immigrants.[20] Shortly afterwards, Soskice

---

Sir C. Osborne, HC Hansard, Oral Answers, 4 June 1964, col. 1226; Lord Hawke, HL Hansard, 10 March 1965, col. 149.

16 See, for example, HC Hansard, Oral Answers, 9 July 1964, cols 617-19; HL Hansard, 23 February 1965, col. 681; HL Hansard, 10 March 1965, col. 94.

17 Lord Elton, HL Hansard, 6 July 1965, col. 1162; the Prime Minister, HC Hansard, 8 July 1965, col. 1812.

18 See, for example, HC Hansard, Written Answers, 30 July 1964, col. 377; Lord Elton, HL Hansard, 30 June 1964, col. 504.

19 HC Hansard, 4 February 1965, cols 1284-8.

20 HC Hansard, Written Answers, 16 March 1965, col. 252.

agreed that there were at least 500,000 Commonwealth citizens with the right of admission, mostly from the West Indies, Pakistan and India, although he did not know whether they intended to come to the UK and he had no intention of removing their rights.[21] Despite this measured response, the numbers question was becoming linked to the abuse issue and genuine dependants with a legal claim to come to the UK were beginning to lose legitimacy. This was made explicit in a parliamentary question by Mr Wingfield Digby, where he asked 'in view of the sharp increase in the number of dependants accompanying or joining Commonwealth citizens subject to immigration control, what steps he is taking to ensure that there is no abuse of dependants?'.[22]

From being regarded as an occasional unfortunate by-product of regulation, the prevention of abuse rapidly became a driving motivation. Some abuse is inevitable under any regulatory regime, but anti-abuse measures are not solely a function of its actual prevalence; the stronger the anti-abuse measures, the less weight is implicitly awarded to recognising, to their fullest extent, the claims of the genuine or innocent.[23] While the measures taken to prevent abuse by dependants in 1965 were minor by later standards, they indicate that the downgrading of dependants' claims had begun, rationalised by the association between numbers and fraud. New Commonwealth immigrants were under scrutiny simply because of their numbers and all began to be tainted with suspicion. Measures that might adversely affect them became increasingly acceptable. From this period there were fewer statements of unequivocal support in favour of family reunion and fewer sentimental paeans to the immigrant contribution to health and other public services. A downward spiral had been initiated which later made possible restrictive measures which would have been inconceivable only a few years before.

After Lord Mountbatten, sent as an emissary in 1965, failed to persuade Commonwealth countries to introduce their own curbs on emigration, he recommended a variety of further restrictions, including health checks for all immigrants, dependants and students. The subsequent White Paper contained a number of proposals for restrictions which clearly went counter to the spirit if not the letter of the 1962 Act.[24] The government could not introduce a compulsory register of dependants or entry certificates without repealing the absolute obligation to admit under the 1962 Act. However, immigration officers would:

---

21 HC Hansard, Written Answers, 1 April 1965, col. 268.

22 HC Hansard, Written Answers, 30 July 1964, col. 377.

23 This has sometimes been openly acknowledged. The government's response to the Select Committee on Race Relations and Immigration in 1979 said that it was 'a regrettable though inevitable consequence of the need to prevent abuse that some genuine applicants suffer inconvenience' (Juss 1997: 54). In 1983, Malcolm Rifkind weighed up the competing claims of applicant and immigration control and said: 'It is no fairer to allow someone in who is not entitled than to exclude anyone who is' ('Fair and foul ways to bring down the immigration barrier', *The Guardian*, 2 March 1983).

24 HMSO, Cmnd 2739, August 1965.

> with a view to preventing evasion, be instructed to apply strict tests of eligibility, and will take into account whether the would-be entrant produces on arrival an entry certificate issued in the country of origin or other appropriate documents establishing his or her identity. An entry certificate will not be issued unless the head of the household, whether resident in this country or intending to come in the future, has furnished ... particulars of his dependants ...[25]

The register of dependants proved both burdensome and ineffective, and was soon dropped.[26] Entry certificates, however, became increasingly important and were presented as being in the interests of immigrants, as it enabled a decision to be made in the country of origin rather than after departure. They remained voluntary, however, and take-up was low at around 20 per cent, even though immigration officers were instructed that a holder should be assumed to be qualified for admission unless there was evidence to the contrary.[27] Take-up was particularly low on the Indian sub-continent, presumably because of the vast distances to be traversed in order to obtain one from the High Commission. In 1969, only one in eight Indians coming for settlement arrived with a certificate.[28] However, the Wilson Committee did not recommend that they become compulsory on the grounds that this would align Commonwealth citizens too closely with those aliens who required visas.[29]

The 1969 Changes: The Ban on Husbands and Compulsory Entry Certificates

After 1965, hostility towards New Commonwealth secondary immigration did not abate. The association between numbers and fraud continued to be made ever more emphatically, and the number of dependants coming to the UK was described by one peer as 'rapidly assuming alarming proportions'.[30] One MP alleged that up to 60 per cent of dependants had been wrongly admitted, although, when pressed, he acknowledged that that he had no evidence for the statistic.[31] As well as the usual calls for the cessation of all immigration, there were calls for children over 14 to

---

25 Ibid., para. 19.

26 Roy Jenkins, HC Hansard, Written Answers, 2 August 1966, col. 91.

27 HMSO, Cmnd 2739, August 1965, para. 14; *Report of the Committee on Immigration Appeals*, Cmnd 3387, 22.

28 HC Hansard, 6 May 1969, col. 1101.

29 *Report of the Committee on Immigration Appeals*, Cmnd 3387, 22.

30 See, for example, Earl of Albemarle, HL Hansard, 26 July 1967, col. 3; Sir C. Osborne and Captain Kerby, HC Hansard, 9 May 1968, Written Answers, cols 125-6; Lord Ailwyn, HL Hansard, 25 October 1967, col. 1650.

31 Mr Anthony Buck, HC Hansard, 22 January 1969, cols 547-51.

be barred.[32] The loss to the Inland Revenue due to alleged fraudulent claims for dependants' allowances was raised, an issue that became central to administrative practice in relation to family admission and is discussed in Chapter 5.[33] The wives and children of polygamous marriages were also the subject of several parliamentary questions. With the exception of some female politicians, critics of polygamous marriages confined their arguments to the number of extra immigrant offspring likely to result as well as the scope for tax evasion. The standard government response was that the number of such families was insignificant (although there was also a defence of the international law principle of recognising lawfully contracted marriages). The dominance of the numbers debate was apparent even in such an apparently culturally charged issue.[34]

The government's tone in response to pressure became more defensive. That the number of dependants was problematic was common ground, so it was a question of demonstrating that they were competent at limiting their entry. The rights of children over 16 to join a single parent and of dependant fathers between 60 and 65 were curtailed in 1968, the fear being that these were disguised workers. Family unity continued to be defended by the government on the grounds of preventing 'social problems in the community' and 'common humanity', but, increasingly, only in terms of the rights of wives and children under 16.[35] It is not surprising that the first moves were against husbands, whose acceptance had always been more conditional than that of wives.

In a written parliamentary answer on 30 January 1969, James Callaghan, the Home Secretary, announced restrictions on husbands.[36] Numbers of male Commonwealth citizens admitted for marriage under a 'concession' had risen in 1968 to 1,676. The rise was said to be on such a scale that marriage was being used as a means of entering, working and settling in the UK outside of the employment voucher scheme.[37] In future, the admission of husbands and fiancés would be limited to those 'presenting special features' and an entry certificate must be obtained prior to departure. Those already present in the UK for temporary purposes would not be permitted to settle there following marriage, save in exceptional circumstances. The new regime was to be implemented through revised instructions to immigration officers. The new measures severely affected non-white New Commonwealth husbands. They were in a worse position than alien spouses, who continued to be allowed to enter in most cases (Dummett and

32 HC Hansard, 14 May 1968, col. 208.

33 HC Hansard , 8 February 1968, cols 1268-9.

34 HC Hansard , 23 April 1968, cols 621-2 and 2 May 1968, cols 1195-200.

35 See, for example, HC Hansard, 7 November 1968, col. 1048, Lord Stonham, HL Hansard, 25 October 1967 or David Ennals, HC Hansard, Written Answers, 5 March 1968, col. 57.

36 HC Hansard, 30 January 1969, col. 367.

37 A counter-view was that rumours of restrictions had fuelled the rise in numbers: see 'Guardian Miscellany', *The Guardian*, 3 June 1974.

Nicol 1990: 206-7). Husbands of white women were less severely affected as their wives were more likely to plead successfully that they could not relocate to places where they would be culturally isolated (Bhabha and Shutter 1994: 57-9 and Chapter 4). Only six South Asian men were permitted entry during the whole of 1973.[38] Particularly badly affected were around 400 stateless Asian husbands expelled from Uganda and refused entry to the UK even though their wives and children held UK passports. The supremacy of the 'numbers' issue is encapsulated by one proposed solution which involved other countries accepting some of these 400 husbands, so that their families who lived in the UK would leave, compensating for other new arrivals.[39] There seems to have been little debate regarding the justification of such drastic measures or their effect upon the rights of UK resident women. It was assumed that males were desperate to gain access to the labour market, that fraudulent applications were commonplace and that these had to be prevented even at a cost to some genuine applicants. The hierarchy of marriages already referred to is more starkly apparent here. Marriages in which a husband sought to join his wife rather than the conventional reverse pattern lacked credibility and legitimacy.

The ban on Commonwealth husbands did not pacify those opposed to secondary immigration; rather, by conceding the underlying argument, it may have made a defence of such immigrants more difficult. Having permitted government competence to become associated with the control of New Commonwealth immigration, ministers had no choice but to continue to play the numbers game.[40] The use of entry certificates was effectively made compulsory for all dependants of Commonwealth entrants by the Immigration Appeals Act 1969. The justification was to protect family members from giving up homes and jobs only to be refused entry on arrival. It was also hoped to prevent long queues and evidential difficulties when applicants arrived at ports tired and confused and had to establish their right to enter with inadequate and incomplete documentation. Immigrants, including the elderly and children, were being detained or returned and their treatment had received adverse publicity.[41] One press report concerned an elderly woman, unable to speak English, who arrived with her sons but was separated from them and detained at Holloway Prison for two months. Her husband worked nights, but visited every day bringing familiar food. Nonetheless, she became so ill that she

38 Ibid.

39 Their position was eventually rectified by Roy Jenkins. 'Uganda cases strike at women's rights', *The Guardian*, 11 January 1973; 'Petition on split Asian families', *The Guardian*, 23 January 1973; 'Plan for Asian husbands', *The Guardian*, 31 January 1973; 'Guardian Miscellany', *The Guardian*, 3 June 1974.

40 See, for example, the exchange between the anti-black immigration MP Sir Cyril Osborne, Home Secretary Merlyn Rees and the backbench Labour MP Sid Bidwell: HC Hansard, 20 March 1969, cols 721-3.

41 'Asians' reception "inhumane", welfare leader says', *The Times*, 23 December 1968; 'Vetting at home for future immigrants', *The Guardian*, 2 May 1969.

was admitted to hospital.[42] A ten-year-old boy was also reported to have been detained for more than two weeks. He could not understand his interpreter and had to rely on other detainees to intercede for him.[43]

In future, migrants would have their claim to enter determined before departure under the entry clearance system. Their interests would be protected by the new appeals procedures. Meanwhile, administrative practice for aliens' dependants was brought into line with Commonwealth dependants, except where agreements for visa abolition prevented this, meeting the objection, at least to an extent, that Commonwealth citizens were being treated less favourably than aliens. The less favourable general treatment of aliens was also maintained.[44]

While those promoting the new system may have sincerely hoped to avoid the problems of eligibility for entry being decided at the port, there were also less noble motives (see Juss 1997: 44-5). The amendment to the Immigration Appeals Bill was introduced late in the Lords shortly before Committee Stage. This was explained as being to 'reduce to a minimum the risk of a rush to enter in advance of the alteration of the law', although an effort was later made to disassociate the government from this suggestion.[45] Clearly, a measure that was in the best interests of immigrants should not give rise to a rush of applicants to beat it. Critical voices argued that compulsory entry certificates would permit bad practice to be concealed and would negate the objectives of the new appeal system, and that delays (already a problem) would inevitably increase, suspicions that were justified, as discussed in Chapter 5.[46] The measure caused the resignation of the National Council of Civil Liberties and the Joint Council for the Welfare of Immigrants from the Home Office Committee on Immigrant Welfare on the grounds that their work had been rendered meaningless.[47]

The assumption of fraud and of the necessity of combating it was now so entrenched that the alternative possibility of reducing queues by carrying out fewer checks was beyond realistic contemplation. Rather, the emphasis was on ensuring adequate systems for advising and supporting applicants in the country of origin.[48] The desire to conceal rather than prevent the harsh treatment

---

42 'Asians' reception "inhumane", welfare leader says', *The Times*, 23 December 1968.

43 HC Hansard, 6 May 1969, col. 1102.

44 See HC Hansard, 1 May 1969, cols 1630-6; HL Hansard, 6 May 1969, cols 1098-142.

45 Lord Stonham, HL Hansard, 6 May 1969, col. 11; Lord Gridley, HL Hansard, 6 May 1969, col. 1126.

46 Lord Gifford, HL Hansard, 6 May 1969, cols 1107, 1110; Lord Foot, HL Hansard, 6 May 1969, cols 1121-6.

47 'Give them a proper chance', *The Guardian*, 20 May 1969; 'Home Office funds for immigrants', *Sunday Telegraph*, 15 June 1969.

48 See, for example, Lord Brockway, HL Hansard, 13 May 1969, cols 83-5 and 'Home Office funds for immigrants', *Sunday Telegraph*, 15 June 1969. However, advice services were not established until the mid-1970s (Lyon 1975).

of immigrants and their family members introduces another recurring theme in immigration legislation: a commitment to providing outwardly palatable answers to public anxiety rather than seeking to dispel or minimise that anxiety.

Reversing the Ban: The 1974 Rule Changes

The Immigration Act 1971 introduced a new framework for controlling immigration. Section 1(5) provided that the Immigration Rules would be formulated so as to protect the pre-existing rights of men settled in the UK prior to 1 January 1973 to bring spouses and minor children to the UK, fulfilling earlier pledges (Hansen 2000: 230). All other Commonwealth citizens and their dependants were to be governed by what Shirley Williams described as the 'weak vessel of the immigration rules'.[49]

Under the first set of rules, the rights of Commonwealth citizens (other than patrials and those exempted under the then s. 2(2) of the Act) were now broadly aligned to those of aliens.[50] Wives of Commonwealth citizens were to be admitted if the husband was already settled or was coming for settlement, provided he was willing and able to support and accommodate them without recourse to public funds.[51] The position of women 'living in permanent association' was also maintained and there were provisions for fiancées.[52] The husbands and fiancés of Commonwealth citizens or aliens were not to be admitted for settlement unless the Home Secretary was satisfied that there were 'special considerations' which rendered exclusion undesirable or, in the case of Commonwealth citizens, he had a grandparent born in the UK.[53] Special considerations included, as an example, the hardship caused to a woman forced to live with her husband outside the UK.[54] Both exceptions would have principally benefited white women. The continuing dependent status of women was reflected in the deportation clauses of the after-entry Rules, which provided that women and children could be deported alongside their husbands in some circumstances.[55]

The implicit hierarchy of acceptable marriages, already alluded to, was now more clearly linked to race. Its maintenance was facilitated both by the actual law and by the discretionary powers of immigration officers, yet its sexism rendered it imperfect. White British men could count on being able to bring in spouses more or less as they chose. Black and Asian men settled in the UK had, formally

49 HC Hansard, 22 November 1972, col. 1350.

50 HC 79, 80, 81 and 82, 25 January 1973; s. 2(1)(a) Immigration Act 1971 (now amended).

51 HC 79, para.41; HC 81, para. 36.

52 HC 79, paras 42, 50; HC 81, paras 37, 45.

53 HC 79, paras 47, 48; HC 81, para. 42.

54 HC 79, paras 47-8; HC 81, para. 43.

55 HC 80, paras 33-48; HC 82, paras 40-55.

speaking, the same rights but were increasingly subject to discrimination through administrative practices in the entry clearance system, an issue discussed in Chapter 5. A woman who married a white male of British descent may have been able to take advantage of the rules on patriality. In other cases, she could claim that she should not suffer the hardship of living in an alien environment, a claim which women of New Commonwealth origin found far harder to make (Bhabha and Shutter 1994: 57-9; see also Chapter 4 below). Nonetheless, white women were adversely affected by the Rules, and the contrast with the new EEC free movement provisions rendered this discrimination more stark.[56]

There were several attempts to bring the matter to the attention of Parliament.[57] On 11 April 1974, the Home Secretary, Roy Jenkins, announced that he was reviewing the wider aspects of the question and that, in the interim, he was issuing instructions for a more 'sympathetic and flexible' approach to be taken.[58] In June 1974, Lena Jeger introduced a Parliamentary Bill to achieve equality for women in immigration and citizenship.[59] Later that same month, Roy Jenkins announced that he would present new rules allowing the admission of husbands and fiancés of women settled in the UK.[60] Almost completely absent from parliamentary debate was reference to women of New Commonwealth descent or origin who had been most severely affected by the ban on husbands. Lord Brockway, in his question to the Lords, gave only examples of hardship caused to women of British descent married to foreign men.[61] Lena Jeger, in moving her Private Member's Bill, stated that, among the enormous postbag she had received on the question, only a few cases concerned Asian countries.[62]

Concerns about arranged marriages started to become explicit during these debates. Lord Harris, speaking for the government, asserted that the arranged marriage system made it more likely that women of Asian origin would contract marriages abroad, so that lifting the ban would lead to considerable increased immigration.[63] Even those sympathetic to change had reservations. Bryan Magee, for example, foresaw a particular danger of them being arranged for payment in order to achieve immigration.[64] Others argued, by contrast, that young Asian people would increasingly reject the international arranged marriage.[65] A few MPs did see

56 For example, it was reported that only ten Australian and six Canadian husbands were admitted during 1973: 'Guardian Miscellany', *The Guardian*, 3 June 1974.

57 See HC Hansard, Written Answers, 21 March 1974, col. 136; HL Hansard, 28 March 1974, cols 774-95.

58 HC Hansard, Written Answers, 11 April 1974, cols 260-261.

59 HC Hansard, 21 June 1974, cols 879-941.

60 HC Hansard, Written Answers, 27 June 1974, cols 535-6.

61 HL Hansard, 28 March 1974, cols 778-80.

62 HC Hansard, 21 June 1974, col. 884.

63 HC Hansard, 28 March 1974, col. 794.

64 HC Hansard, 21 June 1974, col. 936.

65 See, for example, Lena Jeger and Gwyneth Dunwoody, HC Hansard, 21 June 1974, cols 883 and 933.

the question as one of principle and of race as well as of sex equality. Sid Bidwell spoke of the benefit of reform to young women of Pakistani and Indian origin.[66] Martin Flannery pointed out that regardless of whether young Asian women did or did not tend to marry within the UK, 'they have an inalienable right to marry men who live outside this country and be allowed to have these men come here and live with them'.[67] Predominantly, however, the underlying premise was that reform was desirable provided it resulted in only a few Asian males coming to the UK. Roy Jenkins' memoirs (1991: 374) record that the Home Office estimated that a change to the law would result in 5,000 new entrants and, as Home Secretary, he initially declined to act. In subsequent debate, however, he said: 'When I first considered this I believe that I put too high the likely immigration consequences and did not fully allow for the stark and unacceptable nature of the discrimination.'[68] The ban was lifted in 1974. While this was a progressive step, it did not demonstrate a fundamental shift in the assumptions which by that stage underpinned the discussion on marriage and immigration. It represented an evolution in and refinement of the hierarchy of marriages so that the claims of mainly white women were acknowledged. However, the grant of equality depended upon a number of other beliefs also holding true. One was that those of Asian descent brought up in the UK were less likely to enter international arranged marriages. When this expectation was not fulfilled, new measures, discussed below, became necessary.

A number of key assumptions about immigration were by now also firmly in place. Numbers had become the hard currency of debate. Immigration was seen as a one-way process, a simple accretion of numbers posing problems of labour displacement. Immigration from the New Commonwealth was considered to be qualitatively different from other immigration and to be undesirable. The only means of reducing these numbers, it appeared, was through ever-more restrictive measures.

The Defence of Equality

As well as the usual series of parliamentary questions on polygamous wives, arranged marriages, impecunious immigrants and the never-ending queue of dependants, immigration was debated in the Commons in January 1975 and May 1976, in the Lords in June 1976, and again in the Commons in July.[69] During these debates, the major issue remained the admission of husbands, even though between

66 Ibid., col. 910.

67 Ibid., col. 929.

68 HC Hansard, 27 June 1974, cols 535-6. See also 'Guardian Miscellany', *The Guardian*, 3 June 1974.

69 HC Hansard, 23 January 1975, cols 1998-2020, 24 May 1976, cols 33-104; HL Hansard, 24 June 1976, 529-60, 5 July 1976, cols 964-1094.

1974 and 1976, the number of Commonwealth husbands and fiancés arriving rose from around 500 to around 1,800 (Evans 1983: 133), hardly an inundation.

Alex Lyon, the Minister for Immigration, undertook a tour of the Indian sub-continent, during which he criticised the bureaucracy, delays and errors of the entry clearance system. He also recommended that officials adopt the civil standard of proof in immigration cases (unknown to Lyon, the Divisional Court had also found in such terms in 1972, the immigration service having apparently acted unlawfully since then).[70] Lyon was especially concerned with the level of error and the hardship that existing procedures were causing to genuinely married couples. This, he said, had 'to be put into the balance as well as the number of bogus applications'.[71] He also pointed out that the entire notion of a 'bogus' application should be treated with caution. If Western levels of proof were demanded in a largely undocumented society, it was unsurprising that people sometimes turned to those able to furnish them with what was apparently needed. While this reflected the reality that many South Asian marriage procedures were customary and unofficial, Conservative politicians were aghast at the suggestion of any relaxation. They argued that the single biggest cause of delay and hardship was immigrants failing to call over their families promptly and that the absence of documentation and the level of illegal immigration meant that robust and time-consuming checks were necessary. Lyon also argued that there was a finite pool of dependants, so that speeding up the process 'would not be increasing the total commitment of this country towards immigration from the sub-continent'.[72] Whether the 'queue' was finite was the subject of much disagreement.

In 1976, D.F. Hawley, Assistant Under-Secretary in the Foreign and Commonwealth Office, toured entry clearance posts on the sub-continent and wrote a series of confidential reports.[73] They comprised anecdotal reports, impressions and allegations about the extent of fraud, polygamy, the abuse of marriage for immigration purposes (the relaxation of the rules in 1974 was described as a 'bonanza') and the possibility of a never-ending chain of migration. His major thrust was that attempts to implement Lyon's instructions, combined with an appeals system 'weighted in their [applicants'] favour', made the system too favourable to immigrants. Any further move in that direction would turn entry clearance officers (ECOs) into 'rubber stamps' and 'the pride of an ECO in doing a professional job would be destroyed', a perspective considered further in Chapter 5. He also made reference to South Asians being 'men of two worlds', retaining an Asian domicile, building property and marrying locally, an early, and hostile, acknowledgement of transnationalism. Despite the absence of evidence beyond anecdote, the Hawley Report was welcomed by those opposed to New

---

70 *R v Home Secretary ex p. Hussain* (1972) unreported. See also Alex Lyon's response to the Hawley Report in the Runnymede Collection, Middlesex University.

71 HC Hansard, 23 January 1975, col. 2013.

72 Ibid., col. 2011.

73 Available in the Runnymede Collection (and discussed in Juss 1997: 109-21).

Commonwealth immigration. During the debate in May 1976, Enoch Powell referred to the Report as evidence that, far from there being a finite pool, 'we are bailing out an ocean'.[74]

Alex Lyon's confidential reply to Hawley indicates the careful balancing act performed even by politicians sympathetic to the immigrant cause.[75] He defended his record on overturning refusals and the imposition of the balance of probabilities as the standard of proof. His arguments were nonetheless predicated on the assumption that non-white family immigration was problematic but would reduce over time. He was sympathetic to re-assessing the pool of dependants and even to a quota 'to contain the numbers argument'. His public response was also to reiterate that the pool was finite and that the international arranged marriage would inevitably decline as a source of immigration.

It is true that there were finite numbers of Commonwealth immigrants with a statutory right to bring in spouses and children[76] and that some immigrants' children would marry within the UK. At that time, migration was widely regarded as a single act of movement resulting in a definitive new residence, a view that has been challenged by the literature on transnationalism discussed in the introduction to this book. Lyon's argument thus relied almost wholly on a single premise of uncertain validity. It left intact the other premises upon which anti-immigration arguments were based: that numbers were the primary issue and that immigration was solely or principally a New Commonwealth phenomenon (although some Labour MPs did challenge this).[77]

Conservative MPs were openly sceptical about the role of the arranged marriage in immigration. Bhabha and Shutter (1994: 62) refer to comments by Conservative politicians that the liberal regime on husbands was a mistaken concession to 'the women's lobby' and was contrary to both British and Indian culture. Explicit comments were made only by marginal figures, but the premises upon which they were based informed other more measured contributions. Thus, William Whitelaw in opening the July debate recognised the right of a head of household to bring in one wife ('We are a basically monogamous society')[78] and children. There were renewed calls for a register of dependants. Arranged marriages were viewed as being primarily a source of immigration, principally because, it seems, Conservative MPs could not imagine any other motivation for such a marriage.

Thus, neither Conservative nor Labour MPs consistently argued a principled defence of the international arranged marriage. The difference between them

---

74 HC Hansard, 24 May 1976, col. 49.

75 Available in the Runnymede Collection.

76 According to Juss (1997: 190), this particular commitment had been fulfilled by the 1990s.

77 See, for example, Syd Bidwell: 'A certain nonsense emerges if one is thinking genuinely in terms of immigration as a whole-white and black, brown, and black and white' (HC Hansard, 5 July 1976, col. 989).

78 Ibid., col. 969.

was that Labour MPs believed that the arranged marriage would disappear once families had been exposed to superior Western models, while Conservative MPs believed their usefulness as a tool for immigration would ensure their survival. Roy Jenkins took a more sophisticated although less liberal approach than either of these positions. He saw the truth as lying somewhere between the finite pool and the infinite ocean, avoiding reliance on the decline of the arranged marriage. He was committed to preserving the rights of husbands even if he was not willing to go further, and he rejected the assumption that the 'bogus marriage' was a particular characteristic of South Asian immigration, pointing out that arranged marriages 'can be just as real and longlasting as any other marriages' and that '[s]uch contrivances are not confined to those wishing to immigrate from, or avoid removal to, the sub-continent'.[79] Equally, he declined to treat as 'morally reprehensible' the 'lively sense of extended family in Asian culture', even if he was not ready to permit entry by extended family members. He also argued the case for going beyond the numbers debate:

> The basic issue here is not simply one of numbers. We cannot avoid this addition to numbers unless we either keep out all husbands – which would be across-the-board sex discrimination – which would affect the right of English-born wives to bring in an American or Australian husband, or by keeping out those from the sub-continent which would be straightforward racial discrimination. I could not, and would not, defend either of these two forms of blatant discrimination. [80]

Jenkins' approach rested upon the assumption that numbers mattered and that immigration meant New Commonwealth immigration. At that time and in that climate, this was almost the universal view, although MPs such as Joan Lestor and Syd Bidwell did offer some dissent.[81] Jenkins also did not acknowledge the role that administrative measures played in permitting hidden discrimination. Nonetheless, he sought to uphold a position of principle on the admission of husbands in the face of constant and unremitting pressure from both the press and opposition MPs. By the end of 1976, neither he nor Alex Lyon, who had sought to ensure that the rules were applied fairly on the sub-continent, remained in post.

The Birth of Primary Purpose

The association between immigration abuse and the entry of Commonwealth husbands or fiancés was now accepted as fact and was frequently raised in Parliament, although without firm evidence as to the scale of deceit. Government ministers emphasised that it was not confined to New Commonwealth immigrants,

79 Ibid., col. 984.

80 HC Hansard, 24 May 1976, col. 104.

81 See n. 77 above and ibid., cols 73-9.

but such was the clear sub-text of much of the discussion. The Conservative Shadow Home Secretary, William Whitelaw, for example, drew an explicit connection between harmonious race relations and the prevention of abuse.[82] Government competence was now inextricably linked with effective control of New Commonwealth immigration. Dislike of overt sex and race discrimination meant that the rights of New Commonwealth husbands had been, for a period, able to achieve reluctant acceptance as the price of allowing equality to white couples. Once alternative means were found through the strengthening of administrative measures, arranged marriages sponsored by a woman returned to their lowly position in the hierarchy.

Before he left the Home Office, Jenkins had established a small parliamentary group under Lord Franks to look into the feasibility of a register of dependants. Their report was published in February 1977 and the government concluded that such a register would not be desirable or practicable.[83] Following rumours of a revival of the ban on husbands, in March 1977, the government amended the Immigration Rules to prevent men being accepted for settlement through marriages of convenience.[84] The new rules introduced for the first time the concept of primary purpose. However, at that time it was linked closely to the idea of marriages of convenience, a concept from which it later became separated. Thus, entry or settlement would be refused 'if the officer to whom the application is made has reason to believe that the proposed marriage would be one of convenience entered into primarily to obtain admission here with no intention that the parties should live together permanently as husband and wife' (HC 238, para. 47). In addition, husbands were to be admitted or given leave to remain for an initial period of 12 months unless the marriage had taken place more than 12 months previously. The spouses of Commonwealth and non-Commonwealth citizens were now treated in the same way, except that a Commonwealth fiancé, one of whose grandparents was born in the UK, would be admitted for immediate settlement, a privilege which would predominantly benefit white men.

The obligation to find both that the marriage was one of convenience and that the parties should not intend to live permanently together meant that the new rule had only a limited impact at that stage. Evans (1983: 133) suggests that the small numbers of men refused leave to settle after the newly introduced 12-month probationary period indicate that abuse was not a widespread problem at the time. During debate, Alex Lyon argued that the measures were a panicked response to an exaggerated problem.[85] It was also becoming increasingly apparent that the primary means of controlling unwanted immigration would be administrative. The Select Committee Report on Race Relations and Immigration, despite a mostly

82 HC Hansard, 9 February 1977, col. 1435.

83 Ibid., cols 1433-4.

84 'Rees blocks aisle route into Britain', *The Guardian*, 10 February 1977.

85 HC Hansard, 24 May 1977, cols 1336-7.

restrictive tone, drew attention to the lengthy delays and sceptical attitudes of entry clearance officials.[86]

The turn towards administrative measures was, from a government perspective, astute. A government operating in the climate of the time and explicitly committed to the 'numbers game' had to be seen as in control of immigration. However, politicians did not want to confront voters with the actual consequences of this. Administrative practices carried out principally abroad made controls appear more palatable, particularly when backed by the assumption of widespread abuse of the system. By using administrative measures, governments sought to meet their electorate's (and perhaps their own) dual desire to limit immigration and to maintain a clear conscience about how this was achieved. The danger of this strategy is the exposure of the unattractive underbelly of immigration control. This happened when press reports appeared in early 1979 that single women from the sub-continent were being subjected to 'virginity tests', creating an explosive scandal (see Juss 1997: 109-22 and Chapter 5 of this volume for more information). The Home Secretary, Merlyn Rees, refused to order a departmental inquiry or support disciplinary action against the officers involved, merely stating that action had been taken to prevent a recurrence.[87] His replies to parliamentary questions on the subject suggest a strong desire to distance himself from the affair, with terse answers couched in legalistic and bureaucratic terms.[88] It must have been highly embarrassing for it to be so clearly apparent that the government's strategy for controlling immigration permitted such practices. Eventually, the issue was deflected by the Yellowlees Inquiry into medical examinations.[89]

Falling numbers of primary migrants enabled the government to present the immigration 'problem' as being under control, although some Conservative MPs continued to call for further measures.[90] These MPs rejected any moral obligation towards immigrant communities to ensure family reunion and excluded them from the population whom they were tasked to represent, claiming that 'the only moral commitment that matters is the interests of the British people here as a whole'.[91] Government ministers adopted a less crude view, relying on the necessity of good race relations to justify policy: 'The United Kingdom is now, and will remain, a multiracial society. Our overriding responsibility is to do all in our power to make it a harmonious one.'[92]

---

86 *First Report from the Select Committee on Race Relations and Immigration*, HC 303 (HMSO, 1978): 177-87.

87 HC Hansard, 9 February 1979, cols 312-13.

88 See, for example, ibid. or HC Hansard, 14 February 1979, col. 539.

89 *The Medical Examination of Immigrants, Report of Chief Medical Officer*, Home Office, December 1980.

90 See, for example, Mr Dudley Smith, HC Hansard, 6 April 1978, col. 650 or Mr Budgen, HC Hansard, 6 April 1978, col. 651.

91 Ivor Stanbrook, HC Hansard, 6 April 1978, col. 657.

92 Merlyn Rees, HC Hansard, 6 April 1978 col. 648.

Refining Primary Purpose

These differing understandings of what constituted the 'British people' were increasingly crudely drawn after the election of a Conservative government in 1979. Margaret Thatcher was influenced by those who viewed hostility to the 'alien wedge' as natural and morally defensible, a view encapsulated by her famous 'swamping' comment in 1978 (Dummett and Nicol 1990: 238-41). The Conservative manifesto had contained a commitment to preventing the admission of all husbands and fiancés. However, that would have been too crude to implement, affecting white as well as black women, and a more racially discriminatory approach was eventually proposed.

In November 1979, the new Home Secretary, William Whitelaw, announced a series of new measures including several concerning the admission of husbands.[93] The test of primary purpose was to be separated from that of intention to live together. This would have consequences for the meaning attributed to 'primary purpose' in law (see Chapter 4 for further discussion). The proposals also required the parties, whether fiancé(e)s or spouses, to have met, a provision clearly aimed at discouraging Asian arranged marriages. Lord Scarman described it to the Home Affairs Select Committee as 'an attack on the social habits and customs of people who have come to this country and who are living in accord with the customs in which they were brought up'.[94] Equally clearly targeted was the provision allowing entry to only one wife. Of most immediate concern was the proposal that only the husbands or fiancés of British citizen women born in the UK would be eligible to apply at all. Whitelaw conceded that this discriminated but viewed it as necessary to prevent disguised primary male immigration.[95] He saw the ban as 'the price that we have to pay to stop marriage being used as a device to achieve admission to the United Kingdom'.[96] Timothy Raison, Minister for Immigration, meanwhile acknowledged that the affected marriages 'may perfectly well last as enduringly as love marriages', undermining the abuse argument. [97]

The Home Affairs Select Committee warned that the proposals breached the European Convention on Human Rights.[98] Opponents argued that only tiny numbers were actually suspected of abuse and the measure would have only a

93 *HMSO Proposals for Revision of the Immigration Rules*, Cmnd 7750, November 1979.

94 'New immigration rules breach Convention, Lord Scarman says', *The Times*, 18 January 1980.

95 'Immigrant plan has sex bias – Whitelaw', *The Guardian*, 5 November 1979.

96 HC Hansard, 4 December 1979, col. 255.

97 'Immigration needs rules when too many try to play at once', *Daily Telegraph*, 4 December 1979.

98 *House of Commons First Report from the Home Affairs Committee 1979-80, Proposed New Immigration Rules and the European Convention on Human Rights*, HC 303.

limited impact on overall immigration figures.[99] Even *The Times* wondered if it was 'really necessary for the British Government to show itself to be in deliberate breach of its moral and legal international undertakings for such a puny result'.[100] Political opposition was nonetheless muted by the acceptance of the premise that New Commonwealth male immigration was highly undesirable.

Reference has already been made to the hierarchy of acceptable marriages. Fiancés and husbands of black and Asian origin had long been placed on the bottom rung and their interests, although given passing acknowledgement, were easily displaced by the need to prevent even a few non-white immigrants. The refinement here was that the origin of the wife as well as of the husband now determined the extent of the right to decide where to live. The racial distinction between the privileged 'belongers' and those with only a partial status was apparent from the exception eventually incorporated after much public complaint for women born abroad to parents born in the UK.[101]

This implicit notion of who did or did not 'belong' was fluid and was given added complexity by the confused state of the UK's nationality law. Ivor Stanbrook, a prominent anti-immigration MP, asked the Home Secretary to make it clear that 'this country is governed in the interests of its inhabitants and not those of immigrants', suggesting that 'belongers' was a closed category that immigrants could not enter. Tony Marlow was even more explicit, saying that brown and black families 'can go home and rejoin their families in the country of origin'.[102] Senior members of the government avoided such crude rhetoric. Whitelaw's reply to Stanbrook was that the country was 'governed in the best interests of all its citizens', a questionable assertion given that the new proposals discriminated between different types of citizen.[103] There was a lack of congruity between Whitelaw's status as a 'humane Tory' and the discrimination contained in the proposals.[104] Trying to reconcile this involved asserting that 'belongers' included those of immigrant descent as 'girls born in this country, of any race, colour or creed, have exactly the same rights'.[105]

Nevertheless, there was still unease at treating more recently settled communities as complete outsiders. This was resolved by claiming, however unconvincingly, that the measure was in the interests of those affected by it. Thus, Whitelaw said during the debate: 'Many Asian girls in this country would wish to make their own choice. Indeed, that may well happen after the change in the rules rather than at present.' A professed concern to protect women from oppressive non-British practices was becoming a recurring theme in rationalising restriction,

99 'Protest at entry bar on husbands', *The Guardian*, 4 December 1979.

100 'In Breach of the Convention?', *The Times*, 6 March 1980.

101 'New immigration rules could hit overseas appointments', *The Guardian*, 19 November 1979.

102 HC Hansard, 14 November 1979, col. 1344.

103 Ibid., col. 1337.

104 Ibid., col. 1339.

105 Ibid., col. 1345.

called on by Timothy Raison in support of the new requirement for the parties to have met:

> Whatever we may think of arranged marriages, I doubt whether it is right to have an arranged marriage when the parties have never met. In recent weeks I have met large numbers of Asian women. Many of them, when describing what they regard as a satisfactory arranged marriage, agreed that the bride and groom should meet before the marriage.[106]

While the hierarchy of marriages rested upon assumptions about gender and culture, the fear was not of the abuse of marriage alone but also of labour market displacement. Raison also said, during the debate on the new rules, that the arguments as to abuse:

> do not apply with the same force to women entering the United Kingdom to join husbands. In the main, they join husbands who are in the position of having the prime responsibility for providing for their families … Men entering the country to join women settled here … are not joining the family's breadwinner but expect, and are expected to make, a major contribution themselves to the earnings of their new family unit.[107]

Cultural and economic fears intertwined and reinforced each other. Not all marriages where the wife joined the husband were abusive and ministers carefully avoided being led by backbenchers into making such generalisations.[108] However, such a marriage was viewed as more prone to abuse both because it was considered culturally deviant and because it enabled male economic activity. This was compounded by a belief that arranged marriages could, more easily than other forms of marriage, be exploited for immigration purposes. The distinction between crude discrimination and assertions of cultural superiority was often employed as a defence against charges of racism. Thus, Whitelaw argued that the measures were not racist as women of Asian origin born in the UK would be able to bring in husbands.[109] Fears about labour displacement and the belief that arranged marriages were loveless affairs and therefore mere vehicles for immigration should have applied to these women also. The underlying assumption here was that second-generation women, exposed to the superior marriage patterns of the West, would resist such arranged marriages, a belief to which both Labour

106 HC Hansard, 4 December 1979, col. 371. See also 'Immigration needs rules when too many try to play at once', *Daily Telegraph*, 4 December 1979; 'Help for unhappy brides', *Daily Mirror*, 19 April 1980.

107 HC Hansard, 10 March 1980, col. 1026.

108 See, for example, Timothy Raison, HC Hansard, 24 June 1982, col. 424.

109 HC Hansard, 14 November 1979, col. 1337.

and Conservative MPs subscribed. The attack on the arranged marriage thus rested on a combination of economic, cultural and gender assumptions.

The Forced March Back to Equality

In a White Paper 'quietly slipped out', the government 'postponed' a manifesto pledge for a register of dependants.[110] Although the number of dependants admitted was declining, senior politicians were unhappy that, due to second-generation marriages, the 'pool' of family migrants from the sub-continent was not proving to be finite.[111] The White Paper adopted a rather bizarre proposal that the pattern of marriage of Asian men born in the UK should be monitored to assess future long-term trends in immigration, reflecting the reality that there was little now that the government could do to restrict admission further.[112] On the contrary, pressure was mounting elsewhere for liberalisation. The existing law was attracting claims to the European Court of Human Rights and, in May 1982, the European Commission of Human Rights found that the UK government had a case to answer. A discriminatory regime was becoming untenable, particularly when contrasted with the rights accorded to spouses under European law (Sachdeva 1993: 83-4, 165-9).

It was also perhaps becoming less urgent. Sachdeva (1993: 72-4) suggests that, anticipating an unfavourable result, officials were sharpening their use of primary purpose as a means of refusal, perhaps causing the reduction in numbers just alluded to. Certainly, the rate of refusal of husbands and fiancés increased from 10 per cent in 1981 to 47 per cent in 1982 (Bhabha et al. 1985: 69). Moreover, a measure of reform could be rationalised as anticipating the new law on nationality due to come into effect on 1 January 1983. In December 1982, the government introduced proposals to permit all women who were British citizens to sponsor husbands or fiancés, regardless of how that citizenship was acquired.[113] The government aimed to meet objections by introducing two additional restrictions: a probationary period of two years and a shift in the burden of proof to the applicant. Its priority was to head off backbench revolt by those who viewed immigration as purely a question of the numbers of non-white immigrants and who were unable to accept even a modest rise. There was little effort to deny the racist underpinning of the controls. Whitelaw admitted that the rationale for favouring women born in the UK was disappearing, as a new generation of girls of Asian descent born in the UK

110 'The numbers game', *New Society*, 2 December 1982. In fact, the proposal had been effectively discarded following recommendations from the Home Affairs Committee: 'Tories shelve register plan for immigrants' dependants', *The Guardian*, 8 December 1981.

111 'Minister rejects "finite" migration', *The Times*, 27 April 1982.

112 'The numbers game', *New Society*, 2 December 1982.

113 Cmnd 8683.

reached marriageable age.[114] Relying on the assumption that any man coming from abroad to join his wife 'would be doing so primarily for immigration purposes' might have 'awkward consequences with regard to people marrying Australians, Canadians, Americans and so on'.[115] The assumption that the arranged marriage was particularly suited to exploitation for immigration was explicit.[116] Sponsoring a husband to come to the UK was a privilege that should be reserved only for those who truly belonged. This category could now be conveniently redefined as comprising British citizens, a more restricted category than the old CUKC.[117]

However, fear of increased numbers and a misjudgement as to opposition intentions led to a government defeat for the measures through an alliance of its own backbenchers opposed to any liberalisation and opposition members opposed to further restriction.[118] Obliged to lay new rules before Parliament, the government responded with HC 169, which eventually came into effect on 16 February 1983. The extension of the probationary period was dropped, although the critical change, the reversal of the burden of proof, remained. This, coupled with an increasingly hostile administrative climate, was the major factor in enabling the primary purpose rule to be used to such deadly effect in the coming period. Refusals on primary purpose grounds, as a percentage of all refusals of husbands and fiancés, rose from 18 per cent in 1982 to 73 per cent in 1983. It seems that right-wing backbenchers received reassurance that primary purpose would prevent male Asian immigration before accepting the rule changes (Bhabha et al. 1985: 68-9). Debate covered similar ground as in December, although the government's tone was now more confident. Some Conservative MPs such as Nicholas Budgen and Jill Knight, while defending the arranged marriage as appropriate abroad, argued that 'it should not be a means of entering Britain'.[119] This was acceptable as:

> [it] cannot be said that the arranged marriage creates suffering if it is not allowed, because the girl does not know the man who may be selected for her in far away Jullunder. Such a girl is increasingly coming to the view that she does not wish a man to be selected for her in Jullunder.[120]

The belief was that a woman would not be an active or willing participant in an international arranged marriage and the marriage must be made for the benefit of others, principally the immigration advantage of the man. Thus, David Waddington, Minister of State, justifying the reversal of the burden of proof, said

114 HC Hansard, 15 December 1982, col. 361.
115 Ibid., col. 362.
116 Timothy Raison, HC Hansard, 15 December 1982, col. 431.
117 Ibid., cols 429-30.
118 'Misjudgment caused immigration defeat', *The Times*, 18 December 1982.
119 HC Hansard, 15 February 1983, cols 213-16.
120 Ibid., col. 226.

that: 'There cannot be anything wrong in principle with expecting a man who is seeking a major benefit to prove that he is entitled to it.'[121] Meanwhile, primary purpose could be presented as being for the protection of female sponsors. In the wake, for instance, of a sensationalist press report about Asian girls being 'sold' by their parents to Asian men who followed them home from school, Waddington commented that '[t]he so-called "primary purpose" rule has been much attacked but these stories show that it can protect women against exploitation'.[122] Again, assumptions reinforced each other – that of female passivity dovetailed with the denial of the rights of women to choose the place of marital residence. This absence of rights could also be justified in terms of identifying belongers. As Waddington put it, '[i]f they do not wish to be British, why should they have the right to bring in their husbands?'.[123]

This forthright tone was typical of the Conservative government of the time. David Waddington, in particular, adopted an abrasive style that, over the next period, made explicit values, beliefs and assumptions which had been present but were muted or implied under previous regimes. Typical examples included crude head-counts of potential (black and Asian) immigrants, the treatment of all New Commonwealth fiancés and husbands as primary migrants, the unofficial designation of 'pressure to emigrate' countries and a crude assertion of the superiority of life in the UK.[124] This confidence was matched by belief in the ability of the entry clearance service to do the unpleasant work of refusal at a distance, aided, in particular, by the 'primary purpose rule', which was repeatedly described by Waddington as an anti-abuse measure.[125] Complaints about entry clearance procedures were marginalised or dismissed.[126] On occasion, however, the reality of these processes punctured the rarefied parliamentary atmosphere.

121 Ibid.

122 'Scandal of the brides for sale', *Daily Mail*, 5 August 1985.

123 HC Hansard, 15 February 1983, col. 242.

124 HC Hansard, 23 May 1985, cols 1172-3 and 28 February 1985, cols 454-5.

125 See, for example, HC Hansard, 4 July 1985, col. 519. The lack of congruity between the stated intention of preventing marriages of convenience and the true position was occasionally made explicit. On one occasion, a Home Office spokesman acknowledged that it had never been the practice to allow a husband or fiancé to enter simply because it was accepted that the marriage was genuine ('Husband banned from rejoining mother-to-be', *The Guardian*, 3 January 1984).

126 See, for example, Home Affairs Select Committee (1982), where criticism by advisory agencies of entry clearance practices was dismissed. The issue was raised again in evidence given to the Commons Sub-committee on Race Relations, but to little apparent effect: 'Entrants to UK "quizzed in police fashion"', *The Guardian*, 19 March 1985. Again in 1985, the Home Affairs Committee dismissed complaints about the service. The Chair of the Committee, John Wheeler, controversially described the complaints as 'ill-founded allegations and unsubstantiated anecdotes' ('Race equality groups "do serious harm"', *Daily Telegraph*, 27 June 1985; 'In the cause of racial harmony', *The Guardian*, 9 July 1985; 'Liberals slam Home Office department', *Asian Times*, 12 July 1985.

One such instance was the debate on the Commission for Racial Equality report on immigration procedures (Commission for Racial Equality 1985).[127] For the most part, however, there was a severe lack of congruity between the bland assurances by Waddington and others as to the professionalism of entry clearance staff and the actual position, as discussed in Chapter 5.[128]

The government still had to face the challenge of the *Abdulaziz* case in the European Court of Human Rights.[129] The government's defence of its policy in that case rested on labour market protection, the right to control immigration and the necessity of preventing abuse (see Evans 1983: 140-1 and Sachdeva 1993: 92). Its arguments emphasised that these applicant wives remained outsiders. One was described as having 'no strong ties with the United Kingdom, having acquired nationality merely through a very short-lived marriage'. In fact, this applicant had lived in the UK for seven years before marrying her applicant husband and the couple had a UK-born child.[130] The problem for both the government and applicants was that the European Court found only that the sex discrimination involved in the rule could not be justified. A change in the law was required but, in the absence of adverse findings as to race discrimination or violation of Articles 3 or 8 of the Convention, it could be achieved simply by levelling down the rights of women applicants to those of men. Thus, the government could use a forced and minor concession – the extension of the right to sponsor a husband to settled women as well as citizens – as a means of creating an equality of misery for all. The outcome was that all the requirements which applied to husbands and male fiancés now applied equally to wives and fiancées, with additional tightening for all parties with regard to public funds, now defined to include family income supplement and housing benefit.

In debate, Leon Brittan, for the government, relied on the assumptions that had informed previous debates and which do not need reiteration. The obsession with numbers was emphasised by the explicit trade-off between the reluctantly given concession and announced intention to repeal the statutory guarantee in s. 1(5) Immigration Act 1971 of family unity for male Commonwealth citizens settled in the UK on 1 January 1973. This mechanistic and dehumanising approach belies the concern for family unity expressed earlier in Lord Brittan's speech:

> As a result, therefore, of the court's judgement and of this change taken by itself, we expect that the numbers accepted for settlement each year are likely to rise by about 2,000 a year. However, this increase will, at least to some extent, be offset

127 HC Hansard, 23 May 1985, cols 1166-206.

128 Ibid., cols 1166-7.

129 *Abdulaziz, Cabales and Balkandal v United Kingdom*, judgment of 28 May 1985, ECtHR, Series A, no. 94.

130 'Policies for a race apart', *The Guardian*, 25 October 1982.

> by the changes, which I will come to in a moment, concerning the admission of wives and families.[131]

The new Immigration Rules were initially announced only in a Commons Written Answer, a debate being conceded only after strong opposition pressure.[132] The government's approach caused an outcry from immigrant groups, the opposition and the Parliamentary Group on Race Relations, but protest was ineffective.[133] After the new rules came into effect on 26 August 1985, both a man and a woman who were settled in the UK were able to sponsor a spouse or fiancé(e). Entry clearance would be refused unless five separate conditions had been met by applicants. For spouses, these were:

1. that the marriage was not entered into primarily in order to obtain admission to the UK; and
2. that each of the parties had the intention of living permanently with the other as his or her spouse; and
3. that the parties to the marriage had met; and
4. that there would be adequate accommodation for the parties and their dependants without recourse to public funds in accommodation of their own or which they occupied themselves; and
5. that the parties could maintain themselves and their dependants adequately without recourse to public funds.[134]

Similar provisions applied to fiancé(e)s and those seeking extension of stay (with the additional requirements that the marriage had not been terminated, that there had been no breach of the immigration laws and that the marriage did not take place after deportation or removal proceedings had commenced).[135]

The disposability of the family rights of even long-established Commonwealth males was emphasised by the subsequent removal under the Immigration Act 1988 of the statutory guarantee in s. 1(5) Immigration Act 1971, announced as the trade-off for permitting the entry of husbands. Such a summary dispatch of the long-standing family reunion rights of men suggests that principled attachment to them had, for a long period, been superficial and provisional. While wives who joined their husbands stood higher in the hierarchy of deserving unions than husbands who joined their wives, all were subordinate to the need to prevent even a few thousand unwanted black and Asian immigrants. It was claimed that removing the right under s. 1(5) was an attempt to erect additional hurdles when it was realised that DNA testing would make it impossible, in most cases, to refuse entry

131 HC Hansard, 23 July 1985, cols 895-6.

132 'Change in immigration rules to be debated', *Daily Telegraph*, 12 July 1985.

133 'Immigrant wives controversy grows', *The Times*, 12 July 1985.

134 HC 503, para. 46.

135 Ibid., paras 41, 124.

on the grounds that the parties were not related as claimed (an issue discussed further in Chapter 5).[136] The 1988 Act also introduced the requirement to present a certificate of entitlement or passport as evidence of the right of abode under the Immigration Act 1971, restrictions which, it has been claimed, were primarily aimed at hindering family reunification within the Bangladeshi community (Shah 2005: 130).

In 1986, the Rules were amended to prevent entry where the incoming spouse was under 16 and again in 1990 to prevent entry when either spouse was under 16.[137] More recent rises in the minimum age are discussed in Chapters 6 and 7. While the advisability of very young marriages was (and remains) a legitimate subject for debate, the exclusionary context meant that this was understood only as further cultural discrimination. Similar sentiments were evoked by the amendment of the Rules to prevent the entry of more than one wife to a polygamous marriage, an issue which the government eventually acknowledged affected about 25 households per year.[138] This low number was not reflected in earlier and well-publicised claims made by the Select Committee on Race Relations and Immigration. It is not clear from the reports whether these misleading claims were due to misrepresentation by staff at the High Commission in Bangladesh or were wilfully misinterpreted by the anti-immigration Chairman of the Select Committee.[139]

Throughout the period, the government's tone was harsh and overbearing towards those separated by law from their spouses abroad. The implicit assumption was that individuals had themselves rendered their claims illegitimate through marrying in unsanctioned ways. David Waddington, for example, used his usual combative style to reply to a question in the House about constituents separated by the Rules:

> Opinions may differ on whether parents should be encouraging children to marry boys abroad who have been brought up in an entirely different way rather than their contemporaries in British society. But the primary purpose rule is in the general public interest and those cases do not illustrate any defect in the rules, rather the refusal of people to accept immigration requirements approved by a democratically elected Parliament. All too often a girl goes through a marriage and has a child and then the Home Office is asked to pick up the pieces when … anybody with a scrap of sense could have seen before the marriage that the man could not qualify to come here and would have no claim to come here.[140]

136 'Home Office erects further barriers', *New Life*, 23 June 1989.

137 HC 306, para. 1A; HC 555, para. 3.

138 HC 555, para. 3; HC Hansard, 16 November 1988, col. 786.

139 'Inquiry into clash on Bangladesh wives', *The Times*, 28 November 1985; 'MP in retreat on wives claim', *The Guardian*, 28 November 1985; 'MPs scale down claims on immigrant wives', *The Times*, 3 November 1985; 'MPs move to close immigrant loophole', *The Times*, 27 November 1985.

140 HC Hansard, 19 February 1986, cols 457-8.

In the 12 years between 1985 and 1997, many thousands of married couples were separated by the primary purpose rule. There was the occasional chink of light prompted in part by the embarrassing liberality of European Community law, as demonstrated by the well-known case of *Surinder Singh.*[141] Following that case and in the light of domestic case law on 'intervening devotion' (see Chapter 4), concessions were announced in June 1992. Applications would no longer be refused on primary purpose grounds where it was accepted that the marriage was genuine and subsisting, and the parties had been married for at least five years or one or more children had the right of abode in the UK. This provided at least partial relief even if at the cost of a lengthy separation, an unofficial waiting period (Menski 1994: 118). The rule was abolished shortly after the election of a Labour government in 1997.

Conclusion

Although Enoch Powell had praised the contribution of immigrants to the National Health Service in the early 1960s, by 1964 he believed that Commonwealth immigration should be controlled. Nonetheless, he accepted those immigrants already present to be 'part of the community' and stated that 'there is an inescapable obligation of humanity to permit the wives and young children of immigrants already here to join them' (Dummett and Nicol 1990: 196). By 1967, the commitment to family reunification could be best achieved by immigrants returning home (Dummett and Nicol 1990: 196). In 1968, his infamous 'rivers of blood' speech legitimised and gave voice to discontent at the immigrant presence:

> We must be mad, literally mad, as a nation, to be permitting the annual inflow of some 50,000 dependants who are for the most part the material of the future growth of the immigrant-descended population. It is like watching a nation busily engaged in building up its own funeral pyre. (Quoted in Layton-Henry 1992: 80)

Powell was an atypical figure, but the dramatic changes in his position represent, in stark terms, the wider shift in attitudes in the legislature towards the admission of Commonwealth spouses over the period discussed in this chapter. While some politicians expressed themselves more abrasively or acted more directly than others, consistent threads may be identified throughout the many changes of policy described in this chapter.

Immigration policy was viewed as a matter purely to be decided according to the self-interest, enlightened or otherwise, of the nation state. No parliamentarian proposed a different basis for determining policy. Nonetheless, politicians did not

141 Case C-370/90, *R v Immigration Appeal Tribunal ex p. Home Secretary (Surinder Singh case)* [1992] ECR I-4265.

always hold the same conception of national membership. For some, this was only the white population apparently under siege from ceaseless black immigration. Discrimination against those born outside the UK relied on a somewhat more refined view. Others included all those who were lawfully present long-term residents. The shifts in the law over the period discussed here reflect the temporary victory of one or other of these competing conceptions.

Another universal assumption, only challenged by marginal figures, was that non-white immigration was uniquely problematic. White immigration was not counted, scrutinised or even acknowledged, while even small numbers of non-white immigrants provoked drastic measures. The fear seemed to be that permitting a few to enter would open a breach through which hordes might pour in, with dire consequences. In this respect, family migration, particularly by men, was perceived as particularly insidious. The public persona of spouse or dependant, with their humanitarian claim, concealed a less welcome identity as economic migrant and as a link in a never-ending chain. This fearful perspective rested on other beliefs and assumptions: that immigration was a single one-way process and that the pool of potential migrants was infinite, that indigenous workers were displaced by migrants and that the problems of accommodating new migrants by far outweighed the advantages they brought with them. These fears were invoked only by non-white immigration. While immigrants from the sub-continent brought linguistic and cultural challenges, hostility towards earlier immigration from the Caribbean, with its British-oriented culture, suggests that these concerns were, at least to an extent, an indication of deep-rooted racial fears.

Over the period, the constant emphasis on abuse and fraud delegitimised even the act of asking for admission, particularly by men. The main exceptions to this perspective amongst senior politicians were Alex Lyon and Roy Jenkins. Lyon tried to make his defence of immigrants more acceptable by relying on the doubtful premise that non-white secondary immigration was largely finite. Jenkins did not challenge the underlying assumptions of immigration control but was arguably more honest in acknowledging that the issue was the acceptability of non-white immigration within British society rather than 'abusive' applications by immigrants. For the most part, however, reliance on the assumed ubiquity of abuse was dominant.

These beliefs and assumptions about immigration in general reinforced those about the admission of spouses in particular. Despite rhetoric as to the importance of family life, support for the reunification of migrant families was always conditional and became more conditional over time. An implicit hierarchy of acceptable marriages evolved during the period. Race and gender were both dominant factors and were intertwined and mutually reinforcing. As neither race nor (except in the early part of the period) gender discrimination could be publicly acknowledged, they were often expressed using proxies, primarily claims of abuse and, later, oppressive arranged marriages. The arranged marriage was also a source of concern in its own right. Its continuation was one reason why the 'pool' of dependants on the sub-continent did not prove to be finite and it was regarded primarily as a source of unwanted immigration. Lack of sympathy for the emotional claims it embodied made it easy to treat it not only as a cause but as an abusive vehicle of immigration, a familiar elision in immigration control. Marriages where the man accompanied or came to join his wife in particular lacked full legitimacy. In these instances, choosing the 'wrong' husband turned the wife into a partial outsider with consequences that she must accept. The differential treatment of UK residents makes it clear that some the claims of some residents were considered as less weighty than those of others, while the act of marrying an outsider further reinforced their own lack of full belonging.

The claims of all marriages were thus, to a degree, conditional and the arranged marriage was especially vulnerable because it permitted unwanted immigration and because it was poorly understood and viewed as inferior to Western models. Those sympathetic to the claims of immigrants argued that it would disappear as second-generation immigrants grew up. It is likely that some members of a second-generation immigrant community will marry within their country of residence or indeed spouses from other countries. But many MPs under-estimated the centrality of the arranged marriage to the maintenance of the global Asian diaspora and their negative beliefs about it made a principled defence of such marriages more difficult. Those who were anti-immigrant believed that such marriages continued because they were a useful vehicle for immigration. The implied assumption was that Asian parents cared so little for their children's future happiness, howsoever conceived, that they would submit them to an otherwise undesirable marriage purely for an immigration advantage. Arranged marriages where the husband moved to the UK were regarded as doubly illegitimate, resting on a perspective of the South Asian husband as primarily motivated by immigration and of the Asian wife as passive participant. To the extent that such a judgement was unfair, little damage resulted as there was assumed to be no emotional investment in the marriages by either party. Harsh exclusionary policies could therefore be rationalised as causing little distress to the parties involved.

The extent to which the arranged marriage, in itself, created hostility towards South Asian immigration is less clear. Several assertions of cultural superiority have been cited in this chapter. In many cases, these functioned as *post hoc* rationalisations of policy rather than as reasons for it. While a poor understanding of arranged marriages enabled them to be designated as mere vehicles for immigration and while their apparent strangeness reduced sympathy for separated couples, the primary motivation was always the minimisation of South Asian immigration.

If the claims of Asian spouses were regarded as weak, they nonetheless existed, even if they were persistently sacrificed to more urgent political imperatives. The effect of the legislative measures described here was mostly concealed by the entry clearance system (see Chapter 5) or rationalised as a reaction to abuse. This enabled the government to present black and Asian immigration as being under control and the public to avoid confronting the consequences of these policies. This is unsurprising – governments wished to meet the expectations of their largely white electorate and present themselves as competent in controlling immigration. However, it does suggest a more complex public attitude than straightforward hostility towards immigration and immigrant communities. It seems that there were limits to the visible race discrimination which politicians were willing to impose and which the public would accept. The hierarchy of acceptable and deserving marriages might place some marriages on the bottom rung, but the necessity of concealing the hardship involved in their rejection suggests that they had at least some claim. Even under the full force of primary purpose, a proportion of applications succeeded, while efforts were made to rationalise discriminatory policies in non-discriminatory terms. Obligations incurred under statute, such as those to wives and children under the Commonwealth Immigrants Act 1962 and s. 1(5) Immigration Act 1971, were slow to be repealed, although this did eventually happen.

There was not therefore an unlimited public appetite for harsh exclusionary measures at any cost. Rather, governments, anxious to ensure every possible political advantage, aimed to give the electorate what it wanted without making plain the price that was paid for it, upholding the illusion of pain-free immigration control.[142] Immigrant communities and their foreign spouses might be strange and often unwelcome, but the manner in which their applications were dismissed paradoxically recognised the force of their claim.

142 Politicians occasionally acknowledged this. David Waddington defended the policy in 1983 by saying: 'Everyone pays lip service to the need for immigration control. But no one likes to see the logical result – individuals being refused the right to come and stay here and some as a last resort having to be removed' ('Discrimination against women is defended', *Oldham Evening Chronicle,* 28 November 1983).

Chapter 4
Marking the Boundaries of Exclusion: Marriage Migration and the Judiciary before 1997

Introduction

This chapter considers judicial attitudes towards marriage and immigration before 1997, including marriages believed to have been entered into for immigration reasons. It shows that the judiciary was largely indifferent to these before the era of mass non-white Commonwealth immigration. When cases involving New Commonwealth immigrants started to come before the courts, judicial attitudes became more complex and inconsistent. This chapter argues that there was, at least in the early stages, some sympathy. However, this came to be tempered by anxiety about non-white immigration, albeit only occasionally overtly expressed, and a hardening of attitude. The courts did not check and often assisted government and administrators in ensuring that the 'primary purpose' rule applied to marriages that were acknowledged not to be a sham.

Commentators have argued that the judiciary has shown greater deference to executive power in immigration than in other matters (Bevan 1986: 16-22, Legomsky 1987, Desai 1996 and Griffiths 1997: 182-204). However, this has not been uniform and the picture is complex, as these authors and others have acknowledged (see, for example, the discussion in Stevens 2004: Chapter 8, Bevan 1986: 20-21 and Thomas 2003). There have been various explanations for the apparent oscillations in judicial decision-making. Stevens (2004: 365) notes the consistent involvement of particular judges in more liberal decisions. Thomas (2003: 509-10) considers, in relation to asylum, that the courts have been more active and have achieved more long-term successes when intervening in matters of good administration and procedure than in policy. Legomsky (1987: 246) attributes judicial conservatism in immigration matters to political pressure prevailing during periods of high immigration. This chapter argues that in many of the cases discussed here, judges relied on the same beliefs and assumptions about immigration as were held within government and by administrators, resulting in a large degree of congruity in the formulation and application of policy. Specifically judicial values seem to have been relatively muted during the period.

The role of the Immigration Appeals Tribunal during this period is ambiguous. Juss (1997: Chapters 4 and 5) is critical of its tendency to defer to and reinforce the wider discriminatory culture, a point also made by others (Grant and Martin 1982:

355, Harlow and Rawlings 1997: 519). There may have been a tendency towards 'judicialisation' (Thomas 2003: 484), something that is arguably inevitable in dispute-resolving mechanisms (Stone Sweet 1999, 2000: Chapter 1), but, during the period under discussion here, the Tribunal also operated as an administrative body enmeshed with other immigration administrative processes. The decisions that Juss criticises are principally those in which the Tribunal was complicit in supporting the exclusionary culture of the Entry Clearance Service and which did not, on the whole, require the Tribunal to engage in discussions of legal principle. These issues are given fuller coverage in Chapter 5. However, in other respects, the Tribunal was also principally or jointly responsible for the development of aspects of legal doctrine and these decisions are discussed here, alongside higher court decisions. In these cases, the Tribunal was not uniformly complicit with administrative practices.

The era was dominated by the primary purpose rule. Nonetheless, the judiciary was also required to decide other matters relating to immigration through marriage. These are analysed in detail in several sub-sections below, after which the primary purpose case law is considered.

'Having It Both Ways': Judicial Attitudes in Non-Primary Purpose Cases

Bogus Marriages

Bogus marriages for reasons of migration pre-dated control of New Commonwealth immigration. Earlier case law focused on the validity of the marriage rather than on the immigration consequences that flowed from it. The usual rule was that a marriage was valid even if entered into for immigration purposes (*Silver v Silver*; see also Lord Hailsham in *Vervaeke v Smith*),[1] but the courts occasionally adopted a more flexible approach when their sympathies were aroused.

In *H v H*,[2] the wife, a Hungarian national, entered into a bogus marriage with a French citizen in order to leave Hungary, where she was in fear of persecution by the communist regime. In the UK, she successfully applied to have the marriage annulled on the grounds of duress, Karminski J finding that the fear she was under negated her consent to the marriage. *H v H* was followed in *Szechter v Szechter*, involving Polish dissidents.[3] The husband, with his wife's agreement, divorced her and married the petitioner to secure the latter's release from prison and emigration. Once in the UK, they wished to rectify the position. The facts of the case are harrowing: the petitioner in *Szechter* was in more immediate danger than in *H v H* and it is evident that the judge desired to assist the parties. There was tenuous legal authority for these decisions. Duress had always previously been specifically

1 [1955] 1 WLR 728; [1983] AC 145 [152].
2 [1953] 2 All ER 1228.
3 [1971] P 286.

directed towards forcing the petitioner to enter into the marriage.[4] Karminski J in *H v H* cited no authority for his novel interpretation. In *Szechter*, Sir Jocelyn Simon relied on *H v H* and *Buckland v Buckland*, in which the duress was again directed at ensuring that the marriage took place.[5] It is hard not to suspect a willing extension of legal principle in order to justify a desired outcome (Cretney, Masson and Bailey-Harris 2002: 60, n. 60). A further instance of relative liberality was *Silver v Silver*, where a marriage of convenience took place to enable the German wife to cohabit in the UK with a married man. Following his death, she wished to marry someone else. Her husband was by now living with another woman by whom he had three children. The High Court refused a decree of nullity, but exercised its discretion to grant a divorce, viewing this as in the interests of not only the parties and their children but also of the community at large.

In contrast to these benevolent decisions stands the memorable case of *Vervaeke v Smith.*[6] A Belgian woman entered into a marriage of convenience to obtain British nationality and avoid deportation as a prostitute. The price paid to her destitute husband was £50 and a ticket to South Africa. She later underwent a marriage ceremony with a wealthy Italian national who died during the wedding party. To secure her inheritance as a widow, she needed to annul the first marriage. She obtained an annulment only to have it overturned by the High Court due to her perjury. She was then granted an annulment in Belgium and sought recognition of it in the UK. The House of Lords rejected her application on the grounds of *res judicata*, which would have been sufficient. However, they also, by a majority, found against her on the grounds of public policy. Although the case was described as 'a horrible and sordid story', Lord Simon maintained that neither her career as a prostitute nor her previous perjury were relevant to the decision, while the reasoning deployed was consistent with authority. Nonetheless, it is apparent that the court was not, as in *H v H*, looking for a way to relieve the difficulties of a party with whom they were in sympathy.

By contrast, where an undeserving applicant stood to benefit from a finding of validity of marriage, the court sought to negate that benefit. In *Puttick*, Astrid Proll, a member of a terrorist group, fled Germany after being charged with serious criminal offences.[7] She entered the UK under a false identity and used that identity, as well as other forged documents, to marry a British man. To avoid extradition, she sought to have the marriage declared valid so that she could register as a

4 The leading case at the time was *Scott and Sebright* (1886) 12 PD 21, in which the applicant had been subjected to threats of violence and the destruction of her reputation to ensure her compliance. Perhaps aware of the possible dangers of this interpretation, Sir Jocelyn Simon set a very high objective threshold for duress that proved problematic in later cases (see *Singh v Singh* [1971] P 226) until it was replaced by a subjective test in *Hirani v Hirani* (1982) 4 FLR 232. See Deech 1973: 111 and Poulter 1986: 27-32.

5 [1968] P 296.

6 [1983] AC 145.

7 *R v Secretary of State for the Home Office ex p. Puttick* [1981] 1 QB 767.

British citizen.[8] The Family Division of the High Court refused.[9] The Divisional Court extended the existing legal principle to find the marriage valid but to decline to direct registration as a British national.[10]

These cases are too few to permit more than tentative interpretation. However, they suggest that the courts sought to reach decisions congruent with their sense of justice. In all cases, the immigration advantage resulting from the marriage of convenience was a marginal factor in the decision and no concern was expressed over the use of marriage to obtain an immigration advantage. *H v H* and *Silver v Silver* pre-dated mass New Commonwealth immigration and involved European nationalities. *Szechter* came in 1971 but involved persecuted Polish nationals with whom the court had sympathy. *Vervaeke* and *Puttick* in 1983 and 1981, respectively, also involved European nationalities and, despite the dominance of the immigration issue at the time, the courts' disapprobation focused on other aspects of their conduct. Judges in all these cases showed themselves to be flexible and creative in ensuring an outcome consistent with their sense of justice in the particular case.

In contrast to these cases, non-European migrants found to have entered into a bogus marriage were treated with maximum severity. In *Malik v SSHD*, the parties underwent a civil marriage intending to live together after the religious ceremony.[11] This did not take place, as the appellant began a relationship with his wife's sister. As the civil ceremony had taken place early due to the imminent expiry of the applicant's visitor's visa, it was found to be a marriage of convenience and deportation was justified on the grounds that his continued presence was not conducive to the public good under s. 3(5)(b) Immigration Act 1971. In *Cheema*, the court again found that the mere fact of a marriage of convenience justified deportation on public good grounds.[12] These decisions were particularly harsh as there was no appeal against deportation on these grounds. The argument put forward on the applicants' behalf was that public good deportations had been conceived to deal with rare instances of extreme wrongdoing. That argument carried little weight until House of Lords dicta in *Khawaja v SSHD*[13] made it apparent that s. 3(5)(b) was indeed not the appropriate mechanism and that the parties should have been removed as illegal entrants (see *R v IAT ex p. Khan*).[14]

8 Under s .6(2) British Nationality Act 1948, in force at the time, a woman who was married to a CUKC was entitled to be registered as a CUKC.

9 *Puttick v Attorney General* [1980] Fam 1.

10 *R v Chief National Insurance Commissioner ex p. Connor* [1981] QB 758. In *Connor*, it was found that statutory public duties were subject to an implied policy limitation to prevent those guilty of wrongdoing from benefiting. In that case, there was a conviction for homicide. In *Puttick*, perjury and forgery were admitted but there was no conviction.

11 [1981] Imm AR 134.

12 [1982] Imm AR 124.

13 [1983] 2 WLR 321.

14 [1983] Imm AR 32.

Degrees of Hardship

Between 1969 and 1974, Commonwealth husbands were permitted to enter or remain in the UK on the basis of marriage only if 'refusal would be undesirable because of the degree of hardship which, in the particular circumstances of the case, would be caused if the woman had to live outside the United Kingdom in order to be with her husband after marriage'.[15] The courts rapidly became involved in the determining the kind and degree of hardship that would trigger the exception. As Bhabha and Shutter (1994: 57-9) point out, criteria were adopted that were more easily met by white women of British descent.

The first reported case was *Hector*, heard in the Tribunal.[16] The couple, both Mauritian nationals, feared harassment by the husband's former mistress. The Tribunal (at p. 44) considered that, in framing the rule, the Home Department had in mind 'difficulties of a more serious and lasting nature such as, for example, might face a woman settling in a strange country on account of differences in race, language, customs or religion or on account of political intolerance'. The Tribunal here seized on factors that, with the possible exception of political intolerance, would be more likely to affect women of European descent. In the subsequent reported cases, the only claims that succeeded involved white women moving to less developed countries (*Ahmet, Constantinides* and *Papadopoulos*).[17] By contrast, in *Sadhu Singh*, a British-born woman of Sikh descent was reluctant to move to India due to the rural environment, the position of women and her dislike of the food and climate.[18] Her claim was not allowed, as 'there would be no differences in race or religion' (at p. 70) and it was believed that the other problems could be alleviated through financial assistance from her father. The Tribunal quoted the adjudicator without disagreement as saying that the wife was looking for 'the best of both worlds'. She wanted to avoid the scandal that would ensue if she did not fulfil the engagement in accordance with tradition, but she also 'wanted the more free and affluent life of England and detested the idea of becoming the serflike wife of an Indian peasant smallholder'.

An unreported case before the adjudicator shortly afterwards was this time decided in favour of the applicant. In this instance, an Indian woman who had lived in the UK since the age of seven was described as 'extremely involved in the cultural life of the white-born British' with 'firm views on the emancipation of Asian women and the anglicised approach to the status of women'.[19] This appears to have been an exceptional instance and supports the point, made elsewhere in

15 Cmnd 4295, para. 24. For discussion of the political background to this, see Chapter 3.

16 [1972] Imm AR 41.

17 27 June 1972, Imm AR TH/3018/71 (24); 21 June 1973, Imm AR 30 TH/3043/72 (160); [1974] Imm AR 46.

18 19 March 1973, Imm AR 67 TH/581/72 (126).

19 'Asian bride wins appeal for husband to join her', *Yorkshire Post*, 3 July 1973.

this chapter, that the right to bring in a spouse was 'awarded' more readily to immigrants who unequivocally adopted British values. In other instances, the Tribunal refused claims where the wife had also been brought up in the UK, suffered acute anxiety or faced poverty.[20] Differences in race or religion were privileged over those arising from a low standard of living. In *Papayianni*,[21] for example, the Tribunal was deeply critical of the wife's reluctance to live in a village without gas or electricity. Constable (1974) refers to a string of decisions establishing that 'starvation is not hardship'. However, in one case reported in the press, a British woman who had made 'valiant efforts' over seven years in India was permitted to return with her husband after the Tribunal was told of the 'squalor', health hazards, food shortages and economic difficulties facing the family. Class was perhaps a factor, the wife being described as from a 'respectable Gloucestershire family'. She also had difficulty accepting the religion and way of life of the region where she was 'the only English woman living in 50 square miles of the Indian Punjab'. The overall tone suggests that the court wished to rescue this plucky white middle-class adventurer from poverty that other women were expected to endure.[22]

If differences in the standard of living had been routinely brought into account, many more applications by women married to non-white men would have succeeded (Constable 1974). The suspicion that immigration considerations overrode all others is corroborated by the position of Ugandan Asian women who held British passports and who came to the UK with their children after expulsion (this was discussed in Chapter 3). Their non-British husbands who had also been expelled were not permitted to enter the UK and, now stateless, were finding it difficult to gain acceptance by other countries because of their dependants. The Immigration Appeals Tribunal upheld Home Office decisions to refuse admission on the grounds that the hardship, including lack of a settled home elsewhere, was insufficiently severe.[23]

Intention to Live Together

Despite the later predominance of 'primary purpose', there was some early case law on intention alone. The Immigration Rules applicable after 1977 required the Secretary of State always to refuse leave to remain if the marriage was entered into primarily to obtain settlement with no intention to live together, but only normally to refuse when intention was absent, whatever the reason for the marriage.[24] Thus, if the marriage was genuine at inception but had later broken down, there was discretion to grant leave to remain. Tribunal cases on when discretion should be

20 'The "Jenkins husbands" row', *The Observer*, 31 March 1974.
21 [1974] Imm AR 1.
22 'Wife wins place for immigrant husband', *The Guardian*, 11 April 1974.
23 'Uganda cases strike at women's rights', *The Guardian*, 11 January 1973.
24 HC 241, para. 24A.

favourably exercised demonstrated sympathy for hapless husbands whose status was placed in jeopardy due to apparently selfish or inconstant wives.

In *Subhash*, the husband was refused indefinite leave after his wife left him for another man shortly after the wedding. The marriage was not one of convenience and the husband had given up a good job in India and was unlikely to obtain another.[25] The Tribunal agreed with the adjudicator that the reason for the breakdown of the marriage should be brought into consideration when deciding whether to exercise discretion favourably. In *Anseereeganoo*, the parties were living in the same household and shared domestic tasks, although the wife had announced her intention of eventually seeking a divorce.[26] The husband had abandoned work-permit employment at the wife's insistence and was reliant upon his leave as a husband. The Tribunal agreed with the adjudicator that it was incorrect to say that the wife did not have 'any' intention of living with her husband and indefinite leave should be granted. However, the High Court later found that refusing to grant leave was the norm, even where the break-up was not at the instigation of the applicant, as the purpose of the rule was to allow people to stay because of marriage.[27] The judiciary was, it seemed, prepared to show compassion provided the underlying purpose of control was not subverted.

The amendment of the rules in 1979 so that primary purpose became a separate test in all cases made the distinction less important, as primary purpose became the most common reason for refusal, although the relationship between intention and primary purpose was the subject of later case law.

Parties Have Met

The requirement to have met became part of the Immigration Rules in 1979 and particularly affected fiancé(e)s in arranged marriages. There was considerable uncertainty as to the nature and quality of the required meeting. In *Jaffer*, the parties had stayed in the same house when the sponsor was 14 and had seen each other from one room to another but had not spoken.[28] They were found not to have met. The decision made difficult the admission of fiancé(e)s in traditional arranged marriages and was modified in *Hashmi*, where the rule was satisfied when the parties were brought together at a relative's house and saw each other but, in keeping with tradition, did not speak.[29]

In two reported cases, the Tribunal provided guidance.[30] They would not accept a purely nominal interpretation that included parties who had met in early

25 [1979-1980] Imm AR 97.

26 [1981] Imm AR 30.

27 *R v Immigration Appeal Tribunal ex p. Jarnail Singh Sandal* [1981] Imm AR 95.

28 4284.

29 4975.

30 *Rewal Raj v Entry Clearance Officer, New Delhi* [1985] Imm AR 151 and *Mohd Meharban v Entry Clearance Officer, Islamabad* [1989] Imm AR 57.

childhood but had no distinct recollection of each other. Nonetheless, they found that the rule did not require the parties to have met in the context of the marriage arrangements or, as argued by the Home Office, that there must be a degree of personal relationship. They approved the decision in *Hashmi* and adopted an interpretation of 'met' as meaning 'made the acquaintance of'. In this way, the rule was not treated as a meaningless formality, but there was no attempt to undermine fundamentally the practice of traditional arranged marriage (although it was rendered more expensive if an additional meeting had to be organised).

Validity of the Marriage

A major cause of refusal in this period was the allegation that the parties did not have a valid marriage. Barriers included the absence of formalities, uncertainty as to the date, incapacity to enter a polygamous marriage or the invalidity of prior divorce proceedings. Most of these matters were decided by ECOs without involving the courts and are discussed in Chapter 5.

However, the courts were called on to address certain questions and these have been extensively discussed elsewhere (Pearl 1972, Poulter 1976, Jaffey 1978: 38-43, Pearl 1986, Poulter 1986: 11-22, Jones and Welhengama 2000: 109-34, Murphy 2000a and 2000b, Mayss 2000 and Shah 2003). They go beyond immigration questions into the recognition of laws and practices of minority communities, an issue that is beyond the scope of this book. The numbers of polygamous marriages resulting in the admission of additional spouses, for example, was tiny, but there is a long and complex case law and legislative history on the recognition of polygamous marriages (see Poulter 1976 and Shah 2003).

Nonetheless, in dealing with cases that arose in an immigration context, the courts at times betrayed particular attitudes relating to their expectations of immigrants. One such example was the approach taken towards domicile, a question that arose repeatedly in deciding the validity of earlier proceedings. Another was the 'transnational divorce'. The common feature was resistance to immigrants seeking, in the words of the adjudicator in another context,[31] 'the best of both worlds' – to enjoy the benefits of life in the UK while retaining the right to rely, to their advantage, on practices in their country of origin.

Domicile

Domicile was a recurrent issue as the validity of a marriage undertaken in the country of origin might be questioned because it was polygamous, under-age or otherwise did not conform to English law. In these cases, the domicile of the UK party at the time of the marriage was critical. Through domicile, an immigrant of many years' residence, and who may even have naturalised, could retain his or her connection with his or her country of origin, including its legal system. Commentators have criticised the general treatment of domicile by the courts as

31 *Sadhu Singh*, 19 March 1973, Imm AR 67 TH/581/72 (126).

inconsistent (Jones and Welhengama 2000: 109-18) and this inconsistency seems to have extended to those cases where it affected immigration status (see, in relation to the Tribunal, Juss 1997: 125-6). Nonetheless, on balance, a restrictive approach was preferred.

Domicile was critical in spouse applications because, in determining the validity of overseas marriages, the courts used the test of the parties' antenuptial domicile (see Pearl 1986: 41-3). In doing so, they rejected the test of the system of law with which the marriage had a real and substantial connection (*R v IAT ex p. Rafika Bibi*)[32] or the law of the intended matrimonial home (*Radwan v Radwan No. 2*).[33] Thus, the validity of a polygamous marriage depended upon the parties' domicile at the time of the marriage, a position confirmed by s. 11(d) Matrimonial Causes Act 1973.[34]

Domicile of origin was and remains very difficult to lose. There was the 'strongest possible presumption in favour of the continuance of the domicile of origin' (Macdonald and Blake 1995: 328), a position that was maintained (Macdonald and Webber 2005: 595). It could be displaced in favour of a domicile of choice by evidence of intention to continue to reside in a different place 'not for a limited period or particular purpose, but general and indefinite in its contemplation' (Lord Westbury in *Udny v Udny*,[35] quoted in Macdonald and Blake 1995: 327). Given the presumption of domicile of origin, it was for immigration officers to establish that it had been lost. Renunciation must be unequivocal and ascertainable through objective criteria. Statements as to domicile in a will, by a taxpayer on an Inland Revenue form or by an applicant for naturalisation or registration were not reliable according to Macdonald and Blake (1995: 328). Juss (1997: 125-6) argues that, in unreported cases, the Tribunal often wrongly placed the burden of proof upon the applicant to show that he had retained his domicile of origin. Domicile has an awkward relationship with immigration. As recent theories of transnationalism have argued, migration is often not a single discrete movement from country of origin to country of destination. Migrants may initially intend only a temporary stay or become 'international commuters' (Gardner and Shukur, quoted in Shah 2003: 381 and Pearl 1986: 8). Many migrants from the sub-continent did not call for their families until their hand was forced by immigration restrictions and, in doing so, they did not necessarily view themselves as making a definitive choice of residence. Migrants frequently maintain property, business interests and other connections in their country of origin and may anticipate the possibility of a later return, perhaps for retirement. This ambivalence defies easy categorisation and proved problematic for migrants caught between

---

32 [1989] Imm AR 1; see further Fentiman 1985. See Shah 2003: 387-8 for an account of later cases where the test of 'real and substantial connection' was still applied.

33 [1973] Fam 35; see also Pearl 1986: 42.

34 Although Pearl (ibid.: 43) has argued that this approach misunderstands the effect of s. 14(1) Matrimonial Causes Act 1973 on the operation of s. 11(d).

35 (1869) LRI Sc & Dir 441.

two systems. Migrants who returned home to marry had to rely on their domicile of origin to establish the validity of their marriage if it would not be valid in English law. However, they may have been unaware of the significance of domicile when interviewed and over-stressed their commitment to the UK, believing that this would assist their case. Nonetheless, immigration officers and the courts relied upon questionnaires as a means of claiming the adoption of a domicile of choice in the UK, a proceeding that was subject to much criticism (Pearl 1986: 45 and Shah 2003: 382-3). Reported cases on domicile in immigration matters suggest that the courts were also inclined to resist finding a domicile of origin if this brought the immigrant advantages unavailable under UK law.[36]

Two early reported cases involving the adjudicator were decided in favour of polygamous spouses, the husband being found to have retained his domicile of origin.[37] In neither of these cases had another wife already entered the UK, the marriage, in one case, being only potentially polygamous.[38] In these cases, there was a dispassionate consideration of the law that may be contrasted with the emotive tone in the later Tribunal case of *Zahra v Visa Officer, Islamabad*, where immigration factors seem to have been more prominent.[39] In *Zahra*, the sponsor husband had already brought one wife to the UK with whom he had 'a large number of children, four of whom were born in this country' (at p. 49). However, this wife had since returned to Pakistan. The sponsor had made several visits to Pakistan, during one of which he contracted a second marriage. He owned a house, a shop and a bank account in Pakistan but, relying on his answers to a domicile questionnaire, he was found to have adopted an English domicile and the marriage was held to be invalid. The sponsor's lawyer also argued that the second wife should be admitted as a woman 'living in permanent association with a man', a discretionary provision in the Immigration Rules. The Tribunal declined, saying that the measure had been intended to apply only to monogamous relationships, inferring this from the reference to a woman being admitted 'as if she were his wife'. It went on to say: 'If it were otherwise an oriental pasha with a harem of several wives might be entitled to bring them all to this country, even if he were domiciled here, provided that he otherwise satisfied the requirements of this

36 This attitude seems to have been shared by other government departments: see Fransman 1998: 331-2.

37 *Mussarat v SSHD*, 12 January 1971, Imm AR 45 and *Ishiodu v ECO, Lagos*, 29 August 1974, Imm AR 56.

38 At the time, even potentially polygamous marriages were void under English law (a position remedied by the Private International Law (Miscellaneous Provisions) Act 1995). Despite the case law discussed here, it was reported that ECOs persisted in relying on domicile to declare potentially polygamous marriages void. Parties were expected to undergo a new ceremony of marriage in the UK, sometimes after having regarded themselves as married for many years: 'Home Office denies classing Pakistani marriages as invalid', *The Times*, 3 September 1975; 'Anomalies in law on polygamy', *The Times*, 6 September 1975. See also Chapter 5.

39 [1979-1980] Imm AR 48.

paragraph. This is clearly absurd.' The assumption that the wife in a polygamous marriage barely merited description as such recalls the speech of Lord Penzance in *Hyde v Hyde* (1886), quoted in Jones and Welhengama (2000: 111-12; see also the critique in Poulter 1976) and contrasts with the more sympathetic position established after *Hyde v Hyde* (Poulter 1986: 50-8). It arguably reflected the fear that mass immigration might result in large numbers of polygamous marriages. The reference to an oriental pasha places the polygamous marriage in the realm of the exotic, obviating the need to take the claim for entry seriously. The strong impression is that the Tribunal did not wish this application to succeed and the unfavourable decision on domicile was part of that.

The case law after *Zahra* was inconsistent, with some Tribunals adopting a more balanced and sympathetic approach. For example, in *Rokeya and Rably Begum v Entry Clearance Officer Dhaka*, a careful determination found that the burden of proof to establish a domicile of choice had not been discharged.[40] This may have been a more dispassionate Tribunal, but it is interesting that, in this case and unlike the situation in *Zahra*, the first wife had never been in the UK.[41] Shah (2003: 388, n. 75) notes that, in other cases, the Tribunal resisted attempts by ECOs to place immigrants in a Catch-22 situation, whereby their declared intention to live in the UK with their wife, which was necessary if the spouse application was to succeed, counted against them on domicile. Nonetheless, despite these and other cases that took a more sympathetic view, *Zahra* remained the dominant case, permitting officials to use domicile to deny the validity of marriages (Shah 2003: 384-5).

Divorce

In other cases, the contentious issue was whether a previous marriage had been satisfactorily dissolved. The rules for recognition of divorce were complex and changed during the period (see, for example, Pearl 1972, 1974/1975 and 1986, North 1975 and Macdonald and Blake 1991: 255-6) and it is not possible to recite them here. As with other questions of validity, the implications went well beyond immigration considerations. However, one issue that does throw light on the courts' attitudes towards immigrants was the 'transnational divorce', where part of the divorce took place in the UK and the other formalities required under the law of the country of origin were performed in that country.

These divorces fell between two sets of legislative provision. Following *Qureshi v Qureshi*,[42] which had recognised a *talaq* divorce performed entirely in the UK, albeit in the Pakistani High Commission, statutory law was introduced to plug that perceived loophole. Under s. 16(1) Domicile and Matrimonial Proceedings Act 1973, recognition of divorces carried out in the UK was now confined to

40 [1983] Imm AR 631.

41 In 1988, the Immigration Rules were amended to permit the entry of only one wife in any event (HC 555, para. 3).

42 [1972] Fam 173.

those instituted in the UK courts. Thus, a *talaq* divorce pronounced in the UK was invalid under UK law regardless of its validity under the law of the parties' domicile or nationality. Divorces carried out abroad were recognized, provided that either of the parties were habitually resident or a national of the country in question (s. 3 Recognition of Divorces and Legal Separations Act 1971, later amended by s. 46(1) Family Law Act 1986) subject to considerations of policy (s. 8 Recognition of Divorces and Legal Separations Act 1971). Statute thus governed the situation where the parties either sought to divorce within the UK or divorced abroad. However, problems arose when immigrants pronounced the *talaq* in the UK and sent notice of it to a body abroad such as the Union Council in Pakistan. In the Pakistani instances, unless revoked within 90 days, the divorce became effective under Pakistani law (s. 7 Muslim Family Laws Ordinance 1961).

The question of whether such a divorce was also valid under UK law arose in *R v IAT and Saeda Bi and others* in the Queen's Bench Division.[43] The claim of three wives to enter the UK depended upon the validity of the husbands' prior 'transnational' divorces. The court found that these were not recognised under UK law, a view upheld unanimously by the Court of Appeal (under the name *R v SSHD ex p. Ghulam Fatima*)[44] and the House of Lords.[45] Clearly, a *talaq* divorce performed in the UK lacked validity. The question was whether, on the facts, it was performed in Pakistan. The court reasoned that the *talaq* itself formed part of the proceedings and so these could not be said to have taken place wholly in Pakistan. An overseas divorce was only recognised if the entire proceedings took place in the overseas country as, under ss. 2 and 3(1) Recognition of Divorces and Legal Separations Act 1971, an overseas divorce meant a single set of proceedings instituted in that country. Lawyers for the applicants argued that the purpose of that statute was to give effect to the Hague Convention on the Recognition of Divorces and Legal Separations, which aimed to prevent 'limping marriages' where the divorce was recognised in one jurisdiction but not in another. This argument received short shrift, the courts relying on s. 16(1) Domicile and Matrimonial Proceedings Act 1973, passed as indicated above to reverse the decision in *Qureshi v Qureshi*, derecognising a *talaq* divorce performed entirely in the UK.[46]

The decision in *Ghulam Fatima* was criticised for lack of logic (Young 1987: 87-8, Berkovits 1988), as inconsistent with the principles of statutory interpretation (Berkovits 1988: 74) and as increasing the likelihood of a 'limping marriage' (Mayss 2000: 62). Its effect was principally upon the poorer immigrant, as the wealthy could afford to circumvent it by returning to Pakistan to perform the *talaq* (Berkovits 1988: 77 and Mayss 2000: 62). On the other hand, as Lord Ackner made explicit in his speech, having removed recognition of *talaq* proceedings

43 [1983] Imm AR 82.
44 [1985] QB 190.
45 [1986] AC 527.
46 [1972] Fam 173.

performed inside the UK, '(i)t would seem contrary to that policy to encourage the obtaining of divorces essentially by post by Pakistani nationals resident in this country by means of the talaq procedure'.[47]

Two competing values were in play here; recognising divorces valid overseas and preventing (mainly male) British residents from using unilateral and relatively informal forms of divorce to disadvantage wives. As Berkovits (1988: 77-8) comments, the decision 'indicates an unenunciated presumption that the policy of eliminating limping marriages is less important than the policy factor of subordinating all residents of England to a uniform municipal jurisdiction'. He goes on to point out that the parties here were not opportunistically forum shopping but had a close connection with the country and religion under which the divorce had been sought. While there is not space to discuss this issue further here, it is a point that continues to be problematic within and outside the sphere of migration.[48]

Right of Abode

R v SSHD ex p. Phansopkar is worth considering briefly, as Lord Denning's speech brings into strong relief attitudes that were usually more muted and nuanced.[49] The case found that wives who claimed the right of abode in the UK should not be required to wait in the same lengthy queue as those seeking entry clearance. Lord Denning (at pp. 615-17) described the right of abode as 'the most precious right anyone can have' and commented that 'Parliament made it very easy for many an immigrant to become a patrial and get this precious right'. He acknowledged that the rights of these immigrants and of their families who have 'never been to England and cannot speak a word of English' is equal to that of '[y]ou and I and our families ... born here and [who have] lived here from time immemorial', describing the law as 'wide and generous'. He went on to find that this right should be given practical recognition. He did so in equally lofty terms, saying (at p. 621) that the applicant 'can invoke Magna Carta: "To none will we sell: to no one will we delay or deny right or justice"'. Both Lawton and Scarman LJ also made reference to Magna Carta.

The case provided a welcome relief to those who had been frustrated in the exercise of a statutory right (although at a cost to other applicants; see Chapter 5). Even given Lord Denning's predilection for a high-blown style, the emphasis on these applicants' 'outsider' status, the reference to residence as 'a precious right'

47 Berkovits (1988: 79; see also Pilkington 1988) argues that the decision in *Fatima* was inadvertently overruled by Part II Family Law Act 1986. However, this does not seem to be the courts' view: see *Berkovits v Grinberg* [1995] Fam 142 and Reed 1996.

48 See the House of Lords decision in *Quazi v Quazi* (1980) AC 744 and the subsequent case law – for example, *Sulaiman v Jaffali* (2002) 1 FLR 479; see also Chapters 8 and 9.

49 [1975] 3 All ER 497.

and the reliance on the primordial sources of Magna Carta are suggestive. Justice, an ancient and fundamental value, was graciously extended even to those who had been included almost inadvertently and undeservedly in the privileged class of 'belongers'.

Non-primary Purpose Case Law: Discussion

In some respects, there were some sympathetic decisions made within the confines set by the value of respect for the legislature, particularly earlier in the period (see Legomsky 1987: 232-3 and, in relation to the Tribunal, Juss 1997: 163-8). The rule on 'intention to live together' was interpreted, for a period, to take account of the predicament of an immigrant whose marriage ended against his wishes. The requirement to have met was applied in a way that would permit traditional arranged marriages to continue with minimal prior contact between the parties, albeit with the added expense of an additional trip. This latter finding suggests that there was no inclination to undermine the traditional arranged marriage as such, despite the hostile tone of political debate reported in the previous section. In *Phansopkar*, the favourable decision was associated with historical 'British' values, suggesting that too much hostility would be incongruent with the courts' self-perception as an instrument of justice, despite, in the case of Lord Denning, an emphasis on the applicants' outsider status.

In other instances, and particularly as time went on, judicial sympathy was absent or ambivalent. The sympathetic cases on 'intention' were overruled. The case law on domicile indicates that, while there was some resistance to manipulation by immigration officers, the courts were reluctant to acknowledge a domicile of origin where it permitted a well-established immigrant to gain an advantage not otherwise available to him. This was more marked when it would have permitted the entry of more than one wife, even though the immigrant was relying upon well-established legal principles. A similar preoccupation was evident in the rejection of the 'trans-national divorce'. There was resistance to immigrants 'having it both ways', becoming long-term residents of the UK but also relying on their connection with the country of origin to gain advantages that conflicted with British values.

This resistance was expressed overtly during discussion on what constituted the necessary 'degree of hardship' for an exception to the ban on husbands to apply. Criteria were adopted that were clearly likely to favour women of British descent. Differences in race and culture were privileged above differences in living standards, difficulties to which a tribunal expected women to adapt despite the resulting unaccustomed domestic labour. This may have been the result of a calculation that, if differences in living standards were to be a factor, few cases would be refused. While it was perhaps predictable that settled women were considered able to readapt to life in their country of origin, the failure to consistently apply the exception to women of immigrant descent suggests a conditional attitude towards their acceptance. By selecting a husband from their country of origin, such women demonstrated a lack of commitment to the UK and must accept the consequences. A similar sentiment was detectable, as discussed in Chapter 1, in the earlier debate on married women's nationality and, in Chapter 3, during parliamentary debate. As the reproving remarks in *Sadhu Singh* (1972) suggest, such women could not reasonably expect to have 'the best of both worlds'. By contrast, where a woman had wholeheartedly adopted British values, sympathy was more apparent.

Migrants, it seems, were not treated with hostility purely by virtue of being migrants or because their marriage customs were different. When the demands they made were perceived as moderate or reasonable, they were liable to receive a degree of sympathy. However, this soon ran out when migrants' expectations suggested that they wished to retain the benefits of both identities, retaining allegiance to 'foreign' or 'alien' values. This was so even when, as with the cases on domicile, they were not attempting to circumvent or extend the law.

This absence of sympathy became outright hostility when migrants were seen as abusing the UK's hospitality. Thus, the presence of men found to have entered into bogus marriages was considered to be not conducive to the public good, the most serious grounds for deportation. This was particularly harsh in *Malik*, where the marriage had been entered into prematurely but in the expectation that it would endure. In *Vervaeke v Smith* and *Puttick*, the court also disapproved of the parties' conduct, but their abuse of immigration control was not the focus of disapprobation. In the cases involving refugees from Eastern Europe, no moral censure was attached to a marriage of convenience. Instead, the court actively sought to find ways to relieve their difficulties.

It seems that the immigration status of non-white migrants was a defining characteristic in a way that did not occur for other nationalities. This was certainly the case for Lord Denning in *Phansopkar*. It was not that non-white immigrants were necessarily unwelcome, but they were first and foremost immigrants even in the second generation, as *Sadhu Singh* suggests. As tolerated guests, they had particular obligations, both moral and legal, not to abuse the generosity of their hosts, and transgression of these brought sometimes severe retribution.

The case law discussed here was decided prior to the stream of primary purpose cases that began with *Vinod Bhatia* in 1985. Commentators (Scannell 1992a: 3 and Sachdeva 1993: 119-21) observed that early primary purpose case law was also relatively sympathetic to immigrants, although, by the early 1990s, attitudes were starting to change. The reluctance of the judiciary to confront the misapplication of the primary purpose rule was a major characteristic of case law and is considered in the next section.

The Judicial Response to 'Primary Purpose'

As discussed in Chapter 3, from July 1985 onwards, both men and women settled in the UK could sponsor a spouse. Entry clearance for either party would be refused unless five separate conditions had been met. These included:

1. that the marriage was not entered into primarily to obtain admission to the UK; and
2. that each of the parties had the intention of living permanently with the other as his or her spouse.

The following years were a period of intense judicial involvement in primary purpose. There was a wide body of contemporary commentary, including Marrington (1985), Macdonald and Blake (1991: 260-5), Scannell (1992a and 1992b), Vincenzi and Marrington (1992), Pannick and Young Justice (1993), Sachdeva (1993: Chapter 4), Supperstone and O'Dempsey (1994: 207-11), Macdonald and Blake (1995: 336-44) and Griffiths (1997: 182-90).

Relationship between Intention and Purpose

Early Tribunal case law remained unreported but was the subject of commentary (Marrington 1985, Mole 1987 and Sachdeva 1993: 119-27). The central issue was the relationship between primary purpose and intention to live together, which had became separate requirements in 1979. Given this, it was improbable that any court, however sympathetic, would have found that satisfaction of one meant automatic satisfaction of the other. The key issue was the extent to which a favourable finding on intention informed the decision on primary purpose.

Naresh Kumar found that that once the parties had established the necessary intention, the burden of proof was reversed and it was for the Secretary of State to show that the primary purpose of the marriage was nonetheless immigration.[50] The decision was followed in other Tribunal decisions, notably those chaired by Professor Jackson, but this sympathetic approach did not endure. The first major reported case under primary purpose was *Vinod Bhatia* in the Tribunal (unreported),[51] the Queen's Bench Division and finally the Court of Appeal.[52] All agreed that a finding on intention did not remove the obligation upon the applicant with respect to primary purpose. The genius of the primary purpose rule as applied to arranged marriages was that the applicant had to demonstrate that the main purpose of the marriage was something other than immigration. It was immaterial

50 3278.

51 Blake (1984) says that, under pressure from the Home Office, who were unhappy at the guidance in *Naresh Kumar*, this Tribunal was exceptionally constituted for a special hearing before three legally qualified chairs.

52 [1985] Imm AR 39; [1985] Imm AR 50.

how many other motives might be present; unless the applicant could demonstrate that one of these was the primary motive, the application failed. In the High Court, Forbes J ensured this function was fulfilled by minimising the impact of a favourable finding on intention. He rejected engagement with a 'philosophical inquiry into the concept of marriage', preferring to engage in selective legal and factual argument. For example, he supported his interpretation by reference to the rules of statutory interpretation, although these were not appropriate to the Immigration Rules.[53] He also asserted (at p. 46) 'the fact that many marriages in the sub-continent have been entered into whose primary purpose was, in fact, to obtain admission to the United Kingdom', a statement of doubtful validity (see Sachdeva 1993: 115-16) described as 'a piece of expedient political mythology' (Rees 1989: 92). Against this background, an ECO should approach his task with 'cautious pessimism'. It seems likely that Forbes was feeling the pressure of 200 further cases on the same point awaiting his decision.[54] However, he sought to distance himself from the actual consequences of his decision, rejecting any evaluation of the underlying policy of the Rule. The Court of Appeal supported the essential findings in Forbes' judgement, but in a more nuanced fashion. In one respect, the Court of Appeal went further in finding that the primary purpose rule presumed that the purpose of the marriage was admission to the UK. As with Forbes, however, there was also a certain distancing from the impact of the rule. The court noted that no criticism was made of the parties' honesty and that there was no dispute that the proposed marriage was genuine.

In *Vinod Bhatia*, the courts chose to facilitate rather than subvert the discriminatory effects of primary purpose. They did so despite acknowledging that, as in the present case, parties to a genuine marriage would suffer the consequences. It seems that the right of these parties to live in the UK was easily subordinated to the necessity of restricting immigration. Commentators have indicated the difficulties that applicants faced in the period after *Vinod Bhatia* (Pearl 1986: 25 and Sachdeva 1993: 128-30).

In *Arun Kumar*, the Court of Appeal took a more humane approach, finding that the function of primary purpose was to distinguish between 'genuine' and 'immigration' husbands and fiancés (even though this was arguably not the case).[55] Thus, findings on intention would 'often cast a flood of light' on primary purpose. Lord Donaldson (at p. 455) distinguished between a theoretical approach based on speculation about possible motivation and the practical reality of a marriage that was, on the evidence, clearly extant:

> Again, the adjudicator was right to say that under the rules a marriage primarily entered into in order to obtain admission to the United Kingdom would still

53 Lord Roskill in *Alexander v Immigration Appeal Tribunal* [1982] WLR 1076 at p. 1081.

54 O'Connor LJ [1985] Imm AR 50 at p. 50.

55 *R v IAT ex p. Arun Kumar* [1986] Imm AR 446.

> retain its non-qualifying character whatever happened afterwards and even if the husband applied for entry on their Golden Wedding Day. For my part, I do not think that any violence would be done to this country's immigration policy if entry clearance officers put out of their minds the theoretical possibility that a marriage which at the time of application is, on the evidence, undoubtedly a very genuine and soundly based marriage could, at its inception some time before, have had a different character.

As *Vinod Bhatia* had found, primary purpose had to mean something beyond having an intention to live together or it would have been otiose, but its additional import was, in this way, reduced. There were a few other chinks of sympathy, Mole (1987: 32) suggesting that the courts took a more detached view than the Tribunal. She quotes Simon Brown J in *R v IAT ex p. Singh*, who referred to the 'enormity' of binding oneself for life in marriage to obtain entry to the UK and envisaged a primary purpose marriage as one where 'the husband had plainly gone to considerable length[s] to find a wife who could secure him entry to the UK, that plainly being his essential object rather than entry into a lifelong union'.

Scannell (1992a: 3) argues that *Singh* represented the high water mark of judicial sympathy. It was appealed by the Home Office and heard in the Court of Appeal with another case under the case name *IAT v Hoque and Singh*.[56] The court set out ten well-known propositions drawn from the decisions in *Bhatia* and *Kumar*. Approving the passage by Lord Donaldson in *Arun Kumar* quoted above, it found that while a favourable finding as to intention did not 'suffice' to ensure satisfaction of primary purpose, it meant that the applicant was better placed to ensure this. Nonetheless, in Sachdeva's words (1993: 142), 'this apparently liberal stand was immediately nullified by Slade LJ when he said that: "However, in the end, it must be left to entry clearance officers to decide how they do their work"'. In this way, the court respected the separate sphere of authority of the immigration officer, highlighting the problematic relationship between law and fact. The assumption that the quest for fact is a neutral process separate to the application of the law may permit the application of unofficial policy that the law is then powerless to challenge. Sachdeva (1993: 142) argues the Court of Appeal's stance in *Hoque and Singh* 'was as far as one could go without endangering the policy aims of British immigration control'. It suggests that the courts were reluctant to use their powers if this would undermine government policy on immigration.[57]

Debate ensued as to whether a specific finding on intention was needed before considering primary purpose. If so, it would prevent vague and subjective findings on primary purpose being made without considering the essential character of the marriage. Some decisions, mostly unreported, considered this in a broadly

56 [1988] Imm AR 216.

57 The Court of Appeal, perhaps unsurprisingly, declined to find that the primary purpose rule was sufficiently uncertain, unclear and unfair to be *ultra vires* (*R v Home Secretary ex p. Rajput, The Independent*, 8 February 1989).

sympathetic way (see *Bashir* and, for commentary, Rees 1989, Scannell 1989 and Sachdeva 1993: 142-4).[58] Amongst the reported cases was *R v IAT ex p. Shameem Wali*, in which Farquharson J found that the applicant was entitled to be informed of the court's findings on intention.[59] In *R v IAT ex p. Mohammed Khatab*, Henry J saw the finding on intention as 'no formal technical point' but as essential to ensuring adequate reasoning on primary purpose.[60] These cases clearly caused some anxiety. *The Independent* reported that the Treasury Solicitor had written to adjudicators (and possibly tribunal members; the article conflates the two) advising them that High Court judges, and Henry J in particular, had placed 'glosses' on the primary purpose rule which deprived it of its force.[61] The letter referred to an unidentified judgement by Henry J (presumably *Khatab*), saying that 'it represents the high water mark of primary purpose "jurisprudence", in the sense that I do not think anything more can be done to undermine the primary purpose rule than is done in this Judgment. In certain respects, it seems to me the Judge goes much too far'. The report provides a rare glimpse into the intense pressure exerted towards a restrictive policy.

Restraint was more evident in other cases. In *R v IAT ex p. Naushad Amad Kandiya*, Simon Brown J found that a finding on intention was not necessary as an applicant could fail on primary purpose regardless of intention.[62] His tone was exasperated. Provided there was implicit consideration of 'intention', there was no requirement for adjudicators 'to follow slavishly some pre-ordained route, let alone to recite routinely as an incantation certain particular assumptions or conclusions which could as well be implied in their decisions' (at p. 495). A similar conclusion was reached by Roch J in *R v IAT ex p. Aurangzeb Khan.*[63]

Appeals in Kandiya and *Khan* were heard together in the Court of Appeal.[64] In the meantime, the same point came before the Court of Appeal in *Mohamed Numanul Islam Choudhury v Immigration Appeal Tribunal.*[65] In both cases, the court found that, despite the relevance of intention to primary purpose, no specific finding on intention had to be made before a finding on primary purpose was reached. This denied the close connection, in reality if not in theory, between intention and purpose, as acknowledged by Lord Donaldson in *Arun Kumar*, and reduced the likelihood that a favourable finding as to intention would affect the decision on primary purpose. While a few judges continued to assert the link between the two (Scannell 1992b), primary purpose had become a subjective

58 *R v IAT ex p. Bashir (DC)*, 15 March 1988.

59 [1989] Imm AR 86.

60 [1989] Imm AR 313.

61 'Judges' decisions in immigration cases "too liberal"', *The Independent*, 6 June 1989.

62 [1989] Imm AR 491.

63 [1989] Imm AR 524.

64 [1990] Imm AR 377.

65 [1990] Imm AR 211.

free-floating concept devoid of the context provided by an assessment of the reality of the marriage.

Dillon LJ observed in *Choudhury* that 'in an enormous number of arranged marriages between girls settled here and young men coming from the Asian Sub-Continent, the husband wishes to live in the United Kingdom'. This public allusion to contemporary immigration preoccupations stands alone. However, legal reasoning in these cases was also either absent or surprisingly superficial. Thus, Taylor LJ in *Kandiya and Khan* said that, while the propositions in *Hoque and Singh* asserted the 'evidential relevance' of a finding on intention to a finding on primary purpose, they did not demand a 'specific finding' as to intention before proceeding to consideration of primary purpose. This was technically true, but it is difficult to see how a finding as to intention could 'cast a flood of light' on primary purpose unless evidence as to intention was evaluated. This loosening of the relationship between primary purpose and intention was justified, when it was rationalised at all, as enabling decision-makers to act 'sensibly and realistically' (Taylor LJ in *Kandiya and Khan* at p. 385), a debatable proposition. The courts may have feared a rash of technical challenges, but that was not the only practical consideration. Other, more sympathetic decisions referred to 'the intrinsic improbability' of a marriage that satisfied the requirement of intention failing on primary purpose.[66] Sense and realism were fickle resources.

There followed the much-criticised case of *Sumeina Masood v IAT*.[67] It was acknowledged here that the parties, who were cousins, had entered a traditional arranged marriage but for their decision to live in the UK. The couples' economic prospects were far better in the UK and their decision was unsurprising. Despite acknowledging that this was a genuine marriage, the court found that, as it was conditional upon the husband's admission, the necessary intention to live together was not present, a point rather surprisingly conceded by counsel for the couple. Certainly, Lord Prosser believed it was 'wrongly or too widely made' when he considered it in *Raja Zafar Zia v SSHD*.[68] The court then concluded that the applicant must also fail on primary purpose. In doing so, it adopted an unusual interpretation, finding that, if entry was a precondition of the marriage, it was also its primary purpose. This is plainly illogical. It may be that a wedding will not take place before the bride has a dress, but that does not mean that the primary purpose of the marriage is to procure a dress. The court appears to regard the couple as presumptuous in assuming the power to decide where they should live, a matter over which the state should have precedence (see also the comments in Sachdeva 1993: 157). The harshness of the decision in *Sumeina Masood* was a step too far for some members of the judiciary. Schiemann J in *R v IAT ex p. Iram Iqbal* saw the argument as relevant only to intention and declined to follow it on primary

66 Simon Brown J in *R v IAT ex p. Matwinder Singh*, *The Times*, 15 April 1987 and Lord Prosser in *Mohammed Saftar v SSHD* [1995] AR 1 at p. 11.

67 [1992] Imm AR 69.

68 [1993] Imm AR 405 at p. 415.

purpose.[69] In a well-known passage, he also acknowledged the logical fallacy of assuming that because one common motive for marriage was absent, the only alternative explanation must be immigration:

> … the fact that an American heiress was so keen to be a duchess that she was prepared to marry an Englishman whom she did not love, would not lead one to suppose that the primary purpose of the marriage was for her to obtain admission to the United Kingdom. (At p. 276)

Intervening Devotion

As already discussed, *Arun Kumar* was one of the more sympathetic cases.[70] It found that the rules should receive a 'broad common sense construction' and opened the way to use of 'intervening devotion', i.e. correspondence, cohabitation and other evidence of the post-marriage relationship that demonstrated it to have been genuine at its inception. It thus created an arena within which couples could hope to succeed. While the case suggests that, in this instance, there was little desire to use primary purpose for the mass refusal of arranged marriages, there was not unconditional acceptance of this. The endorsement of 'intervening devotion' permitted couples whose marriages were self-evidently genuine to comply with primary purpose, but only after a period of separation.

Although *Arun Kumar* brought a measure of relief, the Tribunal did not always follow its spirit, although sympathy was more likely when the parties had cohabited overseas (Mole 1987: 32). In effect, 'intervening devotion', as well as permitting yet more intrusive questioning, created an unofficial waiting period, a hurdle that became detached from any meaningful conception of 'intervening devotion' and suggests that applicants were expected to prove their merit through endurance.[71] Thus, in the Tribunal decision in *Mohammed Afzal v Visa Officer, Islamabad*,[72] the applicant had been refused as a fiancé by the ECO and the adjudicator, but the parties married before the Tribunal hearing, not unreasonably, given the two-year wait. They then cohabited for three months in Pakistan and argued intervening devotion. The Tribunal took a hostile view of the marriage, saying that it could be interpreted 'as an attempt to force the hand of the Home Office by presenting them with a fait accompli', a further suggestion that couples should defer to state

69 [1993] Imm AR 270.

70 As well as condoning 'intervening devotion', the court rejected the proposition that the rules 'presumed' the purpose of a marriage to be immigration and that, because a marriage was arranged, immigration was a likely motive for the marriage. However, the officer could bear in mind that it was less difficult to achieve an 'immigration' marriage in an arranged marriage as the personal feelings of the parties may be more easily set aside.

71 A similar observation may be made about the concessions granted to couples who had been married five years or had a child (see Chapter 3 and Menski 1994: 118).

72 [1986] Imm AR 474.

power if they wish to gain acceptance. The short period of cohabitation here was compared unfavourably with the longer period in *Kumar*, even though it is arguably the fact – rather than the length – of cohabitation that is the strongest indication of the purpose and nature of an Asian marriage.

Deception

Where parties had misled the authorities, even many years previously, this counted heavily against them. For example, the Court of Appeal found against the applicant in *Pervez Iqbal v IAT* in part because of a deception made when he was 11.[73] There was a drift from the legal issue to moral judgement. Deceit in primary purpose cases might be so major that the parties' statements as to their motives could have little credibility. However, once the relationship was accepted as genuine, it should have had only limited relevance as there are many possible reasons for deception. However, evidence of deception was sometimes reason in itself to dismiss an application.

In *R v IAT ex p. Girishkumar Somabhai Patel*, the application failed on primary purpose despite intervening devotion, including the birth of a child.[74] The Tribunal supported the adjudicator in finding that the intervening devotion 'was outweighed by the deceit practised by the appellant and his wife' and an application for judicial review was refused. However, the deception was not material to the motivation for the marriage. The applicant had entered as a visitor to attend a religious festival (described in somewhat dismissive terms by Farquharson J) and, while there, called the sponsor's family, having been previously engaged to the sponsor. After meeting, the engagement was renewed. After poor legal advice, the couple falsely stated that they met by chance at the festival. Whether they met by chance or by arrangement had little bearing on the purpose of the marriage. Even if the applicant had intended to renew contact, failure to mention this in his application to visit is explicable in other terms. He did not know how he would be received and he may not have been certain whether he wished to revive the engagement. Leaving aside personal reticence, admitting such a possibility was likely to cause refusal for absence of intention to leave the UK. It was a big leap to suggest that his reason for entering had always been marriage and the purpose of the marriage was settlement in the UK.[75] It is perhaps another instance in which the applicant's main defect was his perceived insubordination.

---

73 [1988] Imm AR 469. Another instance was *R v IAT ex p. Sukhivan Singh* [1988] Imm AR 527.

74 [1990] Imm AR 153.

75 Equivocation of any kind, although understandable in matters as personal as marriage, was sometimes unsympathetically treated. In *Sukhinder Singh* (5329, reported in *Legal Action*, November 1987, pp. 15-16), an applicant who was unsure whether he intended to remain in the UK after marriage failed both as a fiancé and as a visitor. The case was particularly harsh, given that a firm declaration of intent to live in the UK

In *R v IAT ex p. Syed Akhtar Hussain*,[76] the applicant was refused after having concealed a previous visit to the UK, which was found to have been the occasion of the parties' first meeting. The subsequent account of the marriage was therefore seen as suspect without considering what light the deception cast upon the motive for the marriage. The negative impact of deception was emphasised by the Court of Appeal in *Mohamed Numanul Islam Choudhury v IAT*.[77] The husband had made some misleading statements about the purpose of his visit and was granted only temporary admission. While in the UK, he married the sponsor. Both parties maintained the marriage was a love match, but the adjudicator believed that it was a marriage arranged before the applicant came to the UK. The applicant was refused on primary purpose grounds and eventually came before the Court of Appeal. In the leading judgement, Dillon LJ said (at p. 218):

> It is one of the unfortunate features of this case that one has the strong suspicion that if the truth, as found by the adjudicator, had been candidly stated at the outset … there would have been no difficulty about the grant of entry clearance … But lies were told and persisted in. I cannot say that the adjudicator was not entitled to consider that the object of telling the untruths was possibly to cover up that the primary object was a marriage to enable the husband to gain entry to the United Kingdom.

Dillon LJ found 'with considerable regret … because it seems likely that the price the parties will have to pay for untruthfulness is so severe' that the appeal should be dismissed. In other words, despite a genuine marriage and the birth of a child, the court would not interfere with an inference of primary purpose arising principally from deception.

Sometimes, deception was treated more dispassionately. In *R v IAT ex p. Kulbander Kaur*, the applicant had told some lies in a previous visitor's application.[78] In the spouse application, the adjudicator disbelieved the applicant as to his desire to live in the UK. McCullough J found that the adjudicator was wrong to leap from a finding that some of the applicant's statements were untruthful to rejecting the applicant on primary purpose. After referring to Sir John Donaldson's speech in *Arun Kumar*, he said, at p. 110, 'it is easy but wrong to treat the fact that a man has lied about the strength of his desire to obtain admission to the United Kingdom as evidence that this was the primary purpose of the marriage'.

---

risked a finding of 'primary purpose'. This point was appreciated by Simon Brown J in *R v Immigration Appeal Tribunal ex p. Rafique* [1990] Imm AR 235, who, adopting the approach of Professor Jackson in an earlier Tribunal case, found that an applicant who was undecided as to permanent residence should be treated as applying for settlement.

76 [1989] Imm AR 382.

77 [1990] Imm AR 211.

78 [1991] Imm AR 107.

However, the weight of the case law did not take such an approach, instead viewing evidence of dishonesty as grounds for an unfavourable finding on primary purpose. The subjective nature of primary purpose, established earlier by the courts, permitted the refusal of applicants who had failed to demonstrate the required qualities.

Deference to the Fact-Finder

In *R v IAT ex p. Naushad Amad Kandiya*, Simon Brown J said that it was trite law that questions of weight (challenges on which basis were described by him in an aside as suggesting 'intrinsic want of promise') are for the fact-finding body.[79] A similar conclusion was reached by Roch J in *R v IAT ex p. Aurangzeb Khan.*[80] The courts, probably fearing a flood of applications on this point, did not often intervene.[81] They were also unwilling to overturn decisions where the decision-maker had not referred to all the relevant evidence. Again, it is likely that the courts feared encouraging a flood of applications based on minor omissions, but the effect was that they upheld decisions that stressed points against the applicant while ignoring those in the applicant's favour.

An example was *R v IAT ex p. Shivprasad Bhagwandas Gondalia*[82] before Henry J in the Queen's Bench Division. The parties damaged their credibility by falsely claiming a love match and the adjudicator found that the applicant was from a poor background and could not marry in India. Thus, there was 'an enormous economic incentive' to make a marriage that could 'result in his achieving settlement in the United Kingdom'. The court did not question the reasoning that, because the applicant could only marry if he emigrated, emigration was the primary purpose of the marriage. It also declined to consider the fact that the applicant had not previously applied for a passport (when the converse was often held against applicants) and that the initiative for the marriage had come from the wife's family. The justification was that, as these matters had been brought before the adjudicator, they must have been considered by him. Similar reasoning may be found in *R v IAT ex p. Aftab Hussain.*[83] Relying on *Kandiya*, the High Court (at p. 214) found that there was no obligation upon the adjudicator to 'isolate every piece of evidence and to indicate whether or not he regards it as being material. What he must do is look at the evidence as a whole in the way that a jury would look at the matter'.

The outcome was that unbalanced decision-making went uncorrected. In this case, only fleeting reference was made to two important factors in favour of the

79 [1989] Imm AR 491.

80 [1989] Imm AR 524.

81 Although they did on occasion; see, for example, *ECO, Islamabad v Mohammad Jahangir Hussain* [1991] Imm AR 476 at p. 480.

82 [1991] Imm AR 519.

83 [1992] Imm AR 212.

applicant, while findings as to his economic circumstances were brought into consideration.[84] In upholding these decisions, judges showed themselves conscious of the presumed limitations of the judicial role. Deference to the decision-maker on findings of fact is correct to the extent that it acknowledges that the court did not hear the parties or observe the interviews. Yet it is arguable that too much restraint results in legal error. The weight attached to a finding of fact engages a question of law if the outcome is that the wrong legal test or standard of proof is applied (see Juss 1997: 148-9). This was a critical issue given the excessive reliance by decision-makers on minor discrepancies (see Chapter 5) and the way in which a finding as to dishonesty would result in an imputation of primary purpose. However, it is not clear that the courts were themselves actively pursuing an anti-immigration agenda. It is equally plausible that judicial self-restraint enabled them to avoid direct confrontation on such a charged issue.

Tradition, Love and Other Reasons for Marriage

The requirement to show that the primary motive for the marriage was not immigration required applicants to demonstrate that another motive was more important. This permitted decision-makers to pass judgement on the likelihood of these other factors predominating. If parties claimed they were marrying in accordance with custom, any departure from perceived tradition could result in rejection by ECOs on primary purpose grounds, an issue discussed in Chapter 5. The courts relied heavily on ECOs' presumed knowledge of custom and did not question its claimed inflexibility (Powell 1992). This potentially affected all male applicants who were found to have apparently deserted the custom of requiring their wives to join them and who thus entered any proceedings at a disadvantage.

Some of these cases were treated sympathetically by the courts. The Court of Appeal in *Arun Kumar* identified the 'Catch-22' for applicants. A British-based wife who wished to remain in the UK would only marry a man who also wished to live there. Yet it was 'fatally easy' to treat that wish as an admission that coming to the UK was the primary purpose of the marriage. The solution was to consider the evidence as a whole:

> What is or was the real, the primary, the basic object of the exercise in this couple agreeing to get married? Was it to live together as man and wife, preferably in the United Kingdom, or was it to enable the fiancé or husband to obtain entry to the United Kingdom, the matrimonial relationship being of subsidiary importance? (At p. 455)

In *R v IAT ex p. Shameem Wali*, Farquharson J found it 'perfectly proper' for a sponsor to insist on remaining in the UK and that no adverse inferences should

84 The reliance upon stereotypical forms of reasoning about, for example, economic background is discussed in Chapter 5.

be drawn from this.[85] In *R v IAT ex p. Mohammed Khatab*,[86] Henry J criticised an adjudication that described a British women's insistence on living in the UK, where she had a job, savings and a home, as a 'whim'. However, he did not consider that the 'unusual feature' of a husband joining his wife should always be left out of the account.

In 1990, the Court of Appeal in *Mohamed Numanul Islam Choudhury v IAT* declined to regard as 'irrelevant' two assumed facts.[87] The first was that Bangladeshi Muslim men would not permit their wives to decide the location of the matrimonial home and the other was that, 'in an enormous number' of such marriages, the husband wished to live in the UK. These 'facts', regularly relied on by entry clearance staff, are discussed in Chapter 5. The harshest decision in this respect was *Sumeina Masood*, already discussed, which found that there was no intention to live together if intention was conditional upon entry. These decisions legitimised the suspicious approach adopted by immigration officers and are discussed in Chapter 5.

Love matches were also subject to inconsistent treatment. Where decision-makers accepted a love match, the parties were better able to show a primary motive other than immigration and could succeed. However, applicants who claimed a love match were often suspected of contriving this and failed accordingly. The courts failed to acknowledge that conceptions of 'love' might vary according to culture and individual expectation (Powell 1992 and Scannell 1993), a problem discussed further in Chapter 5. In *R v IAT ex p. Manjula Jethva*,[88] the applicant was a poor labourer who could not afford to marry in India. He met the sponsor at a circus and the couple said they had fallen in love almost immediately. The adjudicator was sceptical that a love match could arise so swiftly and, in the High Court, Popplewell J said (at p. 455):

> Falling in love is a perfectly normal concept which is understood by everybody in the world, and I do not imagine that falling in love is any different in India than it is in this country; these two people contended that they had in fact fallen in love. The adjudicator said that that was how it was presented to him, and he did not accept it.

The failure to recognise that the concept of 'love' is partially culture-dependent also featured in *Aurangzeb Khan*, discussed above. Roch J supported the adjudicator's rejection of the appellant who, when asked why he wished to go the UK, replied 'I love her and I want to live there'. The adjudicator commented: 'However, the appellant did not speak to the sponsor before the engagement, and I have heard little in evidence which suggests that he is in fact in love with her' (p. 527).

85 [1989] Imm AR 86.
86 [1989] Imm AR 313.
87 [1990] Imm AR 211.
88 [1990] Imm AR 450.

However, by 'love', the applicant may have meant not the romantic attachment associated with being 'in love', but that he was committed to the marriage and his responsibilities towards his future wife's happiness (see Chapter 5). As counsel in *Manjula Jethva* unsuccessfully argued, love is a word with many meanings.

The requirement to show that a motive other than immigration was the primary cause of the marriage invited decision-makers to assess the likelihood and thus the rationality of the stated reasons for marriage. For example, in *R v SSHD ex p. Jagdishchandra Jinabhai Prajapati*, Potts J quoted (at p. 516) the adjudicator as saying:

> I ... find difficulty in accepting that less than a year after her divorce was finalised – this is a reference to the wife's previous matrimonial history – 'she was prepared to embark on a courtship as speedily as this allegedly was. I accept that she wanted to choose her own spouse this time, but it would appear more natural to proceed cautiously bearing in mind her previous experience.'[89]

Potts J upheld the adjudicator's primary purpose refusal despite a subsequent period of cohabitation and resulting pregnancy. This argument seems thin. An early remarriage may have been unwise, but was hardly unnatural and may have been entered into for any number of reasons. As Scannell (1987: 6) observed, in relation to another case, '(t)he Court of Appeal seems to have forgotten that Indian people have independent sexuality'. This tendency to view applicants only through the prism of an immigration motive and thus to diminish their humanity is a marked characteristic of immigration control throughout the period.

Gender

Assumptions about gender lay at the heart of primary purpose. Its successful application depended upon a belief in the powerlessness and passivity of the Asian woman and the absence of any right to determine her place of residence after marriage. Yet, in the majority of cases, the focus of discussion was the credibility of the man's statements as to his motives. The belief that women lacked agency was so widespread that it rarely merited mention.

If the aim was to reduce male non-white immigration, the belief was a convenient one. Stripping women of their responsibilities also enabled their rights to be ignored. When women did demonstrate a degree of power, this could be turned against the couple. In *Sumeina Masood*, already discussed, Glidewell LJ referred to the wife having the 'whip hand' and relied on this to find that, as the wife was unwilling to leave the UK, intention to live together was absent.

In some cases, female agency was acknowledged. One such was *Mohammed Saftar v SSHD*, where Lord Prosser in the House of Session pointed out the

89 [1990] Imm AR 513.

importance of the sponsor's beliefs about the marriage.[90] He also, uniquely in the cases considered here, pointed out that the rules not only granted a right or privilege to the applicant but were 'protecting or preserving for the sponsor, a United Kingdom citizen, the ability to marry and live permanently with the man that she wants to marry and live with, without being forced to leave the United Kingdom in order to do so' (at p. 10). A further instance was McCullough J in *R v IAT ex p. Kulbander Kaur*,[91] in which he criticised the adjudicator for failing to take account of the sponsor's devotion to the applicant when determining the primary purpose of the marriage. He said (at p. 109):

> There can be few young women who are prepared to be married to a man whom they believe is primarily marrying them not for themselves but in order to obtain entry to the United Kingdom. No doubt some are more easily fooled than others, and there are men with such primary purpose who are able to conceal it from the women whom they marry. But the sponsor was young and intelligent …

Lord Prosser also mentioned that the ECO had found the sponsor 'to be a lively, attractive, intelligent young lady who answered his questions honestly and without guile' (at p. 4). It seems that an attractive young woman might persuade a judge that she was an active participant in the proceedings and that the applicant had chosen to marry her for her own merits. Less fortunate sponsors did not have that advantage. One adjudicator dismissed a primary purpose appeal (overturned on further appeal to the Tribunal), commenting that his impression of the sponsor was that:

> she was a rather unimpressive young woman who left school with no qualifications and is of limited intelligence. Her most striking feature is that she wears thick glasses which suggest bad eyesight … some people might find such glasses a discouraging feature but obviously I cannot assess their effect on a young Indian man. (Scannell 1993a: 22)

That underlying beliefs about Asian female passivity conveniently reinforced primary purpose does not suggest that they were insincerely held but that, being congruent with the other major assumption, that non-white male immigration was undesirable, they were unlikely to be displaced. It was only in rare cases that female applicants could persuade judges that they had agency in such matters. These cases seemed to occur when women conformed to the judge's conception of a how a woman with such agency would present herself. Women who were young and, by the decision-maker's standard, attractive and intelligent were thus predictably more fortunate.

90 [1992] Imm AR 1.
91 [1991] Imm AR 107.

Primary Purpose Case Law: Discussion

The underlying premise of 'primary purpose' was that a single dominant motive for a marriage could be identified and that this motive would often, at least for some types of applicant, be immigration. Some decisions, particularly early in the period discussed in this chapter, did acknowledge the improbability of a single instrumental motive being the main reason for a marriage. *Arun Kumar, Hoque and Singh* and other cases enabled some applicants to succeed. Even later in the period, some judges sought a more balanced approach. Lord Prosser in the 1992 case of *Mohammed Saftar*, for example, recognised that the purpose of a marriage could not be identified by looking only at the motives of the individual but by looking at the entire arrangements for the marriage.[92] However, as Sachdeva (1993: 144) observes, there was a slowly growing tone of judicial hostility that focused on the position of the applicant and that dealt cursorily, if at all, with the wishes of the sponsor.

It was not apparent in such cases that judges were necessarily in sympathy with primary purpose. Nonetheless, they were mostly willing to adopt conservative interpretations of the rule. The intense pressure to reinforce highly restrictive practices was made explicit only occasionally, but it is probable that it was present, at least in the background, throughout the period. The outcome was a series of cases in which, with some exceptions, the dispassionate consideration of evidence was displaced by excessive stress on the applicant, as a potential immigrant, rather than on the marriage itself. Decisions often seemed poorly reasoned and the conclusions reached barely justified by the reported facts. These were rationalised by the judicial value of respect for the administrative decision-maker and fact-finder, but, as argued here, this respect amounted, at times, to an abdication of judicial responsibility for ensuring that the correct legal test was applied.

A more critical stance by the courts would have exposed the poor fact-finding and the impossible position in which primary purpose placed applicants. While this would not have exceeded the interpretative function of the courts, it would have inevitably created conflict with the government. With some exceptions, the courts chose to avoid confrontation. Their acquiescence suggests that, for the most part, the judiciary accepted the central premises upon which policy was founded: the urgent necessity of controlling non-white immigration and the small weight to be placed upon the hardship caused by controls. Securing the power to refuse unwanted immigrants was a primary aim, trumping the right of female British residents to decide where to live after marriage. Belief in the passivity of these women made the denial of their autonomy more palatable.

As observed in relation to the non-primary purpose case law, judges did not betray personal hostility towards the non-white applicants before them unless these applicants had transgressed the perceived boundaries of good conduct. Nonetheless, interpretations of aspects of primary purpose, intervening devotion

92 [1992] Imm AR 1.

and the effect of deception had the effect of creating additional unofficial tests of endurance and probity, suggesting that aspiring immigrants had to prove themselves worthy of acceptance.

To avoid a finding of primary purpose, a couple had to present a narrative that matched official expectations as to either a 'traditional' or 'love' marriage. A love marriage had to conform to the pattern familiar in the West. Other types of complexity were ignored or discounted as self-serving. It was assumed that immigrants were motivated overwhelmingly by an urgent desire to come to the UK. As is so often the case, applicants from the sub-continent were defined and confined by their status as aspiring immigrants and every action and decision was viewed through that prism. All other aspects of their lives were invisible, the effect being a one-dimensional and dehumanised portrayal.

Conclusion

With some exceptions, judges rarely passed open comment on the political issues underlying the law. Nonetheless, the outcome of the cases and the reasoning employed suggest that certain attitudes and beliefs were implicitly held. Most obviously, the necessity for strong controls to prevent non-white immigration was rarely challenged, even implicitly. This is unsurprising given its overwhelming dominance. Thus, in a number of instances, the courts adopted interpretations of the law that favoured restrictive immigration policies. The legal reasoning upon which these were based was sometimes questionable. In a few cases, judges did adopt interpretations that assisted the immigrant, but these were relatively few in number.

Another universal and unsurprising assumption was that a foreign applicant was an 'outsider' whose claims should carry relatively little weight. However, the British-based applicant was sometimes also considered to be at least a partial outsider. A comparison with the small number of cases decided before mass non-white immigration suggests that non-white applicants and their British-based spouses were viewed predominantly as immigrants in a way that did not occur for white applicants, even when there was disapproval of the latter's conduct. The lives of these non-white parties tended to be simplified so that complex human relations were explained only in immigration terms.

Perhaps unsurprisingly, given the status of human rights law at the time, there was a marked absence of human rights-related discourse in any of this case law. Applications did not represent the exercise of a right by a British resident but the granting of a privilege by the state, and judicial powers were exercised in ways that deferred to state supremacy in these matters. This privilege was extended only to those who acknowledged such state supremacy and was unavailable to those who deceived or misled. In some cases, only those who proved themselves in various ways were considered worthy. There was resistance to assisting those who, despite extensive residence in the UK, continued to rely on the law or values in their country of origin. The privilege of British residence should be repaid by an unequivocal adoption of British ways. This expectation was not absolute. Judges did not display a dislike of the arranged marriage in the manner of some MPs and there was sometimes sympathy for the distress caused to these by the exclusion of a spouse. However, this was easily displaced.

While there was occasional evidence of direct political pressure, it is not argued that judges generally lacked independence in the formal sense. However, it is arguable that, because they shared the assumptions upon which government policy was predicated, they were over-inclined to support the government's view. It is true that, in the pre-Human Rights Act era, judges may have felt they lacked a mandate for a more challenging approach, but that does not fully explain the degree of deference, which was also noted during that period in other immigration-related areas (see Legomsky 1987 and Griffiths 1997). In the cases discussed here, judges generally expressed themselves formally and in ways that were consistent with their institutional values, rarely commenting on political issues and deferring to the fact-finding role of the primary decision-maker. Decisions were justified in terms of the principles of precedent and statutory interpretation. Yet it has been argued throughout this chapter that this was done selectively, the courts often adopting interpretations that, to those unconvinced of the urgency of strict immigration control, was less coherent than the alternative. These cases, explored in some depth above, suggest that, in these cases, the process of legal reasoning, despite its appearance of ineluctable movement towards a single conclusion, was ultimately based on unprovable (and sometimes tendentious) beliefs and assumptions. These were largely congruent with those held within the other institutions discussed in this section of the book during this period, and their decisions supported and enabled the implementation of policy created elsewhere. In this way, the judiciary largely supported the hierarchy of acceptable marriages implicitly established by the legislature and discussed in the previous chapter, and, in particular, the lowly place occupied by non-white husbands coming to join British citizens or residents of immigrant descent.

Chapter 5

Doubt and Cynicism: Entry Clearance on the Indian Sub-continent 1969-1997

Introduction

This chapter analyses the administration of immigration control on the sub-continent from 1969, when compulsory entry clearance was introduced, although Sondhi (1987: 18-19) suggests that the culture and practices described in this chapter took root soon after the introduction of a voluntary system of entry certificates in 1965. While the sub-continent was the focus of attention, it is not clear that it was the largest source of bogus applications. 'Marriage rackets' were regularly reported in the British press during this period. The nationalities involved were various and included Algeria, 'Arab' nations, Cyprus, Egypt, Ghana, India, Iran, Israel, Morocco, Nigeria, Pakistan, Poland, Portugal, Turkey, the USA and 'West Africa'.[1] Yet, while there was the occasional report of adverse treatment of other nationalities, the overwhelming focus of public discussion was on the 'problem' of South Asian immigration.[2] It was argued in the press and by politicians that pressure to emigrate from poor countries, and most especially the Indian sub-continent, led to frequent forgeries and bogus applications.[3] The entry clearance service was doing an unpleasant task to the best of its abilities.

Immigrant groups and some academics, on the other hand, were deeply critical, judging the service to be discriminatory and unfair. Juss (1997: 22) captured the essence of the critique when he wrote of 'an internal culture of deep-rooted doubt and cynicism'. The Commission for Racial Equality (1985: 52) found that:

> The procedures ... operate on the basis that few applications, and virtually no family cases can be believed without extensive and painstaking cross-checking. The genuine applicant is faced not with a presumption that he or she is genuine,

---

1 See Appendix A for citations.

2 'Britain barred Jamaican clergyman because love letters were too cool', *The Guardian*, 3 February 1984; 'Love story without a happy ending', *The Guardian*, 28 December 1989 (Hong Kong); 'I had to wait 4 years before they let me live with my husband', *Woman*, 11 November 1992 (the Philippines); 'Knickers quiz bars wife from Britain', *The Sun*, 10 December 1992 (Jordan).

3 See Chapter 3 and, for example, 'How many migrants in the queue?', *Daily Telegraph*, 10 January 1975; 'FO official accused of inquiry influence', *The Guardian*, 26 November 1985; 'Immigration: the first hurdle', *Daily Telegraph*, 2 December 1985.

> nor with a presumption of neutrality, but with the requirement in effect to persuade the officer that he or she is not presenting a well-prepared bogus application.

It is not the aim of this chapter to reach a definitive view on such matters as the relative levels of abuse. Rather, by reporting the competing claims that were made, its objective is to demonstrate that decision-makers almost invariably made choices and exercised their discretion in ways that favoured restriction and minimised the chances of an applicant succeeding. The consistency of practice suggests a reliance upon commonly held assumptions and beliefs and that countervailing institutional or other values were weak or absent. These beliefs and assumptions were manifested in the particular ways discussed in this chapter and it is arguable that the burden of proof on the applicant frequently went beyond that of the balance of probabilities (see Runnymede Trust 1977: 22-3 and Chowdhury 1982: 3). It was persistently argued that these practices were part of a deliberate strategy condoned or even directed by government to control covertly the level of non-white immigration.[4] There was much contemporary critical commentary, including the Runnymede Trust (1977), Chowdhury (1982), the Commission for Racial Equality (1985), Sondhi (1987), Powell (1992, 1993a and 1993b) and Juss (1997). Defence of the entry clearance service was confined to occasional newspaper articles and political speeches.

Contemporaneous to the institution of compulsory entry clearance was the establishment of a two-tier appeals system of adjudicators and the Immigration Appeals Tribunal (for detail, see Juss 1997: 124-5). While this aimed to provide a check on poor decision-making, the inability of parties to attend their own appeals made them less effective. Juss (1997: 125-52; see also Chowdhury 1982: 3-4) is critical of the appellate bodies' failure to challenge entry clearance practices. Some of their reported attitudes were similar to those observed and criticised in the entry clearance service.[5] This may have been because they shared similar assumptions or because, lacking expert knowledge of their own, they relied on entry clearance service claims as to local conditions (Chowdhury 1982: 60-1). The outcome was that, while the appeals process assisted some individuals, it had a limited effect upon the daily practices of the entry clearance service.

---

4 'Immigrant entry "being controlled by stealth"', *The Guardian*, 1 November 1983; 'Black marks for Whitehall', *The Guardian*, 9 May 1984; 'Making racism respectable', *The Observer*, 15 July 1984; see also the sections below on delay, medical evidence and primary purpose.

5 See also 'Immigrants' inquisition', *The Guardian*, 14 March 1975; 'The immigration appeal system needs to be made just', *The Guardian*, 23 April 1980; 'Immigration adjudicator under fire', *The Observer*, 26 July 1981; 'Controls "unfair to legal migrants"', *The Guardian*, 11 February 1985. Some applicants did succeed upon appeal (25 per cent of settlement applications in 1978 according to the Home Office in 1978: letter from the Home Office to the Runnymede Trust, 1 September 1978, Runnymede Collection).

The entry clearance service was thus subject to scathing criticism in this period, much of which is adopted in this chapter. This was partly a matter of the conduct of individuals, some of whom appeared to relish their role (see the section below on interviews, for example), but institutional factors also encouraged this style of decision-making. ECOs were obliged to apply a bureaucratic system to a largely undocumented society and to definitively establish matters that could not be proven without extensive investigation and knowledge, for example, the existence of a relationship for which there was no formal record or the compliance of a marriage with the norms of local society. A perusal of refused applications (see, for example, Runnymede Trust 1977: 37-147) reveals some of these difficulties. The service operated in a political climate where the reduction of non-white immigration was a paramount aim of immigration control and played a critical role by deflecting unwanted migrants before they reached the UK. There is some evidence, discussed below, of deliberate manipulation in ensuring that such a function was effective. Certainly, such allegations were widespread at the time and were, in general, consistent with many of the administrative practices discussed here. ECOs may (or may not) have been happy to dismiss claims in the manner discussed here, but the institutional environment encouraged them to do so.

Delay

Delay was endemic throughout the period and was a source of anger within the Asian community.[6] The Home Affairs Committee in 1990 accepted that delays were dictated by deliberate Home Office policy (Juss 1997: 60), a policy that seems to have spanned two decades or more. Before entry clearance became compulsory in 1969, queues on arrival were visible and politically controversial.[7] As previously discussed (see Chapter 3), the rationale for compulsory entry clearance was to prevent lengthy waits in an unsuitable environment and to ensure immigrants did not incur the expense and disruption of emigration only to be refused admission on arrival. However, immigrant groups warned that problems at entry clearance posts were inevitable, given staffing levels.[8] Even immigration staff were dismayed, although their principal concern was that inexperienced staff would issue too many certificates.[9] In response, the government increased the staff at High Commissions, but by only ten.[10]

6 See, for example, the Joint Council for the Welfare of Immigrants, quoted in Juss 1997: 59.

7 'Asians' reception "inhumane", welfare leader says', *The Times*, 23 December 1968.

8 'Migrant attack on Callaghan', *Daily Telegraph*, 3 May 1969; 'New permit rules upset immigrants', *The Times*, 3 May 1969.

9 'Migrant attack on Callaghan', *Daily Telegraph*, 3 May 1969.

10 'Give them a proper chance', *The Guardian*, 20 May 1969. However, ECOs at Dacca were increased from 5 to 12 in 1974 (Martin 1975: 1). In this context, it is interesting

The result was lengthy delays. Even before compulsory entry clearance, applicants might wait a year for a decision.[11] Two-, three- or even four-year delays for interview, which was often only the first step in a lengthy process, were reported for wives in Bangladesh by the mid-1970s, while in Pakistan, the queue was 18 months and in Bombay, six months.[12] Pressure started to mount. In 1975, the Court of Appeal found in *Phansopkar* that the lengthy wait for admission of patrial wives and children was unlawful and those applicants were placed in a priority queue.[13] Following intervention by the Minister for Immigration, Alex Lyon, in 1975, recently married wives and those with small children were also given priority.[14] However, the queue for husbands and fiancés remained long and it was suggested that this was a deliberate policy to limit the number of husbands admitted after the rule change in 1974.[15] Concerns were explicitly linked to the fear, discussed in Chapter 3, of an 'infinite pool' of immigrants.[16]

Queues for interview were generally somewhat shorter in the 1980s but were still between 18 months and two years in Bangladesh and between six months and a year in Pakistan and India (Commission for Racial Equality 1985: 136). Actual resolution of an application frequently took many years. Sondhi (1987: 71) found that, where applications were repeatedly refused, the entire process might take 10–15 years. The Home Office Select Committee found in 1990 that delays remained unacceptable.[17]

At the very least, reducing the queue was not a priority, or more staff would have been appointed. The response to staff shortages was to allow queues to grow rather than to reduce the time taken to consider applications. It was reported that staff at Dhaka, for example, interviewed wives at the rate of three every two days in 1974, although, by 1975, they reportedly managed two interviews per day

that, in 1988, the number of staff employed in the UK to investigate and detain illegal entrants and overstayers was doubled ('Home Office to double number of visa staff', *The Guardian*, 14 November 1988).

11 New permit rules upset immigrants', *The Times*, 3 May 1969.

12 According to Martin (1975: 1), only one case in five at Dacca was, at the time he was writing, settled at first interview: 'Two-year holdup for wives', *The Guardian*, 28 February 1974; 'Pledge to help women waiting to join husbands', *The Guardian*, 30 August 1974; 'Britain to speed up entry of immigrants' dependants', *The Times*, 6 January 1975.

13 *R v Secretary of State for the Home Department ex p. Phansopkar* [1975] 3 All ER 497.

14 Letter from Alex Lyon, 8 August 1975, Runnymede Collection; 'Priority categories for entry clearance applicants in the Indian sub-continent', JCWI briefing, February 1977.

15 'The law's delays', *The Guardian*, 21 May 1975.

16 See 'We must control the numbers of immigrants for their own good', *The Times*, 3 May 1977, in which a Conservative MP stated that ECOs operate a 'sluice gate quota system' and that increasing the number of officials would increase the length of the queue due to raised expectations.

17 *Report on Administrative Delays in the Immigration Department* (1989-90, HC 319), para. 38.

(Martin 1975: 2). This was rationalised by the need to be vigilant against abuse, although a spokesman 'could not give the ratio of fraudulent to genuine claims'.[18] Alex Lyon (1975) pointed out that the standard of proof did not require all doubt to be eliminated so that a more rapid examination was appropriate.[19] However, it seems likely that, save during the brief period when he was minister, delays due to extensive enquiries received political support.[20]

The suspicion that queues were manipulated was a persistent theme. The suggestion that long queues were used to delay the entry of husbands in the 1970s has already been alluded to. Lyon (1975) found that the queue at Karachi had been kept artificially long to match that at Islamabad and there was suspicion at the sudden lengthening of the queue at Bombay.[21] Evans (1983: 128) argues that queues were a form of concealed rationing of all applications, although this was denied.[22] However, his suggestion is given credence by a leaked government briefing written in 1983. The number of ECOs was described as 'the primary regulator' of the numbers of entrants and that 'a system of queues operates to regulate the flow of immigrants ... Provided the queues do not become too long this form of administrative regulation can continue'. The briefing went on to say that this policy of delay, if openly acknowledged, would be unlawful unless backed by legislation authorising quotas.[23]

The 'administrative regulation' of numbers through queues continued and, following the *Abdulaziz* decision in 1985, when husbands and fiancés became entitled to equal treatment, wives and fiancées lost their priority and all spouses and fiancés were placed in a slower queue. Refused applicants making renewed applications, of which there were a considerable number, were put in the final 'dustbin' queue.[24] There were also considerable delays in the appeals process, so that the hearing might take place between one and six years after the first interview (Runnymede Trust 1977: 24). A major factor was the ECO's obligation to draw up an explanatory statement for which there was no time limit (which also raised issues as to their accuracy).[25]

Delays caused obvious distress. However, as sponsors had voluntarily left their families for many years, further delay was regarded as a minor self-imposed

18 'Two-year hold-up for wives', *The Guardian*, 28 February 1974.

19 The impact of Lyon's intervention is discussed later in this chapter.

20 See, for example, David Lane's comment that unless illegal immigration was drastically reduced, there could be no speed-up in the issue of entry certificates on the sub-continent (Runneymede Trust 1974: 6).

21 'The law's delays', *The Guardian*, 21 March 1975.

22 'Queues used to stem immigration', *The Guardian*, 21 March 1985.

23 Ibid.

24 'Long queues separate families', *JCWI Bulletin*, September 1985; 'Asian wives go to back of queue', *The Guardian*, 31 August 1985; 'Migrants face long delays', *Daily Telegraph*, 25 July 1985.

25 See *Interviews Conducted by Entry Clearance Officers Overseas*, paper prepared for submission to the Minister of State by UKIAS, 29 January 1985 (Runnymede Collection).

hardship; the Hawley Report, for instance, quoted approvingly a comment on the 'barbaric' nature of these voluntary separations. Consistent with this was the priority given to the recently married in queues for interview.[26] However, even these individuals were subject to long delays, particularly after 1985. One report (Smith 1984) encapsulated the impossible position facing applicants and their sponsors. Faced with a two-year wait just for an interview, the British wife lived with her husband in Bangladesh despite severe health problems and homesickness. The British High Commission advised her to return but, leaving aside her wish to be with her husband, she feared that doing so would be used against the application when it was eventually heard.

Tax Fraud

Bangladeshi applications often encountered particular problems due to the 'Sylheti tax pattern' (Commission for Racial Equality 1985: 21-5 and Juss 1997: 77-84). Some early immigrants to the UK, not expecting to settle or to call over their families, had claimed income tax allowances for non-existent wives and children. Over time, these men returned home and established real families whom they then wished to bring to the UK. Unless the tax fraud was to be admitted, the prior account had to be reconciled with the true position for entry clearance purposes. Previous fictitious wives had to 'die' or be 'divorced'. Fictitious children might also 'die' or be listed as non-applicants. Alternatively, the true wife and children might impersonate the fictional ones, or another relative might stand in for an invented child. In all instances, an element of deception was involved and aspects of the claim might be misleading. Divorce or death certificates would be absent or faked, wives and children would appear to be younger than claimed and oral accounts would be confused or contradictory.

While the 'Sylheti tax pattern' caused obvious confusion and difficulty, in immigration terms, it was material only if impersonation led to the entry of non-entitled individuals. An internal briefing produced in 1976 by the British High Commission at Bangladesh stated as fact that 'most' applications were artificially constructed to fit a bogus tax pattern and bogus children assumed the identity of those shown in the tax affidavit. This was revised in 1978 to 'many'. Indications of tax fraud were said in this briefing to include a wife who does not look her stated age, a second wife, an early marriage by the husband, age-estimate discrepancies for the children and a sparse family tree.

Fears about tax fraud contributed to the style of questioning and consequent reliance on 'discrepancies', which are described below. However, while many applications did include references to non-existent dependants, it seems that most applicants did not seek entry clearance for anyone other than their real dependants.

26 *Joint Council for the Welfare of Immigrants Briefing Paper*, February 1977 (Runnymede Collection).

The Commission for Racial Equality (1985: 21-4; see also Lal and Wilson 1986: 19) found that, in the cases they observed, this was suspected in only a few instances and that, of wives and children confessed to being bogus up to 1980, fewer than one in six had been applicants for entry clearance. An investigation into 'tax confessions' by the Foreign and Commonwealth Office found that only 6.7 per cent of these involved false applications for entry. It was improbable, in the context of Bangladeshi culture, that a man would seek to present as a wife a woman to whom he was not married (Chowdhury 1982: 40 and Juss 1997: 75, 84).

The problems with tax fraud were, to an extent, of the officials' own making. Difficulties could have been partially avoided had applicants been advised at the outset that there would be no contact with the Inland Revenue, no cross-checking for consistency with tax forms and no investigation of possible tax fraud. However, this was not the approach adopted, although it is not clear at which level the decisions were made, since the Hawley Report suggests ECOs favoured a 'tax amnesty'. Sponsors of applicants from Bangladesh were required to authorise the Inland Revenue to divulge information about their tax affairs (Commission for Racial Equality 1985: 24). Despite an apparent initial reluctance on the part of the Inland Revenue, later reports suggest that information was obtained, the practice being abandoned only after the Commission for Racial Equality Report was published (Chowdhury 1982: 18-19 and Hussain 1994: 18).[27] Principal applicants were also required to list on the application the names of any children not applying for entry clearance. Thus, there was pressure to ensure that applications were consistent with previous tax forms.

The misleading information or inconsistencies that resulted formed the basis of detailed investigations and many refusals (Chowdhury 1982: 18-19 and Commission for Racial Equality 1985: 21-4). Some ECOs disregarded false information that did not represent an attempt to evade control (perhaps recording that they did not accept the existence of the non-applicants). Many however were keen to obtain 'confessions' of tax fraud, concerned that non-applicant children might make a later claim for admission, or considered that the deception cast doubt on the credibility of the whole application. Applicants would be asked for evidence to confirm the claimed history even when ECOs did not doubt that the applicants were, in reality, the wife and children of the sponsor. The Commission for Racial Equality (1985: 37) found that sponsors were frequently threatened with refusal unless they made a 'tax confession'. The 'Sylheti tax pattern' thus provided a rationale for suspicion and exhaustive investigation of credentials. Applicants were seen as tainted by the prior dishonesty, as lacking credibility and as undeserving by both ECOs and adjudicators (see, for example, Sondhi 1987: 54-5 and Juss 1997: 82-3). It also permitted applications from the sub-continent

27 'Why family cannot have entry permit', *Birmingham Post*, 11 July 1969. In this instance, entry clearance had been refused because the sponsor could not obtain a letter from the Inland Revenue showing the dependants for whom he had claimed tax relief.

to be publicly presented as abusive, notwithstanding that it is likely that in only a minority of cases was there an attempt to bring bogus family members to the UK.[28]

Documentary Evidence

In the largely undocumented society from which immigrants came, it was often impossible for them to establish their status in ways that were usual in the UK. Menski (2001: 10-20), for example, describes the absence of state input and the impossibility of ensuring the consistent registration of marriages in India, resulting in a lack of documentary evidence of many marriages. Moreover, 'customary' marriages, whether or not they were supported by registration, varied enormously, so that identifying a valid marriage was not straightforward and, indeed, was a matter that the Indian courts themselves had difficulty in resolving. According to Powell (1992), customary divorces were not recognised by the UK authorities, leading to severe practical problems many years later for some applicants. Providing other evidence of the relationship might also prove problematic. Illiterate people would not communicate by letter and remittances were often sent indirectly (Martin 1975: 2).

Decision-makers chose to deal with this situation in particular ways. The Muslim presumption of marriage appears to have been accorded little weight (see Chowdhury 1982: 43 and Pearl and Menski 1998: 151). Although posts officially maintained that documentation was not essential for a successful application, in reality, an extensive array of documents was expected (Martin 1975: 2, Runnymede Trust 1977: 9-10, Commission for Racial Equality 1985: 30-31, Lal and Wilson 1986: 14-16 and Sondhi 1987: 29). Such demands would have caused anxiety, expense and delay. Yet, while applicants were expected to go to considerable lengths to obtain documents, once presented, they were accorded little weight (Runnymede Trust 1977: 10, Commission for Racial Equality 1985: 31-2 and Sondhi 1987: 30-32). One officer at Dhaka was reported as saying that they counted neither for nor against an application. The Commission for Racial Equality observed no instance where documentary evidence was considered sufficient in itself to justify an issue of entry clearance, although a failure to produce supporting documentation often contributed to a refusal. Producing an 'excessive' number of documents might also lead to suspicion.

Documents were frequently discounted as likely forgeries, although allegations of fraud were rarely investigated. Instead, refusals frequently referred to the ease with which forged documents could be obtained. Thus, in the 58 cases examined by the Runnymede Trust, the documentary evidence in all cases was considered insufficient, but a specific allegation of forgery was made in only 32 cases (Runnymede Trust 1977: 8-11). Internal guidance to ECOs in Pakistan and

28 For press coverage, see 'Immigrant fraud cases "top 2,600"', *The Times*, 16 February 1982; 'Immigrant "confessions"', *The Times*, 26 February 1982.

Bangladesh suggested that forgeries were commonplace and that even genuine documents may have been obtained by impersonation, a difficult allegation to disprove, particularly at a distant appeal. The guidance concluded that relationships can 'only be established with any degree of accuracy by personal interview and exhaustive cross-checking'. Prepared in the mid-1970s, the guidance was still considered reliable in the 1980s (Juss 1997: 90, 106-7).

Martin (1975: 3) argues that local documentation was more reliable than ECOs believed (although see Chowdhury 1982: 15-17). However, some applicants did rely either on forged documents or on genuine documents obtained years after the original event. In some cases, this was on the advice of agents, but Chowdhury (1982: 20-21) argues that ECOs often requested documents during interviews that the applicant then felt obliged to obtain. These may have contained errors and inconsistencies due to misunderstandings or ignorance, or because applicants were trying to make documents consistent with tax affidavits. While ECOs often concluded that they represented a bogus application, this was not necessarily the case (Runnymede Trust 1977: 11-13, Chowdhury 1982: 20-21 and Sondhi 1987: 20, 32).

Scepticism appears to have been extreme on occasion. Until the Tribunal intervened, ECOs and adjudicators refused wives if the date of marriage remained undetermined, even if the fact of marriage was not disputed (Chowdhury 1982: 4).[29] Documents such as correspondence, remittances, voters' lists, land deeds, school records and medical or bank records were described by critics as highly reliable, yet were not requested by ECOs or, if produced, were given little weight (Chowdhury 1982: 22-6, Sondhi 1987: 34-7 and Juss 1997: 91-108). Juss also describes instances, both at post and on appeal, when doubts about the veracity of individual documents resulted in refusal even when, taken together, the evidence overwhelmingly supported the existence of the relationship, or when (often trivial) discrepancies at interview were used to undermine otherwise consistent documentary evidence. Documents produced after an application had been refused were usually disregarded, even when forging them would have required improbable levels of skill and sophistication (Sondhi 1987: 33; see also the rejection of 'intervening devotion' in Powell, 1993a: 116). By contrast, it was claimed that denunciatory letters (even when anonymous) and documents that were unfavourable to the applicant's claim were scrutinised less critically (Sondhi 1987: 38-9).

Juss (1997: 105) argues that scepticism increased over the years. Attitudes seem to have gone beyond a cautious approach to disbelief in the integrity of the entire community (Sondhi 1987: 30-32). Certainly, the problems that sometimes existed in obtaining reliable documentary evidence were used to rationalise the delays, the 'discrepancy system', reliance upon medical examination and other practices described here. In other instances, where documents were beyond doubt, ECOs applied principles such as domicile (discussed in Chapter 4), nationality,

29 *Bibi Barkat*, TH/36849/78 (1761) unreported.

accommodation and maintenance or the requirement to have met to assert that a marriage was not valid or that the parties did not fulfil requirements (Sondhi 1987: 60-3, 102-3 and Menski 1994: 113-14). Where an applicant had previously misrepresented his position, even strong evidence of the true situation was treated sceptically, effectively punishing the applicant for his prior deception (Hussain 1994: 20).

Interviews

As documentary evidence was considered insufficient on its own, applicants were always interviewed (Commission for Racial Equality 1985: 33) which often involved a long journey in difficult conditions. Applicants from Sylhet District, for example, would have to travel to Sylhet town using local transport or foot and then undertake a 13-hour train journey to Dhaka, often accompanied by small children (Chowdhury 1982: 11 and Commission for Racial Equality 1985: 48). Many applicants would not previously have travelled so far, while women were unused even to leaving their own homes (Juss 1997: 68-9). Journeys might take place during the rainy season when travelling was difficult (and ECOs themselves suspended their village visits). Having arrived at the capital, applicants would usually stay overnight as they were expected to report at 7 am. All of this involved immense cost, potential loss of income and significant stress. There was however resistance to the establishment of local consulates (Commission for Racial Equality 1985: 49 and Sondhi 1987: 21-2). There also seems to have been little priority given to minimising discomfort and anxiety. Applicants had to wait long hours in uncomfortable conditions. At Dhaka and Islamabad, for example, the waiting room was the only part of the building not to be air-conditioned (Lal and Wilson 1986: 11 and Sondhi 1987: 22).

Fatigued and aware of the importance for the entire family of a successful outcome to this long-awaited interview, applicants found lengthy questioning by an authority figure, often the first white male they had ever encountered, to be intimidating and exhausting (Chowdhury 1997: 50-51 and Juss 1997: 69). At the outset, applicants should have been asked if they were tired or unwell and if they understood the interpreter, but this did not always occur. Requests for postponement were rare for fear of further delay, although it seems that applicants frequently did feel unwell or were unable to understand interpreters who were sometimes poorly matched to applicants. Translators recruited locally were reported to be incompetent in dialects (Sylheti, for instance, is very different from standard Bengali), leading to fundamental misunderstandings and, on occasion, to be rude, aggressive or even corrupt (Chowdhury 1982: 10-12 and Powell 1992). Given these difficulties and the problems associated with cross-cultural communication, it is unsurprising that misunderstandings were frequently reported (see, for example, Powell 1993a:

109, 170).[30] ECOs were said to ask questions which were misunderstood or whose answers were unknown by the interviewee (Sondhi 1987: 22-3, Chowdhury 1982: 10-2, Runnymede Trust 1977: 14-7). Powell (1993a: 109), for example, cites a woman who understood a question about whether she was related to her husband prior to marriage as one asking whether she had sexual relations with him before marriage and responded with an indignant negative. Adjudicators tended to be dismissive of appeals arising from such errors, despite the critical importance of accurate translation (Runnymede Trust 1977: 14-17 and Sondhi 1987: 22-3).

It was expected that female applicants would be accompanied by a male relative, who was also interviewed. Unaccompanied applicants seem to have been regarded unfavourably (Sondhi 1987: 24). It was usual to interview each family member in turn, and children as young as five were reported to have been included. Following adverse comments at the Tribunal, interviews of children under 14 were officially ended, although, in practice, accompanied children over ten were still interviewed (Commission for Racial Equality 1985: 35, Sondhi 1987: 23-4 and Juss 1997: 63). ECOs usually put questions through the interpreter, failing to address the applicant directly, and were reported as appearing bored, irritated or, in some instances, intimidating. Chowdhury (1982: 58-9) found that the interviews he observed were 'grim', formal and impersonal. Elsewhere, it was found that interruptions, even for personal matters, were frequent but were neither explained nor apologised for. Children reported that they were threatened with being thrown out of the window or into the river. One woman reported that disbelieving staff tore up her affidavit in front of her. Parties described how they were so anxious that they gave inaccurate answers that they were then too frightened to retract or pruned family trees to avoid prolonging the interview (Martin 1975: 9, Runnymede Trust 1977: 16-17 and Commission for Racial Equality 1985: 36-7). Powell (1992) found that out of 69 refused applicants in Pakistan, 38 claimed they had been treated rudely or harshly and 34 said that they had not been given a proper chance to explain themselves. He criticised the reported interviewing style as resembling a cross-examination in which leading questions invited answers that would unfairly condemn the applicant. A typical scenario was a series of reported questions on residence that permitted the inference that applicants were acting against religious principle in seeking to join their wives. Applicants were not encouraged or even permitted to expand on or qualify their answers. In the same work, Powell also reports frequent allegations that interviews were wrongly recorded by the ECO and even that answers and confessions were fabricated.

Each interviewee was asked to provide a family tree and there would follow questions about the family, significant events and the circumstances of the applicants' lives. Taking the family tree was a laborious procedure that the Home Office privately acknowledged was of little probative value (Lal and Wilson 1986: 13). ECOs had discretion over the areas of questioning and practice

30 Ballard (undated) discusses these in relation to the judiciary and many of his points are equally apt here, given the imbalance of power.

was inconsistent. Recall might be expected of events that had occurred years previously, such as a sponsor's visit or a wedding, as well as matters such as the construction and location of the family house or the characteristics of the family's livestock, which might easily be described differently by different people (UKIAS 1985). Sondhi (1987: 45) details an intensive series of questions asked by an ECO concerning the order and circumstances of various marriages and births in an extended family. The implications for refusals on discrepancy grounds are discussed below. Applicants might have felt inhibited from revealing, in such a context, personal matters such as their feelings for a spouse (Powell 1993a: 4) and some reported questions were embarrassing (Martin 1975: 4). There were several press reports, particularly during the early part of the period, of personal questions, such as the use of contraception or the colour of underwear.[31] Most of these involved immigration staff in the UK, but applicants on the sub-continent also complained of questions about their sex lives.[32] Instructions to ECOs issued in 1987 warned against such questions, suggesting it was a continuing problem.

Parties had reason to feel anxious and might confer or take advice beforehand. Evidence that they had been coached or had otherwise prepared would result in a loss of credibility (Sondhi 1987: 33). In some cases, parties did tell untruths or partial truths at interview, often on the advice of others, with predictably damaging results. This was said to result from the widespread perception that the truth would be disbelieved or misinterpreted (see, for example, Powell 1992 and 1993a: 332, 380). ECOs also used interviews to make a visual assessment of the ages, family likeness and general demeanour of applicants. This permitted ECOs to draw subjective and sometimes distressing conclusions about whether an individual was truly a family member (see, for example, Sondhi 1987: 56-7).

A decision might be made immediately after interview or deferred until after a village visit, medical examination or a sponsor interview (Sondhi 1987: 24). The Commission for Racial Equality found that the clarifications sought from sponsors were frequently of a peripheral nature (Commission for Racial Equality 1985: 35-7). Lal and Wilson (1986: 14) cited an instance in which the sponsor was to be asked why he had failed to father a child during a visit to Bangladesh. However, such enquiries could cause considerable delay, particularly if the sponsor happened to be absent from the UK at the time he was called for interview (Martin 1975: 9). After the sponsor interview, a re-interview of the applicants might follow (with a repeat of the lengthy and stressful journey), causing further delay. This was often several years later, involving a different ECO and interpreter. Applicants would be expected to explain discrepancies between the answers given at the first interview, at the sponsor interview and in applications made by other family members (Sondhi 1987: 25).

---

31 'Police carry out sex snoop on migrants', *The Guardian*, 22 April 1977; 'Newly-weds' bloomer', *Daily Star*, 10 December 1992.

32 'Secret immigration guide "biased to refuse entry"', *The Guardian*, 21 March 1984. See also Bhabha, Klug and Shutter 1985: 70.

It is unsurprising that answers at interview were frequently confused or inconsistent. When these were later described in an explanatory statement away from the context in which they were made and without reference to other more consistent answers, they could suggest substantial dishonesty and evasion. It was frequently difficult to persuade appellate bodies to overturn refusals based on these contradictory answers (Juss 1997: 73-4). The Runnymede Trust (1977: 27) cites instances where an applicant's dishonesty or inaccuracy in one aspect caused the whole application to be regarded as discredited on appeal. One adjudicator commented of an applicant who had lied to the ECO: 'If she is hoist on the petard of her own dishonesty (which destroys the whole of her credibility) she must not be surprised.'

The 'Discrepancy System'

The interviewing techniques described above supported the so-called 'discrepancy system'. Discrepancies in the answers given to questions would be used to justify refusal on the grounds that the parties were not related as claimed. There was widespread contemporary criticism of the system (Commission for Racial Equality 1985: 34-6 and Juss 1997: 62-7) centring not only on the way that interviews were carried out but on the evidential weight given to discrepancies. While an interview may have been the only way to assess family relationships on the sub-continent, discrepancies formed the basis of refusal even where other evidence supported the relationship (Juss 1997: 62-3). Of 58 refusals examined by the Runnymede Trust (1977: 6-8, 14), 55 were believed by the investigators to be genuine, two (involving children, not spouses) fraudulent and one inconclusive. Of these 58, 49 were refused at least partly due to alleged discrepancies as to domestic circumstances and 24 due to the family tree. Of these, 12 were refused on discrepancies alone, unsupported by other evidence against the relationship, while in 19 cases, evidence had been taken from children 12 years old or younger (Runnymede Trust 1977: 34). The conduct of interviews has already been discussed. The Runnymede Trust (1977: 16-19) and the Commission for Racial Equality (1985: 34) demonstrate how questions might focus on minor domestic details, be ambiguous, permit more than one correct answer, ask for information that was unknown to one of the parties or permit different recollections. Intimidated by the interview process, applicants gave inaccurate answers rather than admit that they could not answer.

As well as extensive interviews, applications were cross-checked with files relating to previous applications by family members or sponsors' declarations in the UK for tax or nationality purposes to ensure consistency. Applicants who 'pruned' their family trees lost credibility (Chowdhury 1982: 21, Commission for Racial Equality 1985: 36 and Sondhi 1987: 37-8), although this was a natural temptation given the potentially catastrophic consequences of error. Applicants who came from small families were treated with disbelief, even though Powell (1992) argues that infertility was common. Applicants were advised in writing that their application would not proceed further unless an undertaking was made that 'full' or 'complete' details would be given (Martin 1975: 8-9).

Village visits were also a source of possible discrepancies. Sondhi (1987: 50-52) is critical of their execution, arguing that this was perfunctory and aimed at discrediting rather than confirming applications, a criticism also made, in rather more circumspect terms, by Webb (1986). A critique of an unsatisfactory village visit may be found in Powell (1993b: 20-43). The Joint Council for the Welfare of Immigrants (1987) was particularly critical of their execution in Bangladesh, comparing them to 'military operations'. Lal and Wilson (1986: 39) describe them as an exercise in 'neo-colonial administration' and the example they cite does seem to have been characterised by an arrogant highhandedness, typified by the officials driving a Land Rover over newly planted paddy fields (1986: 37-8).

The reliability of the 'discrepancy system' is doubtful. One unnamed official admitted that 'probably you would get as good results by sticking a pin into a list'.[33] In some cases, the system may have detected a bogus applicant's inadequate knowledge of the claimed family. However, as the Commission for Racial Equality (1985: 38) point out, a bogus applicant could be well drilled or familiar with the family while, even leaving aside the difficulties in interview discussed above, those genuinely related may suffer memory lapses, have varying conceptualisations of relationships, use different terminology or misunderstand peripheral matters. Other possible explanations abound. People might be known by a pet name (Chowdhury 1982: 49 and Sondhi 1987: 44) or names might take various forms (see, for example, Runnymede Trust 1977: 151). Elder relatives were often addressed in terms of the relationship rather than by name (Chowdhury 1982: 47-9). Parties might be reticent about revealing information regarded as shameful, such as a divorce, or give incorrect information for reasons of self-interest, ignorance or on the advice of agents (Runnymede Trust 1977: 13, 18-19). Matters that an ECO might regard as elementary, such as dates, intervals of time or the sequence of events, often held little meaning for illiterate people from a culture where events were not recorded and birthdays not celebrated. Questions as to schooling (when children might only attend a *madrasa*) or the numbers of rooms in a house (which might be partitioned or have a partially exposed kitchen) often gave rise to different answers. Parties failed to appreciate the critical importance of accuracy on these matters (Chowdhury 1982: 49-56 and Juss 1997: 67-70).

Examples of discrepancies used to justify refusals are cited in the literature or contemporary reports. Juss (1997: 66) reports refusals based on disagreement as to the number of visits, how long the family had owned their buffalo, the location of a school, the number of children belonging to a relative, the correct full name of another relative and the name of a party's barber and tailor. There were reports of 'discrepancies' as to how many eggs the chickens laid or the number of chairs and tables in a house.[34] Smith (1984) reports a 'discrepancy' relating to the names of

33 'How science can unite families', *New Society*, 22 November 1985.

34 Letter from M. Akram to the Home Office, 28 June 1978, Runnymede Collection.

the sponsor's step-brothers. The applicant said they were Sadad, Azad and Ahad, while the sponsor called them Hahdad, Samad and Ahad. Another applicant's son, who was about 12 but was described as 'slow', did not recall the names of his aunts and made an error as to the number of cousins.

Applications might be refused because of one 'major' discrepancy or an accumulation of minor discrepancies. (For an account of how a multiplicity of minor discrepancies can be otherwise explained, see Runnymede Trust 1977: 155-62.) Chowdhury (1982: 5; see also Runnymede Trust 1977: 21) found that explanatory statements only included those parts of the interview in which discrepancies occurred, presenting a distorted picture. This was not always well received at appeal. Chowdhury (1982: 5) quotes an adjudicator's exasperation at 'a declining standard of objectivity by the Dacca office in assessing the reality or otherwise of family relationships. It seems to me that the search for "kitchen sink" discrepancies is becoming almost an obsession'. Juss (1997: 70-72) also notes that the Tribunal sometimes took a critical stance. However, this was not uniformly the case (see also Runnymede Trust 1977: 24-8 and Juss 1997: 73-4).

Reliance on discrepancies was defended as being the only reliable way to ascertain whether parties were related as claimed. The advent of DNA testing in the 1980s rendered redundant, in most cases, the original stated purpose of the discrepancy system.[35] The claim that its true purpose was otherwise is given credence by the delays and other hurdles put in the way of those who could benefit from DNA testing and by the seepage of the use of discrepancies into other types of application (Lal and Wilson 1986: 13).[36]

Medical Evidence 1: X-rays

X-rays were frequently used to assess age. This was of some approximate use in the case of children (Juss 1997: 111-12), but X-rays of adults were of little evidential value even though they were used until 1979 (Chowdhury 1982: 31-7 and Juss 1997: 117-19). Juss (1997: 118-19), Chowdhury (1982: 31-6) and Lal and Wilson (1986: 17) cite refusals of wives on the basis that X-rays suggested that they were younger than they claimed to be. In some cases, the age gap was minimal (37 as against 40 in one case cited by Lal and Wilson 1986: 17-18). In others, it was more substantial. This may have been related to Sylheti tax fraud (so that they were wives but had misstated their ages to comply with the prior tax declaration). In others, the disparity was more likely due to the very approximate nature of such estimates, particularly given the possible effects of malnutrition

35 DNA testing could demonstrate that children were related to their claimed parents, substantiating the spouse's as well as the children's claim. Where there were no children, DNA testing could not assist.

36 'Renton disowns DNA test memo', *The Independent*, 23 June 1989; 'Home Office erects further barriers', *New Life*, 23 June 1989.

and an impoverished lifestyle. In some instances, however, not only ECOs but adjudicators and the Tribunal preferred such X-ray evidence over other forms of evidence supporting the applicant's claimed age.

The World Health Organization condemned the routine use of X-rays.[37] Their manner of administration also caused concern. It was reported that they had been carried out by unqualified staff at Heathrow, defended on the grounds that 'the requirements ... for health screening owe more to the demands of immigration legislation than to the demands of normal NHS screening programmes'.[38] It was also reported that pregnant women in Dhaka had been subjected to X-rays that were prohibited in the UK other than 'in cases of absolute medical necessity' to avoid possible harm to the foetus.[39] These were subsequently ended, while all X-ray examinations ended in 1982 (Commission for Racial Equality 1985: 40).[40]

Medical Evidence 2: Gynaecological Examinations

Gynaecological examinations or 'virginity tests' first received national attention in February 1979.[41] It was reported that a male doctor carried out an intimate internal examination of a fiancée applicant at Heathrow to establish whether she had given birth or was pregnant. The Home Office's extraordinary defence was to deny that the examination was internal, saying that a 'cursory' examination had taken place to establish 'whether she was, in fact, a bona fide virgin'. They also maintained that the woman had the option of being examined by a female doctor at a local hospital.

The press report led to an international outcry involving immigrant groups, race equality bodies, politicians, the press and pressure groups on the sub-continent, as well as the United Nations Commission on Human Rights.[42] The Home Secretary immediately instructed officials at ports and overseas that these examinations should not occur and established the Yellowlees Inquiry into the object and nature of all medical examinations. Nonetheless, he maintained that the reported instance

37 'Asian emigrants X-rayed by UK officials', *The Guardian*, 8 February 1979; 'X-ray tests on migrants banned', *The Guardian*, 27 February 1979.

38 'Heathrow X-ray risk to migrants', *The Guardian*, 9 February 1979.

39 'Asian emigrants X-rayed by UK officials', *The Guardian*, 8 February 1979.

40 'X-ray tests on migrants banned', *The Guardian*, 27 February 1979.

41 'Virginity tests on immigrants at Heathrow', *The Guardian*, 1 February 1979; 'Medical controls', *New Society*, 8 February 1979.

42 'Medical controls', *New Society*, 8 February 1979; 'Virginity testing: joint statement by CRE and EOC', *Commission for Racial Equality press release*, CR/9/79, 1 February 1979; 'Virginity tests alleged in India', *The Guardian*, 7 February 1979; '"Fiancée tests" end in India', *Daily Telegraph*, 6 February 1979; 'India talks of "retaliation" over virginity tests', *Daily Telegraph*, 5 February 1979; United Nations press release HR/718, 6 March 1979.

was 'exceptional'.[43] This, it soon became apparent, was not the case. Despite official claims that only two other such tests had been carried out at Heathrow, the Indian Workers Association said that it knew of eight cases there, while doctors at the airport admitted that the tests had been carried out for several years.[44] The Commission for Racial Equality referred to reports of instructions given in 1969 for gynaecological examinations to be stopped.[45] The practice was not confined to the UK. Alex Lyon revealed that, when he was immigration minister between 1974 and 1976, he had been aware of examinations being carried out 'fairly frequently' in Dhaka and that he had given instructions to end the practice.[46] Lal and Wilson (1986: 50) report at least one personal examination of a 14-year-old girl. It was alleged in the Indian Parliament that there had been at least 34 instances at the Delhi British High Commission.[47] The High Commission effectively admitted that this was the case, saying that no specific instructions to undertake these examinations had been issued to the doctors involved who, moreover, had all been female.[48]

Medical examination without consent is self-evidently unlawful. Consent on Home Office headed paper 'to a gynaecological examination which may be vaginal if necessary' was obtained from the woman in the Heathrow case, who maintained that she had been too frightened to refuse, reasonably so, given that refusal 'would be taken into account' in reaching a decision.[49] It was claimed that asking for consent to such an examination was not usual practice and it was not known why it had happened in her case.[50] The description of her psychological state afterwards suggests that consent, even if formally obtained, was not freely given, a supposition given strength by a subsequent offer of compensation by the Home Office.[51] Juss' (1997: 110-11) description of the procedure for medical

43 Letter from Merlyn Rees, Home Secretary, to David Lane, Chairman, Commission for Racial Equality, 1 March 1979, Runnymede Collection.

44 'I knew about virginity tests, says former Minister', *The Guardian*, 2 February 1979; 'Row grows over airport virginity test on Indian woman', *Daily Telegraph*, 2 February 1979.

45 Letter from David Lane, Chairman Commission for Racial Equality to Merlyn Rees, Home Secretary, 12 February 1979, Runnymede Collection.

46 'I knew about virginity tests, says former Minister', *The Guardian*, 2 February 1979.

47 'UK "lied" about tests on virgins', *The Guardian*, 21 February 1979.

48 '"Fiancée tests" end in India', *Daily Telegraph*, 6 February 1979.

49 'Virginity tests on immigrants at Heathrow', *The Guardian*, 1 February 1979; 'Ordeal has put our wedding at risk', *Daily Telegraph*, 2 February 1979.

50 'Virginity tests on immigrants at Heathrow', *The Guardian*, 1 February 1979.

51 Her fiancé described how she emerged from the ordeal 'in tears and trembling', was subsequently barely able to speak and refused to eat or leave the house: 'Ordeal has put our wedding at risk', *Daily Telegraph*, 2 February 1979; 'Offer of £500 over airport virginity test', *The Times*, 18 June 1980; 'Indian woman in virginity test row "will reject Home Office cash offer"', *The Guardian*, 19 June 1980; 'Home Office sued over test of virginity', *The Times*, 11 February 1982; 'Virginity test', *The Times*, 13 July 1982. The offer

examinations at posts abroad suggests that applicants there could not be regarded as having given informed consent to such a procedure. It barely needs iteration that, illegality and offensiveness aside, such examinations were an unreliable guide to a woman's status either as a virgin or as a fiancée.

After the scandal became public, no staff involved were disciplined, while the Yellowlees Report assumed that the examinations had ceased, so that the degree of official knowledge and collusion remained unexamined.[52] Yet it is improbable that these examinations would have occurred on such a scale without some official knowledge, if not sanction. The consent form in the Heathrow case suggests otherwise. Moreover, the examinations would have served little purpose (other than intimidation) unless used in reaching decisions. Juss (1997: 119-21) refers to Tribunal cases in which reference was made to gynaecological examinations and argues (at 119) that it is 'difficult to believe that they [the Home Office] were unaware of what went on'.

The Admission of Husbands and the Primary Purpose Rule

In 1983, rule changes led to the burden of proof, including as regards primary purpose, being placed upon the applicants. The significance of this was appreciated by the entry clearance service. New guidance was issued pointing out that where an application is evenly balanced, the application should now be refused.[53] The guidance outlined six areas of questioning to be pursued in assessing primary purpose, including, most critically, the relevance of the sponsor's UK residence to the decision to marry. Three examples were given of hypothetical questions that might help clarify the primary purpose issue:

1. If your fiancée did not live in the UK, would you still go to her home to live?
2. If you were not able to live with your fiancée in the UK, would you still marry her?
3. If your family had asked you to marry a local girl, would you have done so?

According to the guidance, a negative response to any of these would lead to refusal if the applicant's 'general circumstances or background together indicate that the marriage is primarily for immigration purposes'. This implicitly sanctioned greater scrutiny of applicants from poor countries.

---

was rejected and legal action was commenced by the husband (it seems the wife may have returned to India) but was struck out.

52 Letter from Merlyn Rees, Home Secretary, to David Lane, Chairman, Commission for Racial Equality, 1 March 1979, Runnymede Collection.

53 Available in the Runnymede Collection.

Sondhi (1987: 82-4) also demonstrates how even affirmative answers to these questions could result in refusal. A positive answer to the first question when the marriage was otherwise traditional might be considered to lack credibility. If other members of the family had complied with 'tradition', then an emigration motive could be ascribed. On the other hand, where other family members had migrated, an emigration motive might equally be assumed. An applicant who claimed he would have married the sponsor even if she did not live in the UK might not be believed if his home circumstances were such that he could not support a wife. An applicant who answered 'yes' to the third question would be asked about efforts made to find a suitable wife at home. Sondhi (1987: 85-8) points out that characteristics that would normally be commended, such as eagerness to work or remit funds, could now be counted against the applicant.[54]

An application would also be refused if the applicant admitted that the primary purpose of the marriage was to gain entry to the UK or if 'the overall tenor' of the applicants' answers suggested primary purpose. Sondhi (1987: 97) notes the 'remarkable candour' with which applicants admitted to primary purpose, suggesting persistent problems with interpretation or accurate reporting (discussed earlier), although the appellate authorities rarely acknowledged this. Some of these 'admissions' seemed to have been obtained by leading questions inviting an affirmative answer such as '[h]ave you always, since you were a child, wanted to go to the UK? (UKIAS 1985).

Guidance issued in 1987 and reported by Grant (1987) was slightly more guarded. It identified eight likely areas of questioning, including the applicant's prospects if he remained in his country, previous attempts to settle overseas and the relevance of the sponsor's residence to the marriage. However, it was noted that hypothetical questions should not be pursued, while a purported breach with custom was not, of itself, a reason for refusal (although it presumably was still a factor).

'Tradition' and 'Custom'

Despite this slightly more cautious guidance, perceived 'custom' and 'tradition' were often critical factors in applications. Marriages that failed to fit within an ECO's template of a typical marriage could be rejected as 'primary purpose' marriages. The tendency (already noted) to reduce aspiring immigrants to a single dimension, concerned only with emigration and lacking the complexity and nuance

54 The introduction in 1985 of the requirement to show that there would be no recourse to public funds added more complexity, as it was feared that arranging a job would lead to an inference of primary purpose while not having it would cause refusal for reason of public funds ('A Machiavellian policy', *New Society*, 30 August 1985). The guidance issued in 1987 said that having a job should not be held against applicants on primary purpose grounds.

of full human beings, is observable in the treatment of marriage rituals. Powell (1992), for example, is critical of the over-simplification of marriage customs that he encountered in ECO refusals. Marriage traditions and rituals on the Asian sub-continent reflect a rich and complex heritage and are not reducible to a single set of inflexible rules. They vary not only by country or major religion but are subject to myriad differences depending on caste, class, tribe, family or personal preference. A flavour of their complexity may be gained from Menski's (2001: 24-33) description of the many possible versions of the Hindu ritual of *saptapadi.* Families and individuals attached varying degrees of importance to tradition and breaches were commonplace (Powell 1992). Wider social changes will inevitably lead to changes in customary practice and Sondhi (1987: 101-2; see also Ballard 2005: 15) argues that 'tradition' was much less rigid than ECOs believed amongst those communities who migrated.

Questions as to custom and tradition provided a potential trap for the unwary applicant. In practice, and despite judicial dicta to the contrary (see *Arun Kumar*, discussed in Chapter 4), the simple fact of a spouse application by a male was enough to raise an inference of primary purpose (see, for example, Powell 1993a: 50). Applicants would typically be asked whether the wedding had conformed to custom in terms of the arrangements and ceremony. Having gained confirmation that the marriage was 'traditional', the ECO would query why, in this respect only the applicant was breaking with custom by moving to join his wife's family (Sondhi 1987: 81, Powell 1993a: 22). ECOs frequently referred to the practice of a wife joining her husband as a 'religious' requirement and asked applicants if they were 'good Muslims' (see, for example, Powell 1993a: 22, 178). Powell states repeatedly (1990, 1992 and 1993a: 54, 82, 125, 170) that the custom was not a rule, had no religious significance and its strength could not be deduced from the level of societal religious feeling.[55] Rather, it was a flexible custom, a breach of which did not in itself incur disapproval and that might be summarised as that a wife will move to her husband's residence unless there is a good reason to do otherwise. It had previously been breached in India due to patterns of urbanisation (Shah 1979) and another important reason for departure was the difficulty that British resident women had in adapting to life on the sub-continent (Powell 1990). Economic betterment is likely to have played a role. It is usual for a married couple to live where their prospects are better and that decision casts little light on the motive for the marriage.

Marriages that did not conform in other respects, perhaps because the wife was divorced or older, were also treated sceptically (Sondhi 1987: 81). ECOs assumed that a UK-divorced woman would only attract a husband on account of that residency. The belief was that divorce was rare and a catastrophe, particularly for women. Menski (2001: 47-57, 63-72) demonstrates, with respect to India, that, during the period under consideration, while there was resistance

55 It should also be noted that Pearl and Menski (1998) do not include such a practice in their extensive survey of Muslim family law.

to a state-sanctioned system of easy divorce, exit routes from marriage, both official and unofficial, were long-standing and well used. Muslim divorce law is well established in South Asia (Pearl and Menski 1998: 292-382). Powell (1992, 1993a: 121-2; see also, more generally, Ballard 1990 and Butler 1999: 145) argues that, throughout the sub-continent, while divorce was a blow, it was not an insurmountable obstacle to marriage. Divorced women often remarried and not only to other divorcés, widowers or husbands of lower social standing. In particular, women who had suffered at the hands of a violent or drunken husband were regarded sympathetically. The UK-based community was frequently more rigid in this regard, so that a UK-based divorced woman might find it easier to attract a husband from the sub-continent. ECOs also had firmly held conceptions as to the likely relative ages of the parties, the customary ages for marriage, the order of marriage among siblings and the preference for cousin marriages (Chowdhury 1982: 41-2, Sondhi 1987: 45, Powell 1992 and 1993a: 164-6). In all these instances, critics argued that practice was more complex and less rigid than ECOs believed (see, in particular, Powell 1992 for an extended discussion).

Yet adherence to perceived tradition was sometimes insufficient if primary purpose was suspected due to the absence of prior emotional involvement or detailed knowledge of the other (Sondhi 1987: 88-92 and Powell 1993a: 16). In this regard, ECOs were criticised for failing to appreciate the particular nature of the spousal relationship in an arranged marriage. They were suspicious of marriages where the parties were of differing educational levels, a characteristic that Ballard (2005: 21) regards as more probable in Muslim than in Hindu or Sikh marriages. They could not understand how an applicant who claimed to love his wife would not be familiar with her day-to-day activities, interests or friends. Correspondence might be deemed insufficiently affectionate.[56] Critics argued that these beliefs mistook the nature of the South Asian marital relationship. Spouses did not necessarily expect to share intellectual or cultural interests, and daily activities and friendships were not usually matters of discussion between them. They demonstrated the strength of their feelings through the exercise of their marital duties, expressions of concern for their health and physical well-being and by the husband taking account of his wife's wishes (see, for example, Bhabha, Klug and Shutter 1985: 70 and Powell 1992 and 1993a: 145, 244, 268).

It was also argued that ECOs' beliefs in the absolute patriarchy of Asian society misunderstood the nature of gender relations. Thus, where an applicant stated that he wished to live in the UK to please his wife, the assertion would be treated with incredulity if there was no evidence of open affection. ECOs were said to have failed to appreciate that notions of male superiority carried with them

---

56 'Secret immigration guide "biased to refuse entry"', *The Guardian*, 21 March 1984. This tendency was not confined to the sub-continent. In one instance, a Jamaican clergyman was refused because his letters to his wife were deemed insufficiently affectionate ('Britain barred Jamaican clergyman because love letters were too cool', *The Guardian*, 3 February 1984).

concomitant obligations, including consideration of a wife's wishes. These gave wives more agency than might first appear (Powell 1992 and 1993a: 82, 179, 244; for a discussion on Muslim law in this respect, see Pearl and Menski 1998: 177-8, 186-90), despite the asymmetry in formal power (see Siddiqui 2005: 290-94 for a discussion in relation to Bangladesh).

Applicants who established a love match were at an advantage so far as primary purpose was concerned and ECOs enquired closely into such claims. However, they assumed a binary divide between a 'love match' similar to relationships in the West on the one hand and an arranged marriage on the other, failing to acknowledge that the concept of love is at least partially culturally determined and that there is no inevitable opposition between the two. For example, a love match might be presented as an arranged marriage to save face within the wider family or parents might be manipulated by ingenious offspring, assisted by other relatives. Couples, unfamiliar with the extended courtship common in the West, would regard an expression of preference or a few minutes spent alone in shy and formal conversation as sufficient to create a 'love match'. Parents might engineer a meeting so as to permit their children to believe that they had initiated the relationship. Couples would use indirect means of discovering more about the other. Young men might exaggerate and young women might minimise the length and frequency of unaccompanied contact for reasons unconnected with the hope of obtaining a visa (Powell 1993a: 125, 331-2, 357). In none of these cases would a couple experience the familiarity and intimacy of a typical Western couple and ECOs saw the assertion of a 'love match' in the context of an arranged marriage as an attempt to deceive them (see, for example, Divided Families Campaign 1978: 5). Yet many could be credibly described as 'love matches' as well as 'arranged marriages'. As one failed applicant told Powell (1993a: 218), 'they didn't understand that both things are true – it is an arranged marriage and a love match'.

The tone of refusals suggests that ECOs did not accept that, for most, an arranged marriage was an accepted and welcome part of their lives and that they expected to achieve happiness and fulfilment through it. Powell (1992) argues that, contrary to popular Western preconceptions and with some exceptions, parents and children perceived little opposition of interest on the subject of marriage. While this may have been the case for the spouse on the sub-continent, it is less clear that this was always so for British-based families (see, for example, Brah 1978, Bhopal 1999, Ballard 1990 and 2005, and discussion below and in Chapter 6).

ECOs seemed to regard entering an arranged marriage as a grim duty governed by unchangeable rules, from which romantic expectations or consideration for a wife's feelings must be entirely absent. One explanatory statement (quoted in Powell 1993a: 340) expressed this more starkly than most:

> ... as he [the applicant] had clearly demonstrated (as had his father-in-law) that he held strictly traditional views, I considered it pertinent to ask him why he was therefore intending to join the sponsor in the United Kingdom. He had quite simply explained that, though he could happily withstand the rigours of a

> United Kingdom winter, his sponsor would be unable to cope with the heat of a Pakistani summer. Regrettably, I found his contention somewhat unbelievable. Additionally, he informed me that all of the male members of his family had previously complied with tradition in that their wives had joined them after marriage. Had the appellant succeeded in convincing me that his marriage had been motivated by love or even a degree of mutual affection, I would, of course, have disregarded the customary aspect as being largely irrelevant. He had, however, failed to do so. I would therefore respectfully submit that, if one is to expect that the appellant should be granted settlement in the United Kingdom on the basis of a marriage arranged to a girl picked entirely because tradition dictated that she was a suitable choice, one must also accept that the same traditions should be followed to their logical conclusion.

ECOs were criticised for a lack of comprehension of the complexity and flexibility of the arrangements for marriage (Powell 1992 and 1993a: 166, 245, 261; for a general discussion, see Ballard 1982 and 2005). While a male head of household usually undertook formalities, women frequently initiated discussions informally and might continue to play a leading role. Children might not be aware of all discussions, particularly informal ones, or that other offers had been refused because a particular match was desired. A lengthy period of 'understanding' might precede formal negotiations, a first match might not proceed or members of a family might promote different candidates. For reasons of family diplomacy, parties might be permitted to believe that their views carried greater weight than they did or a 'love match' might be presented as an arranged marriage. An individual's inclination for a match could be gauged indirectly without denting a father's ostensible authority. All of these could result in 'discrepancies' as to when and how a match was decided (see, for example, Powell 1992 and 1993a: 377). Meanwhile, a failure to differentiate between the distinct systems of 'dower' or 'bridewealth' and 'dowry' led to claims that men were 'buying' a British-based wife (Shah 1979; on these generally, see Pearl 1976 and 1986: 30-7, Poulter 1986: 40-2 and Pearl and Menski 1998: 178-81). These claims made their way into the British press, with predictably sensationalist results.[57]

Emigration as a Motive for Marriage

By requiring the application to be made abroad, the administrative process created an in-built bias towards detecting an emigration motive. Had, as immigrant groups

57 'Scandal of the brides for sale' and 'Who has caused this heartache?', *Daily Mail*, 5 August 1985. The report, which implied such marriages were commonplace, caused an angry reaction within the Asian community ('Daily Mail sold out to white prejudice?', *New Life*, 9 August 1985; 'Furious Asians plan picket of Daily Mail', *New Statesman*, 9 August 1985).

requested, the sponsor made the application, the 'story' would have been the wish of a British resident to be joined by their spouse.[58] Instead, the initial tone was determined by the applicant's situation, including a wish to emigrate that was an inescapable part of the application but that was, in this way, given immediate prominence.

Critics (for example, Powell 1990 and 1992) argued that the entry clearance service exaggerated the importance of emigration, although some critics, acting within the highly adversarial arena of entry clearance, may, in their turn, have tended to minimise its impact. It is likely that such a major phenomenon would have contributed to decisions about marriage and commentators such as Ballard (2005: 12) suggest that it did. The question was not whether emigration was a factor in deciding whom to marry but its importance in relation to other reasons. This, this is not a question that can easily be retrospectively determined, but it seems likely that the entry clearance service did over-estimate its role. While Asian parents might conceive their children's welfare differently from parents in the West, they were no less interested in securing it. Writers (for example, Commission for Racial Equality 1978: 16-19, Ballard 1982 and 1990) emphasise the corporate nature of Asian families and the expectation that an individual will subordinate individual preference to the family's overall welfare and honour. That does not mean that Asian parents regarded their children's happiness as unimportant, but that it was best secured through supporting and having the continuing protection of the family. Concern for the individual might be compounded by knowledge that their conduct, particularly that of girls and young women, will reflect on the wider family, and parents may be anxious to secure matches for wayward children (Bhopal 1999). However, a conceptual distinction would not necessarily be drawn between the welfare of the child and that of the family. There was obvious potential for tension, particularly when children were exposed to the more individualistic ethos of Western family life, but such tension did not, in itself, connote an absence of affection and, except perhaps for a few blinkered individuals, few parents favoured a marriage that was only or even mainly for immigration purposes. The social importance attached to securing a suitable and lasting union made such a casual disposition unlikely.

The contemporary literature shows that the impetus towards an international marriage did not always originate on the sub-continent. While some British-based groups were more likely than others to seek an international marriage (Pearl 1986: 5), numerous commentators (Commission for Racial Equality 1978: 26, Brah 1978, Ballard 1990, Powell 1992 and Menski 1999) explain why families settled in the UK might have chosen such marriages for their children. Parents, anxious lest children abandon their culture and values, saw marriage as a way to cement these and to reinforce links with their country and culture of origin. They also experienced pressure from the overseas community for an active demonstration of their own

58 This is not an academic point. Appeals frequently succeed because the sponsor, who is more competent than the applicant at negotiating British officialdom, manages to persuade the decision-maker of their case.

continuing adherence to tradition (Poulter 1976: 590 and Butler 1999: 145). UK-based children, by contrast, displayed ambivalent and even contradictory attitudes towards arranged marriages in general and international arranged marriages in particular. Writing in 1978, Brah (199-200) found that, while some young people adopted aspects of British mores outside the home and were critical of traditional arrangements, few displayed a firm intention of defying their parents' wishes. They were not persuaded that the benefits of choosing their own spouse outweighed the loss of familial security and relationships, and they were aware of the particular pressures on such marriages. Writing 20 years later, Bradby (1999: 156) also found that women sought to modify rather than undermine the arranged marriage system. Wholesale rejection of the system was thus elusive, although Poulter (1986: 26-7) reports that while many acknowledged the benefits of an arranged marriage, they were less convinced that it would survive long in Britain. They were also less enthusiastic about marriage to a partner brought directly from the sub-continent (Commission for Racial Equality 1978: 28-9). Ballard (1990: 18-19 and 2005: 13-14) argues that Sikh and Hindu children were more likely than Muslims to resist an international marriage and were more successful at diverting their parents from such a course or at persuading them to look to the wider diaspora.

International marriages nonetheless remained common. Apart from the preference of some children to trust their parents' judgement or comply with their wishes, some British-based young men regarded women raised in the UK as insufficiently domesticated and preferred a wife from the sub-continent. As men found wives from the sub-continent and elsewhere, British Asian women were faced with a growing gender imbalance in the marriage market (Menski 1999). British-born women, particularly those at a disadvantage, might therefore welcome an international marriage. In promoting international marriages, UK-based parents made adjustments to minimise potential difficulties for their children, perhaps preferring families with whom they were already familiar or conceding their children a prior meeting and a right of veto. It was thus plausible that, irrespective of any immigration considerations, some UK-based parents would seek and their children accept a spouse, including a male spouse, from the sub-continent.

Having decided upon an international marriage, there would be little point in having discussions with families unwilling to contemplate emigration. Ballard (1990: 9-10) distinguishes between endogamous marriages undertaken in Hindus and Sikh communities on the one hand and Muslims (in his study, those from Mirpur) on the other, who would feel bound to offer their children to relatives. In the former case, parents could enter negotiations with any suitable family. Ballard (2005: 12) describes British families of Punjabi origin as 'besieged' by offers, including from families of higher status. However, Powell (1992) argues that only a relatively small segment of society was involved. The poor, uneducated or feckless had little hope of making such a match, while the wealthy and educated usually had no need to emigrate. In Muslim families, on the other hand, obligations of kinship meant that UK-based families usually turned first to members of their own family. Failing to do so could have serious implications for family relations.

From the perspective of those on the sub-continent, emigration might be one of the attractions of a UK marriage. However, this is not as straightforward as it first appears. Migration theorists (for example, Smith 2004) have pointed out the complexity of reasons for emigration, including family-related emigration. Powell (1992; see also Ballard 1990: 12) argues that a man who emigrated was not necessarily the primary beneficiary of his move. He exchanged his social networks and personal autonomy outside the home for relatively low social status and poorly-paid unskilled work in the UK. His earnings provided remittances for those left behind and domestic appliances that made his wife's life easier. He might well have preferred not to join his wife's family, regarding it as a comparative loss of status. His own gains except in terms of local prestige were less evident. If emigration benefited his entire family as much as or more than himself, then, even discounting, as ECOs did, aspirations for personal fulfilment through marriage, it is difficult to see how an applicant's primary motive for the marriage was emigration. It would be more accurate to say that his reason was to please or assist his family.

ECOs tended to conflate the two motives. Yet, if the applicant's family is brought into consideration, it becomes even harder to identify a single predominant motive. The previous account describes some of the complexities of the arranged marriage, the multiplicity of interests and the web of spoken and unspoken arrangements that preceded its fulfilment. Emigration may have been a factor, but it was usually only one amongst many (see, for example, Ballard 2005: 12; see also the case studies in Powell 1992, 1993a and 1993b). In most cases, it would be hard to identify a single dominant reason. Certainly, it would be difficult for the applicant to do so with any accuracy in the interview conditions already described. However, failure would, in all likelihood, mean a refusal on primary purpose grounds.

The issue becomes clearer if the question of emigration is separated from that of the arranged marriage. As discussed in the introduction, it is not possible to establish a binary divide between 'good' and 'bad' reasons for marriage. In non-arranged marriages, people may marry for 'love', but they do not fall in love by chance. They seek out and are attracted to those whose qualities and circumstances complement and enhance their own. Those who are interested in emigrating are likely to be attracted to a spouse who can offer that possibility. Yet the 'emigration' motive, like other instrumental reasons for marriage, cannot easily be disentangled from the other reasons, although, in Western discourse, such instrumental motives are often not acknowledged. The problem for those in arranged marriages was that, just as in other forms of marriage, emigration may have been a partial motive but they were unable to persuade ECOs that other motives existed. These often concerned questions of family obligation, caste, social or professional status rather than the individual characteristics that would normally be cited in non-arranged marriages. Such reasons did not mean that the individual was not personally committed to the marriage but, in the absence of the conventional discourse of romance, such reasons were either poorly understood or discounted and the emigration motive was assumed to predominate. As described so often in this book, the ECO viewed the applicant only as an aspiring immigrant.

ECOs could thus over-apply the primary purpose rule. The rule did not state that any immigration motive was fatal. The applicant should fail only if the immigration motive was the primary one. ECOs assumed that a marriage that was not a 'love match', and where the husband wished to join the wife, was predominantly motivated by immigration.

The Invisible Sponsor

If the applicant was perceived only as an aspiring immigrant, the sponsor was largely invisible. In part, this was a function of the process in which, at least until appeal, the sponsor was more bystander than participant. However, this lack of presence was arguably more than an accidental by-product of administrative systems. It represented part of a persistent tendency to marginalise British residents and citizens who, by conducting their personal lives in unapproved ways, displayed insufficient commitment to their country of residence. This was particularly true of women.

The first sponsors were usually male migrants seeking family reunification once free movement in and out of the UK was removed under the Commonwealth Immigrants Act 1962. Ballard (1990: 3) describes them as torn between their desire to be with their families and the gains in these families' material welfare that their emigration permitted. He also describes immigrants' reluctance to reconstitute their families in the alien environment of the UK, a reluctance that was particularly marked amongst Bangladeshis (Ballard 1994: 16). It was only over a period, and at varying paces within the different communities, that men accepted that what had started as temporary was now permanent and called for their families, only to be refused or delayed by many additional years. However, the resulting hardship was regarded as self-inflicted (see, for example, the Hawley Report description of the initial emigration as 'barbaric').

There was also little official contemplation of the hardship caused to female sponsors, often the children of those early migrants, who had been born or raised in the UK. The belief was that, consistent with tradition, such women should join their husbands on the sub-continent. Critics argued that this was often not a practical option as, unused to the climate and environment, women frequently endured continuous ill health and depression-related complaints (see Powell 1992). In the same work, Powell provides a vivid first-person account of a British woman who attempted to live with her much-loved husband and his family in Pakistan. She eventually attempted suicide, became seriously ill and returned to the UK, but her husband's application to join her was nonetheless refused.

The suffering of women who remained in the UK without their husbands was equally invisible. Menski (1999) drew attention to increases in reports of psychological and physical ailments. Outside the small sphere of critics, arranged marriages were discussed principally in terms of immigration, coercion and oppression (see, for example, the comments made by parliamentarians in Chapter 3) that precluded acknowledging the loneliness and sexual frustration of the 'immigration widows', emotions that Asian women had difficulty expressing.[59] Instead, they were criticised for their 'manipulation and selective regard of a tradition' (Powell 1993a: 224; see also at 179-80, 362).

In all instances, the suffering imposed on victims of a restrictive policy was minimised or they themselves were held responsible for their distress. The state declined to enable British residents or citizens to exercise family life in their own country. A recurrent theme in this book has been a hierarchy of deserving marriages, this being determined by both the character of the marriage and the extent to which the sponsor was regarded as belonging to the UK. The parties here suffered the double disadvantage of having entered marriages that were not easily comprehended by the majority population and of being partial outsiders. This was perhaps foreseeable, if regrettable, for those who had themselves previously emigrated to the UK as children or adults. It is more remarkable in the case of those who had been born in the UK. As indicated in Chapters 3 and 4, non-white residents were often seen predominantly as immigrants even in the second generation. They had to prove that they deserved to enter the privileged category of 'belonger'. Non-white males were the least desirable of immigrants and the women who married them had, by that act, further marginalised themselves.

In choosing correctly, sponsors had to reject ambiguity and ambivalence. Hawley, defending restrictive policies, described South Asian men as 'men of two worlds' and the family as having 'a foot in both camps'. There were similar criticisms of female sponsors. An explanatory statement quoted in Powell (1993a: 224) makes the point (punctuation added):

> While I accepted that she had been born in the United Kingdom, had spent most of her life there, might well have preferred to remain there, I considered that by entering into an arranged marriage she had shown herself to be constrained by the traditional dictates of her society.

A woman was either 'traditional', entering an arranged marriage and residing on the sub-continent, or 'modern', which presumably meant marrying a UK spouse. Like the judiciary, ECOs did not view UK residents who attempted to have 'the best of both worlds' favourably. It also highlights another recurring theme – the reduction of complex individual lives to simplistic categories that permitted their marginalisation or exclusion.

---

59 The 'Immigration Widows' were a campaigning group established in 1985; 'She has never seen her father', *The Observer*, 6 January 1985.

The Two-Dimensional Applicant

In more sympathetic accounts, individuals break the bounds of these reductionist categories. Powell (1993a and 1993b), for example, carried out a detailed investigation into refused applicants. His interviews and observations emphasise the humanity of these applicants. He describes their shyness, embarrassment, inexperience and romanticism. Some of his accounts are very affecting, for example, the deaf/mute sponsor whose husband was refused on primary purpose grounds (Powell 1993a: 83-98). The ECO was dismissive, believing the sponsor to be an unattractive prospect and that the applicant would surely have preferred to marry her younger sister. Investigation by Powell revealed that the applicant had been orphaned as a child and had come to live with the sponsor's family. Both had been lonely children and had developed an exceptionally close bond using their personal sign language. The sponsor had moved to the UK because of the better facilities there, but the couple were deeply attached and distraught at the separation.

If Powell's observations bring to mind the empathy and attention to human detail of good literature, the responses of ECOs suggest the stereotyping and over-simplification of poor fiction. It will be apparent from the prior commentary that ECOs regarded applicants as governed by rigid rules of conduct, guided by a single overwhelming motive and ready to compromise their entire future family life for the sake of emigration. This portrayal lacked the complexity and nuance that are characteristically human. From this reductionism, other judgements followed. Applicants were not regarded as capable of the tangled relationships, uncertainty and ambiguity that are the stuff of human life. An ECO, for instance, could not believe that a poor husband would have tolerated an affair between his wife and a wealthy friend who paid money that enabled the family to eat (Powell 1993b: 63-86).

The reference to fiction is deliberately made in a context in which the function of decision-makers was to establish fact. However, decision-makers also interpret facts, constructing a narrative as they do so. An administrative decision-maker does not have the luxury of pondering, as a novelist may, the endless permutations of human motivation. A degree of reductionism and over-simplification is inevitable. The baseline assumptions upon which this is based are thus critical. Unfortunately, in this instance, these were almost entirely unfavourable.

The reductionist assumptions described here were sometimes applied to an entire population. Hawley describes Sylhet in the following terms:

> The villagers themselves are quiet, decent farming folk living in a countryside which is, at least in November, very beautiful. They produce considerable quantities of rice and seem to live relatively well. Their houses are clean and those of the 'Londonis' ... are usually larger and more pretentious than others.

Hawley, it must be recalled, was an advocate of strong restrictions on the admission of dependants. Elsewhere in his report, he talks of an emigration 'industry' and widespread forgery. These 'decent' folk in their 'clean' homes were unwelcome outsiders so far as the UK was concerned. There is even a suggestion that this was for their own good; 'pretentious' is preferred to 'comfortable' or even 'luxurious' in describing the improved homes of 'Londonis'. The tone recalls the paternalistic ideology of colonialism and its representation of the simple native. The reduction, described in this chapter, of complex human beings to cardboard cut-out figures desperate to emigrate did not arise as a purely spontaneous response to administrative pressures. While it conveniently rationalised the refusal of unwanted immigrants, it was also directly connected to the assumptions that had made the immigration of these individuals such an apparently potent threat.

Conclusion

This chapter has shown that the entry clearance service consistently interpreted and responded to applicants' claims in ways that minimised the chances of an application succeeding and, in doing so, reduced applicants to diminished human beings whose every action was dominated by the desire to emigrate. The essential premise was that immigration from the sub-continent must be minimised and that this outweighed the damage caused by the refusal of entitled applicants or the manner of their refusal.[60] The imperative was particularly strong in the case of family members due to fear of an endless chain of migration, and entry clearance staff saw themselves as gatekeepers protecting the integrity of the host society.[61] As such, the premise that non-white immigration must be minimised arguably amounted to an informal internal policy. It was applied with remarkable consistency and thoroughness throughout the period. The reported approach taken towards queues, documentary evidence, interviews, medical examinations, factual findings and local customs all converged towards the same end: that the applicant should be refused if possible. The Commission for Racial Equality (1985: 50-51; see also Lal and Wilson 1986: 21) saw material indicating that 'in some cases, at least, the prospect of securing refusals of entry clearances would generate greater enthusiasm than that of issuing them'. File notes suggested that even where entry clearances were issued, staff did so with reluctance. The Hawley Report argued that applying the correct standard of proof would reduce job satisfaction amongst

60 See 'Natural selection', *Times Education Supplement*, 7 June 1985.

61 The law's delays', *The Guardian*, 21 March 1975; 'The bridal path to Britain', *Daily Mail*, 28 February 1978; 'Immigration: the first hurdle', *Daily Telegraph*, 2 December 1985.

entry clearance staff, who would be nothing more than 'rubber stamps'. Refusal was arguably the unofficial primary function of the service.[62]

In minimising the number of successful applications, decision-makers acted as if certain other propositions were true: that many people wished to emigrate to the UK and that this determined even life-long decisions such as marriage. Applicants would readily forge documents and lie, to a highly elaborate degree, in order to achieve that aim. South Asian people were governed by a set of inflexible social customs, deviation from which was usually the outcome of a wish to emigrate, and arranged marriages took little account of the perceived welfare of the parties who had no feelings of obligation or affection towards each other. The emphasis on fraud and deceit suggests that, as well as the official requirements of the rules, ECOs perceived themselves as moral gatekeepers. Non-white applicants faced the unofficial hurdle of demonstrating that, despite appearances to the contrary, they merited even provisional admission.

Sponsors were less commonly the focus of specific attention, but their claim to live in their home with their choice of spouse carried little weight against the imperative of controlling non-white immigration. Even those born or raised in the UK remained partial outsiders and, in marrying and seeking entry for unwanted immigrants, threw into question even their partial status as 'belongers'. The binary divide between the 'modern' UK and the 'traditional' sub-continent did not permit ambivalence. British-based women, in particular, were afforded little credibility if they claimed to have determined the place of residence when entering an arranged marriage. Female agency was thus confined only to those acting in accordance with Western norms, the stereotype of Asian female oppression and passivity being presumed to be unbreakable.

It was stated above that ECOs acted 'as if' the propositions above were true because if the dominant priority was the minimisation of South Asian immigration, their adoption could have been self-serving. It is likely that not all ECOs believed them to be universally true. The official quoted earlier on the reliability of discrepancies suggests that some individuals had a degree of perspective. The over-simplification of applicants' lives may have been partially the outcome of administrative pressure. The extreme nature of some refusals raises the possibility that decision-makers were seeking to justify what they knew to be unjustifiable, the over-use of discrepancies being the most egregious example of specious reasoning used in aid of a pre-determined end. Yet, had the application of these propositions been utterly incongruent with how most decision-makers viewed the world, it is difficult to see how they could have been applied so consistently. The interviewing style described earlier suggests a degree of personal commitment, and the Commission for Racial Equality (1985: 50) reported that file notes sometimes betrayed a 'contemptuous or dismissive attitude to applicants'. The toleration of intimate physical examinations of women from a culture known for its emphasis on

62 This was widely alleged at the time; see, for example, 'The middle class Asian vote', *New Statesman*, 30 November 1984.

female personal modesty suggests contempt for that culture projected onto its most vulnerable members. There were frequent allegations of racism throughout the immigration service as a whole.[63] Doubtless, some applicants on the sub-continent lacked honesty or were motivated purely by the wish to emigrate, and false documents and incorrect information were put forward, although not necessarily for reasons of deceit. To conclude, as ECOs seemed to, that every application therefore required minute dissection suggests a dismal view of that entire society.

Chapters 3 and 4 demonstrated how political debate and judicial decision-making were underpinned by anxiety about non-white immigration. However, the decisions made by the legislature and judges were subject to some public scrutiny and to countervailing values connected with their self-perception as legislators or as judges. Legislators and judges generally avoided confronting this lack of congruity because, for the most part, the inconsistent acts were performed by the entry clearance service out of sight. Thus, politicians could present the primary purpose rule as an anti-abuse measure or judges could avoid challenging unbalanced decision-making by deferring to the fact-finder. They could still explain themselves in terms that would be considered morally acceptable both by outsiders and, presumably, by the institution's own members. The entry clearance service does not appear to have been subject to these countervailing pressures. The need to minimise non-white immigration was accepted by all three bodies discussed in this chapter, but the entry clearance service did so with the least equivocation. It adopted modes of thinking and procedures that suggest a strong and unregulated culture. Despite having the fewest formal powers, the service was, in practice, the least accountable. This was, it may be argued, not coincidental. Its relative autonomy enabled the unpleasant work of exclusion to be carried on, without compromising the apparent integrity of the other bodies more than necessary. There was a largely invisible but vital connection between the daily prevarication and scepticism displayed by the most junior members of the entry clearance service, the political preoccupations of legislators and government described in Chapter 3 and the pattern of judicial decision-making identified in Chapter 4. This connection consisted of the beliefs and assumptions identified in this chapter and which were also, with modifications, identified in the preceding chapters. These beliefs established that marriages involving non-white male spouses, in particular those from the sub-continent, were at the bottom of the hierarchy of deserving marriages. The extent to which they continued to hold that position after 1997 is considered in Part II of this book.

63 'Migrant "rackets" protest', *The Guardian*, 9 January 1969; 'Fool or liar', *Caribbean Times*, 7 December 1984.

PART II
1997-2010

Chapter 6
A Conditional Welcome: Immigration Policy 1997-2010

Introduction

The previous three chapters were concerned with the regulation of marriage migration from 1962 until 1997. They argued that, while attitudes evolved throughout the period and there was some variation between institutions, there was also a consistent strand of shared assumptions that resulted in common patterns of decision-making and an unofficial hierarchy of acceptable marriages. This part of the book considers the same institutions during the period between 1997 and May 2010. This chapter sets the scene for that study. It considers government policy and the position of minority ethnic groups between 1997 and 2010 and argues that, in comparison with the earlier period, there was more fluidity and ambivalence. The following chapters argue that this is reflected in the treatment of marriage migration by the same institutions as those considered in Chapters 3, 4 and 5.

The first section of this chapter briefly reviews immigration policy generally since 1997. The following section considers the position of the communities of South Asian origin who were the main focus of measures discussed in earlier chapters.

The Right Kind of Immigrant: Immigration Policy since 1997

In the period between 1962 and 1997, despite some occasional deviations, the general direction of policy was consistent. The control of marriage migration took place against a background in which the minimisation of non-white immigration was the most important priority. Marriage was an essential link in the apparently never-ending chain of migration from poor non-white countries, particularly the Indian sub-continent. Attempts to break this chain absorbed large quantities of political and administrative effort. This part of the book picks up the discussion at the election of the 'New Labour' government in 1997, the moment at which new priorities and assumptions became ascendant. The resulting policy changes were not necessarily immediately evident, but they were precipitated by the change in government and they rendered the former terms of analysis outmoded. These changes may be summarised as new approaches towards the desirability of immigration, towards how it should be controlled and towards minorities including ethnic minorities. They reflected the changed global and national context in which the government operated, including the presence of well-established non-white communities, the increased movement of workers, refugees and asylum seekers from all parts of the world, an enlarged European Union, an ageing domestic population and labour shortages (see the discussion in Lewis and Neal 2005: 424-6).

New Attitudes Towards Immigration

In a major departure from preceding policy, the Labour government elected in 1997 was willing to contemplate the benefits of immigration. Flynn (2005: 464) notes that Immigration and Nationality Department policy, as summarised in its Annual Reports, switched in 1997 from being to restrict immigration 'severely' to its 'regulation'. Support within government for new immigration was expressed cautiously at first but was articulated more strongly over time through various policy channels, including a Department of Trade White Paper, the 1999 pre-budget report, a major government review in 2000 and a wave of government-funded research (Somerville 2007: 29-30). In 2000, politicians began to give open voice to this change of emphasis.[1] There followed large increases in economic migration, which began to reverse only towards the end of the period. The number of work permit-related approvals more than tripled between 1997 and 2006, when more than 140,000 approvals were given, after which they fell, a decline which continued under the Points-Based System (PBS) introduced in 2008 (Home Office 2009: Table 1.2, Salt 2009: 109 and Home Office 2010b: Table 1f). These rises in numbers partially reflected liberalisation of the criteria for issue in 2000, following which there was a particularly large increase. However, approvals had already begun to rise from at least 1995, predating the new government.

As significant in policy terms, if not in absolute numbers, was the creation of new avenues for skilled migration where the applicant did not need a job offer: the Innovators Scheme and the Highly Skilled Migrant Programme (HSMP), introduced in 2000 and 2001. These were the first points-based systems in the UK, prefiguring the later conversion of much of the immigration system to the PBS. The HSMP was, by far, the more successful, peaking in 2007 with 28,090 approvals, after which numbers began to decline, partly due to more restrictive criteria. Numbers admitted under Tier 1 of the PBS, which replaced the HSMP, were lower at 18,600 in 2009 (Home Office 2010b: Table 1f). Nonetheless, the government remained committed to encouraging highly skilled migration to the UK. While some changes were made to the Tier 1 criteria after implementation of the PBS, these did not fundamentally undermine the scheme.

---

1 First indications were in a speech by the former Home Office minister Barbara Roche, 'UK migration in a global economy', to a conference organised by the Institute of Public Policy Research in September 2000. See also Sales 2005: 445-6 and Somerville 2007: 29-30.

Another area in which migration was actively encouraged was education, beginning with the Prime Minister's initiative in 1999 to welcome overseas students (see Clayton 2008: 351) and continuing with rule changes that enabled graduating students to remain in the UK for work. Between 280,000 and 370,000 students were admitted in each year between 2000 and 2007 (Home Office 2005a, 18 and 2010a: 60). This policy began to reverse towards the end of the period as recession took hold and claims of abuse mounted (Home Office 2010a: 60, Clayton 2010: 371).

Unskilled workers, by contrast, were less welcome. They were not included in any programmes leading to settlement but did, for a while, have their own short-term entry route, the Sectors Based Scheme. Introduced in 2003 on a quota basis and designed to relieve shortages in particular sectors, problems arose when large numbers of applicants were refused entry clearance even though the employer had paid for the permit (Clayton 2010: 370). The accession of the A8 countries to the EU in 2004 meant a new pool of labour to do unskilled work and the scheme was restricted to A2 nationals from Bulgaria amd Romania, while its PBS equivalent, Tier 3, was not implemented. Even had it been, it would have permitted only 'small tightly managed quota based schemes for specific shortage areas and for fixed periods only, with guarantees that migrants will leave at the end of their stay' (Home Office 2005b: 16).

Thus, the liberal approach to immigration that became evident after 1997 extended only to skilled or educated migrants, a point made repeatedly in government documentation (for example, Home Office 2005b: 15). It was a programme of 'managed migration', emphatically not one of free migration, and the government was determined to control the terms of entry. In that context, marriage migration, one of the few routes open to those who did not possess the necessary skills or qualifications, had the potential to derail the government's control over the quality of entrants. This potential was increased by the rights granted by European law, in particular, under Article 8 ECHR, brought into domestic law under the Human Rights Act 1998, and free movement rights in EU law which applied to EEA nationals and their spouses, including third country nationals.

New Approaches to Controlling Immigration

Given that public opinion is generally either antagonistic or, at best, lukewarm towards immigration (see Somerville 2007: Chapter 12), a government who promotes a policy of increased immigration has a delicate line to tread. An expansive policy is one response to the pressure of unauthorised migration, but if it is to succeed, the government must show itself able to resist the pressures of such irregular migration.

Unauthorised migratory pressures were very strong during the period. In 1997, the year Labour came to power, there were 32,500 asylum applications, a figure that peaked in 2002 at 84,130 (Somerville 2007: 65). Numbers of irregular migrants, who enter without leave and do not claim asylum are, for obvious reasons, difficult to estimate, but it is likely that their numbers also increased. Woodbridge (2005: 1) estimated that, in 2001, there were 430,000 unauthorised migrants present in the UK. A study published in 2009 and using a similar methodology estimated that, at the end of 2007, there were around 618,000 (Gordon et al. 2009: 6). Asylum seekers and irregular migrants (and increasingly migrants in general) were often associated with welfare abuse, criminality, terrorism and other security issues, and became a potent political issue (Chakrabarti 2005, Sales 2005: 448 and Bosworth and Guild 2008). Although the government managed to reduce the numbers of claimants after 2002, a major issue was its inability to remove failed asylum seekers (Home Affairs Select Committee 2006a: 141), adding to the numbers of unauthorised migrants and the impression of official impotence. The immigration service also faced huge administrative problems. Badly managed computer systems and rising numbers of applicants caused long delays, administrative chaos and loss of control, at least over asylum applications (McKee 2005: 254 and Home Affairs Select Committee 2006c: 190). In the meantime, the accession of new EU member states resulted in the entry of many new relatively poor migrants. In comparison with other member states, the government placed relatively few constraints on the labour market participation of A8 nationals who acceded in 2004, after which there was relatively little that could be done to regulate their presence. A2 nationals from Romania and Bulgaria also started to enter in 2007 despite heavy labour market restrictions. Meanwhile, the numbers of third-country nationals entering as the family members of EEA nationals increased.[2] None of these could be easily controlled.

The government responded to these pressures by acting where it could act through a ceaseless programme of organisational and regulatory reform, adopting managerialist terminology such as 'managed migration', 'five year plan' or 'new asylum model' and ambitious rubrics such as 'Fairer, Faster, Firmer' or 'Making Migration Work for Britain'. Nine Acts of Parliament relating to immigration were passed between 1997 and 2010. The Immigration Rules were amended constantly, with more than 25 changes in just the three years between the start of 2004 and the end of 2006 and, under the PBS, migrants and sponsors became subject to detailed and frequently changing guidance. In 2007, the Immigration and Nationality Department became a 'Next Steps' agency, the Border and Immigration Agency, which, in 2009, became the UK Border Agency, an executive agency with responsibility not only for border control but also for visa services and customs detection work. Other aspects of the immigration system, such as welfare support for asylum seekers and asylum decision-making, were also substantially re-organised.

2 See Chapter 1. Figures before 2007 are not available, but there were claims of substantial increases (Home Affairs Select Committee 2006c: 125).

Policy changes included the acceleration of asylum decision-making, the withdrawal of welfare support, prohibitions on unauthorised or short-term migrants moving into other categories and limits on appeal rights. Asylum policy was criticised as failing to differentiate adequately between 'genuine' claimants and the non-entitled (Hassan 2000 and Chakrabarti 2005) and asylum decision-making was described in terms reminiscent of the critique of the entry clearance service made in the previous chapter (see, for example, Amnesty International UK 2004 and Independent Asylum Commission 2008). Concerns about terrorism resulted in security-related measures such as indefinite detention of some foreign nationals, followed, when these were found unlawful, by control orders, a form of house arrest that was also heavily contested.[3] Security concerns also rationalised the adoption of new technologies to control movement, including e-borders, biometric visas and identity cards, combined with increased internal surveillance. These anti-asylum and security-oriented measures became associated with a general authoritarian trend in government that also extended to nationals (Bosworth 2008).

The implementation of the PBS in 2008 re-organised the decision-making framework for almost all migrants other than those entering under family or humanitarian routes. The PBS framework was characterised by increased executive power to micromanage criteria for entry through guidance (although, by the time of writing, this had been found to be unlawful)[4] and the removal of appeal rights. The flexibility usually associated with points systems for immigration was largely absent. However, what was present were increased obligations on employers, educational institutions and others to monitor compliance (see Wray 2009b for a discussion). Pre-entry language tests for economic migrants and tests of knowledge of life and language in the UK were introduced as a precondition first of naturalisation and then of settlement. Towards the end of its period in office, the government legislated to make long-term residence and naturalisation more dependent on compliance with state-generated criteria for demonstrating sufficient integration, introducing a new normative element of active participation, although this was not implemented before Labour's election defeat in 2010 (for a discussion of aspects of this, see McGhee 2009 and Wray 2009a).

However, despite the frenetic pace of change, critics doubted whether control over immigration was a realisable objective given multiple and conflicting internal and external pressures (Flynn 2005). Nonetheless, the aim remained the '*comprehensive management of all forms of migration*, whether forced or voluntary' and the 'reassertion of the capacity for state control' (Flynn 2005: 464-5, emphasis in the original). The increasingly harsh rhetoric and regulatory overload reflected the growing predominance of this goal so that it sometimes trumped even economic benefit, as with the prohibition on asylum seekers working, even when these individuals had skills in short supply. It was also the background to the

3 *A v SSHD* [2004] UKHL 56; *A v UK* (2009) EHRR 29; *E v SSHD* [2009] UKHL 28; *SSHD v AP* [2010] UKSC 24.

4 *SSHD v Pankina* [2010] EWCA Civ 719.

draconian controls on in-country marriage by many groups of migrants, found in ss. 19-25 Asylum and Immigration (Treatment of Claimants, etc.) Act 2004 and which are discussed in the following chapters.

This highly controlling approach brought the government into conflict with the courts who, on several occasions, used legal standards introduced by the government itself to frustrate its more authoritarian ambitions. These conflicts remind us that the government was, itself, torn between liberalising and repressive tendencies, with the latter becoming more evident over time.

New Approaches to Race and Immigration

While the authoritarian aspects of the New Labour government, particularly in the latter half of its period in office, must not be overlooked, nor should its more progressive aspects. All post-war governments have feared racial conflict and race equality legislation had, for many years, been seen as the counterpart of strong immigration control. To that extent, the post-1997 government did not represent a major change of direction when it promoted race equality internally while maintaining immigration controls externally.

However, some new approaches to race and immigration were evident after 1997. Non-white ethnic minorities were, by then, well-established communities in their second or even third generation and formed an important electoral constituency, particularly for a Labour government. Compared to the more diverse immigration that entered throughout this period, they were well integrated and politically powerful. Addressing their concerns was both a principled and strategic position and took the government some distance beyond the old formula of counterposing immigration controls and race equality when it strove, at least to a limited degree, to import considerations of equality and fairness into immigration control.

Paragraph 2 of the Immigration Rules already required immigration officials to carry out their duties without regard to race, colour or religion. The Race Relations (Amendment) Act 2000, passed after the Macpherson Inquiry into the unresolved murder of Stephen Lawrence, was potentially more far-reaching in its effects. The Act, now replaced – although to much the same effect – by the Equality Act 2010, extended the Race Relations Act 1976 by prohibiting discrimination on racial grounds by public authorities, including the Home Office, immigration authorities and the entry clearance service (s. 19(B) of the amended 1976 Act). Public bodies carrying out immigration functions also had to have due regard to the need to eliminate unlawful racial discrimination and promote good relations between persons of different racial groups (s. 71(1)). There were however some significant limitations. Judicial and legislative acts were excluded by s. 19(C) and acts relating to 'immigration functions' that discriminated on the basis of nationality or ethnic or national origin and were carried out personally or authorised by the Secretary of State were still permitted (s. 19D).

Formal protection against race discrimination was also strengthened by application to immigration control of the main ECHR rights through the Human Rights Act 1998. Article 14 ECHR prohibited discrimination in the enjoyment of Convention rights on the grounds, *inter alia*, of race, colour, religion, national or social origin and association with a national minority.

Given that accusations of race discrimination had plagued immigration control and, in particular, the entry clearance service during the preceding decades, the prohibition of race discrimination in the immigration service was a welcome step, but there was relatively little use of the legal remedies provided. In part, this was because of the government's use of ministerial authorisations to permit differential treatment.[5] Establishing the evidential basis of a claim for race discrimination was difficult.[6] In most cases, practical and resource obstacles made proving discrimination almost impossible. The complexity of the rules, the discretion involved in their application and global inequalities made it difficult, in the absence of overt statements of discrimination, to establish that a particular individual was treated less favourably because of their race or ethnicity. Even if this was established, it might not assist the applicant if he or she would have failed for other reasons.[7]

If new laws provided some limited protection against discrimination, arguably more important in practice was the new context of immigration policy. Given the positive yet instrumental attitude towards immigration that characterised government policy in this period, the stereotyped decision-making described in earlier chapters was inefficient, even obsolete. That did not mean that race disappeared as an issue in immigration; rather, it became a less prominent determinant (Flynn 2005: 484, Sales 2005: 458 and Yuval-Davis, Anthias and Kofman 2005: 521). Skilled Indian nationals, for instance, came to dominate the various work entry schemes (Salt 2009: 97). Nonetheless, given global inequalities, many divisions were still perpetuated along ethnic, national or racial lines. Wealthy non-white entrepreneurs and highly skilled migrants may have encountered less resistance, but it is doubtful whether poor migrants, who were often but not exclusively non-white, received better treatment. Throughout the period under discussion and despite efforts discussed later in this book to improve the efficiency and quality of decision-making, both the Entry Clearance Monitor and her successor, the Chief Inspector of the UK Border Agency, were critical of the standard of service at some African and South Asian posts (for example, Lindsley 2005: para. 87 and 2006, and Vine 2009a: 3). Some groups experienced difficulties securing entry for visits, for example, Muslims from poor countries in the period after 9/11 (Citizens Advice Bureau 2003 and Lindsley

5 Although, following the High Court decision in *R (on the application of Tamil Information Centre) v SSHD* [2002] EWHC 2155 (Admin), these had to be made by express permission of the minister based on evidence of breaches by the group in question.

6 For example, *SK (India)* [2006] UKAIT 00067.

7 *CS (Race discrimination: Proper approach) Jamaica* [2006] UKAIT 00004.

2006). Meanwhile, national origin appeared to remain the unspoken standard for judging the moral seriousness of transgression. A national newspaper published a first-hand, humorous account of an American national planning to enter into a sham marriage to remain in the UK, who was deflected only by falling in love at the last moment with another woman (fortunately also British).[8] The skin colour of the protagonists is unknown, but it is difficult to envisage an Asian or African national being uncritically permitted to say that 'I'd viewed marriage as an administrative hurdle to be cleared on my way to a visa'. Immigrants from particular regions might be less unwelcome than before, but they had to establish themselves as the right kind of immigrant. As discussed in the next section, such an expectation was arguably also extended to some British communities of immigrant descent.

An Uneasy Belonging: Residents of South Asian Origin and International Arranged Marriages

Previous chapters argued that some immigrants and even their British-born descendants were perceived as permanent outsiders. Those entering international arranged marriages were often seen as choosing to exclude themselves. This tendency arguably persisted in the post-1997 era, particularly if 'belonging' is understood as more than the ownership of formal legal rights (Yuval-Davis, Anthias and Kofman 2005: 526-9). Nonetheless, emphasis moved from questions of allegiance to less obviously chauvinistic issues of personal liberty, equality and social integration. However, the terms of debate often contained an implied or overt rebuke directed, if not at the parties themselves, then at their families and communities.

The period discussed in the previous chapters ended in June 1997 with the abolition of the primary purpose rule. A Labour government had been elected on a wave of popularity after 18 years of Conservative rule and, as already observed, non-white communities were now a major electoral force. Removal of primary purpose had symbolic as well as practical importance, enabling a clear distinction to be made with the outlook of the preceding regime. Unusually for a liberalising immigration measure, removal of the rule had been promised in the 1997 election manifesto.[9]

However, new concerns were emerging, in particular awareness that long-established communities of migrant origin were living apparently 'parallel lives' while also suffering social disadvantage, leading to widespread debate about 'social cohesion'. Over time and compounded by the fear of terrorism and Islamic extremism, this turned into a widely shared assumption that multiculturalism had 'failed' (for a discussion of this issue, see, for example, McGoldrick 2005: 36-45,

8 *The Guardian*, *Weekend*, 25 May 2002, p. 57.

9 http://www.labour-party.org.uk/manifestos/1997/1997-labour-manifesto.shtml (accessed 11 June 2011).

Ballard 2007, Modood 2007: 10-14 and Finney and Simpson 2009). This became an important discourse in politics with input from government, policy-makers and academics and, while it was often connected to anxiety about security, it pre-dated the events of 9/11. The celebration of diversity by early commentators in this field – for example, Parekh (2000) – was, in some measure, swept away by the breadth and force of the anti-multicultural reaction across Europe, leading, in some instances, to what has been called 'cultural fundamentalism' (Yuval-Davis, Anthias and Kofman 2005: 516).

In the UK, concern crystallised around the 2001 disturbances in towns in the north of England and was later strengthened by the realisation that the perpetrators of the 7/7 bombs in 2005 were educated and (with one exception) born in the UK. Cantle (2001), commissioned to investigate the causes of the 2001 disturbances, saw multifaceted segregation as critical in causing mutual incomprehension and suspicion. He advocated creating a greater sense of citizenship 'based on (a few) common principles which are shared and observed by all sections of the community' (2001: 10). The logic of that conclusion was not entirely evident given that the factors found to characterise better functioning communities related more to practical issues such as police practice, educational policy, good governance, media coverage and poverty than abstract values of citizenship (Cantle 2001: 15-17) and there was much criticism of his conclusions (for example, Yuval-Davis, Anthias and Kofman 2005: 524-5, Ballard 2007: 277-86 and Finney and Simpson 2009: 93-4; see also the discussion in McGhee 2009: 46-7). Nonetheless, his recommendation of a discussion of the 'rights – and in particular – the responsibilities of citizenship' (2001: 46) informed much of the subsequent official discourse.

This was followed by government-led efforts to develop a new paradigm for citizenship (see McGhee 2009: 44-6) as well as a plethora of literature and initiatives aiming at establishing 'social cohesion', understood as involving respect for difference, a 'common vision' and a sense of belonging, equality of opportunity and good inter-communal relationships (see Temple and Moran 2005: 5). Debate in the UK was perhaps expressed more cautiously than elsewhere in Europe and official commentary was careful to avoid an assimilationist discourse.[10] Nonetheless, a search began for common values that did not depend on racial or ethnic exclusion (see, for example, Spencer 1995, Goodhart 2004a and 2004b, and Parekh 2005). This proved difficult given the mutability of national identity and the absence of agreed notions of 'Britishness' (Parekh 1995, Spencer 1995, Ballard 2002 and Ascherson 2005), the problems of separating race, ethnicity and culture (Ballard 2002), the coded meanings that may be present (Gedalof 2007) and the rise of 'cultural fundamentalism' (Kofman et al. 2000: 37). The problem

10 See, for example, Tony Blair's 'Our Nation's Future' speech on multiculturalism and integration, 8 December 2006: http: webarchive.nationalarchives.gov.uk/+/http://www.number10.gov.uk/Page10563 (accessed 11 June 2011). According to Modood (2007: 47-8), assimilation involves adaptation by the incomer so as to comply with norms set by the host society.

was frequently framed as a 'crisis of multiculturalism' (Lewis and Neal 2005: 431), without offering an acceptably nuanced and concrete alternative framework, underscoring for minorities their fragile sense of belonging (see Kymlicka and Banting 2006: 300-304 or Zetter, Griffiths and Sigona 2006 for a more extended discussion).

The debate took place against a complex background. Publicly racist discourse was generally unacceptable, arguably representing a substantive shift in attitudes (Goodhart 2005), although how far it disappeared from private speech is debatable. New waves of immigration made older immigrant communities relatively familiar and there was some incorporation of these longer standing groups (Ballard 2002 and Yuval-Davis, Anthias and Kofman 2005: 521). However, this is not the entire story, as demonstrated by continuing problems throughout this period of poverty, unemployment and under-achievement among these communities (Samad and Eade 2002: Chapter 2 and Peach 2006). Moreover, there remained the danger of underplaying issues of race that were barely submerged beneath the surface. In acknowledging the insecurities of the ethnic British (and particularly the English), it was sometimes difficult to avoid legitimising, even unintentionally, those who saw race as the paramount determinant of difference (see, for example, Hildyard's 2003 critique of Rowthorn 2003). Racism arguably focused on new targets, including ethnic groups less easily distinguishable by skin colour, such as Roma and Travellers, religious minorities, particularly Muslims, and asylum seekers (European Commission Against Racism and Intolerance 2010: 41-51). Some commentators (for example, Ballard 2002) argued that concern at cultural difference replaced visible racial difference as a means of asserting dominance.

Many pointed out how easily the debate could become one-sided, with the predominant emphasis on the failure of minority groups to 'integrate' themselves, which failed to challenge the processes by which white communities also 'segregated' themselves (Parekh 2005, Yuval-Davis, Anthias and Kofman 2005: 527 and Gedalof 2007: 81). The literature demonstrated how practical hurdles such as discrimination, marginalisation and poverty were the major obstacles to social participation (Temple and Moran 2005: Chapter 1). The greatest challenge to traditional concepts of citizenship and identity was arguably the supra-national force of globalisation, which 'brings into question the very meaning of citizenship' (Shaw 2002: 511). Yet, in popular discourse and increasingly in policy across Europe, responsibility for cohesion and for protecting national identity was placed most heavily upon the weakest and most marginalised, whose personal lives were seen as critical in creating the threat to nationhood (Gedalof 2007: 91-2). This focus risked encouraging complacency within the majority population. It is less challenging to frame the debate as one between alien immigrant values and coherent majority values than to acknowledge the divisions within British society (as Wolton 2006 argues in relation to the political elite).

Nonetheless, while 'cultural difference' might rationalise or disguise unequal power relations and while responsibility for maintaining or creating a shared national identity was unfairly distributed within society, the complexities and problems of ethnic identity were real. This critique of multiculturalism, already alluded to in Chapter 1, was frequently made (Goulbourne 1991, Okin 1999, Bano 2000, Samad and Eade 2002: 2, Parekh 2005 and Yuval-Davis, Anthias and Kofman 2005: 523-9, Sales 2005: 523-4). Communities are not 'bounded, homogeneous groupings, each fixedly attached to its ethnicity and traditions' (Parekh 2000: 26). Individuals may define themselves, or be defined, in a multiplicity of ways in addition or in contrast to their ethnicity. Many young British people of South Asian descent choose to identify themselves predominantly as Muslims rather than through their ancestral nationality. Gender, family position, age, sexuality, professional status or other characteristics may be more significant than (or intersect with) ethnic origin. Moreover, the burden of maintaining ethnic identity may be unfairly distributed within groups. Women frequently perform a critical role in the embodiment, preservation and reproduction of culture (Barot, Bradley and Fenton 1999: 15). The difficulties raised by this critique are exemplified by the ongoing debate on forced marriage, which is discussed later in this chapter.

The debate on cohesion, integration, cultural difference and citizenship 'seeped' (McGhee 2009: 47), perhaps inevitably, into immigration policy. Immigration is perceived (whether correctly or not) to be one area in which national sovereignty may still effectively assert itself (Dauvergne 2004), leading to electoral expectations of control that may be difficult to fulfil. In public debate, there were attempts to express reservations about immigration in non-racialised terms (for example, Goodhart 2004a, 2004b and 2006). These arguments usually centred on the compatibility of needs-based state welfare with mass immigration (Lloyd 2002, Gibney 2004: Chapter 2 and Goodhart 2004a), arguments that long preceded this period and were contested (see, for example, Freeman 1986 and Kymlicka and Banting 2006). Arguments about the need to retain social cohesiveness if welfare regimes were to retain public support could and were extended to a 'diverse', i.e. multicultural, society (Goodhart 2004a, Klausen 2000 and Kymlicka and Banting 2006).

The necessity of migrant integration, implied by the debate on social cohesion, became a major element in the official discourse on immigration. Integration has been described as a 'chaotic concept' (Finney and Simpson 2009: 10). Good definitions avoid simplistic, one-dimensional approaches and appreciate its multifaceted and concrete nature, and the need for adjustments by the host country as well as by the migrant (see, for example, the *Common Basic Principles of an Immigrant Integration Policy* adopted by the EU Council).[11] Nonetheless, discourse in immigration policy was largely predicated on the assumption that the relationship between the migrant and the host society had become 'unbalanced', creating not only current problems but threats to future security (McGhee 2009: 42-3). Certainly, government discourse frequently implied that the UK had already

---

11 Conclusions of the European Council adopted at the 2618th Council Meeting, 19 November 2004; press release available at: http://www.consilium.europa.eu/uedocs/cms_data/docs/pressdata/en/jha/82745.pdf (accessed 11 June 2011).

taken all reasonable steps to welcome migrants and that it was now for migrants to show their willingness to adapt (see, for example, the introduction by Jacqui Smith, Home Secretary, in UK Border Agency 2008b: 5).

Several immigration policies, such as pre-entry English language requirements and tests for settlement and naturalisation, were justified by reference to immigrant integration, linking these to wider issues of social cohesion. The White Paper, *Secure Borders, Safe Haven* (Home Office 2002: 10), which introduced the new focus on naturalisation as part of the citizenship project, referred to the 'fractured and divided communities' revealed by the 2001 riots and the need to build 'a sense of common citizenship'. A more challenging tone, referring to migrant criminality and abuse of British hospitality and tolerance, was adopted in *The Path to Citizenship* (UK Border Agency 2008b), which followed Lord Goldsmith's *Citizenship Review* (2008) and proposed drastic changes to the route to settlement and naturalisation. *The Path to Citizenship* was arguably more concerned with ensuring that some migrants did not become a long-term presence than with securing their integration (McGhee 2009: 52 and Wray 2009a; see also the discussion in Etzioni 2007: 353-6). Integration as a tool of immigration policy, while it may be based around civic rather than racial forms of belonging, is nonetheless linked to discourses of exclusion (McGhee 2009: 62-3) and remains liable to manipulation.

Integration and immigration intersected critically in international arranged marriages predominantly involving, in the UK, families of South Asian origin. These marriages were widely seen as reproducing social, cultural and linguistic practices from the country of origin, creating barriers to cohesion and integration not only for the marriage migrants themselves but for their UK-resident spouses and the children of the marriage (see, for example, Joppke 2004: 251). The international arranged marriage, for many years the direct target of immigration policy, thus re-emerged as the focus of scrutiny.

Earlier chapters described how the demise of such marriages had long been predicted. This did not happen. Dale (2008: 2-3) points out that, according to the 2001 Census, people from South Asian backgrounds were the least likely of minority ethnic groups to marry someone from a different group. Many South Asian communities had high marriage rates and women, in particular, tended to marry young. Arranged marriages remained common in South Asian groups, although more common in Pakistani and Bangladeshi communities than amongst Indians (although they were, of course, not confined to those groups).

Many of these marriages were international. Samad and Eade (2002: 48-52) quote statistics as high as 75 per cent in some areas and Cryer stated in 2006 that 80 per cent of marriages by her Muslim constituents were transcontinental.[12] Shaw (2001: 327) found a rate of about 70 per cent amongst the Pakistanis she studied in Oxford, with high rates also of consanguineous marriage. Dale (2008) suggests that the figures are somewhat lower, around half of all marriages in Pakistani

12 HC Hansard, 2 November 2006, col. 165WH.

and Bangladeshi communities and about one-quarter of all marriages in Indian communities being to an overseas spouse. Education seemed to be a material factor, but age of the respondent was not particularly important, suggesting that her findings do not reflect a declining practice.

The reasons for these marriages will be familiar from Chapter 5: a shortage of suitable UK candidates due to gender ratios and endogamous marriage patterns, the pre-emption of rebellion and disaffection in children, the fulfilment of familial expectations and the maintenance of family links (Shaw 2001, Ballard 2005 and Beck-Gernsheim 2007). Young people might have their own reasons for choosing an overseas spouse, which were often connected to the complexities of modern gender politics. Young men might hope for a more compliant overseas wife, while a British woman could hope to gain more leverage in a marriage where in-laws were at a safe distance and she had the advantage of familiarity and language. Both might hope to gain a higher status spouse than would otherwise be available (Beck-Gernsheim 2007: 281-3). However, expectations might not always be realised and, as Samad and Eade (2002: 90) found in the communities they investigated, young people as a whole were less enthusiastic about international marriages than their elders. Beck-Gernsheim (2007: 283) argued that some parents too were beginning to doubt the wisdom of such matches.

Nonetheless, the persistence of the international South Asian marriage was reflected in the immigration statistics after the abolition of primary purpose. A total of 8,810 spouses and fiancé(e)s were admitted from the Indian sub-continent in 1996, the last full year before abolition. Applications and admissions rose immediately after abolition (Jackson and Bennett 1998: 3-4). In 1998, there were 15, 725 admissions, followed by a drop to 12,040 in 1999, after which they climbed again to 17,100 in 2005. The number of spouses entering from South Asia declined after 2005, falling to 10,005 in 2009, although the decline anticipated by only one year a worldwide decline in the number of spouses entering the UK (Home Office 2003: 18 and Home Office 2010a: 62). However, as discussed in Chapter 1, the sub-continent remained the most important source of spouse migration to the UK.

Perceptions of such marriages remained largely negative. Gedalof (2007) reflects upon how family life is viewed as a means of preserving or undermining nationhood. While, as she argues, the arranged marriage, particularly the international arranged marriage, was perceived principally as a threat in this respect, there was occasional recognition of the ability of Asian families to participate in this type of nation-building (Lewis 2005: 550-51; see also the occasional favourable newspaper report).[13] However, this was the exception. As Lewis (2005: 546-7) expresses it:

> While they retain their visibility through their distinctiveness, such communities can never symbolically stand for the nation/national, they can only provide the

13 'Asians fly the flag for traditional family life', *The Guardian*, 18 December 2000; 'Arranged marriages can work, say couples', *Daily Telegraph*, 8 February 2002.

> terrain upon which the 'host' nation can make its claim to tolerance, civilisation and indeed modernity itself.

'Modernity' may most conveniently be asserted through distinctions drawn with more 'backward' communities, removing the Asian family still further from the moral centre of gravity. Gender equality became a primary means of differentiating liberated European and oppressive non-European models of family life (Roggeband and Verloo 2007 and Phillips and Saharso 2008). Over time, the South Asian family was increasingly associated with oppressive or archaic (and often gender-based) practices including forced marriages and 'honour' killings, as well as other disapproved practices such as marriages involving the severely disabled. Reporting of these emphasised the particular cultural context and reinforced suspicion that Asian (and particularly Muslim) family life was inherently oppressive (Samad and Eade 2002: 99-103 and Razack 2004: 156).

Forced marriages are frequently elided with arranged marriages and, in reality, the boundaries are not precise. An-Na'im (2000: 3-4), Phillips and Dustin (2004) and Ballard (2006) all make the point in varying ways that it represents a culturally specific example of the universal phenomenon of family violence. The cultural context includes the conception of the family as a corporate enterprise in which the individual's interests are subordinate to those of the family (see Ballard 2008). While many parents accept more autonomy in their children, some arranged marriages involve psychological pressure stopping short of coercion. Such methods are not perceived as force by many, particularly older, members of the South Asian communities (Samad and Eade 2002: 72 and Gangoli, Razak and McCarry 2006: 9-10). Forced marriages involving duress are thus the end of a continuum rather than a category of their own (Siddiqui 2005: 290-94).

These blurred outlines meant that the forced marriage could taint all arranged marriages, particularly those involving overseas partners and even more so those involving young and poorly educated spouses. Yuval-Davis, Anthias and Kofman (2005: 518) observe that much marriage migration was to those places considered to represent the failure of multiculturalism. Discussion of 'forced marriage' frequently elided immigration, cultural and other concerns. Ann Cryer MP (Home Affairs Select Committee 2006c: 231-6), for example, cited forged documents, forced marriages, sham marriages, chain migration, first-cousin marriages, lack of integration and educational under-achievement as problems associated with immigration control. When government ministers called for 'discussion within those communities that continue the practice of arranged marriages as to whether more of these could be undertaken within the settled community here' (Home Office 2002: 18) or said that the proposed measures aimed at 'ensuring that foreign nationals who come to marry and live in Britain do so happily and successfully' (Border and Immigration Agency 2007a: 3), their words would be read against a background belief that international arranged marriages were often tainted by coercion or were, at best, ill-advised. The forced marriage functioned tacitly as a paradigm rather than an exception and the assumption that the family life of minorities was the arena for insularity and abuse became part of the 'common sense' background against which policy, including immigration policy, was formulated.

Chapter 3 showed how the reluctant bride had previously been frequently deployed to justify restrictive immigration control by those otherwise unsympathetic to Asian communities. Such claims were criticised for their opportunism (Menski 1999: 92). That critique was still made (see, for example, the opening paragraphs of Ballard 2006) and, indeed, the forced marriage was used to claim immigration restrictions were in the interests of young Asian women (Migration Watch 2004: para. 6) or were a feminist cause (Cryer 2003). However, for most of the period and despite the negative connotations just discussed, the government largely desisted from involving the immigration service (although the minimum age of sponsorship and entry was raised to 18), mainly promoting exit from the marriage as the solution (Phillips and Dustin 2004: 534). However, exit alone was increasingly seen as insufficient because the price paid by the victim was so high, and there was a move to a regulatory emphasis through the Forced Marriage (Civil Protection) Act 2007 and, subsequently, the immigration system through increasing still further the minimum age for entry and sponsorship (see Chapter 7). Regulation has benefits but it does not, on its own, obviate the problems caused by exit. In particular, it may be ineffective and fail to promote self-regulation or critical self-examination by communities, regarded by many critics as the only viable long-term solution (Phillips and Dustin 2004: 545-6 and Ballard 2006). The motives for forced marriages are complex (see Samad and Eade 2002: 56-60) and are, at least in part, 'profoundly affected by a community's sense of peril' (Razack 2004: 151-5), including from immigration control. The effective involvement of the immigration service in such a process is thus doubtful, which may be one reason why there was, until quite late in the period discussed in this chapter, caution about its involvement.[14] Nonetheless, as the next chapter will demonstrate, the forced marriage was eventually cited as the rationale for more restrictive immigration policies. However, the effect of these policies went well beyond protecting victims and it may be argued that they fulfilled more instrumental purposes connected to the dilemma that marriage migration created for a government keen to maintain its liberal credentials while minimising the disruption caused by marriage migration to its policy of admitting only the well-educated and easily integrated.

Conclusion

This chapter has attempted to capture some of the fluidity of the period between 1997 and 2010. Attitudes were multifaceted and complex. The Labour government acknowledged that the UK was now a diverse society that included well-established minorities, including but not confined to non-white minorities.

14 See, for example, Angela Eagle, HC Hansard, 17 December 2001, col. 86W.

This was reflected in the adoption of new legal norms relating to discrimination and human rights. The government was also faced with global migratory pressures, which had started prior to its election (see Somerville 2007: Chapter 7) and arose from domestic labour shortages and an explosion in cheap travel and international communications. For some time, labour migration was encouraged and the ability of the country to absorb new migrants was not challenged.

However, there were countervailing pressures, particularly the entry of large numbers of asylum seekers and irregular migrants, followed by the entry of workers from relatively poor new EU member states. This took place against a background in which the UK remained reliant on migrant labour so that restrictive entry policies were undesirable even if they were possible. As a consequence, migration was permitted but migrants were subject to ever-increasing levels of control and surveillance. Meanwhile, fears about security nurtured already extant anxiety about the presence of some non-white, often Muslim, minorities who were perceived to live 'parallel lives' segregated from mainstream society. All these factors combined to make immigration policy more complex than in previous decades. The contradictory pressures that the government faced were not only of its own making but reflected global forces over which it had little control, but against which it perceived itself obliged to act. The result was increased migration accompanied by increased management and control, even though these latter moves were often fruitless, leading to an increasingly authoritarian cycle of regulation.

Marriage migration played an uneasy role in this complicated scenario. The government wished to distinguish itself from its predecessors' hostility to the family lives of some ethnic groups. However, marriage migration had the potential to undermine the government's ability to permit migration only on its own terms. At the same time, the private lives of those minorities who most engaged in marriage migration were coming under increased scrutiny for different reasons. Such marriages were in an ambiguous position because, despite the rejection of open discrimination of the type experienced in earlier eras, they opened the door to an unwelcome pool of potentially unskilled and poorly educated migrants coming to join communities whose family lives were already the subject of scrutiny. Those who continued to choose such spouses were seen, at best, as victims of oppression and, at worst, as reproducing imported archaic family practices.

Chapter 7
No Surrender: Legislative Control of Marriage Migration 1997-2010

Introduction

This chapter considers changes in the legislative control of marriage migration between 1997 and 2010. The role of the legislature between 1962 and 1997 was considered in Chapter 3. As discussed here, the post-1997 government implemented major changes in immigration policy. However, legislative debates may be less revealing than in the past. The sheer bulk of immigration legislation, its density and the broad sweep of delegated powers rendered effective scrutiny more difficult, and the combination of large majorities and 'executive dominance', while hardly a new phenomenon (Seaward and Silk 2003), made Parliament arguably more compliant than in the past. It was not that backbench pressure never counted. The repeated calls for action on forced marriage, for example, provided the context for action taken in 2008 to raise the minimum age of entry and sponsorship. Select Committees also engaged vigorously with particular issues. However, it is arguable that legislative debates and backbench dissent affected the outcome of regulation more rarely than in the period discussed in Chapter 3. As Chapter 8 will explore, the judiciary were perhaps more significant than Parliament in checking the executive during this period.

The legislature was also subject to international forces that had previously been less significant and that it could not control. Free movement rights under EU law had been effective in the UK since its accession to the EEC in 1973. However, their impact in permitting the entry of the third-country national spouses (and other family members) of EEA nationals increased after *Surinder Singh* in 1992, while EU enlargement increased the pool of eligible spouses subject to the more generous EU law provisions.[1] From a government perspective, the European Court of Justice, in interpreting these rights, was more concerned with ensuring that free movement rights were not compromised than with recognising states' concerns about residence rights for third-country nationals.[2] However, the domestic controversy associated with the EU meant that references to the question

1 Case C-370/90, *R v IAT and Surinder Singh ex p. SSHD* [1992] ECR I-4265. See also Chapters 1 and 6.

2 For example, Case C-127/08, *Metock and others v Ministry for Justice, Equality and Law Reform* [2009] QB 318.

were sometimes oblique, as the discussion on ss.19-25 Asylum and Immigration (Treatment of Claimants, etc.) Act 2004 in this chapter demonstrates.

Also significant was the greater impact of the ECHR following the implementation of the Human Rights Act 1998. This question is dealt with mainly in the next chapter, which discusses the judiciary, but, under s. 29 of the Act, the minister responsible for a Parliamentary Bill had either to certify that it was compatible with Convention rights or that the government wished to proceed notwithstanding this fact. The primary legislation discussed in this chapter was declared to be compatible even though some aspects were later found to be non-compliant. It will be seen below that parliamentary debate on human rights aspects of legislation was sometimes superficial, but human rights nonetheless formed part of the discourse and provided a platform for opposition, both within Parliament and outside it.

Control over marriage migration during this period reflected the priorities highlighted in the previous chapter. There was some commitment towards fairness and equality, but an intensive drive to promote state control and legal compliance. In certain respects, the government put in place controls that were more authoritarian than those enacted under 'primary purpose'. In its early years, the post-1997 Labour government, while it also expressed anxiety at the continuation of the international arranged marriage, it avoided enacting measures that would be interpreted as specifically targeting affected communities. This later changed and there was a growing emphasis on issues of integration and belonging that threw the focus back on to the South Asian arranged marriage.

Focus on Compliance, Caution over Culture

In its 1997 manifesto, the Labour Party promised that the current immigration system would be reformed 'to remove the arbitrary and unfair results that can follow from the existing "primary purpose" rule'.[3] Actual abolition came soon after Labour came to power and enabled the government to establish radical credentials on a matter of high symbolic importance which, however, would make only a relatively small difference to immigration totals.[4] It was thus able to position itself as the natural party of the ethnic minority population at relatively little political risk. Jack Straw described the law as 'arbitrary, unfair and ineffective'.[5] He also made reference to the disadvantaged position of British citizens compared with other EU nationals resident in Britain. This must have been an important consideration for a government aiming to be 'new and distinctive' and a 'leader in Europe'.[6] Despite

3 Labour Party manifesto 1997, http://www.labour-party.org.uk/manifestos/1997/1997-labour-manifesto.shtml (accessed 11 June 2011).

4 HC Hansard, Written Answers for 5 June 1997, col. 219.

5 Ibid.

6 Labour Party manifesto 1997, http://www.labour-party.org.uk/manifestos/1997/1997-labour-manifesto.shtml (accessed 11 June 2011).

concerns about the effect of abolition and support for other highly restrictive measures, there was little support even amongst anti-immigration groups for the return of primary purpose.[7] The rule was illogical, ineffectual and outmoded.

Marriage migration soon received renewed attention. In July 1998, the government published a White Paper, *Fairer, Faster, Firmer: A Modern Approach to Immigration and Asylum* (Home Office 1998). It was mostly concerned with asylum but also referred to 'ample evidence to show that large numbers of bogus marriages are being contracted in the UK every year'. Asked in Parliament to estimate the number of 'sham marriages', the Secretary of State for Immigration stated that precise figures were not readily available but that '(t)he perception of some agencies most involved in tackling this abuse is that it is considerable and widespread'.[8] Proposals were limited to giving marriage registrars the power to require documentary evidence of age, identity and marital status (para. 11.5). The Immigration and Asylum Bill that followed went further, also requiring parties to give 15 days' notice of their marriage and attend to give notice personally (now ss. 160-163 Immigration and Asylum Act 1999). More significantly, registrars were also required under s. 24 to report suspected sham marriages to the Home Office, turning a previously informal practice into a statutory obligation.

The Bill was referred to a Special Standing Committee in the Commons. The Immigration Advisory Service, numerous campaigning groups and backbenchers expressed concern at the marriage clauses. The government denied that these represented what Diane Abbott described as the 'domestication of the primary purpose rule', emphasising that they were concerned only with detecting sham marriages, which were stated to have increased substantially.[9] Firm evidence was not provided of their extent, although marriage registrars were already reporting around 500 marriages per year as suspicious.[10] Later in the debate, the government referred to 236 arrests for offences connected with sham marriages, 118 cautions and charges and 42 removals.[11]

Marriages in the Churches of England and Wales were exempted from the proposal. A sham marriage was defined as one entered into 'for the purpose of avoiding the effect of one or more provisions of United Kingdom immigration law or the immigration rules', a definition (now found in s. 24) that was said by commentators to recall the primary purpose rule (Stevens 2001: 420). Critics suggested inserting the word 'sole' before 'purpose' to reflect the wording used by the Council of Ministers in its resolution on marriages of convenience and which would have excluded marriages where immigration was only one of the

---

7 See, for example, Migration Watch UK's briefing, available at: http://www.migrationwatch.org/briefingPaper/document/124 (accessed 11 June 2011).

8 HC Hansard, 16 February 1999, col. 657.

9 Immigration and Asylum Bill, Special Standing Committee, 17 March 1999.

10 Geoff Hoon, HC Standing Committee, part 7.

11 Lord Williams of Mostyn, HL, 12 July 1999, col. 143.

purposes.[12] The government rejected such an amendment, arguing that it would make the registrar's task too difficult and defended the entire set of proposals on the grounds that 'we have the balance right'.[13]

This new clause demonstrated that, from this early stage, the government, under pressure from backbenchers, regarded control of this route of immigration as important, even at the cost of potential discrimination.[14] The limited scope of the measures meant that the values and beliefs implied by them were not widely debated. However, as in earlier eras, relatively anodyne measures paved the way for more restrictive laws later.

During this period, the government also sought to rectify some long-standing injustices. The White Paper had proposed a concession for immigrant spouses suffering domestic violence during their probationary period. This was introduced in 1998 and later incorporated into the Immigration Rules.[15] Implementation, however, proved problematic as, pending a decision, the spouse remained subject to the requirement of 'no recourse to public funds' and victims could not be offered places in refuges. This was the subject of extensive campaigning by Southall Black Sisters but, while it provided limited emergency funds, the government was reluctant to suspend the public funds requirement (Home Affairs Select Committee 2006c: 333-4), prioritising the 'integrity' of immigration control. There were also problems over the evidential requirements of the rule, which led to court challenges that will be discussed in the next chapter.

Debate during the passage of the 1999 Act had avoided adverse commentary on the arranged marriage. However, a more assertive tone was evident in the White Paper *Secure Borders, Safe Haven* (Home Office 2002). The Executive Summary (2002: 18) drew attention to the 'tradition of families originating from the sub-continent wanting to bring spouses from arranged marriages to live with them in the UK'. The succeeding paragraph referred to the 'large profits and financial rewards' obtainable through arranging bogus marriages and went on to say: 'We also believe there is a discussion to be had within those communities that continue the practice of arranged marriages as to whether more of these could be undertaken within the settled community here.' It later said: 'As time goes on, we expect the number of arranged marriages between UK children and those living abroad to

12 Council Resolution 97/C 382/01 of 4 December 1997 (Official Journal C 382 of 16.12.1997); *Immigration Advisory Service Memorandum to the Standing Committee*, 17 March 1999.

13 Lord Bassam of Brighton, HL Hansard, 18 October 1999, col. 808. The debates may be found at HC Hansard, 22 February 1999, cols 37-131; House of Common Special Standing Committee, 17 March 1999; HL Hansard, 29 June 1999, cols 176-257; HL Hansard, 12 July 1999, cols 11-164; and HL Hansard, 18 October 1999, cols 747-926.

14 For examples of backbench pressure, see, for example, HL Hansard, 21 March 2001, cols 1422-3; HC Hansard, 7 March 2002, col. 516W.

15 HC Hansard, 24 June 1998, cols 1026-30; HC395, paras 289A-C.

decline. Instead, parents will seek to choose a suitable partner from among their own communities in this country.'

These passages were regarded by many as an unacceptable intrusion into the personal lives of minorities, although they were defended by the combative Home Secretary, David Blunkett.[16] Gedalof (2007: 84-8) examines how the White Paper, as a whole, presented certain 'alien' forms of family life as problematic. These passages, succeeding paragraphs reiterating the government's refusal to acknowledge polygamous marriages and its disapproval of forced marriage, and the juxtaposition of bogus and arranged marriages were all consistent with that. However, new proposals were confined to increasing the probationary period to two years and an end to switching from other categories, which, while significant in their effects, could be presented as anti-abuse measures. They were also 'balanced' by a proposal to allow immediate indefinite leave to those who had lived together abroad for a lengthy period and relaxation of the requirements for the admission of unmarried partners. There may be detected here the emerging contours of an acceptable 'modern' applicant.

Referring to in-country switching, the White Paper (Home Office 2002: 101) said that it was 'unfair to those applicants who follow the correct procedures by applying for entry clearance overseas and pay for the appropriate visa', an argument that was later criticised by the House of Lords in *Chikwamba* (see Chapter 8). It acknowledged the hardships that result from forcing someone to go abroad for entry clearance to re-enter as a spouse, but argued that hardship was less likely in the case of short-term entrants.

The focus on switching indicated the government's determination to control the terms of entry. The White Paper (2002: 101) stated that, in 1999, 76 per cent of those granted leave to remain on the basis of marriage had been admitted for another purpose and that 50 per cent of those switching did so within six months of entry, although there was no evidence cited for the claim that many of these had lied about their intentions on entry or had entered into sham marriages. These cases were later described as 'literally tens of thousands' of applicants, a claim that seems exaggerated.[17] The published immigration statistics for 2001 (Mallourides and Turner 2002: 3-4) show that there were 23,080 probationary grants of leave to remain as a spouse, i.e. leave granted to those already in-country. If even 50 per cent of these were short-term entrants who switched to marriage, they did not represent tens of thousands in any one year and remained a tiny proportion of the more than 8 million non-EEA visitors who entered the UK annually.

The ban on switching was implemented in 2002.[18] While the stated purpose was to prevent visitors and short-term entrants entering into sham marriages, the measures had a severe impact on asylum seekers and undocumented migrants who

---

16 'Blunkett in clash over marriages', *The Guardian*, 8 February 2002; see also HC Hansard, 24 April 2002, cols 376-7 and 411.

17 Lord Rooker, HL Hansard, 7 February 2002, col. 752.

18 HC 164.

might have spent many years in the UK. The genuine nature of these relationships was not in issue, but they were sacrificed to the government's need to establish its authority in the immigration and, particularly, the asylum arena. These applicants were now required to apply from unstable regions to regularise their position. If the application failed, the government was saved the trouble of removing them. The practical difficulties of this went beyond administrative inconvenience. There were reports of victimisation by the authorities after returning and some applicants allegedly went into hiding. Making a visa application might be time-consuming, expensive or effectively impossible. New passports or exit visas might not be obtainable. Visa facilities in some countries were not available because of security concerns. In those cases, applicants had to travel to neighbouring countries, where they might be refused admission or where they had to keep themselves in hotel accommodation while the application was processed. The delays involved could render documentation such as wage slips or bank statements out of date. At the end of that process, the applicant might be interviewed for only a few minutes and the visa granted or refused.

Where visas could not be obtained, it was usually suggested that the UK resident spouse should accompany the spouse to the country of origin including those that might be unsafe or have poor human rights records such as the Democratic Republic of Congo, Iraq, Iran or Afghanistan.[19] One woman was told that if she wished to live with her husband, she should return with him to Iran and 'submit to the way of life there'. This would have required conversion to Islam, the adoption of Iranian nationality and the loss of British diplomatic protection. Another woman was told that she should accompany her husband to Iraq which, even leaving aside issues of security, meant abandoning her son by a previous marriage. One woman whose poor health needed constant monitoring and medication, who was her disabled parents' main carer and who had shared residence of her eight-year-old daughter was told that it would be 'reasonable' for her to accompany her husband to the Democratic Republic of Congo (Home Affairs Select Committee 2006c: 285-8, 346-54). These letters were signed by government ministers, suggesting government approval (Home Affairs Select Committee 2006c: 351). The court challenges to this rule will be discussed in Chapter 8.

Secure Borders, Safe Haven had shown that the government was determined to force the pace on integration through tests on knowledge of language and life in the UK as a prerequisite for naturalisation, including for spouses.[20] However, despite the combative tone, it refrained from taking major action against the international arranged marriage at that moment, even if backbenchers sometimes tried to draw them on such a commitment.[21] During 2003, the probationary period

19 See, for example, 'Forced to choose ... my husband or my life', *Glamour Magazine*, February 2006, pp. 106-11; HC Hansard, 10 October 2005, col. 129.

20 Sections1 and 2 Immigration, Asylum and Nationality Act 2002.

21 See, for example, HC Hansard, 8 February 2002, col. 1241W; HC Hansard, 9 May 2002, col. 334W.

before settlement was extended to two years and the minimum age of sponsorship was increased to 18, the minimum age for entry also increasing in 2004. There were three adjournment debates on immigration and forced marriage in 2003, during which it was proposed that the minimum age for both entry and for sponsorship should be raised to 21 and that only British citizens should be permitted to act as sponsors.[22] It was assumed that forced marriage was primarily an immigration issue and forced and sham marriages were conflated.[23] Beverley Hughes, the Immigration Minister, showed some sympathy towards these proposals.[24] Raising the minimum age to 21 later received express government support in the 2005 White Paper *Controlling Our Borders* (Home Office 2005b: 22) and was also proposed by the Kirkhope Commission on Immigration (2004: 25-6) established by the Conservative Party. However, the proposal was not implemented until 2008. It seems there was still some hesitancy at this stage despite the increasing interest of parliamentarians in the subject.

Banning the 'Bogus Marriage'

The assertion of state authority over immigration continued with new measures against sham marriages in the Asylum and Immigration (Treatment of Claimants, etc.) Bill. These were not signalled in advance. On the contrary, in February 2004, a written parliamentary question asked whether it was policy to permit people to marry without verification of their immigration status. The reply of the Immigration Minister Beverley Hughes cited the existing law and efforts against suspicious marriages without referring to plans for reform.[25] However, a 'Bogus Marriage Task Force' was later established, while press reports presented 'sham marriages' as an increasing problem associated with organised crime.[26] One figure given wide publicity and quoted in Parliament (although not by ministers) was that one in five register office marriages in London (or 8,000 marriages per year) was

22 HC Hansard, 19 March 2003, cols 276-9WH; HC Hansard, 17 July 2003, cols 517-19; HC Hansard, 17 September 2003, cols 264-71WH.

23 'I believe the solution to all these problems would be for Asian parents to arrange marriages for their sons and daughters within the settled community': Ann Cryer, HC Hansard, 17 July 2003, col. 519; see also HC Hansard, 17 September 2003, col. 266WH.

24 HC Hansard, 17 September 2003, col. 269WH; HC 164.

25 HC Hansard, 23 February 2004, col. 239W.

26 '"I'm asked to conduct many sham weddings" says registrar', *Daily Telegraph*, 21 March 2004; 'Sham marriages soar as illegal immigrants try to beat curbs', *Daily Telegraph*, 15 June 2004; 'Beating the sham wedding cheats', BBC News, 22 September 2004 (http: //news.bbc.co.uk/go/pr/fr/-/2/hi/uk_news/3679482.stm, accessed 11 June 2011), '"Fake marriages network" smashed', BBC News, 22 September 2004 (http: //news.bbc.co.uk/go/pr/fr/-/2/hi/uk_news/3678784.stm, accessed 11 June 2011), '25 jailed for bogus marriage scam', *The Scotsman*, 18 January 2005; '£1m bogus marriage woman jailed', *The Scotsman*, 26 April 2005.

bogus.[27] This claim originated in a questionnaire to marriage registrars sent by the Superintendent Registrar at Brent Register Office, Mark Rimmer. Such evidence might be persuasive and some of the observations reported by registrars suggested possible sham marriages.[28] However, the results were not published and were described as 'impressionistic'.[29] Findings seem to have been based, at least in part, upon subjective judgements made about marriages involving a foreign national and the presence of factors such as a large age gap, religious differences or language difficulties (Home Affairs Select Committee 2006c: 225). In the absence of full publication, it is impossible to evaluate the claims made in the research. Another claim, made in a leaked email, was that 15,000 bogus marriages took place annually, an assertion, however, from which politicians distanced themselves. The Home Secretary David Blunkett commented that: 'We don't think there are anything like the 15,000 that have been outlined, but we think there are more than the 3,000 we have been aware of.'[30] One backbencher claimed that marriage registrars reported 9,000 marriages annually as suspicious under s. 24 Immigration and Asylum Act 1999, although the figures quoted below suggest this was an exaggeration.[31]

The outcome of this focus on the 'bogus' marriage was the announcement by the Home Secretary of plans to restrict the ability of foreign nationals to marry within the UK. Details were sparse but focused on requiring couples to give notice of marriage at a specially designated register office. Plans to allow registrars to refuse to carry out ceremonies were also under consideration. The plans were to be refined following consultation to 'achieve the necessary balance between facilitating the vast majority of genuine applicants and protecting the system from abuse'.[32]

The period for consultation was brief, less than one month, and the resulting clauses went much further than those put forward for consultation (Immigration Advisory Service 2004). They were presented as amendments in the House of Lords, which avoided substantive second-reading debate in the Commons. Restrictions were to be placed on all marriages in which one or both parties were subject to immigration control, except for Church of England weddings.[33] In addition to the requirement to give notice at a designated register office, the marriage could not proceed unless the non-British party had entry clearance for

27 Stephen Pound MP, HC Hansard, 13 May 2004, col. 563; Baroness Carnegy of Lour, HL Hansard, 15 June 2004, col. 693; 'Sham marriages soar as illegal immigrants try to beat curbs', *Daily Telegraph*, 11 June 2004.

28 For example, money changing hands, the bride kissing the wrong man, the wedding rings not fitting or the groom being unable to remember the name of the bride (see HC Hansard, 13 May 2004, col. 563).

29 Telephone interview with Mark Rimmer, 23 August 2005.

30 *The Guardian*, 23 April 2004.

31 HC Hansard, 13 May 2004, col. 564.

32 HL Hansard, 22 April 2004, WS16.

33 This was not stated explicitly in the Act but was a consequence of its application as set out in s. 19.

the purpose of marrying, written permission from the Secretary of State to marry or belonged to a class specified by the Secretary of State.

In arguing for the clauses, the government avoided the tendentious statistics quoted above in favour of more circumspect claims. It relied principally on the increased number of suspicious marriages reported by registrars under s. 24 Immigration and Asylum Act 1999. In 2001, 756 such reports were received, rising by 2003 to 2,712, while 2,251 were received in the first half of 2004 alone.[34] It is not clear if the rise represented increased numbers or increased reporting, or whether suspicion was justified, although marriage registrars believed there was under-reporting.[35] Until April 2004, most reports were not investigated and there was no central record of consequent prosecutions or convictions.[36] However, in 2003, at least 110 people were arrested and 37 people charged.[37] The enforcement effort that began in April 2004 resulted in 200 suspected sham marriages being visited, more than 100 individuals being arrested and 28 marriages that did not proceed.[38] However, these claims were problematic. If existing measures, applied more intensively, were detecting sham marriages, the rationale for new measures was questionable. The number of reports made in the second half of 2004 was just over half those made in the first half, even though the 2004 Act was not in force.[39]

In the Lords, Lord Rooker for the government argued for the necessity of preventing sham marriages taking place, the unfairness of queue-jumping and the importance of detecting sham documentation.[40] His reasoning lacked coherence. He claimed that it was difficult to remove parties after the marriage had taken place.[41] However, the recent no-switching rule already required short-term and illegal entrants to leave the UK and submit to entry clearance to gain leave as a spouse. Those whose documents were not bogus would still be unable to marry if they lacked the necessary immigration status. The Joint Committee on Human Rights (2004: 21-4) foresaw a possible breach of Articles 12 and 14 ECHR due to the failure to discriminate between genuine and bogus marriages and the exemption for the Church of England. There was insufficient time in the Lords debate to respond to their concerns, which caused embarrassment to Lord Rooker in speaking for the government.[42] He conceded that it was unclear whether the rise

34 HC Hansard, 15 June 2004, col. 681.

35 Lord Rooker, HL Hansard, 15 June 2004, col. 686.

36 See the speech by Humfrey Malins MP, HC Hansard, 5 July 2005, cols 261-2; Des Browne, Minister of State (Citizenship, Immigration and Counter-Terrorism), Written Answer, HC Hansard, 8 March 2005, col. 1704W.

37 HC Hansard, 13 May 2004, col. 567.

38 HC Hansard, 15 June 2004, col. 682.

39 HL Hansard, 23rd February 2005, col. 1268; HC Hansard, 18 April 2006, col. 363W.

40 Lord Rooker, HL Hansard, 15 June 2004, cols 680-5.

41 Ibid., col. 682.

42 HL Hansard, 6 July 2004, cols 723-4.

in the number of reports of suspicious marriages was due to increased incidence or increased reporting.[43] He later admitted that he expected a legal challenge to the measures and that he had been placed 'in a position where I cannot do my job of representing the Government to this House'.[44]

If the arguments were unconvincing, it was perhaps because the true motivation was not, at first, given prominence. The measures applied to British and EEA nationals exercising free movement rights who wished to marry those subject to immigration control, but the impact upon the latter was initially only briefly mentioned.[45] However, when other justifications were challenged, the defence switched to the prevention of abuse by EEA nationals.[46] In such marriages, while the government might refuse residence to their third-country spouses on the grounds that the marriage was one of convenience, this was defined narrowly, powers of investigation and enforcement were limited and the burden of proof remained on the government (Macdonald and Webber 2005: 286-9). The ability to remain in the UK after marriage to an EEA national was described as a 'loophole'.[47] It was stated that 61 per cent of reports by registrars of suspicious marriages involved a non-British EEA national and there were some well-publicised arrests.[48] A possible further aim, unmentioned but hinted at in later court proceedings, may have been to minimise the possibility of Article 8 claims succeeding by inhibiting the establishment of family life.[49]

In the Commons third reading, the Minister for Immigration, Des Browne, adopted a more robust tone than Lord Rooker. He defended the proposals as more efficient than investigation of individual cases while human rights concerns were dealt with only cursorily.[50] He alluded to the enhanced rights of those married to a non-British EEA national and it was, by now, apparent that curbing these was a major motive. The clauses became ss. 19-25 Asylum and Immigration (Treatment of Claimants, etc.) Act 2004. Unless they had indefinite leave to remain or entered from abroad on a fiancé or marriage visit visa, all those subject to immigration control had to obtain a certificate of approval to marry in the UK, costing £135 (later raised to £295), creating an estimated income of £1.6 million

43 HL Hansard, 15 June 2004, col. 686.

44 HL Hansard, 15 July 2004, col. 724.

45 For example, HL Hansard, 15 June 2004, col. 684.

46 See HL Hansard, 28 June 2004, col. 70; HL Hansard, 6 July 2004, cols 716-17 and 725-6; HC Hansard, 12 July 2004, col. 1219.

47 Des Browne, Minister for Citizenship and Immigration, HC Hansard, 13 May 2004, col. 569; 'Beating the sham wedding cheats', BBC News, 22 September 2004 (http://news.bbc.co.uk/go/pr/fr/-/2/hi/uk_news/3679482.stm, accessed 11 June 2011).

48 HC Hansard, 12 July 2004, col. 1219; 'Marriage scam for migrants broken', *The Guardian*, 23 September 2004; 'LCCG Bust Sham Wedding Racket', *Interport News*, 13 January 2006.

49 *SSHD v Baiai and others* [2007] EWCA Civ 478 [13].

50 HC Hansard, 12 July 2004, cols 1216-25.

annually (Home Affairs Select Committee 2006c: 288).[51] Under the scheme, those without leave, those whose leave was shortly to expire or those who entered with six months' leave or less were refused. If, in the opinion of the decision-maker, the parties were not free to marry, a certificate would also be refused, arguably usurping the role of the marriage registrar. The refusal template in the Immigration Directorate's Instructions suggested that the burden of proving freedom to marry lay with the applicant.[52]

The measures affected equally those who had complied with immigration law and those who had not. Non-EEA parties refused a certificate of approval had to leave the UK and apply to re-enter unless exceptional circumstances applied, confined to terminal or long-term illness or inability to travel due to pregnancy.[53] Otherwise, parties who had been entirely compliant with immigration control for lengthy periods could be refused because they had applied too late or lacked the necessary form of leave (see Home Affairs Select Committee 2006c: 285-8).

Although the measures were arguably a response to the more liberal EU regime, they could not be wholly successful in that regard, as couples where one party is an EEA national may marry abroad and then apply for a family permit. However, such applications at entry clearance posts were reportedly now subject to more careful scrutiny. Meanwhile, dedicated marriage case working teams were conducting an increased number of interviews with spouses of EEA nationals.[54] In this way, the measures supported efforts by the UK government after *Akrich* (later frustrated by *Metock*) to restrict rights of entry by non-EEA family members to those legally resident in the EU or who met the domestic criteria.[55]

The severity of the 'certificates of approval' regime caused great anger. The failure to distinguish between genuine and sham marriages and the favour shown to the Church of England recalled previous eras of discriminatory policy. The Joint Council for the Welfare of Immigrants immediately announced its intention of making a legal challenge. There was also official censure. As well as the Joint

51 Those who meet the criteria for a fiancé visa may apply to remain in the UK after marriage. Those applying for a marriage visitor visa must demonstrate an intention to leave the UK after the marriage.

52 HL Hansard, 15 June 2004, cols 684-5; HL Hansard, 22 June 2004, col. 1380W; correspondence between Brenda Hawkyard of the Immigration and Nationality Department (IND) and the Immigration Law Practitioners' Association (ILPA) in ILPA members' mailing, March and April 2005, Immigration Directorate's Instructions, Chapter 1, section 15, para. 3 and Annex MM. Ms Hawkyard suggested that 'evidence' of an existing marriage might take the form of a previous statement to an ECO.

53 Immigration Directorate's Instructions, Chapter 1, section 15 and Annex NN.

54 Mandie Campbell, Head of UK Visas, Home Affairs Select Committee 2006b: 88 and a memorandum submitted by the IND to the Select Committee on Home Affairs, Additional Written Evidence, 27 February 2006.

55 Case C-109/01, *SSHD v Akrich* [2004] QB 756; SI 2006/1003. These requirements became unenforceable after the decision in Case C-127/08, *Metock and others v Minister for Justice, Equality and Law Reform* [2009] QB 318.

Committee on Human Rights, already mentioned, the Independent Race Monitor criticised the Act's Race Equality Impact Assessment for failing to analyse the unequal impact of the laws on different nationalities, whether they were proportionate or whether the same goal was achievable in other ways (Coussey 2005: 33). It was reported that this sketchy analysis was deliberate, a 'quick and dirty' assessment being necessary to ensure inclusion of the clauses in the Bill (Home Affairs Select Committee 2006b: 84).

The compatibility of ss. 19-25 Asylum and Immigration (Treatment of Claimants, etc.) Act 2004 with the Human Rights Act 1998 was later successfully challenged in judicial review proceedings in 2006, in the Court of Appeal in 2007 and in the House of Lords in 2008 (the case law will be discussed in the next chapter). The government responded slowly and unsatisfactorily to these judgements. The fee, which was found to be too high, was not removed until April 2009 and refunds were available only to those who could show they had suffered 'real financial hardship'. While those who were previously refused could now marry, the scheme remained in place and migrants had to provide extensive evidence in affidavit form of such matters as the arrangements for the wedding and reception, the couple's plans for the future and details of the relationship. Parties were warned that enforcement action might be taken against applicants who had no leave and for undocumented migrants, the scheme was a clear disincentive to marry. The government announced its intention of abandoning the scheme in autumn 2009 and, in July 2010, a remedial order was laid before Parliament. In the meantime, the scheme remained in place, albeit in modified form, for more than two years after the unfavourable House of Lords judgement.

Until its enforced partial suspension, the new regime had a dramatic effect on the number of marriages in certain areas. By June 2005, there were about 60 per cent fewer notices of marriage in some London boroughs and around 25 per cent fewer in areas such as Birmingham or Leicester.[56] In 2005, the number of reported suspicious marriages fell to 247.[57] The number of marriages celebrated in the UK fell by 10 per cent between 2004 and 2005 to their lowest level since 1896 and this was attributed to the commencement of the new laws on 1 February 2005.[58] Defenders of the measures argued that the reduction vindicated their claim that bogus marriages were widespread.[59] This is doubtful given that the rules affected all marriages involving non-EEA nationals. There was a surge in marriages before implementation, many involving, according to one registrar, 'Asian couples who legitimately want to marry a partner from abroad'.[60] Entry clearance applications took time to organise and process so that a short-term drop in numbers was

56 *Migration News Sheet*, June 2005, p. 5.

57 *Migration News Sheet*, May 2006, p. 9.

58 'Marriage rates fall to lowest on record', Press Release, National Statistics, 21 February 2007.

59 'Tough rules expose scale of bogus marriages', *Daily Telegraph*, 16 May 2005.

60 *Migration News Sheet*, June 2005, p. 5.

probable. Entry clearance might be refused for reasons – such as failure to meet financial criteria – that were unconnected with whether the marriage was genuine. The number of overseas applications by spouses of EEA nationals increased after implementation, suggesting displacement rather than prevention.[61] Nonetheless, it is likely that the measures prevented some sham marriages taking place; the issue was the price paid by genuine applicants.

Back to Culture

The government's focus on bogus marriages reflected both concern at the perceived abuse of EU free movement rights, the 'super-diversity' that resulted from new immigration (Vertovec 2007) and its frequently unregulated character. South Asian communities were particularly affected because of their involvement in marriage migration and the measures were, in part, objectionable because of the discrimination in favour of Church of England marriages. However, the measures did not seem targeted at a particular nationality or region of origin. Fears about forced marriage, on the other hand, were much more specifically located. While official documentation referred to the range of nationalities involved, South Asian and in particular Bangladeshi and Pakistani Muslim communities were, in practice, overwhelmingly implicated.

Forced marriages were raised in Parliament nearly 100 times between 1997 and the introduction of the *Marriage to Partners from Overseas* Consultation Paper in December 2007, and became the explicit or implicit backdrop for almost any discussion on marriage migration. As argued in the previous chapter, the boundaries between a forced marriage and a voluntary arranged marriage are blurred, rendering otherwise illiberal measures more palatable. Meanwhile, elsewhere in Europe (including Belgium, Denmark, Germany, the Netherlands and Norway), these issues resulted in significant immigration restrictions (see, for example, Razack 2004, Roggeband and Verloo 2007, Human Rights Watch 2008, Block 2010, Bonjour 2010 and Schmidt 2011). Such measures were often described as necessary for ensuring the successful integration of immigrants, highlighting the fuzzy conceptual boundaries of the question.

As already suggested, despite David Blunkett's comments and the work of activist MPs such as Ann Cryer, during the early part of the period, British immigration control played only a limited role in preventing forced marriages through raising the minimum age to 18, a measure which did not have a great impact on minority communities.[62] Forced marriage units were established at

61 In the first three months of 2006, 51 applications were made from Ghana compared to nine in the same period of the previous year (Home Affairs Select Committee 2006c: 125).

62 According to Samad and Eade (2002: 22), fewer than ten per cent of Bangladeshis in Tower Hamlets, one of the largest concentrations of the Bangladeshi population in the

Dhaka and Islamabad, but they were not part of the entry clearance post and were staffed independently. Entry clearance staff observed during the field trip described later in this book were not proactive in identifying forced marriages.

A change in approach was heralded by two Consultation Papers issued in December 2007, *Marriage to Partners from Overseas* and *Marriage Visas: Pre-entry English Requirement for Spouses* (Border and Immigration Agency 2007a and 2007b). The former contained a number of proposals and the latter proposed the introduction of a pre-entry English language test.

Because the proposed measures involved rule changes or guidance, no parliamentary debate was required and the consultations and response were announced via written statements.[63] The context in which the minister did so was revealing. While the given rationalisation for *Marriage to Partners from Overseas* was the prevention of forced marriages, it was introduced alongside a Statement of Intent on the PBS and proposals on simplification as 'key aspects of our migration reform programme'. Despite the human rights discourse that is often associated with forced marriages, the changes were firmly placed within the government's managed migration programme.

Marriage to Partners from Overseas featured several traumatic accounts of forced marriages and made a string of proposals, including raising the minimum age for entry and sponsorship to 21, requiring a declaration of intention to marry before leaving the UK, confidential interviews and a Code of Practice for visa officers, with the suggestion that a visa could be refused even in the absence of a victim statement. Indicators of a forced marriage might include significant disparities in age, language, education and time spent in the other's country. The Consultation Paper also proposed revocation of indefinite leave if the marriage route was abused or the UK spouse was abandoned, more investigation of and sanctions against abuse of the marriage route and more protection and information for abandoned spouses.

These proposals seemed concerned only with British sponsor victims of forced marriage, undermining the universalist claims made about the issue. Many of the proposals, for example, revocation of indefinite leave, had little direct relation to forced marriage but appeared to be additional anti-abuse measures. Others, such as the power to refuse a visa where a forced marriage was suspected but not established, risked re-invoking the wide administrative discretion and stereotyped decision-making associated with earlier eras discussed in Chapter 5. Meanwhile, raising the minimum age to 21, while it might benefit some victims, would make UK cohabitation impossible for young partners to international marriages. Suspicions of a wider agenda were reinforced by the tone of the Consultation Paper, which, in places, more closely resembled a relationship manual than proposals to safeguard human rights. The proposed minimum age of entry and sponsorship was justified by reference to the higher average age of first marriage in the UK, itself

UK, marry before the age of 20.

63 HC Deb, 5 December 2007, c72WS; HC Deb, 19 June 2008, c61WS.

a misleading statistic given that many couples cohabit before marriage, and failed to acknowledge that the minimum age for in-country marriage remained 16 with parental consent and 18 without. It also said that the government:

> … does see benefits in requiring people to take time to establish themselves through a period of higher education or work in the country to which they belong before seeking to sponsor a marriage partner from overseas … Where one of the partners is from overseas, we consider that sufficient time should be allowed for the person in the UK to have completed their education, as well as allowing them to gain in maturity and possess adequate life skills. That will help them to navigate the different pressures and opportunities that they face and should help them prepare to participate in the social and economic opportunities around them in this country. (Border and Immigration Agency 2007a: 6)

Of all the proposals, raising the minimum age was most debated. Many well-known pressure groups were opposed because of the interference in young voluntary international marriages, which would mainly affect minority ethnic groups, and fears that it would prove counter-productive, particularly if sponsors were kept abroad until they were of an age to sponsor, although the government did not accept that this was widely the case (Home Affairs Select Committee 2006c: 334 and UK Border Agency 2008a: 15). Of 11 online responses available, 8 were opposed, 2 were in favour and one was ambivalent.[64] However, the results of the consultation showed equal numbers (27) of organisations in favour of and opposed to the proposal, with three ambivalent answers, a tiny majority of individuals in support (15 in favour, 14 against) plus three other unidentifiable favourable responses. This was taken as sufficient endorsement to raise the age to 21, which duly followed in November 2008.[65] There were favourable responses to the other proposals, except that of giving decision-makers power to refuse a visa without an evidential statement. However, of these, only a relatively anodyne Code of Practice was implemented.

The role of consultations would benefit from extended examination, for which there is not space here. Their deployment in immigration increased dramatically after 2006, with 25 taking place between 2006 and 2009. Public consultation can be problematic and the marriage consultations were no exception. *Marriage to Partners from Overseas* juxtaposed dramatic stories from victims of forced marriages with immigration enforcement measures whose impact would go far beyond protecting these. Responses from individuals, who may or may not have

64 Opposed to the proposal were: Rights of Women, Migration and Law Network, Runnymede Trust, Engender, Southall Black Sisters, ILPA, UK Advocacy Group, and Refuge. In favour were the Church of England's Mission and Public Affairs Council and the Social Justice Foundation. The Family Justice Council was ambivalent. The survey was carried out on 2 November 2010.

65 HC Deb, 19 June 2008, c61WS.

appreciated the full range of immigration powers already in place, were given equal weight to those from long-standing and expert pressure groups, raising suspicions of manipulation. More generally, the fundamental purpose of such consultations was unclear. Relying on consultation responses to reach decisions would introduce a highly flawed referendum process into government, yet ignoring them would raise questions as to their utility. Given the limited parliamentary discussion of administrative rule changes, consultations risked becoming a flawed substitute for the democratic process, providing cover for executive action rather than acting as a contribution to informed debate.

The second Consultation Paper, *Marriage Visas: Pre-entry English Requirement for Spouses*, proposed requiring a minimum standard of English language competency before entry. This was rationalised by the benefits for integration, but a more instrumental motive was suggested by the reference to the language requirements of the PBSand to labour market access (Border and Immigration Agency 2007b: 6). The response to the consultation showed a substantial majority opposed (68 against, 31 in favour) with particularly strong opposition from organisations (UK Border Agency 2008a: 34-5). The government backed off from immediate implementation, announcing that its 'medium term goal' remained the introduction of pre-entry testing 'linked to benchmarks about the availability of English tuition worldwide' (UK Border Agency 2008a: 7).[66] This failed to take account of more fundamental objections based on the scope for discrimination between different types of migrant, depending on their country of origin and standard of education, and practical objections, given the much greater ease with which language skills can be acquired in-country. An opinion obtained by Liberty from Matrix Chambers foresaw a possible breach of Articles 8 and 14 ECHR.[67]

The suspicion among many of those opposed to the proposals was that increased involvement by the immigration service in forced marriage was a means of hindering marriage migration, particularly where it involved marriages already barely acceptable to the majority, such as international arranged marriages involving young, often related and sometimes poorly educated parties. At the very least, such marriages might be considered a fair even welcome sacrifice. This argument has force, given the tone and structure of the consultations and the government's failure to publish sponsored research which questioned the

66 However, the Coalition government implemented pre-entry language tests in November 2010, ahead of the two-year lead-in announced by the previous government and despite criticism that there was insufficiently consistent provision across the globe. See, for example, Migrant Rights Network, 'Marrying someone from abroad – how easy will it be for them to take the new English test?', 26 August 2010, http://www.migrantsrights.org.uk/migration-pulse/2010/marrying-someone-abroad-how-easy-will-it-be-them-take-new-english-test (accessed 11 June 2011).

67 Available at http://www.liberty-human-rights.org.uk/human-rights/asylum/pre-entry-language-req-matrix-legal-advice-sept-2010.pdf (accessed 11 June 2011).

benefits of the move, allegedly due to methodological flaws despite the strong academic credentials of the researchers.[68] The Home Affairs Select Committee, while generally supportive of regulation, recommended more research before implementation (Home Affairs Select Committee 2008: 139). The role of these proposals as part of an immigration control strategy is also suggested by their inclusion in a list of measures aimed at *Securing the UK Border* (Home Office/ Foreign and Commonwealth Office 2007: 4).

The numbers of victims of forced marriage, as well as the efficacy of the measures, was uncertain. In 2008, the Forced Marriage Unit took up 420 cases, but the number has been estimated to be around 4,000 incidences annually, calculated by scaling up complaints made to one organisation.[69] It is not clear how many of this higher estimated total involved international marriages where the parties were under 21. The FMU calculated that, between 2005 and 2008, 28 per cent (200) of its cases involved those aged between 18 and 20, who would be affected by the change. However, in the same period, 9.5 per cent were 17-year-olds while, in 2008, 14 per cent of its cases involved those under 16, suggesting that existing restrictions on those marriages were not effective in preventing forced marriage.[70]

The uncertainty about both the efficacy of the measure and the number of likely beneficiaries must be placed against the drastic nature of the curb on young married life. In 2006, for instance, 3,420 spouses aged between 18 and 21 were granted leave to enter and 520 leave to remain.[71] The effects would be felt not only in Muslim communities but also in other less stigmatised groups such as the Jewish community.[72] The government stated in its Equality Impact Assessment that '[w]e consider that this measure is necessary to ensure we do everything to protect vulnerable people from being pressured into sponsoring a marriage visa', revealing the very small weight that was attached to permitting the continuation of such international marriages.[73] However, issues of proportionality were not

---

68 A summary of the research is available at: http://www.mhs.manchester.ac.uk/projectprofilesfiles/1308/FM_RESEARCH_SUMMARY_08.pdf (accessed 11 June 2011).

69 HC Deb, 16 July 2009, c608W; 'Forced marriages: who counts?', *The Guardian*, 11 March 2008, available at http://www.guardian.co.uk/commentisfree/2008/mar/11/forcedmarriageswhocounts (accessed 11 June 2011).

70 See Equality Assessment Impact, p. 8 at http://webarchive.nationalarchives.gov.uk/20100422120657/http://www.ukba.homeoffice.gov.uk/sitecontent/documents/aboutus/consultations/marriagetopartnersfromoverseas/marriagevisasequalityia.pdf?view=Binary (accessed 11 June 2011); HC Deb, 16 July 2009, c608W.

71 Equality Impact Assessment, p. 4 at http://webarchive.nationalarchives.gov.uk/20100422120657/http://www.ukba.homeoffice.gov.uk/sitecontent/documents/aboutus/consultations/marriagetopartnersfromoverseas/marriagevisasequalityia.pdf?view=Binary (accessed 11 June 2011).

72 'Marriage visa plan need a re-think', www.guardian.co.uk/commentisfree/2008/jul/29/immigration.religion (accessed 11 June 2011).

73 Equality Impact Assessment, p. 14 at http: //webarchive.nationalarchives.gov.uk/20100422120657/http: //www.ukba.homeoffice.gov.uk/sitecontent/documents/aboutus/

aired within Parliament and were generally submerged by more emotive aspects of debate.

The proposals in the two marriage consultations went beyond controlling forced marriages and were consistent with the shift in emphasis away from skin colour alone as a criterion for entry discussed in the last chapter. They were unmistakably aimed at poorer, less well-educated and less well-integrated immigrants, an increasingly common strand in European immigration policy that was also evident in the proposals, published in the same year, to reform the route to settlement and naturalisation (Border and Immigration Agency 2008a and 2008b). At the time of writing, the application of the age restriction had been found by the Court of Appeal to breach Convention rights.[74]

Conclusion

The legislative changes discussed here are consistent with the themes identified in the previous chapter. They were promoted by a powerful executive who wished to demonstrate commitment to democratic processes while sometimes being willing to manipulate or abridge them. Examples discussed in this chapter include the truncated debate on the certificate of approval scheme and the unsatisfactory consultation on raising the minimum age of entry and sponsorship to 21. They also betrayed changing approaches towards ethnic minority and immigrant communities. Favour was now based less on race or skin colour and more on conformity to cultural and legal norms and, arguably, on considerations of social class. Out of the myriad changes described here emerged the contours of an acceptable spouse and an acceptable 'victim'. An acceptable spouse was not too young, keen to integrate, economically active and compliant with any hurdles that British immigration law might erect. They did not need to be married or heterosexual. Some vulnerable individuals aroused compassion, notably (and to a limited extent) the victims of domestic violence or forced marriage. However, there was a telling absence of sympathy in other cases, such as for those separated by the rules on switching or refusal of a certificate of approval. Such couples might eventually be reunited, but only after considerable hardship, recalling the ordeal by endurance noted in earlier chapters. Nor was there regret at the effective prohibition on early international marriages within the UK; such marriages were seen as largely unacceptable (despite remaining legal within the UK), suggesting new forms of cultural discrimination.

Previous chapters suggested an implied hierarchy of acceptable marriages based primarily on gender and race. Race and gender still featured, although more implicitly than before, but married status and a heterosexual relationship

---

consultations/marriagetopartnersfromoverseas/marriagevisasequalityia.pdf?view=Binary (accessed 11 June 2011).

74 *Quila and another v SSHD* [2010] EWCA Civ 1482.

were no longer central, providing an implicit contrast with less 'modern' forms of family life such as the arranged marriage. Marriages that did not conform to the cultural standards of majority British society were increasingly regarded with disfavour, a tendency noted in previous chapters, and were present but somewhat muted during the early part of the period before becoming more dominant. This distinction between 'modernity' and problematic 'tradition' intersected with the other division discussed here of those who accepted the state's authority and those who did not. Attempts to demote the non-compliant included the ban on switching and certificates of approval.

All these measures suggest that those who married in officially unapproved ways, whether sponsor or applicant, might find themselves outside the realm of inclusion. The assumptions and beliefs that shaped the policy described here were not identical to those discussed in earlier chapters, but the conditional nature of acceptance and belonging remained. While freedom and plurality in personal matters were prioritised for the majority settled population (Eekelaar 2006: 23-6), there was little sign that the state was retreating as far as families of migrant descent were concerned; in fact, the developments discussed here suggest that the reverse was true.

Chapter 8

Marking New Boundaries: The Judiciary and Marriage Migration 1997-2010

Introduction

Chapter 7 argued that legislative control of immigration through marriage between 1997 and 2010 was subject to sometimes contradictory forces. On the one hand, there was a commitment to non-discrimination and human rights values, but there was also a strong impetus towards government control of immigration. This chapter considers the judicial response over the same period. The discussion in Chapter 4 noted that the judiciary mainly endorsed government efforts to control marriage migration through regulatory mechanisms, such as the primary purpose rule and unfavourable judgements on questions such as 'credibility'. This chapter will discuss high-level case law, some of which, particularly towards the end of the period discussed here, challenged government supremacy in immigration control. The means of doing so was the Human Rights Act 1998 and the question, which it is too early to answer with any certainty, is whether this marks a new era of more robust judicial oversight in immigration mandated by the Human Rights Act.

Primary purpose, as we saw in Chapter 4, generated much case law. After its removal, issues such as intention to live together, domestic violence, the validity of marriages and divorces and third party support continued to receive some attention. However, a major issue, discussed first in this chapter, was the regularisation of undocumented migrants who had entered marriages or relationships while in the UK. This issue, important in its own right, was also the conduit by which major questions on the judicial function in human rights cases were determined.

Regularising Irregular Marriage Migrants

The Regulatory Framework

The legal framework for these cases evolved during this period. The power of removal was introduced in s. 33 Immigration Act 1971, but only for illegal entrants or those refused entry. Other cases were subject to deportation. Section 10 Immigration and Asylum Act 1999 extended removal to overstayers, those who breached conditions of leave or who obtained leave by deception. However, until 2002, in-country switching to a marriage visa was possible so that such migrants could regularise their position. As discussed in the previous chapter, the possibility of switching was removed in 2002 for those without leave or who had entered with less than six months' leave. These individuals had to leave the UK to apply for a marriage visa. Sections 19-25 Asylum and Immigration (Treatment of Claimants, etc.) Act 2004, also discussed in the previous chapter, implemented the certificates of approval scheme, which aimed to prevent the majority of such migrants, together with others coming to the end of their leave, from even getting married without government sanction and also forcing them abroad for regularisation.

At the start of the period, most of those considered here were liable to deportation while, after the implementation of s. 10 of the Immigration and Asylum Act 1999, they became subject to removal. A deportation order must expire or be lifted before the deportee can apply to re-enter the UK. Married life in the UK might be deferred for years and case law focused on whether it could continue abroad. Those who were removed could apply immediately to rejoin the UK-based spouse (automatic re-entry bans introduced in 2008 did not apply to family migrants) and the focus switched to difficulties in obtaining entry clearance. Until implementation of the Human Rights Act, those resisting removal due to marriage could rely only on Home Office policy or the general exercise of discretion. Until 1996, policy was set out in DP2/93, which purported to incorporate the UK's obligations under the ECHR. This was succeeded by DP3/96, which did not explicitly refer to the ECHR. After the implementation of the Human Rights Act, most applicants argued their claim on Article 8 grounds, although DP3/96 remained occasionally relevant until its abolition in 2008 (Clayton 2006b: 589; see also *AB* and *CH*[1]). After that, cases could be argued only on the basis of Article 8 ECHR – that removal would breach the right to respect for private and family life.

DP2/93 provided that enforcement action should not normally be initiated if the marriage pre-dated enforcement action or there was conclusive evidence of a genuine and subsisting relationship akin to marriage. Other factors included a spouse of long-standing residence or who could not otherwise be reasonably expected to live abroad, and children by a former relationship if these had the right of abode and lived with or had frequent contact with the resident spouse. DP3/96 was more restrictive. It did not acknowledge unmarried relationships and required marriages to have pre-dated enforcement action by two years and for it to be unreasonable to expect the resident spouse to accompany the deported spouse abroad. Marriages that post-dated enforcement action would only end action in 'the most exceptional circumstances'. Article 8 ECHR requires governments to respect family and private life.

The Strasbourg case law on the effect of Article 8 on immigration control is well developed and demands a structured approach, summarised by Lord Bingham in *Razgar*:

1 *AB (Jamaica) v SSHD* [2007] EWCA Civ 1302; *CH (Jamaica) v SSHD* [2007] EWCA Civ 792.

> (1) Will the proposed removal be an interference by a public authority with the exercise of the applicant's right to respect for his private or (as the case may be) family life? (2) If so, will such interference have consequences of such gravity as potentially to engage the operation of article 8? (3) If so, is such interference in accordance with the law? (4) If so, is such interference necessary in a democratic society in the interests of national security, public safety or the economic well-being of the country, for the prevention of disorder or crime, for the protection of health or morals, or for the protection of the rights and freedoms of others? (5) If so, is such interference proportionate to the legitimate public end sought to be achieved?[2]

In practice, questions of whether family life exists between spouses and has suffered an interference (i.e. questions (1), (2) and (3)) are not separately considered or, if it is, is answered in the affirmative. It is generally assumed that immigration controls fulfil at least one of the interests in question (4) and is thus 'necessary in a democratic society', although which interest is engaged is rarely considered.[3] The question for the courts in marriage cases is usually one of proportionality, which involves weighing up the public interest implied by question (4) with the severity of the interference. Decisions are fact-sensitive, although some principles may be observed. In particular, Article 8 does not require parties to live together in the country of their choice, although when obstacles make the expectation of cohabitation abroad unreasonable, this may be contested (see the discussion on 'insurmountable obstacles' below).[4] Factors include the circumstances under which the relationship was formed as well the difficulties that face the parties in relocating. Irregular migrants who enter marriages knowing that the future is precarious are consequently at a disadvantage. However, as the discussion below demonstrates, Article 8 is a more flexible, individually oriented way to reach decisions than government policies that relied on bright line demarcations.

Although the precise legal arguments have been different, certain issues have persistently presented themselves in these cases: the extent to which the court will intervene in immigration decisions and the circumstances that trump the imperatives of immigration control.

---

2 *R (on the application of Razgar) v SSHD* [2004] UKHL 27 [17].

3 Although the question has arisen in the context of differentiating proportionality decisions in criminal deportations from those in administrative removal: *JO (Uganda) v SSHD* [2010] EWCA Civ 10.

4 *Abdulaziz, Cabales and Balkandali v United Kingdom*, ECtHR, Series A, no. 94, 28 May 1985, para. 68 and several subsequent cases; see also Thym 2008: 104 and, for an interesting new perspective, Sedley LJ in *Quila v SSHD* [2010] EWCA Civ 1483 [43]-[45].

The Role of the Courts

Prior to the implementation of the Human Rights Act in 2000, applicants refused leave to remain in the UK because they did not comply with the Immigration Rules could have recourse only to the policies referred to earlier or to executive discretion. The courts were frequently asked to review cases which fell outside the precise terms of the policies, but where discretion might be exercised or where the Secretary of State did not accept factual assertions that would bring applicants within the policies. These cases were decided according to judicial review principles. ECHR considerations might be imported only to the extent permitted by the law as it then stood.[5] The policies represented the balance struck by the government between Article 8 and immigration control, and could not be disturbed by the domestic courts for non-compliance with ECHR.[6] Cases were rarely decided in favour of the immigrant because the bar for intervention was set so high. Provided all relevant factors had been considered, the decision stood. Hardship was not, without procedural error, enough to suggest irrationality. In *Gbadegesin*, for example, the court found that, provided the interests of the child had received consideration, the court would not interfere with a decision that separated a parent and child.[7] Home Office refusals were often formulaic, being described by one representative as 'incantations'.[8] The rationale was the need for consistent treatment. Yet there was a tension that the courts declined to acknowledge between use of standard wording and the obligation to demonstrate that all factors in a case had been properly taken into account.

After the commencement of the Human Rights Act, there was extensive debate as to the role of the court in determining Article 8 questions, which was often played out in marriage cases. In *Mahmood*,[9] a judicial review case, Laws LJ in the Court of Appeal found that while 'anxious scrutiny' was demanded, the judicial function required that a 'margin of discretion' be permitted to the executive so that the court's function remained that of 'anxious scrutiny'. This was despite a contrary approach previously approved by the Court of Appeal in B.[10] *Mahmood* was a problematic case which acted as a constraint on the courts for several years. It was decided only very shortly after the implementation of the Human Rights Act and involved a decision made prior to the Act. It is perhaps unsurprising that even senior judges were wary about adopting an expansive approach at that stage. Laws LJ expressed the court's hesitation as follows at para. 33:

---

5 See *R v Secretary of State ex p. Brind* [1991] 1 AC 696. As regards Article 8, see the speech of the Master of the Rolls in *R v Ministry of Defence ex p. Smith* [1996] 1 All ER 257 [263].

6 *R v SSHD ex p. Gangadeen and another* [1997] EWCA 2799.

7 *R v Chief Immigration Officer ex p. Gbadegesin* [1998] EWHC Admin 408.

8 *R v SSHD ex p. Otusi* [1997] EWHC Admin 1165 [15].

9 *R v SSHD ex p. Mahmood* [2000] EWCA Civ 315.

10 *B v SSHD* [2000] Imm AR 478.

> The Human Rights Act 1998 does not authorise the judges to stand in the shoes of Parliament's delegates, who are decision-makers given their responsibilities by the democratic arm of the state. The arrogation of such a power to the judges would usurp those functions of government which are controlled and distributed by powers whose authority is derived from the ballot-box. It follows that there must be a principled distance between the court's adjudication in a case such as this, and the Secretary of State's decision, based on his perception of the case's merits.

Despite criticism the following year in the House of Lords, the deferential approach in *Mahmood* was followed in many subsequent immigration cases, which also failed to determine whether it should be confined only to judicial review cases or applied to appeal hearings also.[11] In 2005, in *Huang*, the Court of Appeal found that it was for the court (including the adjudicator) to form its own judgement as to whether a particular case 'is so exceptional on its particular facts that the imperative of proportionality demands an outcome in the appellant's favour notwithstanding that he cannot succeed under the Rules' (Laws LJ at para. 59).[12] While adjudicators and the Tribunal now had authority to decide issues of proportionality for themselves, the requirement of exceptionality meant that successful Article 8 claims remained rare. Cases decided prior to *Huang* were upheld on appeal after *Huang*.[13]

The House of Lords subsequently upheld the Court of Appeal's decision that appellate bodies should decide questions of proportionality for themselves, but overturned their finding that such cases must be exceptional.[14] The House of Lords' decision in *Huang* was important at several levels. It established two critical points of law and it set the tone for later Article 8 cases, some of which are discussed below. The first legal point was that appellate bodies must reach their own decision on Article 8. This did not always mean a different outcome. Shortly afterwards, the Court of Appeal emphasised that, in normal circumstances, interference in family life will still be justified.[15] After *Huang*, courts did remit some cases for rehearing as the wrong test had been applied but, in others, unfavourable decisions were upheld due to an insufficiently strong claim.[16] In reaching its own decision as

11 *R v SSHD ex p. Daly* [2001] UKHL 26 at para 27; *R v SSHD ex p. Isiko* [2000] EWCA Civ 346; *Samaroo and another v SSHD* [2001] EWCA Civ 1139; *Noruwa (Proportionality appeal: assessment, not discretion) Nigeria* [2001] UKIAT 00016; *Blessing Edore v SSHD* [2003] EWCA Civ 736; *M(Croatia)* [2004] UKIAT 00024.

12 *Huang and others v SSHD* [2005] EWCA Civ 105.

13 For example, *Chikwamba v SSHD* [2005] EWCA Civ 1779.

14 *Huang (FC) v SSHD* [2007] UKHL 11.

15 *LK (Serbia) v SSHD* [2007] EWCA Civ 1554.

16 For example, *J (Uganda) v SSHD* [2007] EWCA Civ 802, as compared to *R (on the application of Bujar Semanaj) v SSHD* [2007] EWHC 1704 (Admin); *PM (Jamaica) v SSHD* [2007] EWCA Civ 937; *R (on the application of M) v SSHD* [2009] EWHC 1545 (Admin).

to what Article 8 required, the court would agree frequently with the government and Article 8 cases remained difficult to win. Nonetheless, unfavourable decisions could at least be challenged on their own terms rather than by the more deferential standards of review.

The other major point in *Huang* was the disapproval of any test of exceptionality. Their Lordships found that, in imposing such a condition, lower courts and tribunals had confused a prediction – that it would be relatively rare for the demands of immigration control to be trumped by Article 8 considerations – with a precondition (para. 20; see also Clayton 2007). The test of an Article 8 claim was:

> … whether the refusal of leave to enter or remain, in circumstances where the life of the family cannot reasonably be expected to be enjoyed elsewhere, taking full account of all considerations weighing in favour of the refusal, prejudices the family life of the applicant in a manner sufficiently serious to amount to a breach of the fundamental right protected by article 8. (Para. 20)

In so finding, the court opened the way to the rejection of the requirement of 'insurmountable obstacles' discussed below.

In the judgement, their Lordships focused on the essential purpose of Article 8, which had been arguably distorted by the 'tendency …to complicate and mystify what is not, in principle, a hard task to define, however difficult the task is, in practice, to perform' (para. 14). They observed the need to balance not only the competing interests of state and individual but also of individual and society. The individual should not bear consequences that are too severe and they referred to 'the core value', which Article 8 exists to protect:

> Human beings are social animals. They depend on others. Their family, or extended family, is the group on which many people most heavily depend, socially, emotionally and often financially. There comes a point at which, for some, prolonged and unavoidable separation from this group seriously inhibits their ability to live full and fulfilling lives. (Para. 18)

The language used in *Huang* also suggested a particular role for the courts in protecting the rights of migrants who were excluded from the democratic process. Rejecting an analogy with case law involving disputes between public sector landlords and occupiers, their Lordships stated, at para. 17, that 'the Immigration Rules and supplementary instructions … are not the product of active debate in Parliament, where non-nationals seeking leave to enter or remain are not in any event represented'. This recognition of the particular and personal nature of Article 8 rights and their role in enabling the family lives of the excluded was reflected in subsequent case law, some of which is discussed below.

Consistent with this approach, their Lordships later found in *Beoku-Betts* that judicial power to determine human rights questions under s. 84 Nationality,

Asylum and Immigration Act 2002 (formerly contained in s. 65 Immigration and Asylum Act 1999) permitted the court to take account of the entire family unit and not only of the appellant.[17] This settled an issue that had been litigated over for a long period and avoided the artificiality of the appellant's human rights being decided in one forum while those of his family members were decided in separate proceedings elsewhere.

Living Together Abroad

This section considers those numerous cases where it was argued that the UK resident spouse should join the non-resident spouse abroad either because the spouse was subject to a deportation order and was forbidden entry or because the parties could not meet the criteria for entry. Such an expectation was subject only to domestic law prior to the implementation of the Human Rights Act 1998 and the plight of the spouse and children carried little weight, even when these were UK nationals or faced extreme hardship.[18] In part, this reflected the review function to which the courts were then confined. The planned deportation to India of a step-father, for example, was described by the family's GP as 'catastrophic' for the children, 'who have for the first time in their lives had stability'. The wife and children had no prior connection to India. One child had severe asthma and a consultant paediatrician was concerned about adequate treatment in rural India. However, as the impact upon the children had been considered, the decision to deport was upheld.[19]

The standard formulation adopted after the implementation of the Human Rights Act was that the couple had to establish 'insurmountable obstacles' to living abroad, a term used by the European Court of Human Rights (ECtHR) in *Poku* and elsewhere.[20] Lord Phillips had quoted from *Poku* and relied on the phrase when setting out his conclusions on the ECtHR jurisprudence in the early case of *Mahmood*.[21] As Lord Justice Sedley pointed out some years later in *LM (DRC)*, the phrase 'insurmountable obstacles' was not a term of art and had merely formed part of the ECtHR's illustrative checklist. If taken literally, it could result in almost no claims succeeding and was inconsistent with Lord Phillips' later use of the term 'not reasonable to expect'. It was, in any event, qualified by its context in Lord Phillips' speech so that it did not represent the only circumstances in which he found that a claim might succeed.[22]

Nonetheless, the phrase was taken up as the test for determining whether a migrant should be removed. It rapidly became a way to defeat almost any claim,

17 *Beoku-Betts v SSHD* [2008] UKHL 39.

18 *R v SSHD ex p. Ahmed and Patel* [1998] EWHC Admin 453.

19 *R v SSHD ex p. Singh* [1997] EWHC Admin 59.

20 *Poku v United Kingdom* (1996) 22 EHRR CD 94.

21 *R v SSHD ex p. Mahmood* [2000] EWCA Civ 315, para. 55.

22 *LM (DRC) v SSHD* [2008] EWCA Civ 325, paras 11-12.

including those involving UK-resident refugees returning to their country of origin. In *PK*, for instance, the Tribunal found that it was for the parties to establish that there were insurmountable obstacles preventing the refugee wife from accompanying her husband to the Democratic Republic of Congo.[23] In *SS*, the Secretary of State had acted lawfully in finding no insurmountable obstacles to the return of the refugee husband to Sri Lanka, given changes in the situation there.[24] In both instances, the Tribunal denied that their findings required the parties to re-litigate their asylum claim. Unsurprisingly, given these findings, it was also found that a spouse with exceptional leave could not demonstrate insurmountable obstacles to return.[25] Moses J in the Administrative Court found that insurmountable obstacles required impossibility due to external factors such as refusal by the state to admit the parties.[26] It was not sufficient to show disruption to the spouse or children. In *EH*, it was acknowledged that the appellant's pregnant wife could not accompany him to Iraq, but this was due to security considerations alone. In all other cases, state supremacy should prevail: 'All the other factors, language, family and social conditions were factors which represent the consequences of her choice of husband. They cannot impose their choice of residence upon the United Kingdom for those reasons.'[27]

Rarely, when there was an identifiable flaw in the reasoning, the court intervened. In one instance, a psychiatrist reported that forcing the family abroad would aggravate the mother-in-law's heart condition. The Home Office responded that the increased stress would not be long-lasting. The court quashed the decision as failing to deal properly with the medical evidence. The judge, however, counselled against over-optimism, warning that the Secretary of State could take such evidence properly into account and still reach the same decision.[28] By contrast, the Tribunal often found that decisions by adjudicators in favour of spouses were outside the range of reasonable responses.[29] In one case, the Tribunal agreed that the family could not move to Bangladesh but considered that the adjudicator had erred in finding the Secretary of State unreasonable in ordering the husband's deportation, even though the family would not be reunited for at least three years.[30]

The requirement for 'insurmountable obstacles' was clearly inconsistent with both the general tenor of *Huang* and the specific finding that Article 8 applies 'in circumstances where the life of the family cannot reasonably be expected

---

23 *PK (Article 8, Return, Marriage-Refugee) Democratic Republic of Congo* [2002] UKIAT 05220.

24 *SS (ILR, Article 8 return) Sri Lanka* [2004] UKIAT 00126.

25 *R (Sri Lanka)* [2003] UKIAT 00093; *V (Democratic Republic of Congo)* [2003] UKIAT 00131; *JF (Article 8: inconsistency, family members) Angola* [2005] UKIAT 00173.

26 *R (on the application of Surinder Singh) v IAT and SSHD* [2003] EWHC 248.

27 *EH (Palestinian – entry clearance- proportionality) Iraq* [2005] UKIAT 00062.

28 *R v SSHD ex p. Khaira* [1998] EWHC Admin 355.

29 *R (Serbia & Montenegro)* [2003] UKIAT 00187; *F (Jamaica)* [2003] UKIAT 00152; *J (Serbia and Montenegro)* [2003] UKIAT 00151; *A (Pakistan)* [2004] UKIAT 00034.

30 *MD (14 years not disproportionate) Bangladesh* [2004] UKIAT 00208.

to be enjoyed elsewhere' (para. 20). After *Huang*, the Court of Appeal began to adopt a more flexible approach. In *AB*, it found that where there was reliance upon a third party's refugee status, the starting point for the Tribunal is that this person cannot reasonably be expected to return to the country of origin unless there is some basis to suppose otherwise.[31] In *AB (Jamaica)*, the wife's prior breach of immigration control had been minor and rapidly acknowledged, while the Home Office had acted tardily. The husband was a British national and it was disproportionate for him to disrupt his life to follow his spouse.[32] While the Tribunal was still finding that the test of 'insurmountable obstacles' remained extant, the Court of Appeal in *LM (DRC)*, mentioned above, emphasised that 'insurmountable' should not be interpreted literally; it meant not realistic or reasonable rather than not possible.[33]

The requirement of 'insurmountable obstacles' was finally buried by Lord Bingham in *EB (Kosovo)*, who found (at para. 12) that 'it will rarely be proportionate to uphold an order for removal of a spouse if there is a close and genuine bond with the other spouse and that spouse cannot reasonably be expected to follow the removed spouse to the country of removal', although, for some time afterwards, the higher courts had to correct lower level decisions made before (and sometimes after) *Huang* and *EB (Kosovo)*.[34] In *VW and AB*, Sedley LJ explained the correct test:

> [W]hile it is of course possible that the facts of any one case may disclose an insurmountable obstacle to removal, the inquiry into proportionality is not a search for such an obstacle and does not end with its elimination. It is a balanced judgment of what can reasonably be expected in the light of all the material facts.[35]

While 'reasonably expected' imposes a lower threshold than a requirement of 'insurmountable obstacles', it is also a different type of test, one that requires evaluation of all the circumstances. It does not make 'insurmountable obstacles' irrelevant (the term has been and continues to be used by the Strasbourg court).[36]

---

31 *AB (Democratic Republic of Congo) v SSHD* [2007] EWCA Civ 1422.

32 *AB (Jamaica) v SSHD* [2007] EWCA Civ 1302.

33 *VW and MO (Article 8: insurmountable obstacles) Uganda* [2008] UKAIT 00021; *LM (DRC) v SSHD* [2008] EWCA Civ 325.

34 *EB (Kosovo) v SSHD* [2008] UKHL 11. Examples where the courts had to correct findings of 'insurmountable obstacles' include *R (on the application of CM (Jamaica)* [2008] EWHC 2778 (Admin); *AF (Jamaica) v SSHD* [2009] EWCA Civ 240; and *TF (Angola) v SSHD* [2009] EWCA Civ 905. An instance where the higher courts had to correct a decision based on 'insurmountable obstacles' even after *EB (Kosovo)* was *YD (Togo) v SSHD* [2010] EWCA Civ 214, although the immigration judge in the earlier hearing had perhaps been influenced by the ECtHR's use of the term in a recent decision.

35 *VW (Uganda) v SSHD, AB (Somalia) v SSHD* [2009] EWCA Civ 5 at para. 19.

36 In, for example, *Omoregie v Norway* [2009] Imm AR 170.

All cases depend on their facts and the proportionality argument will be harder to win in some cases than in others. It may, on the facts, be reasonable to expect some people to return unless obstacles are indeed insurmountable. However, the House of Lords has unequivocally established that, contrary to the domestic case law after *Mahmood*, obstacles certainly do not need to be insurmountable for a claim to succeed.

'Temporary Removal'

After 2000, most irregular marriage migrants became subject to administrative removal rather than deportation. There was nothing to prevent such a migrant from making an application to rejoin his or her UK spouse at the earliest opportunity and argument increasingly shifted towards whether it was right to require the migrant to leave in order to apply for entry clearance as a spouse. Two issues were usually involved: the position of an applicant who would not come within the Immigration Rules, particularly if this was due to the disruption of removal, and the degree of hardship an applicant should endure in accessing entry clearance facilities, particularly if these were absent or difficult to access in the country of origin.

The first question received attention in *Mahmood*.[37] It was argued that the applicant met all the criteria for entry as a spouse except for valid entry clearance. Leaving the UK might cause the loss of his employment and, as a consequence, failure of the entry clearance application. The court found that it would be unfair to other more compliant applicants if individuals who breached immigration law were permitted to jump the queue. Article 8 considerations would be brought into account during the entry clearance process. Following *Mahmood*, the Tribunal found in *BS India*[38] that only in 'exceptional circumstances' would an Article 8 claim succeed where the possibility of entry clearance existed. Moses J supported this approach in the High Court, finding that any interference with Article 8 rights arose from the couple's decision to marry despite the husband's precarious immigration status rather than from any action of the state.[39] That the application for entry clearance might fail could not be a factor according to the Court of Appeal in *Ekinci*, Simon Brown LJ finding that '[i]t would be a bizarre and unsatisfactory result if, the less able the applicant is to satisfy the full requirements for entry clearance, the more readily he should be excused the need to apply'.[40] This principle was upheld in numerous succeeding cases. Even where the applicant's child was severely disabled, the mother was unable to cope alone and the family's sole income would be state benefits, the case was insufficiently exceptional to waive an application for entry

37 *R v SSHD ex p. Mahmood* [2000] EWCA Civ 315.

38 [2002] UKIAT 00660.

39 *R (on the application of Surinder Singh) v IAT and SSHD* [2003] EWHC 248.

40 *R (on the application of Ekinci) v SSHD* [2003] EWCA Civ 765 [17].

clearance.[41] As this instance demonstrates, removal of the main earner might not only make compliance with the rules more difficult but could create new reliance on public funds, something immigration control usually seeks to avoid.

Applicants had still to leave the UK even if there was no entry clearance post in the country of origin, provided that facilities could be accessed in a neighbouring country.[42] Consequently, the Tribunal became involved in assessing the feasibility and danger of travel in various troubled locations. For instance, in *HC*, the applicant was required to return to a highly unstable Iraq, obtain travel documents, negotiate Jordanian border controls and endure the cost and danger of travelling from Iraq to Jordan in order to obtain a visa.[43] '[A] reasonable likelihood that the claimant could not make the journey without adverse consequences or a violation of his human rights' was not established. A similar view was taken in *SA*, where the Tribunal held that: 'Although there are extensive dangers, we are not satisfied in the light of this evidence that the dangers are so extensive that it is unreasonable to expect the appellant to make the same journey being made regularly by others seeking entry clearance.'[44]

Some decisions acknowledged the difficulties. In *AM*, the Tribunal found that the impossibility of obtaining entry clearance in Somalia prevented the removal of the husband of a Somalian refugee, given that it would probably result in permanent separation.[45] In *KJ*, the Tribunal found that travel within Iraq was too dangerous for a Kurd and that the parties' precarious financial position made the cost disproportionate.[46] It found in *SM Afghanistan* that, as there was no queue to join, allowing Afghan applicants to remain in the UK did not legitimise queue-jumping.[47] In *R(S)*, Collins J found that the absence of entry clearance facilities in Afghanistan and the delay in considering the asylum claim meant that the claimant could make his marriage application in-country.[48] Collins J referred (at para. 203) to the human cost of such decision-making: 'People cannot be expected to put their lives on hold, particularly if they are young. The claimant was when he arrived in genuine need of protection and he has been condemned to a cruel limbo of worry and uncertainty over his future.'

Many of the unfavourable decisions drew upon the test of 'exceptionality' disapproved in *Huang*. The punitive tone of some judgements, which prioritised compliance with immigration procedures over protection of family life or even

---

41 *LH (Truly exceptional – Ekinci applied) Jamaica* [2006] UKIAT 00019.

42 *J (Serbia and Montenegro)* [2003] UKIAT 00041.

43 *HC (Availability of Entry Clearance Facilities) Iraq* [2004] UKIAT 00154.

44 *SA (Entry clearance in Jordan – proportionality) Iraq CG* [2006] UKAIT 00011 [32].

45 *AM (Inability to make entry clearance application) Somalia* [2004] UKIAT 00276.

46 *KJ (Entry clearance proportionality) Iraq CG* [2005] UKIAT 00066.

47 *SM and others (Entry clearance, proportionality) Afghanistan GC* [2007] UKAIT 00010.

48 *R(S) v SSHD* [2007] EWHC 51 (Admin).

personal safety, was inconsistent with the recognition of the emotional lives of migrants found in *Huang*. Nonetheless, *Huang* did not make much immediate material difference to the bulk of decision-making, as, for example, *SM Iraq* demonstrates.[49] The question fell to be resolved by the House of Lords decision in *Chikwamba*.[50] This case involved a failed Zimbabwean asylum seeker permitted to remain when removals to Zimbabwe were suspended. She married a Zimbabwean refugee and the couple had a small daughter. Once removals were reinstated, the government intended to remove her so that she would have reapply for entry, giving her the choice of taking her child from her father to the harsh conditions of Zimbabwe or being separated from them both for the time necessary for the application to be made and, it was assumed, granted. The judgement was unusually trenchant. Lord Scott expressed 'astonishment' that the case had come so far, given the inevitability of the outcome. He was critical of the failure to acknowledge the particular circumstances of applicants: '… policies that involve people cannot be, and should not be allowed to become, rigid inflexible rules. The bureaucracy of which Kafka wrote cannot be allowed to take root in this country and the courts must see that it does not' (para. 4). The real aim of the policy was to deter illegal entry rather than to prevent unfairness or queue-jumping. Requiring the applicant to return to Zimbabwe for a visa was disproportionate to such an aim. According to Lord Brown, 'only comparatively rarely, certainly in family cases involving children, should an Article 8 appeal be dismissed on the basis that it would be proportionate and more appropriate for the appellant to apply for leave from abroad' (para. 44). This was for reasons not only of humanity but also of efficacy. An entry clearance refusal could be appealed on Article 8 grounds, but the appeal would be heard in-country in the absence of the appellant. It was consistent with streamlined appeal procedures for all such issues to be aired and decided at the same time and with the appellant present.

Chikwamba represented another critically important decision in which the House of Lords sought to mitigate a minimalist, over-technical and over-deferential approach to Article 8. In *MA (Pakistan)*, the Court of Appeal found that the principle applied to all family cases, not just those that involved children.[51] This is clearly correct. Article 8 relates to the totality of the parties' circumstances and a claim does not depend upon establishing a single fact, although, of course, the presence of children, particularly young children, will strengthen a claim. The court suggested that previous decisions prioritising immigration control had not only asked the wrong question but had failed to frame the issue correctly as '[t]he real question was not whether there were "insurmountable obstacles" to the applicant returning to Pakistan in order to make an application for entry clearance

49 *SM (Entry clearance application in Jordan, proportionality) Iraq CG* [2007] UKAIT 00077.

50 *Chikwamba v SSHD* [2008] UKHL 40.

51 *MA (Pakistan) v SSHD* [2009] EWCA Civ 953.

from there, but whether there was any sensible reason as to why he should be required to do so'(para. 9).

Given that applications for leave to remain can be made from within the UK, it might seem that almost any case might succeed under *Chikwamba.* However, limits were implied by the *Chikwamba* judgement, which drew a distinction between the position of that appellant and the appellant in *Ekinci* who, despite having a child, also had 'an appalling immigration history' (para. 30) and faced only a brief return to Germany.[52] The objective of deterring illegal immigration was not 'necessarily objectionable' and it might sometimes be 'reasonable and proportionate' to require return (para. 42). Subsequent applicants did not always succeed if their personal circumstances and 'immigration history' were insufficiently compelling to outweigh the 'requirements of firm and fair immigration control'.[53]

In *Chikwamba*, no doubt was expressed as to the ultimate success of the entry clearance application. That the application would succeed anyway under the rules only added to the artificiality of requiring the applicant to apply from abroad and the court in *VW (Uganda)* made the point very cogently:

> It has in the past been urged by the Home Office that there is relatively little hardship in breaking up a family by removal where the removed spouse can immediately apply for entry clearance in order to return. The decision of the House of Lords in *Chikwamba* [2008] UKHL 40 ... has called a halt to this false logic. The likelihood of return via entry clearance should not be ordinarily treated as a factor rendering removal proportionate; if anything, the reverse is the case.[54]

However, that left open two questions: the position of those who could not comply with the Immigration Rules and the type of leave to be granted to those who did. On the first question, it was subsequently held by the High Court that *Chikwamba* only applied to those who had 'an unassailable case for entry clearance'.[55] That seems to be an excessively formalistic approach. Although visa officers decide Article 8 questions, Article 8 appeals are normally heard in-country and it is preferable for all claims to be decided at once, as Lord Brown pointed out in *Chikwamba.* Besides, *Chikwamba* was not only about the difficulties of returning to turbulent countries in order to make the application but was also about the damage to family life in the meantime. These were not issues that could be considered separately to a substantive Article 8 claim for leave to remain. Lord Brown said, at para. 46 of *Chikwamba*, that '[n]o one apparently doubts that, in the longer term, this family will have to be allowed to live together here'. Whether that was because the claim would succeed under the rules or outside the rules under Article 8 did not seem

52 *R (on the application of Ekinci) v SSHD* [2003] EWCA Civ 765.

53 *R (on the application of Kussin) v SSHD* [2009] EWHC 358 (Admin), para. 29.

54 *VW (Uganda) v SSHD* [2009] EWCA Civ 5 [43].

55 *R (on the application of GA Iraq) v SSHD* [2009] EWHC 2403 (Admin), para. 18.

critical (although the nearness of the miss may affect proportionality).[56] In fact, some doubt about the parties' ability to maintain themselves had previously been canvassed before the Court of Appeal (Seddon 2008).

On the second question, leave to remain as a spouse requires prior leave of a particular type. Applicants in *Chikwamba*-type situations do not meet this requirement of the rules and so do not qualify for a spouse visa, which normally leads to indefinite leave after two years. By contrast, successful Article 8 claimants are awarded discretionary leave under which indefinite leave is available only after six years. In *Abdelghani*, the applicant, who had been granted discretionary leave due to the ill health of his wife, argued that the only reason he did not have a spouse visa was that he could not travel abroad and thus meet the Immigration Rules and he should not be disadvantaged by having to wait six years for a secure status.[57] The High Court was sympathetic to his predicament and found that the application of a six-year wait would be unlawful if routinely applied and might always be so in a *Chikwamba*-type case. However, the solution lay in a challenge to the discretionary leave provisions rather than to the Immigration Rules. Leave that is granted for Article 8 reasons should not itself become subject to the rigid requirements that cases such as *Chikwamba* aimed to remedy, an argument that could presumably be extended to those granted discretionary leave because they did not meet other more substantive requirements of the rules.

Delay

Delay by the UK immigration authorities was endemic throughout this period. Such delay was often argued to make a case 'exceptional' and resulted in some successes before the Tribunal.[58] Given the extensive delays in decision-making, many applicants might rely on family life established while awaiting a decision to resist refusal and the issue soon came before the higher courts. In *Shala*, the Court of Appeal found that the four years taken to decide the applicant's asylum status made removal after his marriage disproportionate.[59] Had his claim been dealt with more promptly, he would have been granted exceptional leave to remain, entitling him to make an in-country marriage application. Later cases distinguished *Shala*, limiting its potential impact, although some cases that were exceptional even by the abysmal standards of the Home Office succeeded.[60] The Court of Appeal

56 *MB (Article 8 – near miss) Pakistan* [2010] UKUT 282 (IAC).

57 *R (on the application of Abdelghani) v SSHD* [2010] EWHC 1227 (Admin).

58 *GX v SSHD (Kosovo)* [2002] UKIAT 03352; *MH v SSHD (Pakistan)* [2002] UKIAT 04685.

59 *Shala v SSHD* [2003] EWCA Civ 233.

60 *N (Kenya)* [2003] UKIAT 00102; *K (Russia)* [2003] UKIAT 00082; *RS (Spouse's pending claim: removal bar?) Sri Lanka* [2004] UKIAT 00195; *Strbac v SSHD* [2005]

sought to establish some general principles in *HB*.[61] It emphasised that *Shala* was concerned with procedural rather than substantive questions. The applicant had a claim under the Immigration Rules and the only question was whether he should be required to leave the UK to apply for entry clearance.

In the House of Lords judgement in *EB Kosovo*, Lord Bingham found that delay could affect the strength of an Article 8 claim in three ways:

- families ties will intensify over time;
- consciousness that status is precarious and that the relationship may be disrupted will weaken as time goes on; and
- a dysfunctional system, which yields unpredictable, inconsistent and unfair outcomes, reduces the weight to be attributed to a 'firm and fair immigration control' (Lord Brown dissenting).[62]

The clarity of the judgement cut across the complexity of the previous case law and, in particular, distinctions between those who had a 'right' to enter independent of delay and those who did not. While the strength of the original claim might be a factor, it should not, under Article 8, be determinative. Of the three factors, the most potentially far-reaching was the third. Delays were endemic within the asylum system during this period and it might be argued in many cases that the system was dysfunctional, although there does not seem to be any indication that the principle was widely applied, either because the delay was less damaging than in *EB (Kosovo)* or the applicant's claim was less pressing.[63]

Summary

This section of the chapter has highlighted some significant cases relating to Article 8 and family, including marriage, migration. In successive cases, the House of Lords considered issues that affected migrants, often with irregular status, who faced removal despite family ties in the UK. In each instance, lower courts had taken a restrictive view of Article 8, relying on criteria such as 'insurmountable obstacles' or 'exceptionality' to defeat the claim and deferring to the demands of immigration control. The House of Lords, as it then was, returned to the spirit of Article 8 and the Strasbourg case law, insisting both on a flexible approach, as mandated by Article 8, and on a true recognition of the human claims at stake.

The cases discussed here were the not the only ones issued by the House of Lords or, latterly, the Supreme Court in the field of family migration. Two more

---

EWCA Civ 848; *Jaha v SSHD* [2005] EWCA Civ 968; *SSHD v Abbas* [2005] EWCA Civ 992; *SSHD v Akaeke* [2005] EWCA Civ 947.

61 *HB and others v SSHD* [2006] EWCA Civ 1713.

62 *EB Kosovo v SSHD* [2008] UKHL 41 [14]-[16].

63 See, for instance, *R (on the application of Omoruyi) v SSHD* [2008] UKHC 3120 (Admin).

important cases, *Mahad* (not determined on Article 8 grounds) and *Baiai* (an Article 12 case), are discussed in the next section. The overall significance, in terms of the concerns of this book, of this wave of high-level case law is discussed in the conclusion to this chapter.

Other Case Law

As well as the human rights issues already discussed, the courts continued to consider the questions that had also concerned them in the preceding period, together with some new ones.

Intention to Live Together

After the abolition of the primary purpose rule in 1997, the main test for deciding if a marriage was genuine became the requirement for the parties to show that the marriage was 'subsisting' and that the parties intended 'to live permanently with the other as his or her spouse or civil partner'.[64] 'Intention' did not become the source of controversy in the same way as 'primary purpose' and relatively few cases came before the courts or the Tribunal. Some of those that did involved cases where visa officers had confused the motive or purpose of the marriage with the parties' intentions for the future, thereby applying a test that was closer to 'primary purpose' than 'intention'.[65] Other cases included *Olofinusi*, in which Sullivan J found that intention was present, although the UK-settled spouse was unwilling to live elsewhere than in the UK, an issue that had previously been decided the other way in *Sumeina Masood* (see Chapter 4).[66] In *BK*, the parties had experienced difficulties in their marriage but now intended to cohabit.[67] The Tribunal found that a marriage is subsisting if it exists in law. The requirement to show intention provides the opportunity to investigate whether it has substance. However, in the starred determination of *GA*, the Tribunal held that this was mistaken and that 'subsisting' refers to the present state of the marriage while 'intention' looks to the future.[68]

Not every married couple cohabits all the time. In some unreported cases, the Tribunal was sympathetic to couples separated by economic necessity or similar circumstances (Clayton 2006b: 293-4). The reported cases, however, demonstrated little sympathy for unorthodox relationships. Where the husband was in prison, intention was found to be absent as cohabitation would have been unlawful in the

64 HC 395, para. 281(iii).

65 For example, *ECO Islamabad v Nasir Mahmood* [2002] UKIAT 01034; *Anju Malik v ECO New Delhi* [2002] UKIAT 00738. See also Wray 2006c.

66 *R (on the application of Olofinusi) v IAT* [2002] EWHC 2106.

67 *BK and others v ECO Ankara* [2005] UKAIT 00174.

68 *GA ('Subsisting' marriage) Ghana* [2006] UKAIT 00046.

circumstances.[69] Sometimes the absence of sympathy took a more cultural turn. Where a polygamous husband intended to spend six months of the year in the UK with his second wife, intention was considered to be absent even though the couple had a child. The Tribunal distinguished this instance from others involving periods of separation because of the regularity and permanent nature of the polygamous arrangement.[70] A troubling case was *ZB and HB*.[71] This case also concerned the validity and recognition of marriage and these concerns seem to have infected the findings on intention. The sponsor in this case was disabled mentally and physically. He had visited his wife, who was also his second cousin, in Pakistan and she had given birth to a child of the marriage. The wife now applied for entry. The Tribunal clearly found the facts of the case disturbing. However, they seemed to veer close to a primary purpose finding in holding her lack of knowledge of the sponsor and her wish to improve her son's educational opportunities against her. They found that she had not established that she wanted to be with the sponsor 'as his wife' (para. 16), yet they acknowledged that the parties had cohabited and had had sexual relations, that she wished to care for the sponsor and that, as an uneducated, illiterate woman, she had few other prospects in the UK. It seems likely that they regarded a companionate relationship as the missing element in the marriage when they said: 'The requirements of sub-para 281 (iii) are not met simply by a wish to share a house, nor by a wish to look after the (non-disabled) sponsor, or a wish to alleviate the care responsibilities imposed upon the sponsor's mother by her relatives' (para. 16).

There are policy issues surrounding the recognition of marriages involving those with mental disabilities concerning the necessity for meaningful consent to marriage and sexual relations. These issues are usually presented as questions of validity, although questions as to the ability of the disabled party to have an intention might be relevant (as was also the case here). However, by focusing on the applicant's intentions, the Tribunal extended the question of 'intention to live together' into more value-laden territory. If some marriages are regarded as unacceptable, such a view should not be disguised by misapplying a test that is designed for different purposes.

Maintenance, Public Funds and Third Party Support

The Immigration Rules require that the parties should be able to maintain and accommodate themselves adequately without recourse to public funds.[72] Such requirements are not usually regarded as objectionable in principle, even though they disadvantage some sections of the population, because barring new entrants from access to welfare is seen as a precondition of public acceptance of immigration.

69 *SB v Entry Clearance Officer, Islamabad* [2002] UKIAT 06623.

70 *AB Bangladesh* [2004] UKIAT 00314.

71 *ZB and HB (Validity and recognition of marriage)* [2009] UKAIT 00040.

72 HC 395, para. 281.

The minimum requirements in the UK are also not onerous compared to some other European states and are equivalent to minimum income under the welfare regime (although parties who can live more frugally are not permitted to do so).[73] Nonetheless, maintenance and accommodation requirements are an area of policy into which other policy considerations have sometimes intruded, as demonstrated by disputes around disabled sponsors and third party maintenance.

The government was strongly opposed to permitting reliance on third party support of married couples and other family members, seeing it as insufficiently reliable and verifiable.[74] This argument was not entirely persuasive. Other more acceptable sources of support, for example, a sponsor's employment, may, on the facts, be more precarious than a well-established parent's offer of assistance. Evidential questions can be decided on a case-by-case basis. The resistance to third party support seemed to favour the European model of the nuclear family, in which only the immediate family undertakes financial support. In *Arman Ali*, Mr Justice Collins found that, given that the underlying purpose of the rules was to prevent reliance on public funds, it would breach Article 8 to exclude reliance on third party maintenance or accommodation.[75] Following *Arman Ali*, short-term support for spouses was upheld in the starred determination of *Amjad Mahmood*.[76] The Immigration Rules were subsequently amended to require children to be maintained by and accommodated with the sponsoring relative, and the Tribunal in *AA* found that *Arman Ali* could no longer be relied upon for children, a position upheld 'with some regret' (para. 20) by the Court of Appeal in *MW*.[77] Meanwhile, tribunal decisions on third party maintenance for spouses were inconsistent.[78]

The issue eventually came before the Court of Appeal and then the Supreme Court. The Court of Appeal hearing in *AM (Ethiopia)* brought together five appellants, including a 76-year-old Somali man whose wife, a British citizen, and five children lived in the UK.[79] A daughter and a cousin were providing financial support. One of the other parties was also a spouse, while the other appellants were different family members. The court was sympathetic to the applicants' plight but found that the rules did not permit third party financial support, although assistance with accommodation was permitted. The rules did not embody any underlying purpose such as the enabling of family life and did not have to be

---

73 *KA (Pakistan)* [2006] UKAIT 00065, para. 6.

74 *Mahad (Ethiopia) v ECO* [2009] UKSC 16 [18].

75 *Ex p. Arman Ali v SSHD* [1999] EWHC Admin 830.

76 *Amjad Mahmood v ECO Islamabad* [2002] UKIAT 01819.

77 *ECO (Dhaka) v AA* [2005] UKIAT 00105; *MW (Liberia) v SSHD* [2007] EWCA Civ 1376.

78 *AK and others (Long term third party support) Bangladesh* [2006] UKIAT 00069; *KA and others (Adequacy of maintenance) Pakistan* [2006] UKAIT 00065; *AM (Third party support not permitted R281(v))* [2007] UKAIT 00058; *AB (Third party provision of accommodation) v ECO Islamabad* [2008] UKAIT 00018.

79 *AM (Ethiopia) v Entry Clearance Officer* [2008] EWCA Civ 1082.

construed to comply with Article 8, which could be applied outside the rules. The court proposed joint sponsorship as a possible solution, although without ruling on whether this was currently permitted.

The appeal from *AM (Ethiopia)* was heard in the Supreme Court as *Mahad*.[80] The court, in a unanimous judgement, agreed that the rules did not embody any particular policy and were to be interpreted according to their natural and ordinary meaning. From such a reading, in the context of the Immigration Rules as a whole, it was apparent that the overall purpose of the rules on maintenance and accommodation was to prevent recourse to public funds and that they did not contain any prohibition on third party assistance, including to children. Lord Brown, giving the leading judgement in forthright terms, found that 'third party promises' were not necessarily less reliable than other types of support and asked at para. 19: 'Are rich and devoted uncles (or, indeed, large supportive immigrant communities such as often assist those seeking entry) really to be ignored in this way?' The reliability of the evidence was, of course, for the applicant to establish, but there was no reason why it should not be considered. Whether, if the rules had not been so construed, they would have to be read to comply with Article 8 was not a question that had to be decided given the interpretation they had already been given. While the findings on third party support made the joint sponsorship question less pressing from the applicants' point of view, it remained open to the Secretary of State to seek sponsorship undertakings from more than one person.

Mahad also upheld a finding in the Court of Appeal that a recipient of disability benefits could use these to sponsor a spouse.[81] This had overturned decisions in the Tribunal that such benefits recognised the disabled person's additional needs and were not a 'bonus' to be spent as the sponsor chose.[82] This finding, with its controlling overtones, had, in its turn, overturned older cases that such enhanced benefits could be used to sponsor, provided sufficient surplus income was established (Clayton 2006b: 287-8). The sole note of caution was a dissenting judgement in the Court of Appeal by Pill LJ, who hinted that he feared abuse of disabled spouses. This concern reflected wider concerns about the exploitation of disabled sponsors, already alluded to on the question of 'intention' and discussed below in relation to the validity of marriage. However, where abuse is not specifically alleged, it is difficult to see why disabled sponsors should be denied agency in the use of their funds. They may prefer that care and services are provided by a spouse than by a paid carer, for example.

80 *Mahad (Ethiopia) v Entry Clearance Officer* [2009] UKSC 16.

81 *MK (Somalia) v Entry Clearance Officer* [2008] EWCA Civ 1521.

82 *MK (Adequacy of maintenance-disabled sponsor) Somalia* [2007] UKIAT 00028; see also *AM (Third party support not permitted R281(v))* [2007] UKAIT 00058.

Domestic Violence

The two-year probationary period for spouses meant that vulnerable migrants might remain in an abusive marriage to avoid removal, particularly if they feared hostility or ostracism in their country of origin due to the failed marriage. A concession permitting indefinite leave if the marriage ended during the probationary period due to domestic violence was, in 2001, incorporated into the Immigration Rules.[83] Some problems in using the provision were discussed in Chapter 7. Another difficulty was that the rule required an applicant to 'produce such evidence as may be required by the Secretary of State'. The Immigration Directorate Instructions (IDIs) specified the types of evidence that should be produced.

In a series of cases, the courts were asked to decide whether the list contained in the IDIs was exhaustive or whether other forms of evidence might satisfy the rule. Two competing values were in play. From the government's perspective, the domestic violence provisions represented an exceptional concession whose boundaries must be strictly delineated to avoid abuse. The opposing view was that decisions should be made according to the merits of the case, not the ability to produce evidence in a particular form. A restrictive view was adopted in earlier cases.[84] However, in *JL*, the Tribunal found that the evidential requirements contained in the IDIs were not binding on them.[85] Parliament would not permit one party to control an independent tribunal's fact-finding. The outcome was supported by the Court of Appeal in *Ishtiaq*, which found that the rule should be interpreted purposively to further the policy aim of allowing victims to acquire indefinite leave.[86]

Nonetheless, victims of domestic violence faced formidable hurdles. They had to establish that violence caused the break-up of the relationship during the probationary period. The requirement assumed expectations and knowledge that might be absent in immigrant women struggling with language, culture, shame and dependency. The courts showed some sympathy. In *B*, the wife left the matrimonial home after the husband made an allegation of assault against her (she was later acquitted on the grounds of self-defence).[87] After divorce and termination of her leave, but in response to continued harassment, she obtained an injunction against her former husband. The Court of Appeal accepted that the husband's violence predated the parties' separation and that, while his assault allegation had been the precipitating cause of the separation, it was his prior conduct that caused the marriage to break down. The Tribunal in *LA (Pakistan)* pointed out that, while a

83 HC 395, para. 289A.

84 For example, *S (India)* [2003] UKIAT 00162; *R (on the application of Manpreet Kaur)* [2004 EWCA Civ 818; *RH (Para 289A/HC395-no discretion) Bangladesh* [2006] UKAIT 00043.

85 *JL (Domestic violence: evidence and procedure) India* [2006] UKAIT 00058.

86 *Ishtiaq v SSHD* [2007] EWCA Civ 386.

87 *R (on the application of B) v SSHD* [2002] EWCA Civ 1797.

relationship formally ends at the moment one or both parties decide to leave, the cause of the breakdown can only be assessed by looking at the relationship as a whole.[88]

On the other hand, in *IN*, the violence was not reported until after the expiry of the wife's probationary period.[89] She told her GP that she did not complain earlier 'because of the Asian culture' and even the sceptical immigration judge accepted that there had been 'difficulties ...at a relatively low level' during the probationary period, including at least one incident of physical and verbal abuse. However, because the wife attempted reconciliation and did not finally leave her husband until after more incidents, the Tribunal found that the separation was not due to the earlier violence and that the domestic violence rule could not be used to remedy overstaying. These findings ignored victims' vulnerability. As happened here, an abusive spouse may prevent a timely indefinite leave application being made or a confused and disoriented applicant may not appreciate the need to apply in time.

The requirement also penalised those who tried to save their marriage. In the words of the out-of-time applicant in *Begum*: 'I wanted the marriage to work for the sake of our children.'[90] The judge found that this admission conflicted with the requirement to show that the relationship ended before the expiry of the probationary period. However, he drew a distinction between the end of the marriage and the breakdown of the relationship, pointing out that the relationship may end before the parties stop cohabiting.

Given that the application presupposed the end of the married relationship, Article 8 applications in this area faced difficulties. In *NG*, the Court of Appeal found that a woman with two small children who left a violent marriage could not rely on Article 8 to remain in the UK.[91] Following *Beoku-Betts*, the relationship between children and the UK-resident parent should be taken into account by the court. However, here the Court of Appeal upheld earlier findings that the relationship could continue through visits and other contact. In *Begum*, discussed above, the young age of the children and the absence of contact between them and their father also meant that the Article 8 claim failed even though the children were British citizens.

The Certificate of Approval Scheme

The legislative history and nature of this scheme were discussed in Chapter 7. In essence, the scheme required migrants to obtain permission to marry in the UK, which would be refused to irregular and short-term migrants. The scheme did not apply to those marrying in the Church of England. There were three High Court

88 *LA (Pakistan) v SSHD* [2009] UKAIT 00019.

89 *IN (Domestic violence – IDI policy) Pakistan* [2007] UKAIT 00024.

90 *R (on the application of Parven Begum)* [2010] EWHC 1897 (Admin), para. 15.

91 *NG (Pakistan) v SSHD* [2007] EWCA Civ 1543.

decisions on the scheme, a Court of Appeal decision and a judgement in the House of Lords.[92]

The combined effect of the High Court decisions was that, so far as those lawfully present were concerned, the scheme breached Articles 12 (right to marry) and 14 (prohibition of discrimination) ECHR as it was not rationally connected to the legislative purpose, was disproportionate and discriminated by race and nationality. However, refusal of a certificate of approval to an unlawfully present applicant remained compatible because of the weight awarded to the interests of immigration control, reasoning that was not entirely congruent with the court's other findings. The Court of Appeal found that the High Court had accorded too much deference to the Secretary of State. Although Article 12 was qualified, these qualifications did not permit interference with genuine marriages for the purposes of immigration control. The protection afforded by Article 12 extended to those present without leave (although the court suggested that a differently constructed scheme might be compatible).

The House of Lords found unanimously that the scheme and its application breached Article 12 ECHR, which was a strong right that could be regulated but that could not be made subject to conditions that impaired its essence. The only part of the statutory scheme that breached the ECHR was the distinction between Church of England and other ceremonies, which was discriminatory. Otherwise, the incompatibility was in its application and would be remedied if, where there was no evidence of a sham marriage, a certificate of approval was granted and the scheme as a whole (including the fee) did not 'unreasonably inhibit' the exercise of the right to marry. The government's defective implementation of the judgement was discussed in Chapter 7.

Validity of Marriage and Divorce

The Immigration Rules require that a marriage visa applicant 'is married'. This simple phrase conceals the need to make complex judgements across legal and cultural boundaries. Some earlier case law was discussed in Chapter 4. Cases in the period discussed here were dominated by two concerns: the continuing issue of the validity of a marriage ceremony or of the preceding divorce and a new question – marriages entered into by UK residents that might be valid under local law but that conflict with majority norms and values in the UK.

The first issue was essentially one of correcting mistakes made by visa officers. These cases do not usually come before the higher courts and tribunal findings are most appropriately discussed in the next chapter, which considers whether the

92 *R (on the application of Baiai and others) v SSHD* [2006] EWHC 823 (Admin); *R (on the application of Baiai and others) v SSHD* [2006] EWHC 1035 (Admin); *R (on the application of Baiai and another) v SSHD* [2006] EWHC 1454 (Admin); *SSHD v Baiai and others* [2007] EWCA Civ 478; *R (On the application of Baiai and others) v SSHD* [2008] UKHL 53.

visa service found it excessively difficult to resolve issues of validity correctly. The second question involved broader policy questions. The key case here is *KC*, which was heard in the Court of Appeal.[93] This was not an immigration case but it raised critical questions for the control of transnational marriage migration. It involved a young British man (IC) of Bangladeshi descent and British domicile who suffered from severe mental disabilities, having skills below those of an average three year old. Through his guardian and father, he entered into a telephone marriage with a Bangladeshi woman. The court accepted that the marriage had been conducted in Bangladesh and was valid under Bangladeshi and Muslim law even though, under the law of his domicile, IC lacked the capacity to enter into a marriage. The marriage was thus voidable according to UK law but not void, i.e. it remained valid until a court order of nullity. The question was whether it should be recognised by the UK court as a valid marriage, as had occasionally happened on previous occasions where overseas marriages involving UK domiciles did not conform to UK rules on capacity, for example, because of consanguinity. The case thus became one where a policy decision had to be made. Although the court had the power to recognise the marriage, in this case, it chose not to because the question of consent was regarded as critical.

The case revealed clear differences in the way marriage was conceptualised. As the court pointed out, it was unthinkable, according to British cultural and legal norms, that IC should marry. He was incapable of understanding and consenting to such an arrangement and any attempt at sexual relations would be regarded as abusive and criminal. Marriage was, from that perspective, likely to be harmful to him. The family's perspective, based on their Bangladeshi and Islamic heritage, was different, as Wall LJ acknowledged in his judgement. They regarded marriage as being to his benefit as it procured his long-term care. His guardian, who was his father, could consent on his behalf. Given the deep-seated moral objections from a majority perspective, going to the heart of how intimate relations are conceptualised, it is unsurprising that the court refused recognition even if the profoundly different view was acknowledged and accorded some respect. The case perhaps indicates where the outer limits of mutual accommodation between different cultures and normative systems may be located.

IC's lack of capacity was manifest and the case was not itself concerned with spouse immigration, although such an application was contemplated. However, the same question arose in the spouse entry case of *ZB and HB*, already discussed in relation to the question of intention, where the danger of blurred boundaries in such cases is demonstrated.[94] The sponsor in this case was less disabled than IC and, while the Tribunal therefore could not reach an unequivocal conclusion on capacity, its doubts on the issue seeped, as already discussed, into discussion of the parties' intentions, leading to a refusal based, at least partly, on distaste

93 *KC v City of Westminster Social and Community Services Department* [2008] EWCA Civ 198.

94 *ZB and HB (Validity and recognition of marriage) Pakistan* [2009] UKAIT 00040.

for the marriage arrangements rather than on the fundamental objections given expression in *KC*.

Judicial Decision-Making: Conclusion

This chapter has been divided thematically into two parts, one concerned with the courts' application of Article 8 ECHR to married couples and families facing separation, and the other addressing judicial treatment of specific aspects of the marriage migration rules. In fact, another division could have been imposed: one between decisions by the House of Lords, later the Supreme Court, together with a handful of cases from elsewhere within the court system and the rest.

Most lower court decisions maintained the deference or caution in immigration matters that characterised the period before 1997.[95] In particular, their application of Article 8 was, in most respects, conservative, upholding the exclusion of spouses regardless of the hardship faced by the UK resident party, who often faced exile or separation due to their choice of spouse. The maintenance for a long period of a review function and the rigid application of criteria such as 'insurmountable obstacles' or 'exceptionality' arguably reflected an out-of-date approach to Strasbourg jurisprudence and failed to take account of more recent developments (Rogers 2003, Macdonald and Webber 2005: 430-1 and Macdonald 2008). Meanwhile, in decisions relating to public funds, domestic violence and the meaning of 'subsisting', the lower courts often (although not always) tended towards supporting and enabling control mechanisms. Of course, they were not always wrong to do so. Not every immigrant's claim is rightly made according to the law. Nonetheless, there were many instances where the judicial conservatism in immigration that was widely noted in the past (see the discussion in Chapter 6) seems to have continued even after the implementation of the Human Rights Act.

Without a full evaluation of the range of case law, it is not possible to assert that judges demonstrated more restraint in immigration issues than in other areas under the Human Rights Act, although some have suggested the possibility (see Leigh 2002: 276-7 and Clayton 2007: 317 for a critique of *Mahmood* and *Samaroo* in relation to other Article 8 cases). Nonetheless, for a period, many were disappointed by the courts' overall approach to deference, arguing that this was mandated neither by the Human Rights Act itself nor by the ECHR jurisprudence (Edwards 2002, Leigh 2002, Clayton 2004 and Ewing 2004). The legal formulation of deference, the 'margin of discretion', was a domestic judicial creation and was arguably applied too broadly and uncritically (Craig 2001 and Edwards 2002).

This self-limiting must be seen in the particular contemporary context. The Human Rights Act represented 'an unprecedented transfer of political power from the executive and legislature to the judiciary' (Ewing 1999: 79) and there was much

95 The term 'deference' is used here, although it is argued by some to be unsuitable as it suggests that the judiciary is refraining from legitimate intervention; see Dickson 2006: 340-1.

anxiety prior to its enactment at the 'serious question of democratic legitimacy' it posed and at the potential politicisation of the judiciary (Stevens 1999: 368-72). Judicial self-restraint acknowledges that the legitimacy of judicial intervention remains contested (Nicol 2006) and may bring legislative retaliation, as in the failed attempt to impose a judicial review ouster clause (Rawlings 2005). Judicial reticence has perhaps had more to do with judges' 'self-limiting institutional norms' (Judge 2004: 693) than with attitudes towards litigants. However, Judge (2004: 691-2) also comments that such reticence is 'based upon an idealised conception of parliamentary sovereignty rooted in an acceptance of the Westminster model. Rarely does the reality of executive dominance and "executive" sovereignty intrude into this view'. Failing to acknowledge this reality arguably permitted an impoverished view of democracy to prevail.

However, this critique of the judiciary must be read in the light of the series of House of Lords/Supreme Court cases discussed here beginning in 2007, all of which found against the government in key respects (*Huang*, *Beoku-Betts*, *Chikwamba*, *EB (Kosovo)*, *Mahad* and *Baiai*). Taken together, this case law suggests a more value-driven approach and that the upper courts 'have begun to see human rights as constitutive of democracy rather than ranged against it' (Fredman 2006: 54). The House of Lords judgement in *Huang* recalls that human rights apply to human beings even if their presence is unsanctioned. There is also the assertion of a distinct role for the courts in protecting those excluded by majoritarian politics. *EB Kosovo* and *Chikwamba* demonstrate a readiness to place greater weight on the human cost of immigration control. *Beoku-Betts* suggests a will to give practical effect to human rights. *Mahad* was decided according to principles of interpretation rather than human rights, but its ethos was consistent with the other case law. *Baiai* makes it clear that government schemes must bear some relation to their stated aims.

Some Court of Appeal judgements towards the end of the period discussed here (*AB Jamaica* or *LM (DRC)*, for example) suggest that this new emphasis was having an effect on the lower courts, although it was less visible in Tribunal decisions. In 2006, Fredman (2006: 80) argued that the 'UK courts are beginning to construct a system of fundamental values, based on liberty, democracy and equality: but so far only the contours of such values are visible'. The recent higher court decisions discussed here support her contention. Whether, over the long term, the courts will better protect those whom immigration control has otherwise stripped of rights remains to be seen. Others have previously warned against undue optimism (Ewing 2005).

The House of Lords cases discussed in this chapter principally concerned the application by the UK courts of Article 8 ECHR after the implementation of the Human Rights Act. Together, they changed the legal landscape for such migrants even though, in practice, it is likely that only a small number of additional migrants received leave to remain as a consequence. Their significance was twofold. Firstly, they brought the courts into line with the approach taken in Strasbourg towards Article 8, which represented a major cultural shift for courts used to reaching decisions based on pre-determined categories and deciding, often by analogy with previous cases, whether applicants fitted within them. Now, they had broad principles to guide them and were required to apply these to individual circumstances, rather than review their application by another. It seemed that the lower courts were wary of this function, although it was one that the Human Rights Act now required them to undertake. In the words of Lord Bingham in para. 12 of *EB (Kosovo)*, '[t]he search for a hard-edged or bright-line rule to be applied to the generality of cases is incompatible with the difficult evaluative exercise which article 8 requires'.

Secondly, these cases talked about migrants in a different way. In lower level case law, they were usually defined by their irregularity. The predominant consideration was ensuring that immigration controls were not undermined. The tone often implied opportunism and the exploitation of humanitarian impulses. British residents who permitted themselves to be implicated in such wiles had to accept the consequences, however severe these were in terms of the disruption, even destruction, of their family lives. By contrast, the House of Lords cases more fully recognised migrants' humanity. Their lives and their affective and family ties, as well as their breach of immigration controls, were the context for the decisions made. Even the narrative structure of judgements reflected this change of emphasis. In *EB (Kosovo)*, for instance, Lord Bingham opened his judgement with the appellant's history. Before reaching the legal discussion, the reader learns about a boy who, at 13, was forcibly separated from his family and passed through refugee camps before coming to the UK, where he stayed with foster carers before being reunited with an uncle. In his late teens, he met a young pregnant Somali woman, Laetitia, who had also fled her home country and who had been abandoned by her baby's father. The couple lived at the uncle's house and the appellant raised Laetitia's fatherless daughter as his own. By this stage, the reader is emotionally engaged with the story and appreciates how precious such family life must have been. When Lord Bingham goes on to explain that Home Office delays resulted in the appellant missing out on a policy that would have given him secure status as a minor, his proposed removal to Kosovo is elegantly and effectively framed as an act of bureaucratic inhumanity rather than a necessary discipline to preserve the integrity of immigration control.

That does not mean that the legitimacy and importance of immigration control were questioned in these cases. However, they were not given unquestioning priority. A flexible, individuated approach is undoubtedly mandated by the ECHR and correction was necessary. However, reading these cases in succession gives the impression of something more. The strength of expression and the frequency with which reference is made to the emotional lives and human circumstances of the parties suggest a sincere wish to soften the hard edges of government policy, using tools that the same government had given them. Without the Human Rights Act, these cases were unlikely but, even with the Act, they were not inevitable. The Strasbourg jurisprudence is complex, sometimes ambiguous and, on some of the questions decided by the House of Lords, for example, *Chikwamba*, the margin of appreciation would have permitted a more conservative reading.[96] These cases suggest that the highest judiciary, while not unsympathetic to the dilemmas faced by the government, were not willing to permit any means possible for them to be resolved.

This book has argued that the regulation of marriage migration involves an implicit hierarchy of marriages. In the previous chapter, it was argued that, after 1997, questions of compliance and legality became an increasingly critical factor for the government. However, the government did not have its own way in all respects and the courts have, through the cases discussed here, given irregular migrants and their families a somewhat higher standing. In Chapter 7, it was also argued that questions of cultural conformity were gaining in importance. This new approach did not result in any legal challenge during the period discussed here, although the application of the new minimum age for entry and sponsorship was successfully reviewed in the Court of Appeal in late 2010 and it seems probable that any such further measures will also be subject to critical if not unsympathetic scrutiny.[97]

These cases, although immensely important, were nonetheless principally discussions about migrants, their legal and moral rights and deserts. The position of their British-based spouses was acknowledged and it sometimes informed the decision (as required according to *Beoku-Betts*), but they were not at the centre of the argument. That was a natural consequence of the migrant being the applicant, but it also meant that an area of conceptual debate around the rights and expectations of British residents and nationals was not fully explored in the courts or, for the most part, elsewhere. This is a gap to which this book will return in Chapter 10.

96 Contrast, for example, the judgements in *Rodrigues Da Silva and Hoogkamer v Netherlands*, 50435/99, 31 January 2006 with *Omoregie v Norway*, 265/07, 31 July 2008; see also the discussion in Thym 2008 and De Hart 2009.

97 *R (on the application of Quila) v SSHD* [2010] EWCA Civ 1482.

Chapter 9

A Partial Reorientation?: Marriage Migration and the Visa Service 1997-2010

Introduction

Chapter 5 provided a critique of entry clearance decision-making prior to 1997. It argued that administrative attitudes, which resulted in the dismissal of thousands of claims for family reunification from the sub-continent and elsewhere, were congruent with and contributed to broader policy aims. This chapter revisits the entry clearance service, although here it is called the 'visa service' and ECOs are generally called 'visa officers' as the names changed part way through the period (although the term 'entry clearance officer' is used in the account of the field trip as that was the term then in use). The new terminology more accurately reflects the recent position. Most applicants, including Commonwealth nationals, are now visa nationals and apply for visas rather than entry clearance.

This chapter also considers the visa service's role in regulating marriage migration between 1997 and 2010. It argues that the link between administrative practice and policy aims was still present but was more indirect. In the earlier period, entry clearance was seen as unaccountable and secretive, qualities that enabled it to engage in mass refusal from certain regions with little outside scrutiny. There was also evidence of official collusion in exclusionary practice. After 1997, the service was still criticised, but with less vehemence than before. In contrast to the frontier mentality described in Chapter 5, the modern service was integrated into a reorganised immigration service and became subject to modern forms of administrative scrutiny, although the ability of individuals to challenge decisions did not necessarily increase. The service became more efficient and there were at least some efforts to move away from crude stereotyping of applicants, although how far and how deep this went is uncertain.

Entry clearance was formerly run by the Foreign and Commonwealth Office (FCO) and was jointly staffed by the FCO and the Home Office. In 2000, the two departments established the Joint Entry Clearance Unit, which became UK Visas, although it still operated under the umbrella of the FCO. In 2006, the Home Secretary John Reid, addressing the Home Affairs Select Committee, described the immigration system as 'not fit for purpose' and in need of a 'fundamental overhaul' (Home Affairs Select Committee 2006c: Q.866). The Home Affairs Select Committee (2006a: 6) found that '[f]ragmentation and lack of communication is a systemic problem not just within the IND but within the entire immigration system which ought, ideally, to work as a whole'. Reorganisation followed and, in 2009, UK Visas became the 'International Group', one of five operations (the others being Borders, Immigration, Intelligence and Criminality and Detention) within the UK Border Agency (UKBA), a newly-established government agency overseen by the Home Office. Institutionally and organisationally, the visa service was now a branch of immigration control rather than an aspect of British foreign relations, giving it a more control-oriented and defensive function, particularly in the context of the restrictive objectives adopted by the Agency in 2008 and discussed below. However, given the critique made of entry clearance in the past, it is not evident that, in practice, this made a significant difference to how decisions were made, but it did have implications for the role of the visa service in the overall immigration system, as will be discussed below.

During the period discussed here, there was a range of material, much of it officially generated, which scrutinised or explained aspects of the visa service. UK Visas and, later, UKBA published annual reports, five-year business plans and a 'customer strategy', and were subject to public sector performance targets. From 1993, an Independent Monitor for Entry Clearance reviewed refusals where there was no right of appeal. In 2008, the Independent Monitor's functions were taken over by the Chief Inspector of the UKBA, who had a wider remit and more resources. While their reports are not directly relevant to marriage applications, which retained their right of appeal, they provide an insight into the workings of the service. There was also a User Panel, established in 2000, which met twice-yearly and published minutes, which showed discussion between senior staff and leading practitioners and user groups. The Home Affairs Select Committee reported on immigration control, including the visa service, in 2006 (Home Affairs Select Committee 2006a, 2006b and 2006c). The Public Accounts Committee examined entry clearance in a 2005 report (Public Accounts Committee 2005) and there was a detailed Audit Commission report in 2004 (National Audit Office 2004). Meanwhile, policies and guidance that were previously either secret or difficult to access were published on websites.

There was thus a greater degree of official scrutiny of and information about the visa service in comparison with the past. Much (although not all) of this dealt with questions of efficiency and value for money rather than the quality of decision-making. This focus on process and efficiency is not unimportant; the endless delays reported in Chapter 5 created a major obstacle for applicants. But where a visa was wrongly refused, there was little recourse for dissatisfied individuals through these mechanisms. For marriage applicants, redress was through appeal to the Tribunal.

The Role of the Tribunal

Chapter 8 analysed the role of the higher courts who, particularly at the highest level, imposed some constraints on decision-making. However, such cases were relatively few and were generally the result of many years' litigation at lower levels. In reality, the Tribunal had the critical oversight in ensuring compliance on a day-to-day basis.[1] In this respect, it was not wholly successful. Entry clearance appeals were heard in the absence of the applicant (although the sponsor or legal representatives might be present). The ability of each appellate body to determine questions of fact as well as law were complex, but generally became more restricted over the period.

Even where findings of fact could be challenged, evidence of facts arising after the initial decision could not usually be introduced. Until the implementation of s. 85(5) Nationality, Immigration and Asylum Act 2002, the position on that issue had been governed by the 1982 case of *R v IAT ex p. Kotecha*, which held that account could be taken of arrangements which were reasonably foreseeable at the time of the decision.[2] Section 85(5) authorised the Tribunal, in refusal of entry clearance cases, to consider the circumstances at the time of the decision, not the time of the hearing. Post-decision evidence might be used only to establish that the decision was wrong at the time it was made. Thus, post-decision evidence of cohabitation or 'intervening devotion' might show that the visa officer was wrong to disbelieve the parties about their intention to live together.[3] In other cases, reversing the original decision was more difficult. Evidence of post-decision employment, for example, would only be relevant if it showed that the original decision-maker had been wrong to find, on the evidence then available, that parties would be unable to maintain themselves satisfactorily. Good luck would not assist the parties, although the fulfilment of a pre-existing legal entitlement might.[4] The inability of the Tribunal to take account of new circumstances was explained by Lord Hope in the House of Lords decision of *AS (Somalia) v SSHD* as follows:

> ... it is in the best interests of the effective working of the system of immigration control that the facts which an adjudicator has to examine in entry clearance cases should be those found locally by the entrance clearance officer. Questions of credibility and reliability may be in issue which the local officer is likely to be

1 The appeals system was amended twice during the 1997-2010 period. The two-tier system of adjudicator and tribunal established in 1969 was replaced by a single Asylum and Immigration Tribunal in 2005, although there remained the possibility of a second appeal on a point of law within the single Tribunal. In early 2010, immigration appeals were brought within a new unified Tribunal system. Initial appeal was to the Immigration and Asylum Chamber of the First Tier Tribunal, with a further appeal on an error of law to the Upper Tribunal. Here, the term 'Tribunal' is used to refer to any of these appellate bodies, although, in the early part of the period, an immigration adjudicator might have heard the appeal.

2 [1982] Imm AR 88.

3 *OA and OA (Intention to co-habit 'intervening devotion') Nigeria* [2005] UKIAT 00026; *DR Morocco* [2005] UKIAT 00038.

4 *Hashim v ECO Karachi* [2002] UKIAT 00928, where an award of a back-dated benefit increase could be taken into account.

> best placed to determine. He may also be best placed to assess the significance of any fresh information in the overall context.[5]

This approach did not, of course, preclude an appellant arguing that the initial decision had been wrongly decided on the facts as they then stood, but Lord Hope's words articulated continuing deference to the initial decision-maker on factual questions that also characterised judicial decision-making prior to 1997 (see Chapter 4). This deference raised the bar in appeals based on incorrect factual findings. As the Tribunal expressed it in *TM*, 'it is appropriate for an Adjudicator to give proper weight to the views of the entry clearance officer'. While it is true that a Tribunal must consider the case made by either side, the degree of 'weight' given may amount to giving the service an in-built advantage.[6]

The Tribunal also tended to adopt conservative interpretations of the law, as demonstrated by the discussion on the application of Article 8 ECHR or domestic violence in the previous chapter. Even where appeals were successful, the visa service sometimes failed to implement them at least in a timely way or to act upon principles established in unreported findings (see, for example, Shah 2011). As the discussion later in this chapter demonstrates, the visa service appeared alienated to a degree from the legal system. There was also resistance to implementing unfavourable legal decisions at higher levels. It took more than four years from the first High Court decision and more than two years from the House of Lords decision for the discriminatory certificates of approval scheme to be dismantled. With such an example from above, it would not be surprising if lower level decision-makers also sometimes adopted a cavalier approach to the law.

A Changing Role for the Visa Service after 1997?

In the period discussed in Chapter 5, entry clearance had been the single most significant hurdle facing applicants. It was often a formidable obstacle but, once traversed, the remainder of the journey was usually straightforward. Until 1977, parties gained immediate settlement. In that year, a one-year probationary period was introduced for husbands and extended to both spouses in 1985.[7] However, settlement and, if desired, naturalisation were relatively easy to obtain. In contrast, the period after 1997 saw a major expansion in both pre- and post-entry controls. As the Home Affairs Select Committee (2006a: 155) commented, the focus of control could 'no longer remain so heavily weighted towards initial entry and border control'.

---

5 [2009] UKHL 32 [20]. Their Lordships found that Article 8 may sometimes require a different approach, but that was to be decided on a case-by-case basis. More often, the remedy would be a new application based on the new facts.

6 *TM (views of ECO-Weight Attached) Pakistan* [2005] UKAIT 00044.

7 HC 238, HC 503.

Expanded borders were not confined to the UK. Their emergence within immigration control was the subject of an extensive debate in political and sociological theory (some of which is discussed in Wray forthcoming) and in law (Ryan and Mitsilegas 2010), and represented a response to the dual challenges of global migration and global travel which made retaining the focus of control along the frontier both ineffective, as it could not prevent unwanted migration, and inefficient, as it would also disrupt sanctioned movement.

In the UK, pre-entry controls accelerated, particularly after 2006, when new technologies began to be more fully exploited and the immigration service was reorganised to form a single entity. According to a Home Office document, *Securing the UK Border*, published in 2007:

> Border control can no longer just be a fixed line on a map. Using new technology, particularly biometrics, and new approaches to managing risk and intelligence, we must create a new offshore line of defence, checking individuals as far from the UK as possible and through each stage of their journey. (Home Office/Foreign and Commonwealth Office 2007: 2)

Securing the UK Border and a later document, *A Strong New Force at the Border* (Home Office/UK Border Agency 2008a), set out an ambitious programme including biometric visas to 'fix' identity and enable tracking in and out of the UK, increased official powers, a more systematic visa regime, more carrier controls and a tightening of some immigration rules. These added a new layer to existing off-shore controls that already included a widespread visa regime, juxtaposed controls and carriers' liability regimes. They were to be supported by new forms of information sharing and technology, the concentration of functions within the UKBA and increased co-operation with other bodies (Home Office/UK Border Agency 2008a: 23-4).

Post-entry controls also expanded the Public Accounts Committee (2005: 4) and the Home Affairs Select Committee (2006a: 155) both stressed the growing role of these, given that external controls and the traditional border had failed to prevent irregular migration. Powers of deportation were strengthened and increasing removals became a priority, although implementation was problematic. Criminal offences connected with irregular entry or stay multiplied. Appeal rights for asylum seekers were curbed and increased detention and 'fast-tracking' of claims were introduced. Welfare entitlements and working by those in the asylum system were also curbed. Biometric immigration documents (BIDs) were issued progressively to groups of migrants. The points-based system, introduced in 2008, drew employers, educational institutions and other sponsors more deeply into monitoring compliance. Naturalisation and then settlement became conditional on passing language and integration tests. The proposals in *The Path to Citizenship* (Border and Immigration Agency 2008a and 2008b), enacted but not implemented before the 2010 General Election, aimed at making the route to a secure status longer or even impossible for some. Even naturalisation no longer represented unassailable security as powers of deprivation of citizenship were expanded progressively until they mirrored the grounds of deportation.[8]

The traditional border, i.e. the physical frontier, was also strengthened through increased investigative powers and greater use of technology such as electronically chipped passports and information sharing systems.[9] The new technologically-oriented border aimed at ensuring the straightforward passage of those permitted to enter while unwanted migrants were detected and diverted. However, its renewed significance somewhat depended upon the work already undertaken elsewhere, while the rhetoric used suggested that its function was partly symbolic, aiming to restore shaken public confidence: 'At our borders the public is increasingly noticing that our controls are for real' (Home Office/UK Border Agency 2008a: 15). Staff became more 'visible' and even had new uniforms.

Marriage migrants were subject to these new forms of control as well as to some specific new controls. Most of these latter were mentioned in Chapter 7: pre-entry English language testing, raising the minimum age of entry and increasing the probationary period before settlement. By prohibiting in-country switching and introducing the certificate of approval scheme, both discussed in Chapters 7 and 8, the government also attempted to force marriage migrants out of the UK so as to re-enter (or not) through approved channels. As discussed, these efforts were substantially undermined by the courts.

These changes expanded the border, in the sense of points of control over migrants, both temporally and spatially, creating, in the words of Balibar (2002: 85; emphasis in original), a '*grid* ranging over the new social space'. Visa services were an important node on the grid, particularly for legal migration, but other points were coming into existence and gaining in importance, partly because irregular migration often bypassed visa services altogether and partly because there were limits to what they could achieve. The consequence was that while visa services still mattered, they were now only one amongst a range of tools.

However, the argument is not only that visa services were increasingly only one point of control amongst many. There were also new demands on visa services given the different context in which they were now operating. The account of entry clearance in Chapter 5 focused on practices in one region. It was clear that the acceptability of migrants depended very largely on their nationality. For the entry clearance service to treat all applicants from particular countries or regions in the same sceptical or accepting way met the perceived needs of policy at that time. Yet, as argued in Chapters 6 and 7, in the post-1997 period, differentiating between acceptable and unacceptable migrants, including marriage migrants, was no longer only dependent on race and nationality. Not all migrants from previously stigmatised regions were now unwelcome. The previous focus

8 Section 56 Immigration, Asylum and Nationality Act 2006.

9 This arguably reversed a previous tendency to export more responsibility for control to the visa service, for example, the extension to the service in 2000 of the power to grant leave to enter.

on preventing as much migration as possible from the Indian sub-continent was particularly outmoded given that communities of South Asian descent were significant numerically and electorally and that the region represented an increasingly important trading partner and source of skilled migration. A culture of refusal acted against the UK's wider interests in a globalised economy.[10] Of course, other countries, particularly newer countries of emigration, might have less leverage; as discussed in Chapter 6, global inequalities and the security agenda meant that nationality was still relevant. Nonetheless, moving to a more careful and differentiated style of decision-making would seem a rational response to the changing immigration context and would also perhaps represent an acceptable risk given the expansion in other sites of control. UK Visas' 2006/2007 Annual Report, for example, stated that new forms of information 'will allow us to move away from using crude indicators of risk such as nationality'.

The purpose of this chapter is therefore to consider whether such a shift is observable. The analysis is divided into two parts. The first part considers the published documentation in the form of Independent Monitors' reports, select committee reports, etc., while the second part focuses on the role of the visa service in relation to marriage migration and draws on some recent literature and the author's field trip to the sub-continent in 2006.

A Changing Outlook in the Visa Service?

In Chapter 5, it was observed that, of the three institutions considered in this book, the entry clearance service was the least accountable. Complaints about its decision-making and culture of refusal were widespread. Criticisms of the entry clearance process continued after 1997. In 2005, the Joint Council for the Welfare of Immigrants described entry clearance decision-making as 'poor and inconsistent between UK missions, manifesting a lack of understanding of the law, lack of transparent criteria which can be understood by applicants and a reliance on personal value judgements as reasons for entry refusal' (Home Affairs Select Committee 2006b: 82-6). The question explored here is whether, as this criticism suggests, there was direct continuity from the past through to 2010 or whether, as hypothesised in the previous section, the changing role of the service resulted in attempts to raise standards and improve the quality of decision-making.

From 1993, Independent Monitors had reported on decision-making in areas where there was no right of appeal and these reports provide regular snapshots of the condition of the service, although some caution in interpretation is necessary. Monitors brought their own style and priorities to the task. The appointment in 2008 of a Chief Inspector, supported by a team, brought more continuity and resources but also represented a move away from the detailed overview provided by previous

10 A point made explicitly by the High Commissioner at one of the posts visited during the field study discussed below.

monitors. Nonetheless, the reports provide valuable insights into trends in decision-making, although they do not, of course, deal with marriage applications. Reading a selection of reports throughout the period suggests that, while some aspects of poor decision-making proved difficult to eradicate, there was an institutional commitment to improvement.[11] Recurrent problems were familiar and included onerous and inconsistent documentary requirements, excessive scepticism, poorly reasoned refusals and the application of an unlawfully high burden of proof. While posts identified as problematic varied across reports, they were most often found in Africa and Asia, including South Asia, although Eastern Europe also featured. In some instances, serious errors were identified, for example, the treatment of family visitor applications in Accra in the 2003 report (Lindsley 2005). The same report cited many examples of poor decision-making in relation to students and non-family visitors. However, good practice was cited in both that report and earlier ones, and there were many reports of serious efforts to improve efficiency and reduce delays albeit at some cost to quality. The National Audit Office (2004) confirmed that staff were meeting targets as to efficiency (despite rising numbers of applicants) but possibly at the expense of quality. It recommended an increased focus on good quality decisions. The Home Affairs Select Committee (2006a: 34-43) was also concerned that pressure to make decisions on applications compromised the quality of decision-making. Although it was 'impressed by the care and diligence with which entry clearance staff worked ... we felt that they were not always in a position to be able to make good decisions' (Home Affairs Select Committee 2006a: 36). The investigation by the Public Accounts Committee of 2005 found that UK Visas had already made 'significant efforts to streamline its entry clearance procedures in many posts to provide a better and faster service to applicants ... [but] ... also recognises the importance of reaching the right decisions so as to manage immigration effectively and combat terrorism, and is increasing its emphasis on this area' (Public Accounts Committee 2005: 7).

Efficiency mattered, given the delays associated with earlier eras and reported in Chapter 5, but did not necessarily represent improved attitudes towards all applicants. However, the critique in these documents was generally premised on the assumption that good decision-making not only involved the refusal of the ineligible but also the admission of those who did meet the rules. The Home Affairs Select Committee (2006a: 4) expressed the task as follows:

> Refusing applications which should have been allowed is not good customer service, can have significant consequences for applicants and their family and friends, and can lead to increased costs further down the system (from complaints, appeals or fresh applications). On the other hand, allowing applications which

11 The author looked at reports for 1999 (Anson 1999), 2000 (Singh 2001), 2003 (Lindsley 2005), 2005 (Costelloe Baker 2006), 2006 (Costello Baker 2007), 2009 (Vine 2009a and 2009b) and 2010 (Vine 2010a).

> should have been refused weakens the control and public confidence in it and may increase the risk of overstaying and other forms of illegal migration.

The use of the term 'customer', which appears repeatedly in documentation in this part of the period, is revealing in this context. Even if the consumerist language disguised the nature of the rights at stake and the term was inappropriately used by a body with a monopoly over supply, it suggests some commitment to meeting the needs of users.

Consonant with this, the official aims of UK Visas at that time included facilitating the entry of legitimate travellers through provision of an efficient entry clearance service while preventing the entry of those who did not qualify, dealing 'honestly, fairly, sensitively and openly with people', providing value for money and maintaining 'the highest possible professional standards' (Home Affairs Select Committee (2006a: 26). UK Visas' mission statement, as set out in its 2006/2007 annual report, included bringing 'communities together and improv[ing] the UK's competitiveness as a destination for travel, trade, migration and investment through programmes that prevent immigration abuse, deliver value for money and earn public confidence' (UK Visas 2007: 6). Such aims certainly required efficiency but also implied good decisions.

Other evidence also suggests some momentum towards improvement. In 2005, a new Independent Monitor made similar criticisms to those in earlier reports but also found an 'improving trend toward the end of 2005' and a 'willingness to tackle the problem of lack of consistency', even if this was not yet sufficiently focused.[12] In the introduction to her report for the first part of 2006, she wrote:

> On one of my visits to visa issuing Posts overseas, an Entry Clearance Officer told me that had the visa operation remained as it had been when he was first involved some years ago, he would not have wanted to do similar work again. In those days, he explained, in a big and busy Post the apparent aim was to refuse as many applicants as possible. Nowadays he liked being expected to treat applicants courteously; he enjoyed people, not just shifting papers. As Independent Monitor, I am pleased to record a significant improvement in the quality of UKvisas' work as it began to focus more firmly on balance and customer service. The comments from this experienced Officer confirm the marked shift in the way UKvisas approached its work in 2006 – 'How many? How fast?' started to be replaced by 'How good?'[13]

In that report, the Independent Monitor noted ECOs' 'open-minded responsiveness' and 'thirst for good practice development and guidance' (Costelloe Baker 2006:

12 Letter from the Independent Monitor to the Secretary of State for Foreign Affairs, October 2006, accompanying Costelloe Baker 2006.

13 Letter from the Independent Monitor to the Secretary of State for Foreign Affairs, March 2007, accompanying Costelloe Baker 2007.

8). In 2007, UK Visas told the User Panel that '(m)uch work has also been done with visa-issuing Posts to improve ECO decision making'.[14] Risk assessment units were established at most large posts (for a discussion of these, including some problematic issues, see Wray 2006b) and a structured approach to decision-making was promoted (UK Visas 2007: 15), suggesting efforts to reach better reasoned decisions. Customer Service Teams were also announced in 2007 (although the context does not make it clear how far this represented an innovation).[15] The following year, it was announced that the UKBA was developing a 'global customer service delivery strategy' and 'customer service standards' were set.[16]

It is not easy to know whether this drive for improvement was deep or sustained, nor whether it reached all those posts that had suffered from poor treatment in the past. The Chief Inspector's 2008 inspections of particular visa sections were less positive, with decision-making in Abuja described as of poor quality and 'poor value for money to customers who have paid for this service' (Vine 2009a: 3) and Rome as only 'fair' (Vine 2009b: 3). Decision-making in Islamabad was severely criticised in another report, with the suggestion that the additional checks made on applicants there amounted to unlawful race discrimination (Vine 2010a: 26). In his annual report for 2009-10, the Chief Inspector commended the service's openness and willingness to improve, but found that the quality of service provided was uneven and that the quality of decisions was affected by the emphasis on productivity, with the result that customers received a service that was 'not always fair and equitable' (Vine 2010b: 14). As the public mood turned against immigration, new priorities emerged and it is possible that emphasis on customer satisfaction declined. In its 2008-2011 Business Plan, the UKBA's three strategic objectives had become protecting the border, tackling border- and immigration-related crime and, only finally, implementing fast and fair decisions (Home Office/ UK Border Agency 2008b: 10-11). Nonetheless, it seems that both the efficiency of the service and the quality of decision-making were, for at least some of the period discussed here, the subject of official and institutional concern. That does not mean that all applicants necessarily benefited, but it does suggest that there was an attempt to ensure more finely calibrated decisions, moving, in the words already cited of the visa service itself, 'away from using crude indicators of risk such as nationality' (UK Visas 2007: 32).

Marriage Migration and the Visa Service after 2010

If there was some momentum towards improving the quality of decision-making within the visa service, was this extended to marriage migrants and, in particular, to marriage migrants from those regions which had previously received such poor

14 Minutes of User Panel meeting, 12 April 2007.

15 Minutes of User Panel meeting, 25 October 2007.

16 Minutes of User Panel meeting, 21 May 2008 and 9 December 2008.

treatment? There is relatively little evidence on this question, but the available information is considered first, followed by a report of a field trip by the author to the sub-continent.

After the abolition of the primary purpose rule in 1997, there was an improvement in acceptance rates in applications from the sub-continent. In 1995, 66.3 per cent of husbands and fiancés and 27.8 per cent of wives and fiancées were refused. By 2000, the percentages had dropped to 24.89 per cent and 16.8 per cent respectively. While this represented a significant change, refusals were still much higher than in the developed world. While separate statistics for marriage applications were not available for other regions, the overall settlement rate (which would include marriage and other family members) gives an approximate indication. Overall, the refusal rate in 2002 for settlement in the Indian sub-continent was 22.39 per cent and, in Africa, 18.8 per cent. The rate for Oceania was 0.082 per cent and for the USA 0.37 per cent (Wray 2006c: 166). Unfortunately, comparisons over time are not possible as the presentation of statistics changed. On their own, such figures suggest some improvement but little else. Differential refusal rates might be linked to discrimination and stereotypical decision-making or to an inability to meet the criteria in poorer countries.

In a small-scale study of cases near the start of the period, Wray (2006c) found that the Indian sub-continent was over-represented compared to other countries in appeals on 'intention to live together', many of which were successful. However, it was not the only region represented. She also recorded three Tunisian determinations, all involving older women married to younger men they met on holiday. Given that the marriages were shown to have substance in all three instances, refusal seems to have been predicated on the sheer incredulity that relationships between middle-aged women and younger men could have any content beyond exploitation even when, as in one case, the applicant husband was only 14 years younger than the sponsor wife, an age gap which, if reversed, would barely merit comment.

However, the majority (two-thirds) of cases involved the Indian sub-continent while none involved developed countries and many refusals reflected on motive in a way that evoked the 'primary purpose' rather than the 'intention' test, looking at the motivation for the marriage rather than the parties' plans for the future. Other early commentators also found that 'intention to live together' seemed, to some extent, to have replaced 'primary purpose' as a way of refusing (McKee 1999: 3-5 and Macdonald 2001: 430-1). The appeals in the study were heard between 2001 and 2004 and, in all likelihood, related to decisions originally made only shortly after 'primary purpose' was removed. While the legacy of 'primary purpose' and of the culture of refusal that accompanied it lingered after abolition on the sub-continent, it is not clear whether it continued. Certainly, the issue rarely appeared amongst later reported Tribunal cases.

In fact, the marriage rules featured in relatively few reported Tribunal cases throughout the period. One question which attracted some comment was the recognition of marriage and divorce. It was discussed in the previous chapter in the context of recognition of overseas marriages when the UK-based party lacked capacity. However, in practice, such issues usually arose in more mundane circumstances and concerned the validity of either an unofficial or customary marriage or of prior divorce proceedings. A handful of reported Tribunal cases suggested that the visa service was wary of unofficial ceremonies even where these were valid locally. In *NA (Customary marriage and divorce – evidence)*, the Tribunal found that, contrary to the officer's decision, there was no obligation to register a ceremony if to do so was optional under local law.[17] Proxy marriages also occasionally caused problems.[18] There were also a few cases concerning the validity of *talaq* divorce proceedings.[19]

Anecdotally, it appears that problems of recognition of marriage and divorce were more widespread than this small number of reported cases suggests and commentators have been critical of decision-making in this area (Shah 2008, 2010 and 2011a). For instance Shah (2011a) highlights the failure to recognise an unregistered *nikah*, a common and recognised form of marriage solemnisation in India, and a divorce issued by a Bangladeshi court. Elsewhere, Shah (2010) discusses the refusal to accept a telephonic marriage, a proxy marriage and a 'temporary' marriage. It is clear from both Shah's work and that of Menski (for example, 2007) that such cases were not isolated incidents, although how often they arise is not clear. Nor is it known whether the benefit of any doubt was ever given to the applicant as, in those instances, there would be no appeal. It is thus difficult to estimate just how widespread such problems were.

Judging the degree of official failing is also difficult in such cases. Officers may sometime make a poor decision when a better one might reasonably be expected given even minimal knowledge of local norms, for example, the failure to recognise a *nikah*. Of course, like all decision-makers, visa officers occasionally make errors, although major mistakes should be remedied before the appeal hearing. In other instances, the legal issues were more complex or may have been inadequately presented, and some hesitancy is understandable. In the case of the telephonic marriage, for example, which took place between Saudi Arabia and Somalia, even Shah, appointed as an expert in the case, could not be unequivocal. Problems might also be compounded when the parties sought to remedy apparent defects through the use of post-dated or forged documents or the re-enactment of ceremonies, raising questions of forgery as well as validity. The interaction between aspiring migrant and officialdom is, for the migrant, fraught and expensive and, particularly if poorly advised, they may sometimes adopt inappropriate strategies that backfire.[20]

17 [2009] UKAIT 00009.

18 *CB (Validity of marriage: proxy marriage) Brazil* [2008] UKAIT 00080.

19 *Baig v ECO Islamabad* [2002] UKIAT 04229; *NC (Bare talaq – Indian Muslims recognition) Pakistan* [2009] UKAIT 00016.

20 Another instance, reported by Charsley (2006), was the delay by Pakistani Punjabi couples of critical rituals and the preservation of chastity until after the spouse application

If the difficulty of these cases is accepted, the issue becomes one of judgement: was the visa officer using uncertainty about the formal validity of a marriage to refuse applications which were clearly based on extant relationships and which should have been accepted as substantively meeting the criteria? And if this was the case, was it because these types of marriage were associated with particular types of applicant? Against such a perspective, the visa service would doubtless argue that the Immigration Rules require a valid marriage and that it was for the applicant to establish his or her case. Visa officers are not legal experts and their budgets do not extend to obtaining legal opinions on the behalf of applicants. They also work under considerable time constraints and may see it as reasonable to expect the applicant to make his or her own case.

Shah (2011a) takes a sceptical view of these refusals, linking the cases he discusses to 'repeated official attempts to extinguish such [i.e. non-Western] marriages'. He is right to point to the hostile political climate that developed around certain types of marriage and the association between, in particular, Islamic marriage practices and oppressive family norms. As Menski (2007) demonstrates, it was not only the visa service but also the courts and even legal representatives who failed to understand different forms of marriage, with the result that parties might be mired in a series of unproductive legal proceedings. The larger question is whether this was a question of incompetence, official hostility or something in between. Once a refusal was issued, official inertia or intransigence could explain a reluctance to reverse the decision. On the other hand, it seems improbable that the cultural context of these marriages was not a factor, although there is little evidence of official or even unofficial attempts to restrict recognition. The guidance to decision-makers did adopt a conservative and arguably unlawful approach to telephonic marriages (Clayton 2010: 317). One such error is insufficient to argue a consistent policy of non-recognition, but, as Shah points out, the difficult cases cited by him did not show visa officers and their superiors, who review refusals and appeals, making efforts to accommodate doubtful cases, as they might have were they more sympathetically inclined. Perhaps the more likely, although unproven, hypothesis is that such marriages, which showed a reluctance or inability to comply with European norms of documentation and record-keeping, were associated with problematic marriage migrants. Some decision-makers (although how many and how often is undetermined) may have been unwilling to make sufficient efforts to understand marriage practices that were so alien to their own sense of the importance of state-sanctioned rituals.

The approach adopted on third party financial support also suggests some institutional resistance to apparently alien family norms. Guidance to decision-makers adopted a conservative interpretation, ignoring the decision permitting third party support in *Arman Ali*, an omission described as 'regrettable' by the Supreme

had succeeded. This seemed a sensible precaution given the vagaries of immigration control, but it invited suspicions by entry clearance staff, aware of the importance of these rituals, that the marriage was bogus.

Court in *Mahad* (at para. 11; see Chapter 8 for a discussion of these cases).[21] As a result, appeals were made to the Tribunal, which also failed to follow *Arman Ali*. This uncertainty enabled a restrictive approach to be maintained. Applications that cited third party support were likely to involve poor marriage migrants who relied on extended family or community support. On this question, therefore, there seems to have been an institutional tendency to maintain distinctions based on social status and cultural conformity.

If some marriage migrants were thus marginalised in semi-official ways, the arguments made earlier in this chapter would lead one to expect that the decision-making in other cases would be more sympathetic, including in regions where this had previously been so heavily criticised. Given the absence of other evidence on the point, the author undertook a brief field trip to three posts on the Indian sub-continent. The analysis that follows is based on that visit.[22]

The Visa Service on the Sub-continent

Chapter 5 described an entry clearance service in which the unofficial aim, refracted through institutional practice and myriad individual decisions, seemed to be the refusal of as many applicants from the sub-continent as possible. The foregoing discussion suggests that this situation should now be different and that was indeed the impression received during the field trip, although there were also indications of continuing problems.

By the time of the visit, the visa service had become a large-scale process administered by a relatively small number of staff, creating significant administrative pressures.[23] Yet all the posts visited seemed to be efficiently run. The long delays that characterised entry clearance in the earlier periods had almost entirely disappeared. Applications were now made through private agencies in various locations with no significant wait to make an application and much reduced travelling time. Many applicants could attend an agent's office and complete their

21 The incorrect guidance was originally to be found at Immigration Directorate Instructions (IDI), chapter 8, Annex F, para. 5.1 (http://www.ind.homeoffice.gov.uk/policyandlaw/guidance/IDIs, accessed 21 June 2011) but was subsequently amended.

22 This took place in January 2006. Three posts on the Indian sub-continent were visited over ten days. In total, 13 ECOs, entry clearance managers, five locally appointed staff and three senior staff were interviewed, using semi-structured interviews. The author observed all aspects of the decision-making process, including 22 interviews (not all marriage-related), looked at pending appeals at each post and, at one post, had meetings with the High Commissioner and Forced Marriage Unit. She also spent social time, outside working hours, with staff at two posts.

23 For example, one of the posts visited processed more than 150,000 applications during 2005. At the time of the visit, there were three entry clearance managers (due to be increased to 4), 13 ECOs, due to be 14, and 50 local staff, who mainly undertook administrative functions. Temporary staff were recruited to deal with seasonal increases.

application in little more than an hour. Applications were processed the next working day. Where a decision could be made on the papers, it was delivered on the same or the following day, depending on the location. Waiting times for settlement interviews were vastly shorter than in the past, varying between one month and six weeks, within the objectives set in UK Visa's public service agreement (National Audit Office 2004: 12). A decision was made and, where appropriate, a visa was issued immediately after interview. However, a few applicants still faced longer waits. There was, for example, a four-month queue at one post for those previously refused.[24]

ECOs, later called visa officers, remained central to the process as they made the decision to issue or refuse a visa. Unofficial discretion and institutional culture has been recognised as critical to this type of decision-making, often more so than formal or legal constraints (see, for example, Hawkins 1984, 1994, 2002, Loveland 1994 and Halliday 2000) and the individual attitudes of visa officers would both shape and be shaped by the environment in which they worked. Many staff, during interviews and in social situations, expressed an interest in local culture and the dismissive attitudes that might be expected from the account in Chapter 5 were largely absent. Officers spoke sympathetically about the wish of diasporas to maintain family links and of local family life and marriage arrangements. The official (not a visa officer) who ran the forced marriage unit at one post had a sophisticated understanding of the problem, its extent and the limits of intervention. She opposed raising the minimum age for entry and sponsorship to 21 because of the genuine marriages it would affect. It is possible that the officials interviewed or encountered socially during the visit were, on average, more knowledgeable about and accepting of cultural difference than the majority UK-based population. It is, of course, also possible that those individuals who held different views concealed them or chose not to be interviewed, but it was firmly maintained that they represented a tiny minority.[25]

These qualities were reflected in much of the visa work observed during the visit. Officers were seen to treat applications pragmatically, in one instance, issuing a visa to a son, who was just over-age, when the rest of the immediate family were entering the UK. Officers also searched an application for evidence

24 The queue for working holiday-maker interviews was also much longer, being over one year at one post.

25 There were however factors that may have inhibited a full understanding of the country in which they were posted. Most rotations lasted only three years, limiting opportunities to become fully immersed in local life. Relationships between local and UK staff were cordial, but there seemed to be relatively little mixing on a social level with them or with others in the local population (see also Home Affairs Select Committee 2006a: 39). Staff seemed tightly knit, often socialising with each other or with other High Commission staff. In two posts, accommodation and facilities such as a bar, shop and swimming pool were available on the High Commission compound. Their personal lives therefore unsurprisingly tended to revolve mainly around the ex-pat community.

that could satisfy them and expressed regret when they felt obliged to refuse. One application failed on maintenance, but the sponsor had applied for a job with the police. Issuing the refusal, the ECO commented: 'I hope he gets his job before the appeal.'[26] Most interviews (with some exceptions, which are discussed below) were conducted courteously, with efforts to elicit information favourable to the application. Where documents were suspected to be forgeries, they were referred to the Risk Assessment Unit for verification rather than rejected on unsubstantiated grounds.

There were serious discussions between managers and staff about doubtful cases and senior staff seemed greatly preoccupied with efficiency and quality of decision-making. At one post, notorious for its delays and exclusionary culture during the period discussed in Chapter 5, senior staff asked the author to brief them on her findings and she was later advised that some of her suggestions had been adopted. Errors that did occur sometimes favoured applicants. For instance, one officer was ready to issue a visa to the children of a British resident even though the other parent was able to care for them in India.[27] There was no evidence of pressure either from managers or elsewhere in the system to refuse applicants. Administratively, it was easier to issue than to refuse a visa, as refusal entailed obtaining senior approval and writing a refusal notice. Several ECOs commented that, far from there being an institutional bias towards refusal, the pressure was to issue (an argument made elsewhere in the immigration system; Woodfield at al. 2007: 22). ECOs did issue visas where they had some doubts, but it was not clear that, taking the standard of proof into account, they were wrong to do so.

The foregoing account reflects the impressions gained over three visits of three days each and is subject to the qualifications that must apply to such short visits. However, the findings were consistent with the impressions of the independent monitor made at about the same time and cited above. In general, they support the contention made earlier in this chapter that there were efforts to improve the quality of decision-making, at least on the Indian sub-continent. However, the picture was, perhaps unsurprisingly, more ambiguous than the foregoing rosy picture might suggest. There was also evidence that raising the quality of decisions was difficult and that improvement was uneven. In particular, an examination of outstanding appealed decisions (which were waiting for review in-post) showed that there were still a number of poorly formulated refusals that relied on the type of reasoning that characterised earlier decisions. In the context of a marriage application, one applicant was told that the absence of intervening devotion 'does

---

26 The ECO could have issued the visa even without the job if he was satisfied on the balance of probabilities that there would be adequate maintenance, perhaps because employment was likely. However, such a judgement would have been difficult to make on the information available to him. He was also incorrect to assume that the appeal would succeed just because employment was obtained in the interim; see Clayton 2010: 315-6. ECOs' understanding of law is discussed below.

27 See HC 395, para. 297.

not demonstrate a strong bond of affection between you'. Several were told that the ECO was aware that the marriage 'would not be regarded as a suitable match' on the sub-continent. These reasons suggest a focus on motive, as required by the repealed 'primary purpose' rule, rather than the correct approach of considering the parties' intentions for the future. Other refusals relied on minor discrepancies, for example, an applicant (from a small rural village) believed the sponsor's house was rented when it was owned, or on inconsistencies that were easily explicable in other ways, for example, wage slips from a temp agency that showed different amounts each week.

A minority of the interviews observed were also poorly conducted. In some, the questions and the decision were appropriate but the manner was unnecessarily brusque, with no greeting or eye contact. In another, the applicant was an Indian national and failed asylum seeker seeking a spouse visa to regularise his position. The officer involved commented that such applicants 'riled' him because of their non-compliance with the rules and it seemed that the principal purpose of the interview was to inconvenience the applicant. He had established a business, bought a house, was married with children and therefore represented an 'easy issue', as the officer acknowledged. Little was asked during the interview about his compliance with the spouse visa rules, but he faced a series of hostile questions about his entry to the UK, his failed asylum claim and his absconding. This interview suggested sympathy with the priority awarded by the government to formal compliance, although it is not clear how widespread such a practice was.[28]

Occasionally, officers had a poor grasp of the information they needed to reach a decision. One otherwise well-intentioned officer was convinced that he needed evidence of a Western-style marriage to reach a favourable finding on 'intention to live together' even though the applicant was an illiterate village woman with two children. He asked repeatedly about the level of mutual interaction and the parties' hobbies and interests. These questions were met with bafflement. However, after some persistence, he managed to elicit agreement on a few elementary matters (such as their mutual enjoyment of eating rice) and, to his visible relief, he felt able to issue a visa.

It therefore seemed that consistently good decision-making remained elusive. In a few cases, as with the failed asylum seeker, the applicant was personally regarded unfavourably. More often, however, problems arose from institutional pressures or a poor understanding of legal questions. As already discussed, the emphasis of internal reform had largely been upon improving efficiency, with some welcome results. However, the drive towards efficiency, combined with growing numbers of applications, had also increased pressure on staff. Several officers mentioned that they found the job pressurised (for more discussion on

28 Evidence submitted by Brides Without Borders to the Home Affairs Select Committee suggests varying attitudes to those in the position of this applicant. Staff conduct at Jordan is described as 'wonderful' and at the Democratic Republic of Congo as 'unacceptable' (Home Affairs Select Committee 2006c: 346-54).

this issue, see Home Affairs Select Committee 2006a: 40-3 and Wray 2006b: 115-17). It is likely that officers did not always have time to ensure that refusals were well-formulated, an observation also made elsewhere (Costelloe Baker 2006: 39-40, Home Affairs Select Committee 2006a: 37 and Wray 2006b: 122). For speed and convenience, officers relied on standard paragraphs that were adapted to the particular case and some of these were of poor quality. Quality control mechanisms, which mainly consisted of review by managers, were not as effective as they might be (see Wray 2006b: 127-8 for a discussion of this).

Officers were recruited as administrators, not as lawyers, and, particularly under pressure, seemed to adopt routinised patterns of decision-making that precluded an indepth consideration of legal requirements. Officers commented that those outside the service did not understand the pressures they were under, a common complaint in many jobs. However, this sense of misunderstanding extended to the legal system. This alienation has been observed elsewhere, the Home Affairs Select Committee (2006a: 150) referring to 'a lack of mutual confidence between front-line staff and Immigration Judges'. Following a recommendation by the National Audit Office (2004: 26), posts were reviewing successful appeals to identify trends, but some officers expressed private doubts about the value of the exercise and it sometimes ceded priority to other work. Officers interviewed for the study described immigration judges as failing to understand the reality of visa work, of having a romanticised view of the sub-continent and of being over-persuaded by sponsors.[29] Officers sometimes issued visas because they believed an appeal would succeed rather than because they were persuaded of the application's merits. Thus, while almost all aspired to be fair and correct, officers saw judicial oversight as exterior to and even in tension with this aspiration, a hurdle to be negotiated rather than as integral to their decision-making.

Some officers had an uncertain understanding of the standard of proof and the probative value of evidence. While most officers who were asked correctly identified the standard of proof as being on the balance of probabilities, not all appreciated that this required a visa to be issued even if there were substantial doubts. In some cases, this resulted in an unbalanced approach to certain types of evidence. Assessing evidence is not straightforward. Forgery was a preoccupation at all the posts visited and certainly some documents appeared suspicious, for example, the same head superimposed on several wedding photos or a PAYE slip purporting to originate from 'Norwitch'. However, only a small number of applications involved clearly forged documentation. More frequently, the issue shaded into questions of the value of certain types of evidence, for example, wage slips, tenancy agreements, bank statements and used phone cards. Officers correctly pointed out that these could easily be forged or misleading but that they

---

29 Another explanation of the high success rate when sponsors appear was the absence of a Home Office representative at many appeals (around 35 per cent in 2003-2004, although the position subsequently partially improved: Home Affairs Select Committee 2006a: 248-9).

might equally have represented the best evidence available. The result was that officers became involved in making judgements on the 'credibility' of certain propositions. For example, one doubted the probability of a new immigrant without English being offered the post of manager in a jewellery shop. Despite the support of Risk Assessment Units at all the posts visited, it was sometimes impossible for officers to do anything other than reach their own judgement as to the probative value of any document.

The officers interviewed held a range of attitudes. Some were pragmatic, recognising that onerous evidential requirements encouraged the submission of forged documents in otherwise genuine applications (see Costelloe Baker 2006: 27) and that almost any document, including those usually considered highly probative, may be forged or misleading if, for example, a sponsor took employment only for the duration of the entry clearance process. Some also regretted that they were not allowed to consider third party support (see the discussion above and in Chapter 8) and said that they did not investigate documents too closely if they were confident that a couple would be supported. Others however were more preoccupied with detecting fraud or misleading evidence and felt it important to send a clear message of deterrence, arguing that an appeal was available or a new application could be made.

The scope for subjectivity extended to the discovery of the parties' 'intention to live together', the principal test for determining whether a marriage was genuine. Decisions on such a difficult question had to be made in ignorance of the actual extent of sham marriages (Home Affairs Select Committee 2006c: 90). Management at the posts visited advised that refusals on intention alone were rare and, judging by the appealed refusals surveyed, this seemed to be the case. However, 'intention' did appear more frequently in combination with other grounds, suggesting that it was used to 'strengthen' a refusal on other grounds.

A refusal on 'intention' would not be made without an interview. In the interviews observed, officers could not rely on official guidance as to the characteristics and likelihood of a bogus marriage. Although there had been attempts to establish local information, this was confined to financial and related issues (see Wray 2006b: 126-7). Instead, officers had to draw on their personal template of a genuine marriage in the region. Suspicions might be aroused by characteristics such as a large age gap, disability, a prior divorce or even, according to one officer, a male applicant. Officers sometimes articulated their impressions as they made their decisions. These were highly subjective, for example, that sophisticated urban Indians would have substantial knowledge of their spouse, that a loving couple would happily live anywhere or that adultery 'does not happen' in traditional Bangladeshi society. Aspects of the marriage such as hasty arrangements, the absence of photographs and lack of communication between or knowledge of each other might also be significant, particularly if the marriage was otherwise atypical, but an arranged marriage between spouses deemed to be of typical age and involving a typical relationship received relatively little attention. For example, an officer considering what he regarded as a typical sub-continent marriage application between cousins said that he was unconcerned at the absence of contact between them. However, in less conventional cases, evidence of the relationship was critical and was the subject of lengthy interview. In these cases, the application was not pre-destined to fail, but officers were alert to a possible bogus marriage, although, consistent with the attitudes described above, officers seemed to will the parties to succeed, reformulating questions to get the desired answer and making comments such as ‘that’s better’ when applicants gave the ‘right’ answer.

Nonetheless, some applicants failed to give an account regarded as sufficiently likely and refusal followed. Only one such refusal on ‘intention’ grounds was observed during the field visit. The applicant wife (aged 31) had married a man 27 years her senior. Her previous application had been refused partly on the grounds that the match would not be considered suitable in India. Before the interview, the officer commented that parents might well consider that marriage to an older man in the UK was the best option for their daughter and that the previous refusal was reminiscent of primary purpose. There was thus a willingness to revisit that decision. However, the interview went badly. When asked to account for her husband’s divorce, the applicant said that the first wife had a boyfriend whereas, in the first application, she ascribed it to the parties’ inability to have children. She also said that her husband worked in a clothes shop, whereas she previously said he worked in a grocery store. There were problems with maintenance and the application was refused on those grounds and on intention to live together. Despite the ECO’s good intentions, the renewed intention refusal also seemed weak. The applicant maintained that her husband did not previously disclose the boyfriend out of embarrassment, which was a plausible explanation. The inconsistency as to the job was puzzling, but seemed insubstantial to support a conclusion that this was a sham marriage. This particular omission was perhaps the only tangible evidence of more subjective suspicions arising out of the applicant’s off-hand manner and brief answers. This unfavourable impression may be contrasted with a fiancée interview (by a different officer). The applicant had a sister and brother in the UK. No plans had been made for the wedding and, while she recited the names of her fiancé’s employer and his immediate family, she knew little else. The officer issued the visa, in part because of her ‘straightforward and honest demeanour’. He also commented that he would not have issued the visa had the applicant been male.

The subjectivity and unreliability of decisions on intention were further illustrated by another interview. The UK husband was divorced and it was the wife’s first marriage. Before the interview, the officer said that he suspected the husband’s bank statements were forged as the totals did not tally with the entries. Already suspicious, he found himself dissatisfied with the parties’ inability to explain the bank statements and with the wife’s lack of familiarity with the grounds of divorce. He intended to refuse both on maintenance (as, discounting the bank statements, there was insufficient evidence of his finances) and intention to live together. However, a final perusal at the end of the interview revealed that he had misunderstood the statements and that they were genuine. The 'intention' point fell away and the visa was issued.

In the instances discussed here, officers were obliged to make a series of judgements as to the probability of certain things being as claimed. Many of these eluded precise definition and perhaps corresponded to what Woodfield et al. (2007: 25) describe as the 'instinct' felt by immigration officers at ports. Others, such as a greater suspicion of male migrants, were more familiar. This series of judgements explains why decisions could go wrong. Officers were generally well-intentioned but had little firm evidence to rely on so that small calibrations in their views might make a significant difference in a few cases. An atypical marriage was scrutinised more intensely, making misinterpretations more probable. Suspicion as to one aspect of the application might affect the view taken of other aspects. Personal impressions, however misleading, clearly counted (as they do elsewhere in the immigration system: see Woodfield at al. 2007: 20). Experienced and skilled officers might usually avoid these pitfalls. Others might not. When these factors were added to the other institutional characteristics posited earlier, such as the need to reach decisions rapidly, insufficiently rigorous quality control and a degree of institutional resistance to legal supervision, errors (an inevitability in any regulatory system) were more likely to occur and less likely to be rectified. However, while the style of errors often betrayed the historical legacy, there was no evidence that these were systematic or the outcome of an institutional commitment towards large-scale refusal for its own sake.[30]

Conclusion

This chapter has argued that post-1997 changes in attitudes to immigration and the UK's ethnic minorities meant that former patterns of entry clearance decision-making, as discussed in Chapter 5, would no longer be appropriate to the fulfilment of modern policy aims. The available evidence suggests that there were efforts to make visa decision-making more suited to new conditions and priorities and, despite some areas of concern, there was little evidence of engagement in an unofficially sanctioned culture of refusal on the Indian sub-continent of the type discussed in Chapter 5, even if, as suggested above, the service as a whole tended to be slow to acknowledge legal constraints. There were some problematic areas, for example, the reports of poor decisions relating to the validity of marriages, but it is not possible to establish that these amounted to an unofficial policy and the cultural concerns that started to become apparent in the latter part of the period were not widely apparent during the field trip. In fact, the reverse was the case.

30 While personnel was, by the time of the visit, almost entirely different from that present in the earlier era, many officers said that they learnt their craft largely through observation, so that patterns of decision-making may pass through generations of officers.

Early marriages, first-cousin marriages and other traditionally arranged marriages, seen as normal in the local context, were the least likely to attract scrutiny.

There remained a number of refusals that were reminiscent of the attitudes described in Chapter 5, but these were conditioned by a range of institutional and personal characteristics and there was no suggestion that they were systematic or represented attempts to fulfil a policy objective in the manner described in Chapter 5. Visa officers and management were preoccupied with efficiency and quality (and also forgery). These preoccupations were, however, arguably aligned at a deeper level with the broader policy aims identified in this part of the book, which meant that crude discrimination based primarily on nationality was no longer an efficient policy tool. That certainly does not mean that immigration control had lost its ability to exclude but that tools of exclusion were somewhat more finely honed than before or had been displaced elsewhere, for example, to the asylum system. Nor can it be known how widespread or long-lasting such efforts within the visa service were. Regions or countries that were less strategically important than the sub-continent may never have benefited and, even on the sub-continent, policy may have partially reversed as other concerns, particularly around security, became more prominent. Nonetheless, and despite some evidence of continuing poor decisions, it would not be right to characterise the visa service as carrying on uninterrupted the exclusionary practices that had created such distress and anger before 1997.

This book has argued that those engaged in the control of marriage migration tend to rank migrants according to an unofficial and unarticulated hierarchy, the ordering of which depends on values and beliefs held at a particular moment and in a particular institution. When these were held in common, they resulted in a degree of congruence in how marriage migrants were treated across institutions, as was seen in the period between 1962 and 1997. Previous chapters have suggested a partial reordering of the hierarchy in the post-1997 era, although with some differences between the approach of the government and that of the higher courts. The findings of this chapter suggest that the visa service also reoriented itself, if only partially, towards a more refined hierarchy, even if old institutional habits proved difficult to eradicate.

Chapter 10

Conclusion: A Stranger in the Home

Regulating Marriage Migration 1962-2010

As an immigration issue, marriage migration is particularly problematic because it cannot be 'managed' in the same way as labour migration. The invocation of marriage and family has always been a potent (if risky) political weapon serving a variety of ends, but, in relation to immigration, the emotional significance and nurturing function of marriage have been minimised in favour of a reliance upon its role as a cause of immigration. Family formation or reunion has often been seen as a kind of Trojan horse, the apparently straightforward humanitarian claim to live with one's family members carrying less desirable consequences: the importation of unwanted – often male – workers and the recreation on British soil of alien forms of family life. It says much about attitudes towards non-white immigrants that, for many years, their family life was seen to be so potent a danger that they could not be permitted to exercise it within the UK.

This book has traced the regulation of marriage migration to the UK by the legislature, the interpretation of regulation by the judiciary and its application by the entry clearance or visa service. The main part of the book started in 1962, when immigration from the Commonwealth was first formally regulated, and ended in 2010, with a break at 1997 with the election of the Labour government. During much of the 1962-1997 period, the minimisation of non-white immigration was a major political priority. Non-white migrants and their families, often including their UK-born children, were generally regarded as outsiders whose presence was a problem to be resolved in various ways. Skin colour was a defining characteristic, although race discrimination legislation aimed to minimise domestic tensions. As time went on, there was partial incorporation of older immigrant groups who, by 1997, represented a significant electoral force, but new concerns about integration and cohesion soon emerged alongside anxieties about new forms of immigration. Race and racism became more complex and diffuse phenomena.

When Commonwealth immigration was first formally controlled in 1962, there was a strong commitment to enabling the entry of wives and children to join their Commonwealth immigrant husbands. Husbands seeking to join wives were always treated more conditionally. Over time, this gave way to deep suspicion about claims by both husbands and wives, particularly when these originated on the Indian sub-continent. During this period, various measures including a ban on Commonwealth husbands, the primary purpose rule and administrative practises prevented many husbands, wives and children from entering the UK to reunite or form families. These harsh measures were rationalised by claims of abuse and fraud, despite tenuous evidence, and their full effects were disguised by the displacement of implementation onto the sub-continent through the entry clearance system. Nonetheless, their public acceptability suggested widespread resistance to continued non-white immigration. After 1997 and abolition of the primary purpose rule, entrants from the region generally found it easier to enter, although, over time, arranged marriages among migrant communities became increasingly associated with the archaic and coercive and were the subject of renewed scrutiny, while 'modern' relationships such as cohabitating couples and same-sex relationships gained official recognition. Yet, until close to the end of the period in 2010, the government did not act decisively against the arranged marriage, circling around the issue without daring to strike. It appeared cautious about introducing measures that might alienate well-established communities. To that extent, these communities had achieved a protected status of belonging that had previously eluded them, although this was not without reservations.

Meanwhile, others felt the full force of exclusionary measures, particularly the unauthorised or non-compliant – asylum seekers and irregular migrants whose numbers increased after 1997 and who entered marriages while in the UK. They were targets not specifically because of their racial or national origins (although these arguably increased the perception of threat) but because they lacked officially sanctioned status. Government-imposed hurdles (subsequently partially dismantled by the higher courts) represented an ordeal unrelated to the quality of the marriage but which ensured that only those with sufficient commitment succeeded. In all cases of refusal, UK-resident spouses had to choose between separation and exile. The frequently dismissive manner of their treatment suggests that their choice of spouse placed into question their own status of belonging where this challenged the primacy of state power.

Judicial decision-making between 1962 and 1997 engaged not only in the major battlefield of primary purpose but in other less well-publicised areas, including marriages of convenience, domicile, intention to live together and the requirement that the parties had met. Exclusionary measures, particularly primary purpose, were largely supported by the judiciary. While there were some indications of judicial ambivalence, doubts were subordinated to deference both to legislators and administrative decision-makers. During much of the post-1997 period, the judiciary was also unwilling to interfere with government priorities even when government power seemed overbearing and disproportionate. This seems to be connected to wider institutional concerns about the role of the courts after the Human Rights Act 1998 reinforced by traditional deference in immigration matters. Later, particularly after *Huang*, the higher courts became less willing to be complicit in the exclusion of individuals because of their immigration status. However, they were careful to ground their authority for doing this in the legal principles of the ECHR, which they were now mandated to observe, even if they arguably went beyond the minimum necessary for compliance. By setting their challenge to government supremacy within the confines of judicial authority, the difficult political questions involved were minimised.

From the early 1970s onwards, entry clearance played a vital role in ensuring the exclusion of undesirable spouses and, during the 1970s and 1980s, the entry clearance service achieved notoriety for its exclusionary decision-making, particularly on the Indian sub-continent. The service worked in a largely unregulated environment where countervailing pressures and values were absent. Its work, largely hidden from view, permitted other institutions to distance themselves from the practices necessary to achieve a widely-shared aim: the minimisation of non-white immigration. Thus, there was not only congruity in the assumptions upon which all institutions worked but a degree of symbiosis also.

While some entry clearance decisions after 1997 were reminiscent of this earlier period and contributed to a continuing poor public perception of the service, the available evidence suggests that the service was less engaged in perpetuating an exclusionary style of decision-making and, in fact, there was some momentum, at least from about 2005-2006, to improve quality. This was not because harsh decisions were no longer made throughout the service as a whole but because, given new priorities, an exclusionary visa service on the sub-continent no longer served dominant goals of policy so effectively.

A Hierarchy of Marriages

This book has demonstrated that marriage migrants and their spouses were placed on an unofficial and unarticulated hierarchy that depended upon beliefs and assumptions held by decision-makers and which evolved and were readjusted over the period. The chapters that discussed the period between 1962 and 1997 (Chapters 3, 4 and 5) found that the hierarchy was consistent across the three institutions discussed. There was less congruence after 1997. Throughout both periods, the same issues struggled for pre-eminence in determining the form of the hierarchy, although, at various moments, some were less and others more prominent.

Race

Underlying almost all discourse between 1962 and 1997 was the assumption that skin colour mattered and that further non-white immigration was undesirable. The racial aspect of this was often understated and 'immigration' was treated as synonymous with 'non-white immigration'. Decisions made by all three institutions considered here were predicated on the basis that its minimisation was a priority.

Government figures usually avoided explicitly racial discourse, although some were more outspoken than others. However, whatever their private beliefs, almost all tolerated or encouraged administrative practices that were directed towards the exclusion of particular national groups. Aspects of administrative conduct suggest that attitudes within the entry clearance service went beyond willingness to execute a distasteful but necessary task to contempt for these communities. This manifested itself through the reduction of human beings to two-dimensional caricatures governed only by their desire to emigrate, and through humiliation, including sexual humiliation (as with virginity tests), for their presumption in making claims for entry. The judiciary expressed opinions only very rarely, but decision-making mostly supported exclusionary purposes, particularly as the period went on. Although non-white individuals were occasionally treated sympathetically by the courts, skin colour and national origin were almost always critical defining characteristics. For all three institutions, the perception of the threat posed by non-white immigrants and their families resulted in their reduction to stereotypes, a flattening of their individuality.

In the period after 1997, there was some challenge to these assumptions due to increases in immigration, including white immigration, and the partial integration of non-white communities. Signifiers of difference now arguably centred more on culture or religion with some regard for social class. This did not represent an abrupt switch. Cultural difference had always been intertwined with hostility towards non-white immigration, as the distaste for the arranged marriage discussed in earlier chapters demonstrates. However, the role played by skin colour alone arguably diminished and certain types of cultural difference increased in importance, explaining the renewed focus on the transnational arranged marriage.

The Arranged Marriage

Attitudes towards the arranged marriage intersected with assumptions about race. During the period discussed in Chapters 3, 4 and 5, the arranged marriage was openly seen as inferior to Western models. Many assumed it would die out over time; others believed it would continue as a vehicle for immigration. It was widely assumed that there was little or no emotional investment in such marriages and that separation would cause little hardship. The complexity of the system, its place in Asian family life and the personal commitment of protagonists towards its fulfilment were barely understood.

After 1997 acknowledgement of the plurality of relationships did not, for the most part, extend to international arranged marriages. The government made clear its reservations about their continuation and their inferiority was still largely assumed. While aspects of these marriages were indeed problematic, the uniquely critical focus suggested something more, 'an intense gaze upon their "alien" traditions … an Orientalist [re]construction of family norms of the non-Western other' (Shah 2011b).

Nonetheless, and perhaps against expectation, this book found some disparity between this hostility and post-1997 entry clearance practice. Provided marriages conformed to an officer's preconception of a traditional arranged marriage, they were usually accepted. Refused cases tended to be those perceived as atypical, although more ideological reservations may have been expressed through the reported focus on questions of validity and recognition.

UK restrictions on migration through international arranged marriages were generally less ferocious than in some other European states and, despite anxiety about the perpetuation of family forms seen as archaic and oppressive, there appears to have been hesitation at renewing the aggressive approach that had characterised the pre-1997 period.

Immigration

If, for much of the period between 1962 and 1997, the non-white character of immigration was seen to be its fundamental problem, this was reinforced by many other beliefs. Immigration was seen as an accretion of numbers sharing a limited pot of resources and a single one-way journey rather than part of a pattern of global movement. While emigration did not usually feature in accounts, immigration was widely perceived as fundamentally disadvantageous to the host society, causing labour displacement and a drain on social resources. Its benefits, both economic and social, were rarely if ever articulated in the UK and gains were assumed to be purely made on the immigrant's side.

Family migration was viewed through the prism of these beliefs. It posed a particular threat because, under the guise of humanity, it permitted the entry of new workers and established a potentially endless chain of migration. These beliefs, compounded by the attitudes towards race and arranged marriages just described, ensured that male family migrants in particular were viewed with deep scepticism and abuse was assumed to be ubiquitous and endemic.

The benefits of immigration were better appreciated by the government after 1997, provided it involved the right sort of immigrant entering in a state-approved manner. The rise of the 'sham marriage' and the treatment of those without leave who married or sought to marry in the UK reflected these priorities. Concerns at coercive aspects of the international arranged marriage were arguably a proxy in this period for resistance to the entry of migrants perceived as unskilled and difficult to integrate.

Gender

Assumptions about gender were a major force manifested in several ways. It was for many years assumed that only men moved for work and that wives and children were 'secondary' migrants. Parties who conformed to this conventional pattern were treated more favourably than those who did not. In the early period of Commonwealth immigration control, married men with families were seen as a safer prospect than single (impliedly sexually predatory) men. This was consistent with the particular protection offered to wives and children in the Commonwealth Immigrants Act 1962, which was not repealed until 1988, although the entry of these family members soon became the focus of administrative measures. By contrast, where husbands sought to join wives, they were assumed to be disguised 'primary' migrants entering for economic purposes. This assumption was given explicit expression in immigration control through the ban on husbands. When overt sex discrimination was no longer possible, the primary purpose rule was applied as if male immigrants moved primarily for economic reasons.

Also present were corresponding assumptions about women. In particular, they were often seen as the passive instruments of the wills of their husbands and fathers, their identity subsumed into that of their male relatives. This was literally the case with the rules on married women's nationality discussed in Chapter 2 but was implicitly so during most of the period under discussion here, particularly where South Asian women were concerned, when assumptions about race and gender dovetailed. Paradoxically, however, women were expected to accept the consequences of marriages that had been, it was implied, decided almost without the operation of their will, even where this meant leaving the country of their birth or long-term residence. Women who married outsiders lost their British identity and became outsiders themselves. In this respect, the assumptions of decision-makers recall the underlying premise of much nineteenth-century fiction: that women make only one significant decision in their lives, which is whom to marry. All else leads up to or flows from the wisdom of that choice.

Attitudes towards gender changed over the period discussed here. Sexually discriminatory rules would have been unacceptable in the period after 1997 and not only for legal reasons. The debate became framed in different terms. 'Modern' forms of relationship, including unmarried and same-sex partnerships, were officially acknowledged. 'Modern' marriages, including those where the husband joined the wife, were largely seen as normal. Nonetheless, there were still implicit boundaries of 'normality' that were gender-determined and relationships that fell outside these were still treated sceptically. Thus, men who married much older women were subject to particular doubt. Men were also still more likely to be considered as economic migrants, particularly if the relationship was not otherwise 'modern'. Women in such relationships were sometimes constructed as victims of patriarchy.

Who Belongs?

In this book, there were frequent references to 'belongers' and 'outsiders'. The distinction was essential in determining who might enjoy family life in the UK on their own terms. Decision-making, as analysed in this book (and as the literature suggests; see Yuval-Davis, Floya and Kofman 2005: 526-31), suggests that belonging is a fluctuating, not a static concept and cannot be determined solely by reference to nationality or other formal status. The discussion here has argued that non-white residents, including nationals and those born in the UK, were often not unqualified 'belongers'. This status had to be earned through adoption of a British identity in certain key respects. Thus, men who relied on domicile in the sub-continent to assert legal rights to certain forms of divorce or marriage were treated unsympathetically. Women who married 'wrongly' and, in consequence, wished to import unwanted male immigrants faced loss of belonging as they were unable to enjoy married life in their country of residence.

In the period between 1962 and 1997, demarcations between those with a strong claim to belong and those without were perhaps easier to make. Recent arrivals and their children were generally easily distinguished and were widely regarded as having only a contingent claim. Of course, even those with a strong claim, such as white British-born women, could find their status downgraded through making the wrong marriage and might have to choose between their home and their spouse, as happened as a result of the ban on Commonwealth husbands. However, the position of such women was somewhat mitigated by the courts before the rule was replaced by the more refined tool of primary purpose. After 1997, skin colour and 'belonging' became more decoupled so that some white immigrants (notably those from Eastern Europe) were seen as a threat, while factors such as cultural conformity, social class and compliance with state regulation became more critical in determining the belonging status of the non-white population.

While physical characteristics and origin may have mattered less as time went on, more recent demarcations between different categories of resident or citizen that refer back to ethnic divisions may still be observed. One of the objections to raising the minimum age of entry and sponsorship to 21 was that it would affect groups, such as the Jewish community, that were not tainted by forced marriage – although it did not affect them more than young people from affected communities in voluntary marriages.[1] Determining what claim a person has without reinforcing, even unintentionally, older divisions of ethnicity and race is not straightforward.

State Power

The assertion of state power in immigration matters has always been central to immigration control and the right to enter or remain in the UK was a privilege to be accorded only to the compliant. For the most part, this was assumed and did not need iteration. It drew its legitimacy from the apparently overwhelming public support for firm immigration control and was an unspoken assumption during most of the period between 1962 and 1997, being rarely articulated or challenged by any of the institutions discussed. The post-1997 period brought new challenges, particularly large-scale irregular migration, requiring institutions to act decisively and explicitly on behalf of the state. The assertion of state hegemony became ever more emphatic with repeated attempts at legislation and other forms of regulation. Submission to state-generated criteria became, not only substantively but also in terms of process, a condition for acceptance, even while such compliance became more difficult given almost continuous legal change. Yet there was also the distinct impression of overkill – if the state could control immigration, it would not be necessary to keep legislating on the subject (an issue that has been pursued further

1 http://www.guardian.co.uk/commentisfree/2008/jul/29/immigration.religion (accessed 22 June 2011).

in the general literature on migration; see, for example, Harris 2002 and Juss 2006). Furthermore, there was a price for 'firm' immigration control paid not only by the unwanted immigrant but by all members of society (for more discussion on this, see Joppke 1998 and Hollifield 2000). The point at which accepting state authority causes irreconcilable conflict with other deeply held values will vary by individual and institution, but the account given in this book suggests that this point was reached towards the end of the period by some members of the higher judiciary.

The excessive quantity of legislation and the first stirrings of judicial resistance suggest that the assumption of state authority became something less powerful, a value that must compete with other values. This might have been a transitory event provoked by an excess of government zeal. The discussion of case law in Chapter 4 suggests that the judiciary also briefly entertained moments of rebellion during the era of primary purpose without lasting effect. On the other hand, global forces are here to stay, while the style of judgement in, for example, *Huang* and *Baiai* suggests that judges began to draw inspiration from human rights discourse that may have indicated a deeper shift in their sense of their responsibilities. The judicial history of the recent period suggests that amongst the values competing with the supremacy of state power was a belief in limits upon its powers.

Institutional Factors

It is plausible that decision-making and the hierarchy would also be affected by particular institutional values. However, it is arguable that institutional factors mostly affected the style rather than the content of decisions. In the period between 1962 and 1997, there was a strong degree of congruity in the values that underpinned decision-making. Judges, for example, mostly expressed themselves 'judicially' but, as discussed in Chapter 4, made decisions that supported exclusionary purposes, sometimes at the expense of more coherent legal alternatives. In a few cases, though, such as those regarding the interpretation of the requirement to have met, decision-making suggested reservations about excessive intrusion into personal arrangements, perhaps reflecting institutional caution in this area. Parliament rationalised its decisions through its electoral mandate, but rarely questioned whether its values extended beyond majoritarian politics that apparently demanded rigorous controls. It was also able to maintain a formal commitment to family reunification, knowing that the entry clearance service ensured that unwanted family members were refused. The entry clearance service was largely unregulated and had little sense of any institutional purpose beyond exclusion. It certainly had an institutional culture but it was one that, except for excesses such as 'virginity tests', complemented and fulfilled political aims.

The position was less clear after 1997. Parliament retained its strong commitment to majoritarian politics, tempered only marginally, if at all, by human rights or other countervailing values, despite their formal adoption. However, the judiciary in some instances became more assertive, drawing added authority from human rights in ways that had arguably not been anticipated, thereby disrupting the government-sanctioned hierarchy. The visa service was less enmeshed in the execution of an unofficial policy of exclusion and was more preoccupied by institutional concerns such as efficiency, reflecting new political priorities. A local culture was still observable on the sub-continent, inherited through generations of officials, but its continuing role was ambiguous.

Yet, in general and over the period as a whole, institutional factors were less powerful than might have been anticipated at the start of the book. It is arguable that decision-makers relied most heavily upon unspoken assumptions shared throughout society, the invisible atmosphere in which they functioned.

Ordering the Hierarchy

The place that a marriage occupied in the hierarchy depended partly upon formal legal rules but also upon the assumptions made about it.[2] At the top were those marriages that commanded acceptance in that entry of the non-resident spouse was virtually assured. At the bottom were those where entry was very difficult or even impossible. These marriages may be designated as 'bogus' because they lacked credibility or the non-resident party might belong to a category whose entry was considered undesirable. Very often, the two reasons were conflated.

Gender, race and class were important factors in determining the place of a marriage on the hierarchy. Male entrants married to British-resident women were usually placed below women joining British husbands. The measures described in Chapters 3, 4 and 5 ensured that non-white applicants, particularly from the sub-continent, were most frequently refused. After 1997, non-white countries remained the major source of refusals, but it became difficult to disentangle issues of race from other more amorphous questions such as education, culture and social class. Maintenance and accommodation requirements meant that poor entrants had more difficulty securing entry, while questions of validity of marriage and measures that purported to prevent forced marriage most affected poor, often Muslim families.

The role played by various factors in determining the hierarchy fluctuated. At the beginning, gender arguably predominated over or acted as a proxy for race. By the 1970s, race was the single most important factor and this became more explicit as sex discrimination became more difficult. More recently, there was renewed emphasis on the cultural conformity of the marriage, economic self-sufficiency, the capacity for integration and compliance with state authority in immigration matters. However, the race, gender, class and compliance of the applicant were not the only factors. There was also the question of the UK-resident spouse. Women in particular who persisted in choosing to live with the 'wrong' spouse would

2 The spouses of EEA nationals, for example, had a strong legal right but were poorly regarded and were arguably the target of restrictive policies, particularly the certificate of approval scheme.

find themselves excluded, although, despite formal equality, policy often sought to distinguish between those who might be regarded as having the strongest claim to belong and those whose claims were weaker by reason of their own or even their ancestral entry.

Reconciling the Irreconcilable in Marriage Migration

Like many areas of immigration control, the regulation of marriage migration has often seemed to be based on contradictory values. Family unity has competed with instrumentality and exclusion, race equality with discriminatory measures, and assertions of state sovereignty with uncontrolled entry. Arguably underpinning these has been electoral demand for 'tough' immigration controls in tension with a desire to feel morally comfortable with them.

Reconciling these has not been straightforward. The predominant discourse surrounding control has generally been 'abuse'. Measures were often rationalised by the need to prevent fraudulent applications (or, more recently, applications that abuse or oppress individuals) even though the evidence was often contested or flimsy and measures had a much wider impact. The reliance on abuse and fraud, playing on long-standing anxieties about invasion and difference, became so familiar that its function was not often articulated even when its inconsistencies were observed. In fact, what they revealed was that the electorate might want a restrictive immigration policy but it also needed to be assured that it was justified ethically.

Other prevarications may be noted. Overt racist sentiment was almost never expressed by leading political figures, despite the racially discriminatory content of much policy. The discussion of the period between 1962 and 1997 suggests that the judiciary and the legislature were able to maintain at least a superficial appearance of fairness by refusing to acknowledge the highly discriminatory but mostly covert practices of the entry clearance service. The assumption that underlay reliance on this type of argument or conduct was that, without it, support for measures would be more equivocal. This does not mean that a more honest approach would have removed all support for immigration control, but it might have resulted in less comfort and more ambivalence. In other words, as well as wishing for firm controls, many individuals acknowledged that claims to enter as a spouse had some validity and needed a morally valid peg on which to hang their wish to exclude. However, few politicians attempted to pose the question honestly and those that did tended not to remain at the centre of power.[3]

Linked to this implicit acknowledgement of the need to reconcile the irreconcilable was the tacit recognition, at least by policy-makers, that whatever the government and the electorate might wish to happen, there are limits on what can be achieved, at least if other essential values were not to be unacceptably

3 Alex Lyon and, to a certain extent, Roy Jenkins were the clearest examples (although Jenkins' departure was for other reasons).

compromised. Over-restrictive immigration controls may be incompatible with the values of a liberal state and impossible to implement without interfering excessively in the freedoms of those entitled to circulate. As Joppke (1998: 292) expresses it: 'At the risk of stating a tautology, accepting unwanted immigration is inherent in the liberalness of liberal states.' Whether this was always completely true is debatable given the long policy stasis once primary purpose was put in place, during which many spouses were successfully excluded. However, it certainly seems to capture the position of the post-1997 period where migration seemed an unstoppable force, where once-marginal populations had achieved a degree of incorporation and where migrants had recourse to a wider range of legal rights, even if one does not necessarily accept that they had thereby acquired 'postnational membership' (Soysal 1994).

Caught up in the race to demonstrate competence in immigration matters and the impossibility of pre-empting migratory pressures while not going just that bit too far, governments have, certainly in the recent period, promised more than they can deliver. The result has been recurrent and ceaseless legislation, organisational reform and complexity. New measures might bring immediate results, but pressure often rapidly appeared elsewhere in the system or measures were found to be unlawful, necessitating a further round of changes so that, paradoxically, repeated legislation served only to underline the growing difficulty faced by states in preventing unwanted arrivals.

Marriage migration, which was subject to repeated scrutiny and control, shared this pattern of over-regulation. In fact, the incoherence of immigration control is perhaps more evident in marriage migration policy than elsewhere because it reaches so deeply into the intimate lives of British residents. Whom one chooses to marry is regarded as telling in terms of values, culture and allegiances, particularly for women who, as previously noted, have special responsibility for morality and culture and are still assumed to absorb more than they transmit where these diverge within a relationship. Refusing the marriage migrant entails disapproval of a fundamental choice by the British-based spouse that reflects upon their personal identity as well as on their relationship. Refusing to allow a UK resident the right to live in his or her own home with his or her chosen partner undermines claims that immigration controls are about protecting the interests of the entire populace. In reality, the controls are about sacrificing the intimate lives of some parts of the population, which may often be ethnically or racially distinct, to the expectations of the rest. The consequence may be alienation and strategic resistance, which are presumably unintended and undesired consequences given the 'integration' discourse. Yet, given also the centrality of immigration control to political credibility, it is improbable that any government could cease to regulate marriage migration even if it wanted to.

Marriage Migration: Future Directions

As Chapters 1 and 6 demonstrated, marriage migration has become a major source of new long-term entrants and South Asian communities remain well-represented in such marriages. International marriages also remain common in other communities who have traditionally practised arranged marriages (Beck-Gernsheim 2007: 275-7). Even where, as with the indigenous British population, international marriages are less common, a proportion will enter into them and this is made more probable by increased global migration and travel. Marriage migration looks likely to remain a live issue for the foreseeable future. As discussed in Chapter 1, transnationalism, provided it is used with care, offers an invaluable framework for relating such marriages to wider patterns of migration and social change. While many international marriages are not arranged, the international arranged marriage remains the most controversial category of all such marriages. At the same time, the extended South Asian family with its international links, of which marriage forms a major strand, is a paradigmatic transnational family. The resulting ties may be much wider than a simple binary connection between the UK and the country of origin. Marriages may be contracted with those who have migrated elsewhere in the world, forming a complex web of international links. As demonstrated in Chapter 6, the international arranged marriage system has continued to thrive, despite both government efforts to disrupt it and evidence of ambivalence by the young people involved. This is arguably because, not despite, of the distance involved (Beck-Gernsheim 2007: 277). It seems likely that the regulatory problems it provokes will not disappear in the near future. The Labour government of 1997-2010 clearly regarded continued intervention in these marriages as legitimate, although measures were necessarily of general application. Nonetheless, it did not go as far as some other European countries, suggesting anxiety about alienating well-established if still sometimes problematic groups.

Thus, while some marriage migration is often problematic, regulation is not straightforward. It is becoming more difficult to divide the population into a homogeneous native community who may occasionally draw in an outsider and distinct peripheral groups with links to one country of origin (Beck-Gernsheim 2007: 274-5) and fewer tools are available. Distinctions directly based on nationality or race are no longer possible. Human rights discourse, as interpreted by the British courts, no longer permits intimate lives to be discounted as thoroughly as before. Broad polices such as the certificate of approval scheme are liable to successful legal challenge. Measures that affect too many marriages also risk electoral unpopularity, particularly now that populations of immigrant descent form a significant part of the electorate. The challenge for the government is to formulate non-discriminatory measures that target the undesired immigrant without unduly alienating minority communities and parties to other more acceptable marriages. The most recent moves, discussed in Chapter 6, rationalised by the forced marriage and targeted at only a segment of the population of immigrant descent, show a possible direction of travel. Nonetheless, as the recent successful legal challenge to the age limit, involving two British-born young women (one of Pakistani and the other of British descent), demonstrates, the task is a difficult one given the incorporation of previously marginal groups and the inclination of some parties in all groups towards apparently unsuitable international marriage.[4]

There are no easy answers for the government. Perhaps the most coherent way forward is to turn the issue round. Marriage migration is not primarily a migration question but a question about the inclusion of residents and citizens. This is not a new insight. Carens (2003) noted that states recognise an obligation to admit family members of citizens and residents due to the moral claim of these latter individuals who should not have to choose between home and family. Others have reached the same conclusion by varying normative routes, for example, Lister's (2010) focus on intimate relationships as a sub-species of freedom of association. Very often in this book, the UK resident has been marginalised, with the focus being placed almost exclusively on the consequences of the applicant's entry. The structure of immigration control, with applications usually (and, from the government's perspective, preferably) made abroad by the migrant, reinforces that perspective. Yet, in the past ten years, government has enthusiastically promoted a version of citizenship that goes beyond a purely legal formulation. If citizenship is to mean more than the right to a passport, that means accommodation by the government as well as by migrants. To live in one's most intimate chosen relationship in one's home is surely central to any meaningful conception of belonging and the right should not be sacrificed for instrumental or ideological motives. There should not be implicitly defined classes of citizen in this area and the state should interfere only in pursuance of clearly defined and important public interests.

Marriage (and family) migration cannot be treated in the same way as other forms of migration. In most cases, excluding a particular class of immigrants does not directly impinge personally on those already within the polity. It may do so indirectly if individuals perceive that those similar to themselves are generally rejected. However, there are ways to minimise a close identification. For example, domestic race equality legislation was for many years the explicit trade-off for race-orientated immigration control. Long-term residents have not usually encountered many obstacles to obtaining nationality and formal equality for themselves and their children, although the route to settlement and naturalisation has recently become more complex. Immigration control may be understood as economically necessary rather than as a reaction to an external threat. These techniques have not always been successfully applied, but they do provide a form of discourse that is, on the surface, inclusive.

However, these rationalisations work less well where family migration is concerned, as the UK resident or citizen will feel personally implicated in the rejection of a close family member. There may also be a visible contrast between the quality of family life that he or she enjoys and that of others who are more fortunate. This, on its own, may qualify that individual's own sense of belonging.

4 *Quila v SSHD* [2010] EWCA Civ 1482.

The problem is accentuated in the case of marriage migration. This is not only because marriage or an equivalent relationship may be the necessary core to an individual's well-being, so that being able to enjoy it in a particular place becomes a strong indicator of whether one belongs in that place; it is also because, from the point of view of both the decision-maker and the affected individual, marriage represents a choice in a way that a blood tie does not. As such, it is doubly significant as an important and personal relationship which is chosen, and rejection feels very personal. Such a rejection should occur only in exceptional cases, if at all.

This citizenship perspective does not address all issues. Long-term residents do not possess legal citizenship and they will generally have an alternative nationality, so their claim is less clear-cut. While distinctions between citizens are not justifiable so that measures, including controls on marriage migration, should not implicitly or explicitly permit discrimination between them, if migration controls are accepted at all, some distinctions between citizens and migrants, and between more or less recent migrants, are permissible. However, long-term residents (or 'denizens'; see Hammar 1990) may, in reality, be unable to return or be more deeply connected to this country than to their place of origin.[5] Carens (2003) argues that long-term residents have a progressively stronger claim that eventually entitles them to make the same claims as citizens. Moreover, that claim is a strong one from the outset. Family reunification for migrant workers is necessary for the well-being of the workers themselves and is in the interests of the receiving state because it minimises marginalisation (John 2003: 1-2). Family migration is a natural and inevitable consequence of migration and cannot be short-circuited.

Questions of stratification of citizenship and residence rights have become more pressing and more complex following recent increases in both long-term migrants and naturalised citizens. Enhanced powers of deprivation of citizenship suggest that, for some citizens, nationality is becoming an enhanced immigration status rather than a final end-point, undermining government claims of a 'civic nationalism' framed by legal citizenship (Wray 2011). If a unitary and ethnically non-discriminatory conception of citizenship is to be defended, it becomes more difficult not to differentiate to some increased degree between nationals and long-term residents.[6] Quite obviously, the position of long-term residents should be no weaker than that of more recently arrived non-nationals who may be accompanied

5 These were questions that were raised by the proposals in *The Path to Citizenship* (UK Border Agency 2008b), which promoted naturalisation but had to recognise that this was not viable for all who might remain long term.

6 See, for example, the distinction inferred by Sedley LJ in *Quila v SSHD* [2010] EWCA Civ 1482 [43] between citizens and residents in *Abdulaziz.* As well as being a well-made legal observation, it is conceptually both inclusive, as it places the child of Pakistani migrants on a completely equal footing to a woman of British descent, and exclusive, as it suggests the critical difference is between residence and citizenship. Where this would place a long-term resident or a naturalised citizen with dual nationality was not discussed (as it did not need to be).

by their families. In fact, the UK conditions for the admission of workers' spouses have generally mirrored those for residents and nationals.[7] However, if there is an argument for further expanding the rights of citizens, it must also be acknowledged that many denizens are not positioned closer to recent migrants or even midway between them and nationals but are, in most senses other than the legal sense, citizens (as the law currently acknowledges). Certainly, the legal demarcation between nationals and residents should not axiomatically be taken as a formal break point.

It is unrealistic to suppose that governments will cede their right to control marriage migration, just as it would be naïve to imagine that bogus marriages never take place. Subject to the boundary-related questions discussed above, it is more a question of moving the frame away from migration towards the fulfilment of citizenship rights. If that were done, several recurrent aspects of policy would also be reframed. If some hurdles remain inevitable, they should be constructed at the minimum level necessary to protect clearly identified public interests and not for the sake of administrative convenience or to meet other policy objectives.[8] The constraints on third party support for family migrants is an example of policy that, while purporting to be about protection of the public purse, was in reality about the latter two purposes. Similarly, the requirement for a valid marriage should not become a bureaucratic search for technical grounds of refusal where the evidence shows that parties believe and behave as if they are married. The government should resist the temptation to raise maintenance and accommodation requirements to match the more demanding criteria recently adopted elsewhere in Europe and should ensure that such criteria do not hinder the effective implementation of humanitarian exceptions to the rules, such as those relating to domestic violence. Measures that disrupt marriage migration for other purposes should be critically scrutinised to determine whether they are the best and most effective means of achieving that aim and their benefits explicitly weighed against the interference in the right of British residents to reside with their spouse. It may not be that all measures against forced marriage that are channelled through the immigration system are wrong. An opportunity for exit might be offered in some cases (although practical obstacles to exit at the visa stage are formidable unless ongoing support is also available). However, measures that create additional substantive hurdles or delays or that stigmatise certain marriages need far more careful consideration of their benefits and drawbacks than was evident in the forced marriage consultations discussed in Chapter 7. It was not just that the benefits for forced marriage victims were unsubstantiated but that the problems for affected parties in voluntary and

7 However, there must be an intention to leave the UK and indefinite leave has been obtainable only alongside the primary migrant. In fact, the current rules for points-based migrants are more generous, in that the new minimum age of 21 does not apply.

8 Article 8 jurisprudence rarely examines the Article 8(2) issue of public interest, which immigration controls profess to protect, usually deferring to states' margin of appreciation on such questions. A more specific and critical analysis might yield some surprising results.

entirely lawful marriages were not properly brought into account.[9] There can be little doubt that the acceptability of these types of measures is connected to the belief amongst the majority of the population that international arranged marriages involving young and/or related parties are often unwise. However, a liberal society permits its members to consent to many things in their personal lives that may be unwise, even when these have some adverse consequences for the rest of society, and there seems little principled basis for not extending this freedom to voluntary international arranged marriages merely because they most often happen in the context of a minority community and entail immigration.

In similar vein, the 'bogus' or 'sham' marriage needs to be carefully defined and measures against it confined to its prevention. Most measures that have purported to prevent sham marriages have been vastly over-inclusive and this has not usually been accidental. The certificate of approval scheme, for example, failed in large part because it distinguished only on immigration grounds. Primary purpose prevented entry in many marriages where the parties intended to cohabit as married couples. Again, these measures may seem more palatable because of suspicion that some international marriages do involve opportunism by the overseas partner and naïvety by the UK resident. As discussed in Chapter 1, exploitative or manipulative sexual relationships happen everywhere and, unless consent in an issue, it is not for the state, any more than in the case of arranged marriages, to act as marriage counsellor merely because a marriage entails international migration. Over-inclusive definitions are wrong in principle.

As argued in Chapter 1, while the bogus marriage exists, defining it, except through the absence of all characteristics associated with marriage, is difficult. One returns, as always, to the EU definition: a marriage concluded 'with the sole aim of circumventing the rules on entry and residence'.[10] This narrow definition was adopted precisely because the free movement of EU citizens should be minimally obstructed. There is an argument for also adopting it into national law, not only to give full expression to the citizenship rights of British nationals within their territory but to minimise reverse discrimination against these same citizens that does so much to undermine the credibility and effectiveness of national laws.

Of course, this is currently unlikely. The test, alongside the burden of proof placed on governments, is widely regarded as too liberal and as permitting too many doubtful marriages. But, despite attempts by member states to weaken its effect, the EU clearly sees it as critical. Presumably, it regards the possibility that some bogus marriages may escape detection as a worthwhile price for the complete fulfilment of other aims. Certainly, the opportunistic exercise of rights, so often the target of domestic measures, must be tolerated.[11] Without straying into

9 On this, see Sedley LJ in *Quila v SSHD* [2010] EWCA 1482 [51]-[62].

10 Council Resolution 97/C 382/01 of 4 December 1997 (Official Journal C 382 of 16.12.1997).

11 See Case C-109/01, *SSHD v Akrich* [2004] QB 756; Case C-127/08, *Metock v Minister for Justice, Equality and Law Reform* [2009] QB 318.

debates around the meaning of EU citizenship and its relationship with economic rights, it is perhaps appropriate for national states to also focus more intently on how to maximise the rights of citizens rather than on how to minimise unwanted migration regardless of the cost. If the choice is between bringing strangers into the home or making citizens into strangers, it is not axiomatic that the latter should prevail.

Appendix A

Newspaper Sources

'Wife with 50 husbands', *Daily Express,* 24 July 1976
'Counsellor's advice led to dismissal', *The Times*, 26 July 1976
'Marriage swindle inquiry urged', *The Times*, 26 July 1976
'Asian "married sister to beat ban"', *Daily Telegraph*, 4 August 1976
'Marriage swindle', *The Guardian*, 7 August 1976
'Pakistani's marriage "not a reason to stay"', *The Times*, 25 January 1977
'Five held in marriage check', *The Times*, 31 January 1977
'Woman given £50 to "marry" Iranian', The Guardian, 15 February 1977
'Till the Home Office rules do us part', *The Observer*, 15 January 1978
'Mr Fix-it offered us cash to wed immigrants', *Daily Star*, 26 February 1979
'Buy a bride', *Daily Mail*, 16 November 1982
'Freedom for the "bride" who cashed in on marriage', *Daily Mail*, 13 October 1984
'Migrant racket in fake bridegrooms revealed', *Daily Telegraph*, 21 October 1984
'Immigrants "run marriage racket"', *The Times*, 17 March 1989
'"Thousands" in immigrant weddings rackets', *Daily Telegraph*, 17 March 1989
'Brides for sale scam mother is jailed', *The Sun*, 7 November 1989
'Groom for hire nicked at wedding', *News of the World*, 24 December 1989
'Bogus marriage plots uncovered', *The Times*, 26 February 1990
'MPs demand action to stop immigration marriage fraud', *The Times*, 27 February 1990
'Cops charge three after wedding swoop', *News of the World*, 29 April 1990
'Curb on fake marriages threatened by EC court', *Daily Telegraph*, 8 July 1992
'"Hundreds" in bogus weddings to beat law', *Evening Standard*, 13 August 1993
'Migrants' Mr Fixit forged a fortune', *Daily Mail*, 4 February 1995
'How yet another illegal migrant beats the system', *Sunday Express*, 26 February 1995
'Council crook runs marriage fix scam', *News of the World*, 30 April 1995
'Immigrants will face a marriage of inconvenience', *Daily Mail*, 5 July 1995
'Civil servant "set up weddings for illegal migrants"', *Daily Telegraph*, 7 July 1995

Bibliography

Achato, L., Eaton, M. and Jones, C. 2010. *The Migrant Journey.* London: Home Office.

Allott, A. 1980. *The Limits of Law.* London: Butterworths.

Amnesty International UK. 2004. *Get It Right: How Home Office Decision-Making Fails Refugees.* London: Amnesty International.

An-Na'im, A. 2000. *Forced Marriage.* CIMEL and Interights: http://www.soas.ac.uk/honourcrimes/resources/file55689.pdf (accessed 11 June 2011).

Anson, E. 1999. *Report by the Independent Monitor (Asylum and Immigration Appeals Act 1993).* London: Migration and Visa Division.

Anwar, M. 1986. *Race and Politics: Ethnic Minorities and the British Political System.* London and New York: Tavistock Publications.

Ascherson, N. 2005. Britain Rediscovered. *Prospect Magazine*, 109.

Balibar, E. 2002. *Politics and the Other Scene.* London and New York: Verso.

Ballard, C. 1978. Arranged Marriages in the British Context. *New Community*, VI(3), 181-96.

Ballard, R. Undated. *Culture and Communication.* Centre for Applied South Asian Studies: http://www.casas.org.uk/papers/law.html (accessed 11 June 2011).

Ballard, R. 1982. South Asian Communities, in *Families in Britain*, edited by R.N. Rapoport, M. Fogarty, and R. Rapoport. London: Routledge & Kegan Paul.

Ballard, R. 1990. Migration and Kinship: The Differential Effect of Marriage Rules on the Processes of Punjabi Migration to Britain, in *South Asians Overseas: Contexts and Communities*, edited by C. Clarke, C. Peach and S. Vertovec. Cambridge: Cambridge University Press, 219-49.

Ballard, R. 1994. The Emergence of Desh Pardesh, in *Desh Pardesh: The South Asian Presence in Britain*, edited by R. Ballard. London: C. Hurst & Co.

Ballard, R. 2002. Race Ethnicity and Culture, in *New Directions in Sociology* edited by M. Holborn. Ormskirk: Causeway.

Ballard, R. 2005. *Riste and Ristedari: The Significance of Marriage in the Dynamics of Transnational Kinship Networks.* Centre for Applied South Asian Studies: http://www.casas.org.uk/papers/law.html (accessed 11 June 2011).

Ballard, R. 2006. *Forced Marriages: Just Who is Conspiring against Whom?* Centre for Applied South Asian Studies: http://www.casas.org.uk/papers/law.html (accessed 11 June 2011).

Ballard, R. 2007. Living with Difference: A Forgotten Art in Urgent Need of Revival?, in *Religious Reconstruction in the South Asian Diasporas: From One Generation to Another*, edited by J. Hinnells. Basingstoke: Palgrave Macmillan, 265–301.

Ballard, R. 2008. Inside and Outside: Contrasting Perspectives on the Dynamics of Kinship and Marriage in Contemporary South Asian Transnational Networks, in *The Family in Question: Immigrants and Minorities in Multicultural Europe*, edited by R. Grillo. Amsterdam: University of Amsterdam Press, 37-70.

Bano, S. 2000. Muslim South Asian Women and Customary Law in Britain. *Journal of South Pacific Law* 6(4): http://www.paclii.org/journals/fJSPL/vol04/6.shtml (accessed 11 June 2011).

Banton, M. 1998. Judicial Training in Ethnic Minority Issues in England and Wales. *Journal of Ethnic Minority Studies*, 24(3), 561-72.

Barot, T. Bradley, H. and Fenton, S. 1999. Rethinking Ethnicity and Gender, in *Ethnicity, Gender and Social Change* edited by T. Barot, H. Bradley and S. Fenton. Basingstoke: Macmillan Press, 1-26.

Baty, T. 1936. The Nationality of a Married Woman at Common Law. *Law Quarterly Review*, 52, 247-52.

Bauböck, R. 1991. Migration and Citizenship. *New Community*, 18(1), 27-48.

Bawdon, F. 1997. The Abolition of the Primary Purpose Rule Has Not Eased the Task of Immigration Solicitors. *Law Society Gazette*, 94(38).

Beck-Gernsheim, E. 2007. Transnational Lives, Transnational Marriages: A Review of the Evidence from Migrant Communities in Europe. *Global Networks*, 7(3), 271-88.

Berkovits, B. 1988. Transnational Divorces: The Fatima Decision. *Law Quarterly Review*, 104 (January), 60-93.

Berthoud, R. 2000. *Family Formation in Multi-Cultural Britain: Three Patterns of Diversity.* Institute of Social and Economic Research, University of Essex: http://www.sociology.org.uk/as4fm1.pdf (accessed 11 June 2011).

Bevan, B. 1986. *The Development of British Immigration Law.* London: Croom Helm.

Bhabha, J. 2007. Border Rights and Rites, in *Women and Immigration Law*, edited by S. Van Walsum and T. Spijkerboer. Abingdon and New York: Routledge-Cavendish, 15-34.

Bhabha, J. Klug, F. and Shutter, S. 1985. *Worlds Apart: Women under Immigration and Asylum Law.* London: Pluto Press.

Bhabha, J. and Shutter, S. 1994. *Womens Movement: Women under Immigration, Nationality and Refugee Law.* Stoke-on-Trent: Trentham Books.

Bhamra, M. 2007. On Cultural Diversity: The Importance of Normative Foundations for Legal Responses, in *Law and Ethnic Plurality: Socio-Legal Perspectives* edited by P. Shah. Leiden: Martinus Nijhoff, 9-30.

Bhopal, K. 1999. South Asian Women and Arranged Marriages in East London, in *Ethnicity, Gender and Social Change*, edited by T. Barot, H. Bradley and S. Fenton. Basingstoke: Macmillan Press, 117-34.

Blake, C. 1984. How Wives Became Widows. *New Society*, 11 October 1984.

Blanchet, T. 2008. Bangladeshi Girls Sold as Wives in North India, in *Marriage, Migration and Gender*, edited by R. Palriwala and P. Uberoi. Delhi: Sage Publications, 152-79.

Block, L. 2010. *Gendered Institutional Responses to Marriage Migration in Germany.* Paper to the Workshop Panel 'New Family Migration Policies in Europe: A Gendered Perspective 15th Metropolis Conference: Justice and Migration: Paradoxes of Belonging', The Hague, 7 October 2010.

Bloom, C. 2006, Grounds for Proceedings in Nullity, in *Butterworths Family Law Service*, edited by J. Montgomery and R. Sax. London: Butterworths.

Booth, H. 1986. Immigration in Perspective: Population Development in the UK, in *Towards a Just Immigration Policy*, edited by A.Dummett. London: Cobden Trust, 109-36.

Bonjour, S. 2010. Between Integration Provision and Selection Mechanism: Party Politics, Judicial Constraints, and the Making of French and Dutch Policies of Civic Integration Abroad. *European Journal of Migration and Law*, 12(3), 299-318.

Border and Immigration Agency. 2007a. *Marriage to Partners from Overseas: A Consultation Paper.* London: Border and Immigration Agency.

Border and Immigration Agency. 2007b. *Marriage Visas: Pre-entry English Requirement for Spouses: Consultation Paper.* London: Border and Immigration Agency.

Border and Immigration Agency. 2008a. *The Path to Citizenship: Next Steps in Reforming the Immigration System.* London: Border and Immigration Agency.

Border and Immigration Agency. 2008b. *The Path to Citizenship: Next Steps in Reforming the Immigration System, Government Response to Consultation.* London: Border and Immigration Agency.

Bosworth, M. and Guild, M. 2008. Governing through Migration Control: S*ecurity and Citizenship in Britain, The British Journal of Criminology*, 48, 703–719.

Bourn, C. and Whitmore, J. 1996. *Anti-discrimination Law in Britain.* London: Sweet & Maxwell.

Bradby, H. 1999. Negotiating Marriage: Young Punjabi Womens' Assessment of their Individual and Family Interests, in *Ethnicity, Gender and Social Change*, edited by T. Barot, H. Bradley and S. Fenton. Basingstoke: Macmillan Press, 152-66.

Brah, A. 1978. South Asian Teenagers in Southall: Their Perceptions of Marriage, Family and Ethnic Identity. *New Community*, VI(3), 197-206.

Brah, A. 1987. Women of South Asian Origins in Britain: Issues and Concerns. *South Asia Research*, 7(1), 39-54.

Brodie, A. 2007. UKVisas response to 'Guiding the gatekeepers: entry clearance for settlement on the Indian sub-continent'. *Immigration, Asylum and Nationality Law*, 21(2), 147-54.

Browne, A. 2002. Does Britain Need Immigration?, *Prospect Magazine*, July: http://www.prospectmagazine.co.uk/2002/07/doesbritainneedimmigration (accessed 22 June 2011) .

Butler, C. 1999. Cultural Diversity and Religious Conformity: Dimensions of Social Change Among Second Generation Muslim Women, in *Ethnicity,*

Gender and Social Change, edited by T. Barot, H. Bradley and S. Fenton. Basingstoke: Macmillan Press, 135-51.

Calavita, K. 2006, Gender, Migration and Law: Crossing Borders and Bridging Disciplines. *International Migration Review*, 40(1), 104-32.

Cantle, T. 2001. *Community Cohesion: A Report of the Independent Review Team.* London: Home Office.

Carens, J. 1987. Aliens and Citizens: The Case for Open Borders. *Review of Politics*, 49, 251-73.

Carens, J. 2003. Who Should Get In? The Ethics of Immigration Admissions. *Ethics and International Affairs*, 17(1), 95-110.

Castles, S. and Miller, M. 2009. *The Age of Migration: International Population Movements in the Modern World*, 4th Edition. Basingstoke: Palgrave Macmillan.

Chakrabarti, S. 2005. Rights and Rhetoric: The Politics of Asylum and Human Rights Culture in the United Kingdom. *Journal of Law and Society*, 32(1), 131-47.

Chang, H. 2000. The Economic Analysis of Immigration Law, in *Migration Theory: Talking Across Disciplines*, edited by C. Brettell and J. Hollifield. London: Routledge, 205-301.

Charsley, K. 2006. Risk and Ritual: The Protection of British Pakistani Women in Transnational Marriage. *Journal of Ethnic and Migration Studies*, 32(7), 1169-87.

Charsley, K. 2011. *Marriage Related Migration to the UK: A Brief Overview of Trends.* Paper delivered to Marriage and Migration Workshop, Bristol University, 20 January 2011.

Cheney, D. 1994. *Daughters of the Danaïdes: An Orature on Women and the Operation of UK Immigration Control.* PhD thesis, University of Kent at Canterbury.

Chowdhury, Z. 1982. *Split Families: An Examination of the British Immigration Control System Relating to Dependants in Bangladesh.* London: UKIAS.

Chowdhury, Z. 1994. Admission of a Polygamous Wife and Some Legal Aspects of Conflict of Laws. *Immigration and Nationality Law and Practice*, 8(3), 83-6.

Citizens Advice Bureau. 2003. *Family Visitor Visas: An Analysis of Entry Clearance Officer Decision-Making in 2002.* London: Citizens Advice Bureau.

Clayton, G. 2006a. Entry Clearance and Human Rights: Challenging the Boundaries of Jurisdiction. *Journal of Immigration, Asylum and Nationality Law*, 20(4), 255-69.

Clayton, G. 2006b, *Textbook on Immigration and Asylum Law*, 2nd Edition. Oxford: Oxford University Press.

Clayton, G. 2007. Prediction or Precondition? The House of Lords Judgment in *Huang and Kashmiri. Journal of Immigration, Asylum and Nationality Law*, 21(4), 311-23.

Clayton, G. 2008, *Textbook on Immigration and Asylum Law*, 3rd Edition. Oxford: Oxford University Press.

Clayton, G. 2010, *Textbook on Immigration and Asylum Law*, 4th Edition. Oxford: Oxford University Press.

Clayton, R. 2004. Judicial Deference and 'Democratic Dialogue': The Legitimacy of Judicial Intervention under the Human Rights Act 1998. *Public Law*, 33-47.

Cockburn, A. 1869. *Nationality: Or the Law Relating to Subjects and Aliens, with a View to Future Legislation.* London: W. Ridgway.

Cohen, R. 1991. East-West and European Migration in a Global Context. *New Community*, 18(1), 9-26.

Cohen, S. 1990. *A Hard Act to Follow: The Immigration Act 1988*. Manchester: South Manchester Law Centre.

Cohen, S. 2000. Never Mind the Racism ... Feel the Quality: The Announcement on the Suggested 'Relaxation' of Immigration Controls. *Immigration, Nationality, Law and Practice*, 14(4), 223-6.

Cohen, S. 2001. Do You Take this Man to Be Your Lawfully Wedded Immigration Officer? *Immigration, Asylum and Nationality Law*, 15(3), 157-62.

Collinson, S. 1993. *Beyond Borders: West European Migration Policy towards the 21st Century*, London: Royal Institute of International Affairs.

Commission for Racial Equality. 1978. *Between Two Cultures: A Study of Relationships between Generations in the Asian Community in Britain.* London: Commission for Racial Equality.

Commission for Racial Equality. 1985. *Immigration Control Procedures: Report of a Formal Investigation.* London: Commission for Racial Equality.

Constable, J. 1974. Immigration Appeals. *New Society*, 18 April.

Costelloe Baker, L. 2006. *Independent Monitor for Entry Clearance Refusals Without the Right of Appeal: Report for 2005*, London: Foreign and Commonwealth Office.

Costelloe Baker, L. 2007. *Independent Monitor for Entry Clearance Refusals Without the Right of Appeal: Report for January to September 2006.* London: Foreign and Commonwealth Office.

Cotterell, R. 2009. Spectres of Transnationalism: Changing Terrains of Sociology of Law. *Journal of Law and Society*, 36(4), 481-500.

Coussey, M. 2005. *Annual Report 2004-5: Independent Race Monitor.* London: Home Office.

Coussey, M. 2006. *Annual Report for 2005-6 of the Independent Race Monitor.* London: Home Office.

Craig, P. 2001. The Courts, the Human Rights Act and Judicial Review. *Law Quarterly Review*, 117 (October), 589-603.

Cretney, S. Masson, J. and Bailey-Harris, R. 2002. *Principles of Family Law*, London: Sweet & Maxwell.

Cryer, A. 2003. Feminism in Retreat from Male Tradition. *Tribune*, 26 September, 16-17.

Dale, A. 2008, *Migration, Marriage and Employment amongst Indian, Pakistani and Bangladeshi Residents in the UK.* CCSR Working Paper 2008-02. Manchester: University of Manchester.

Dauvergne, C. 2004. Sovereignty, Migration and the Rule of Law in Global Times. *Modern Law Review*, 67(4), 588-615.

Deech, R. 1973, Immigrants and Family Law. *New Law Journal*, 1 February 1973, 110-112.

De Hart, B. 2006. Introduction: The Marriage of Convenience in European Immigration Law. *European Journal of Migration and Law*, 8(3), 251-262.

De Hart, B. 2009. Love Thy Neighbour: Family Reunification and the Rights of Insiders. *European Journal of Migration and Law*, 11, 235-52.

Del Rosario, T. 2008. Bridal Disapora: Marriage and Migration among Filipino Women, in *Marriage, Migration and Gender*, edited by R. Palriwala and P. Uberoi. Delhi: Sage Publications, 78-97.

Desai, L. 1996. *Judicial Supervision of Administrative Decision-Making in the Immigration and Asylum Law of the UK.* PhD thesis, University of Oxford.

Dickson, B. 2006. Safe in their Hands? Britains Law Lords and Human Rights. *Legal Studies*, 26(3), 329-46.

Digruber, D. and Messinger, I. 2006. Marriages of Residence in Austria. *European Journal of Migration and Law*, 8(3), 281-302.

Divided Families Campaign. 1978. *Give Us a Happy Ending: How Families Are Kept Apart by British Immigration Law.* London: Divided Families Campaign.

Dudley, J. et al. 2005. *Control of Immigration: Immigration Statistics 2004*, Statistical Bulletin 14/05. London: Home Office.

Dummett, A. 1986. Nationality and Immigration Status, in A. Dummett, ed., *Towards a Just Immigration Policy*, London: Cobden Trust.

Dummett, A. and Nicol, A. 1990. *Subjects, Citizens, Aliens and Others.* London: Weidenfeld & Nicolson.

Dummett, M. 2001. *On Immigration and Refugee.* London and New York: Routledge.

Dustin, M. and Phillips, A. 2009. Whose Agenda Is It? Abuses of Women and Abuses of Culture in Britain. *Ethnicities*, 8(3), 405-24.

Düvell, F. and Jordan, B. 2003. Immigration Control and the Management of Economic Migration in the United Kingdom: Organisational Culture, Implementation, Enforcement and Identity Processes in Public Services. *Journal of Ethnic and Migration Studies*, 29(2), 299-336.

Edwards, F. 1914. The Effect of a Certificate of Naturalisation. *Law Quarterly Review* 30, 433-47.

Edwards, R. 2002. Judicial Deference under the Human Rights Act. *Modern Law Review*, 65(6), 859-82.

Eekelaar, J. 2006. *Family Law and Personal Life.* Oxford: Oxford University Press.

Eekelaar, J. and MacLean, M. 2004. Marriage and the Moral Bases of Personal Relationships. *Journal of Law and Society*, 31(4), 510-38.

Eisenberg, A. and Spinner-Halev, J. eds. 2005. *Minorities within Minorities: Equality, Rights and Diversity.* Cambridge: Cambridge University Press.

Elliott, M. 2001. The Human Rights Act 1998 and the Standard of Substantive Review. *Cambridge Law Journal*, 60(2), 301-36.
Enright, M. 2009. Choice, Culture and the Politics of Belonging: The Emerging Law of Forced and Arranged Marriage. *Modern Law Review*, 72(3), 331-59.
Etzioni, A. 2007. Citizenship Tests: A Comparative, Communitarian Perspective. *Political Quarterly*, 78(3), 353-63.
European Commission Against Racism and Intolerance. 2000. *Second Report on the United Kingdom.* Strasbourg: Council of Europe.
European Commission Against Racism and Intolerance. 2005. *Third Report on the United Kingdom.* Strasbourg: Council of Europe.
European Commission Against Racism and Intolerance. 2010. *Fourth Report on the United Kingdom.* Strasbourg: Council of Europe.
Evans, J. 1983. *Immigration Law.* London: Sweet & Maxwell.
Ewing, K. 1999. The Human Rights Act and Parliamentary Democracy. *Modern Law Review*, 62(1), 79-99.
Ewing, K. 2004. The Futility of the Human Rights Act. *Public Law*, 829-52.
Ewing, K. 2005. The Futility of the Human Rights Act: A Long Footnote. *Bracton Law Journal*, 37, 41-7.
Faist, T. 2000. *The Volume and Dynamics of International Migration and Transnational Social Spaces.* Oxford: Clarendon Press.
Favell, A. and Hansen, R. 2001. Markets Against Politics: Migration, EU Enlargement and the Idea of Europe. *Journal of Ethnic and Migration Studies*, 28(4), 581-601.
Fentiman, R. 1985. The Validity of Marriage and the Proper Law. *Cambridge Law Journal*, 44(2), 256-79.
Finney, N. and Simpson, L. 2009. *Sleepwalking to Segregation?: Challenging Myths About Race and Migration.* Bristol: Policy Press.
Flynn, D. 2005. New Borders, New Management: The Dilemmas of Modern Immigration Policy. *Ethnic and Racial Studies*, 28(3), 463-90.
Foblets, M-C and Vanheule, D. 2006. Marriages of Convenience in Belgium: The Punitive Approach Gains Ground in Migration Law. *European Journal of Migration and Law*, 8(3), 263-80.
Fransman, L. 1998. *British Nationality Law.* London, Edinburgh and Dublin: Butteworths.
Fredman, S. 2006. From Deference to Democracy: The Role of Equality under the Human Rights Act 1998. *Law Quarterly Review*, 122, 53-81.
Freeman, G. 1986. Migration and the Political Economy of the Welfare State. *Annals of the American Academy of Political and Social Science*, 51-63.
Freeman, G. 1994. Can Liberal States Control Unwanted Migration? *Annals of the American Academy of Political and Social Science*, 534, 17-30.
Freeman, G. 2002. Winners and Losers: Politics and the Costs and Benefits of Migration, in *West European Immigration and Immigrant Policy in the New Century*, edited by A. Messina. Westport, CT: Praeger Publishers, 77-96.
Gainer, B. 1972. *The Alien Invasion.* London: Heinemann Educational Books.

Galligan, D. 1976. The Nature and Function of Policies within Discretionary Power. *Public Law*, 332.
Galligan, D. 1986. *Discretionary Powers – A Legal Study of Official Discretion.* Oxford: Clarendon Press.
Galligan, D. 1996. *A Reader on Administrative Law.* Oxford: Oxford University Press.
Galligan, D. 2001. Authoritarianism in Government and Administration: The Promise of Administrative Justice. *Current Legal Problems*, 54, 79-102.
Gangoli, G., Razak, A. and McCarry, M. 2006. *Forced Marriage and Domestic Violence among South Asian Communities in North East England.* Bristol: School for Policy Studies, University of Bristol.
Gans, H. 2007. Acculturation, Assimilation and Mobility. *Ethnic and Racial Studies.* 30(1), 152-64.
Garrard, J. 1971. *The English and Immigration – A Comparative Study of the Jewish Influx 1880-1910.* London: Oxford University Press.
Gartner, L. 1960. *The Jewish Immigrant in England 1870-1914.* London: George Allen & Unwin.
Gedalof, I. 2007. Unhomely Homes: Women, Family and Belonging in UK Discourses of Migration and Asylum. *Journal of Ethnic and Migration Studies*, 33(1), 77-94.
Gibney, M. 2004. *The Ethics and Politics of Asylum: Liberal Democracy and the Response to Refugees.* Cambridge: Cambridge University Press.
Goldsmith, Lord. 2008. *Our Common Bond.* London: Ministry of Justice.
Goodhart, D. 2004a. The Discomfort of Strangers. *The Guardian.* Available at: http://www.guardian.co.uk/politics/2004/feb/24/race.eu (accessed 12 June 2011)
Goodhart, D. 2004b. Diversity Divide. *Prospect Magazine*, 97.
Goodhart, D. 2005. Not Black and White, *Prospect Magazine*, 110.
Goodhart, D. 2006. National Anxieties. *Prospect Magazine*, 123.
Goodwin-Gill, G. 1978. *International Law and the Movement of Persons Between States*, Oxford: Clarendon Press.
Goodwin-Gill, G. 1986. Immigration, Nationality and the Standards of International Law, in *Towards a Just Immigration Policy*, edited by A. Dummett. London: Cobden Trust.
Gordon, I et al. 2009. *Economi Impact on the London and UK Economy of an Earned Regularisation of Irregular Migrants to the UK.* London: Greater London Authority.
Goulbourne, H. 1991. Varieties of Pluralism: The Notion of a Pluralist Post-Imperial Britain. *New Community*, 17(2), 211-27.
Gran, K. and Clifford, E. 2000). Rights and Ratios? Evaluating the Relationship Between Social Rights and Immigration. *Journal of Ethnic and Migration Studies*, 26(3), 417-47.
Grant, L. 1987. Applications by Husbands, Wives and Fiancé(e)s. *Immigration and Nationality Law and Practice*, July, 26-31.

Grant, L. and Martin, I. 1982. *Immigration Law and Practice.* London: Cobden Trust.

Grillo, R. 2007. Betwixt and Between: Trajectories and Projects of Transmigration. *Journal of Ethnic and Migration Studies*, 33(2), 199-217.

Griffiths, J. 1997. *The Politics of the Judiciary.* London: Fontana Press.

Grossbard-Shechtman, S. 2003. *Marriage and the Economy.* Cambridge: Cambridge University Press.

Halliday, S. 2000. The Influence of Judicial Review on Bureaucratic Decision-Making. *Public Law.* 110-122.

Hammar, T. 1990. *Democracy and the Nation-State: Aliens, Denizens and Citizens in a World of International Migration.* Aldershot: Avebury.

Hansen, R. 2000. *Citizenship and Immigration in Post-War Britain: The Institutional Origins of a Multicultural Nation.* Oxford: Oxford University Press.

Harlow, C. and Rawlings, R. 1997. *Law and Administration.* London: Butterworths.

Harris, C. 1983. *The Family and Industrial Society.* London: George Allen & Unwin.

Harris, N. 2002. *Thinking the Unthinkable: The Immigration Myth Exposed.* London and New York: IB Tauris.

Hassan, L. 2000. Deterrence Measures and the Preservation of Asylum in the United Kingdom and United States. *Journal of Refugee Studies*, 13(2), 184-204.

Hawkins, F. 1986. Immigration Law and Management in the United States, Canada and Australia, *Towards a Just Immigration Policy*, edited by A. Dummett. London: Cobden Trust.

Hawkins, K. 1984. *Environment and Enforcement: Regulation and the Social Regulation of Pollution.* Oxford: Clarendon Press.

Hawkins, K. 1994. The Use of Legal Discretion: Perspectives from Law and Social Science, in *The Uses of Discretion*, edited by K. Hawkins. Oxford: Clarendon Press.

Hawkins, K. 2002. *Law as Last Resort.* Oxford: Oxford University Press.

Heath, T., Jeffries, R. and Pearce, S. 2006. *Asylum Statistics United Kingdom 2005.* Statistical Bulletin 14/06. London: Home Office.

Hildyard, N. 2003. Rowthorn is Wrong. *Prospect Magazine*, 84.

Hollifield, J. 1992. *Immigrants, Markets and States: The Political Economy of Postwar Europe.* Cambridge, MA and London: Harvard University Press.

Hollifield, J. 2000. Migration and the New International Order: The Missing Regime, in *Managing Migration: Time for a New International Regime*, edited by B. Ghosh. Oxford: Oxford University Press, 75-109.

Holmes, C. 1988. *John Bulls Island: Immigration and British Society 1871-1971.* London: Macmillan.

Home Affairs Select Committee. 2006a. *Immigration Control: Fifth Report of Session 2005-6, Volume 1.* HC 775-I, London: HMSO.

Home Affairs Select Committee. 2006b. *Immigration Control: Fifth Report of Session 2005-6, Volume 2.* HC 775-II, London: HMSO.

Home Affairs Select Committee. 2006c. *Immigration Control: Fifth Report of Session 2005-6, Volume 3.* HC 775-III, London: HMSO.

Home Office. 1998. *Fairer, Faster, Firmer: A Modern Approach to Immigration and Asylum.* Cmnd. 4018, London: HMSO.

Home Office. 2002. *Secure Borders, Safe Haven.* Cmnd. 5387, London: HMSO.

Home Office. 2003. *Control of Immigration: Statistics United Kingdom 2002.* Cmnd. 6053, London: HMSO.

Home Office. 2004. *Control of Immigration: Statistics United Kingdom 2003.* Statistical Bulletin 12/04, London: Home Office.

Home Office. 2005a. *Control of Immigration: Statistics United Kingdom 2004.* Statistical Bulletin 14/05, London: Home Office.

Home Office. 2005b. *Controlling Our Borders: Making Migration Work for Britain.* Cmnd. 6472, London: HMSO.

Home Office. 2006. *Control of Immigration: Statistics United Kingdom 2005.* Cmnd. 6904, London: HMSO.

Home Office. 2007. *Control of Immigration Statistics: United Kingdom 2006.* Cmnd 7197, London: HMSO.

Home Office. 2009. *Control of Immigration Statistics United Kingdom 2008.* Statistical Bulletin 14/09. London: Home Office.

Home Office. 2010a. *Control of Immigration Statistics United Kingdom 2009.* Statistical Bulletin 15/10, London: Home Office.

Home Office. 2010b. *Control of Immigration 2009: Supplementary Tables.* London: Home Office.

Home Office/Foreign and Commonwealth Office. 2007. *Securing the UK Border: Our Vision and Strategy for the Future.* London: Home Office.

Home Office/UK Border Agency. 2008a. *A Strong New Force at the Border* London: Home Office.

Home Office/UK Border Agency. 2008b. *UK Border Agency Business Plan April 2008-March 2011.* London: Home Office.

Home Office/UK Border Agency. 2009. *UK Border Agency Business Plan April 2009-March 2010.* London: Home Office.

House of Commons Home Affairs Committee. 1982. *Immigration from the Sub-Continent.* Cmnd. 8725, London: HMSO.

House of Commons Home Affairs Committee. 2008. *Domestic Violence, Forced Marriage and 'Honour'-Based Violence, Volume 1.* Sixth Report of Session 2007-8. HC 263-I, London: HMSO.

Howard, E. 2008. Race and Racism: Why Does European Law Have Difficulty with Definitions? *International Journal of Comparative Labour Law and Industrial Relations.* 24(1), 5-29.

Human Rights Watch. 2008. *The Netherlands: Discrimination in the Name of Integration – Migrants Rights under the Integration Abroad Act*: http://www.hrw.org/backgrounder/2008/netherlands0508/ (accessed 12 June 2011).

Hunter, A. and Wray, H. 2010. Members of the Family, in *Free Movement of Workers: UK Implementation of Free Movement of Workers 2009/10*, edited by E. Guild. Brussels: European Commission.

Hussain, B. 1994. Validity of Marriage: The Burden of Proof in Context. *Immigration and Nationality Law and Practice*, 8(1), 18-20.

Imman Ali, M. 1987. Dower/Doweries in Bangladesh and Primary Purpose. *Immigration and Nationality Law and Practice*, January, 125.

Immigration Advisory Service. 2004. *Asylum and Immigration (Treatment of Claimants etc) Bill: Briefing on Third Reading Debate, House of Lords, Tuesday 6th July 2004*. London: Immigration Advisory Service.

Immigration and Nationality Directorate. 2006. *Fair, Effective, Transparent and Trusted: Rebuilding Confidence in our Immigration System*. London: Immigration and Nationality Directorate.

Independent Asylum Commission. 2008. *Fit for Purpose Yet?* London: Independent Asylum Commission.

Jackson, J. 1986. *Aspects of Modern Sociology*. London: Longman.

Jackson, K. and Bennett, A. 1998. *Control of Immigration: Statistics United Kingdom, Second Half and Year 1997*. Statistical Bulletin 13/98, London: Home Office.

Jackson, K. and Chilton, T. 1999. *Control of Immigration: Statistics United Kingdom, Second Half and Year 1998*. Statistical Bulletin 11/99, London: Home Office.

Jackson, K. and McGregor, R. 2000. *Control of Immigration: Statistics United Kingdom, Second Half and Year 1999*. Statistical Bulletin 11/00, London: Home Office.

Jaffey, A. 1978. The Essential Validity of Marriage in the English Conflict of Laws. *Modern Law Review*, 41 (January), 38-50.

Jastram, K. 2003. Family Unity, in *Migration and International Legal Norms*, edited by T. Aleinikoff and V. Chetail. The Hague: TMC Asser Press, 185-202.

Jenkins, R. 1991. *A Life at the Centre*. London: Macmillan.

John, A. 2003. *Family Reunification for Migrants and Refugees: A Forgotten Human Right?* EMA thesis, European Inter-University Centre for Human Rights and Democratisation (Venice-Coimbra): http://www.fd.uc.pt/igc/hrc_investigacao_uk.html (accessed 29 January 2011).

Joint Committee on Human Rights. 2004. *Asylum and Immigration (Treatment of Claimants etc) Bill: New Clauses (Fourteenth Report of Session 2003-4)*. HL 130/HC 828, London: HMSO.

Joint Council for the Welfare of Immigrants. 1987. *Immigration from the Indian Sub-Continent: JCWI Briefing on the Select Committee Report*. London: Joint Council for the Welfare of Immigrants.

Jones, J. 1947. *British Nationality Law and Practice*. Oxford: Clarendon Press.

Jones, P. and Shah, S. 1980. Arranged Marriages: A Sample Survey of the Asian Case. *New Community* 8(3), 339-43.

Jones, R. and Welhengama, G. 2000. *Ethnic Minorities in English Law.* Stoke-on-Trent: Trentham Books.

Joppke, C. 1998. Why Liberal States Accept Unwanted Immigration. *World Politics*, 50 (January), 266-93.

Joppke, C. 2004. The Retreat of Multiculturalism in the Liberal State. *British Journal of Sociology*, 55(2), 237-57.

Judge, D. 2004. Whatever Happened to Parliamentary Democracy in the United Kingdom? *Parliamentary Affairs*, 57(3), 682-701.

Juss, S. 1993. *Immigration, Nationality and Citizenship.* London and New York: Mansell.

Juss, S. 1997. *Discretion and Deviation in the Administration of Immigration Control*, London: Sweet & Maxwell.

Juss, S. 2004. Free Movement and the World Order. *International Journal of Refugee Law*, 16(3), 289-335.

Juss, S. 2006. *International Migration & Global Justice.* Aldershot: Ashgate.

Kaushal, R. 1986. The Continuing Paradigm of Immigration Control: Institutional Racism British Style, in *Towards a Just Immigration Policy*, edited by A. Dummett. London: Cobden Trust.

King, D. 1999. *In the Name of Liberalism: Illiberal Social Policy in the USA and Britain.* Oxford: Oxford University Press.

Kirkhope Commission on Immigration. 2004. *Building a Fair Immigration System*: http://www.conservatives.com/pdf/kirkhopecommission.pdf (accessed 22 June 2011).

Klausen, J. 2000. Other People. *Prospect Magazine*, 58: http://www.prospectmagazine.co.uk/2000/12/otherpeople (accessed 21 June 2011).

Klug, F. 1989. Oh To Be in England: The British Case Study, in *Woman-Nation-State*, edited by N. Yuval Davis and F. Anthias. London: Macmillan.

Koehn, P. and Rosenau, J. 2002. Transnational Competence in an Emerging Epoch. *International Studies Perspectives*, 3, 105-27.

Kofman, E. 2004. Family-Related Migration: A Critical Review of European Studies. *Journal of Ethnic and Migration Studies*, 30(2), 243-62.

Kofman, E. and Meetoo, V. 2008. Family Migration, in *World Migration Report 2008*, edited by the International Organisation of Migration. Geneva: International Organisation of Migration, 151-72.

Kofman, E. et al. 2000. *Gender and International Migration in Europe.* London: Routledge.

Kymlicka, W. 1995. Introduction, in *The Rights of Minority Cultures*, edited by W. Kymlicka. Oxford: Oxford University Press, 1-27.

Kymlicka, W. and Banting K. 2006. Immigration, Multiculturalism and the Welfare State. *Ethics and International Affairs*, 20(3), 281-304.

Lal, S. and Wilson, A. 1986. *But My Cows Aren't Coming to England*, Manchester: Manchester Law Centre.

Lambert, H. 2006. The EU Asylum Qualification Directive, its Impact on the Jurisprudence of the United Kingdom and International Law. *International and Comparative Law Quarterly.* 55(January), 161-92.

Landa, M. 1911. *The Alien Problem and its Remedy.* London: PS King & Son.

Layton-Henry, Z. 1992. *The Politics of Immigration: Immigration, 'Race' and 'Race Relations' in Post-War Britain.* Oxford: Blackwell.

Legomsky, S. 1987. *Immigration and the Judiciary: Law and Politics in Britain and America.* Oxford: Clarendon Press.

Leigh, I. 2002. Taking Rights Proportionately: Judicial Review, the Human Rights Act and Strasbourg. *Public Law*, 265-87.

Leigh, S. 1986. Family Settlement Problems, in *Towards a Just Immigration Policy*, edited by A. Dummett. London: Cobden Trust.

Levitt, P. 2004. *The Transnational Turn in Migration Studies.* Geneva: Global Commission on International Migration.

Levitt, P. 2009. Roots and Routes: Understanding the Lives of the Second Generation Transnationally. *Journal of Ethnic and Migration Studies*, 35(7), 1225-42.

Lewis, G. 2005. Welcome to the Margins: Diversity, Tolerance and Policies of Exclusion. *Ethnic and Racial Studies*, 28(3), 536-58.

Lewis, G. and Neal, S. 2005. Introduction: Contemporary Political Contexts, Changing Terrains and Revisited Discourses. *Ethnic and Racial Studies*, 28(3), 423-44.

Lindsley, F. 2005. *Report by the Independent Monitor (Immigration and Asylum Act 1999).* London: UKVisas.

Lindsley, F. 2006. 'Monitoring the UK Entry Clearance System', in P. Shah and W. Menski, eds, *Migrations, Diasporas and Legal Systems in Europe.* London: Routledge Cavendish.

Lister, M. 2010. Immigration, Association, and the Family. *Law and Philosophy*, 29, 717-45.

Lloyd, J. 2002. Poor Whites. *Prospect Magazine*, 75.

Loveland, I. 1994. Irrelevant Considerations? The Role of Administrative Law in Determining the Local Connection of Homeless Persons, in *Administrative Law and Government Action*, edited by G. Richardson and H. Genn. Oxford: Clarendon Press.

Lyon, A. 1975. *Immigration from the Sub-Continent – Report from Mr Lyon to the Home Secretary on his Visit to Bangladesh, India and Pakistan in January 1975.* London: Home Office.

Macdonald, I. 2001. *Immigration Law and Practice in the United Kingdom.* London: Butterworths.

Macdonald, I. 2008. ECHR Article 8: Bringing the UK Courts Back in Step with Strasbourg. *Journal of Immigration Asylum and Nationality Law*, 22(4), 293-302.

Macdonald, I. and Blake, N. 1991. *Immigration Law and Practice in the United Kingdom.* London: Butterworths.

Macdonald, I. and Blake, N. 1995. *Immigration Law and Practice in the United Kingdom.* London: Butterworths.

Macdonald, I. and Webber, F. 2005. *Immigration Law and Practice in the United Kingdom.* London: Butterworths.

Mallourides, E. and Turner, G. 2002. *Control of Immigration: Statistics United Kingdom 2001.* Statistical Bulletin 11/02. London: Home Office.

Marrington, D. 1985. Legal Decisions Affecting Ethnic Minorities and Discrimination. *New Community*, XII(3), 536-45.

Martin, I. 1975. *Entry Certificate Delays in Dacca: Report of a Visit to Bangladesh.* London: Joint Council for the Welfare of Immigrants.

Mau, S., Mewes, J. and Zimmerman, A. 2008. Cosmopolitan Attitudes Through Transnational Social Practices? *Global Networks*, 8(1), 1-24.

Mayhew, K. 1986. Immigration and the Economy in *Towards a Just Immigration Policy*, edited by A. Dummett. London: Cobden Trust.

Mayss, A. 2000. Recognition of Foreign Divorces: Unwarrantable Ethnocentrism, in *Ethnic Minorities, Their Families and the Law*, edited by J. Murphy. Oxford: Hart Publishing.

McCrudden, C. 2006. Legal Research and the Social Sciences, *Law Quarterly Review*, 122, 633-50.

McGhee, D. 2009. The Paths to Citizenship: A Critical Examination of Immigration Policy in Britain since 2001. *Patterns of Prejudice*, 43(1), 41-64.

McGoldrick, D. 2005. Multiculturalism and its Discontents. *Human Rights Law Review*, 5(1), 27-56.

McKee, R. 1999. Primary Purpose by the Backdoor? A Critical Look at 'Intention to Live Together'. *Immigration and Nationality Law and Practice*, 13(1), 3-5.

McKee, R. 2005. More Than It Can Chew. *Immigration, Asylum and Nationality Law*, 19(4), 254-7.

McKee, R. 2008. Party Time. *Journal of Immigration Asylum and Nationality Law*, 22(2), 154-7.

McNair, A. 1919. British Nationality and Alien Status in Time of War. *Law Quarterly Review*, 35, 213-32.

Menski, W. 1994. Family Migration and the New Immigration Rules. *Immigration and Nationality Law and Practice*, 8(4), 112-23.

Menski, W. 1999. South Asian Women in Britain, Family Integrity and the Primary Purpose Rule, in *Ethnicity, Gender and Social Change*, edited by T. Barot, H. Bradley and S. Fenton. Basingstoke: Macmillan Press, 81-98.

Menski, W. 2001. *Modern Indian Family Law.* Richmond, Surrey: Curzon Press.

Menski, W. 2007. Dodgy Asians or Dodgy Lawyers? The Story of H. *Journal of Immigration, Asylum and Nationality Law*, 21(4), 284-94.

Migration Watch. 2004. *Immigration and Marriage: The Problem of Continuous Migration.*: http://www.migrationwatchuk.com/Briefingpapers/other/Immigration_Marriage.asp (accessed 12 June 2011).

Modood, T. 2007. *Multiculturalism: A Civic Idea.* Cambridge and Malden, MA: Polity Press.

Mole, N. 1987. *Immigration: Family Entry and Settlement.* Bristol: Jordan & Sons.

Morris, L. 2002. Britains Asylum and Immigration Regime: The Shifting Contours of Rights. *Journal of Ethnic Minority Studies*, 28(3), 409-25.

Murphy, J. 2000a. Rationality and Cultural Pluralism in the Non-Recognition of Foreign Marriages. *International and Comparative Law Quarterly*, 49 (July), 643-59.

Murphy, J. 2000b. The Discretionary Refusal of Recognition of Foreign Marriages, in *Ethnic Minorities, their Families and the Law*, edited by J. Murphy. Oxford: Hart Publishing.

National Audit Office. 2004. *Visa Entry to the United Kingdom: The Entry Clearance Operation*, HC 367, London: HMSO.

Nicol, D. 2006. Law and Politics After the Human Rights Act. *Public Law*, 722-51.

North, M. 1975. Recognition of Extra-Judicial Divorces. *Law Quarterly Review.* 91 (January), 36-67.

Office for National Statistics. 1999. *Social Trends 29.* London: Stationery Office.

Okin, S. 1999. Is Multiculturalism Bad for Women?, in *Is Multiculturalism Bad for Women?*, edited by S. Okin. Princeton: Princeton University Press.

Okin, S. 2005. Multiculturalism and Feminism: No Simple Question, No Simple Answer, in *Minorities within Minorities: Equality, Rights and Diversity*, edited by A. Eisenberg. and J. Spinner-Halev. Cambridge: Cambridge University Press, 67-89.

Page Baldwin, M. 2001. Subject to Empire: Married Women and the British Nationality and Status of Aliens Act. *Journal of British Studies*, 40(4), 522-56.

Palriwala, R. and Uberoi, P. 2008a. Introduction, in *Marriage, Migration and Gender*, edited by R. Palriwala and P. Uberoi. Delhi: Sage Publications, 7-20.

Palriwala, R. and Uberoi, P. 2008b, Exploring the Links: Gender Issues in Marriage and Migration, in *Marriage, Migration and Gender*, edited by R. Palriwala and P. Uberoi. Delhi: Sage Publications, 23-60.

Pannick, D. and Young Justice. 1993. *The Primary Purpose Rule: A Rule with No Purpose.* London: Justice.

Parekh, B. 1995. The Concept of National Identity. *New Community*, 21(2), 255-68.

Parekh, B. 2000. *Rethinking Multiculturalism: Cultural Diversity and Political Theory.* Basingstoke: Macmillan.

Parekh, B. 2005. British Commitments. *Prospect Magazine*, 14.

Paul, K. 1997. *Whitewashing Britain: Race and Citizenship in the Postwar Era.* Ithaca, NY and London: Cornell University Press.

Peach, C. 2006. Muslims in the 2001 Census of England and Wales: Gender and Economic Disadvantage. *Ethnic and Racial Studies*, 29(4), 629-55.

Pearl, D. 1972. Muslim Marriages in English Law. *Cambridge Law Journal*, 30(1), 120-43.

Pearl, D. 1974/1975. Foreign Marriages and Divorces: Recent English Legislation. *New Community*, IV(1), 119-21.

Pearl, D. 1976. The Legal Rights of Muslim Women in India, Pakistan and Bangladesh. *New Community*, V(1-2), 68-74.

Pearl, D. 1986. *Family Law and the Immigrant Communities.* Bristol: Jordan & Sons.

Pearl, D. and Menski, W. 1998. *Muslim Family Law.* London: Sweet & Maxwell.

Phillips, A. 2003. When Culture Means Gender: Issues of Cultural Defence in the English Courts. *Modern Law Review*, 66 (July), 510-31.

Phillips, A. and Dustin, M. 2004. UK Initiatives on Forced Marriage: Regulation, Dialogue and Exit. *Political Studies.* 52, 531-52.

Phillips, A. and Saharso, S. 2008. The Rights of Women and the Crisis of Multiculturalism. *Ethnicities*, 8(3), 291-301.

Pilkington, M. 1988. Transnational Divorces under the Family Law Act 1986. *International and Comparative Law Quarterly*, 37 (January), 131-43.

Piper, N. 2005. *Gender and Migration.* Geneva: Global Commission on International Migration.

Plender, R. 1988. *International Migration Law.* Dordrecht and London: Nijhoff.

Poulter, S. 1976. *Hyde v Hyde*: A Reappraisal. *International and Comparative Law Quarterly*, 25, 475-508.

Poulter, S. 1986. *English Law and Ethnic Minority Customs.* London: Butterworths.

Poulter, S. 1987. Ethnic Minority Customs, English Law and Human Rights. *International and Comparative Law Quarterly*, 36, 589-615.

Powell, P. 1990. Custom and Tradition in Primary Purpose Cases: Does the ECO Really Know Best? *Immigration and Nationality Law and Practice*, July, 107-9.

Powell, P. 1992. *Notes for UK Immigration Lawyers on Custom and Practice in the Indian Sub-Continent.* London: P. Powell.

Powell, P. 1993a. *Immigration Cases: Volume 1.* London: P. Powell.

Powell, P. 1993b. *Immigration Cases: Volume 2.* London: P. Powell.

Public Accounts Committee. 2005. *Seventh Report: Foreign and Commonwealth Office: Visa Entry to the United Kingdom: The Entry Clearance Operation.* HC 312 (Session 2004-5), London: HMSO.

Rawlings, R. 2005. Review, Revenge and Retreat. *Modern Law Review*, 68(3), 378-410.

Razack, S. 2004. Imperilled Muslim Women, Dangerous Muslim Men and Civilised Europeans: Legal and Social Responses to Forced Marriages. *Feminist Legal Studies*, 12, 129-74.

Reed, A. 1996. Extra-Judicial Divorces since Berkovits. *Family Law*, February, 100-103.

Rees, E. 1989. Recent Judicial Developments on 'Primary Purpose'. *Immigration and Nationality Law and Practice*, 3(4), 92-4.

Reitmann, O. 2005. On Exit, in *Minorities within Minorities: Equality, Rights and Diversity*, edited by A. Eisenberg. and J. Spinner-Halev. Cambridge: Cambridge University Press, 189-208.

Roche, T. 1969. *The Key in the Lock: A History of Immigration Control in England from 1066 to the Present Day.* London: John Murray.

Rogers, N. 2003. Immigration and the European Convention on Human Rights: Are New Principles Emerging? *European Human Rights Law Review*, 1, 53-64.

Roggeband, C. and Verloo, M. 2007. Dutch Women are Liberated, Migrant Women are a Problem: The Evolution of Policy Frames on Gender and Migration in the Netherlands, 1995-2005. *Social Policy and Administration*, 41(3), 271-88.

Rowthorn, B. 2003. Migration Limits, *Prospect Magazine*, 83.

Rowthorn, B. 2006. Numbers Matter, *Prospect Magazine*, 125.

Runnymede Trust. 1974. *The Crisis of the Pakistani Dependants.* Briefing Paper 2/74, London: Runnymede Trust.

Runnymede Trust. 1977. *Appeal Dismissed: The Final Report of the Investigation into Immigration Control Procedures in the Indian Sub-Continent.* London: Runnymede Trust.

Ryan, B. and Mitsilegas, V. 2010. *Extraterritorial Immigration Control: Legal Challenges.* Leiden and Boston: Martinus Nijhoff.

Sachdeva, S. 1993. *The Primary Purpose Rule in British Immigration Law.* Stoke-on-Trent: Trentham Books.

Sales, R. 2005. 'Secure Borders, Safe Haven': A Contradiction in Terms. *Ethnic and Racial Studies*, 28(3), 445-62.

Salt, J. 2005. Migration Matters. *Prospect Magazine*, 110.

Salt, J. 2009. *International Migration and the UK. Annual Report of the UK SOPEMI Correspondent to the OECD.* London: Migration Research Unit (UCL).

Samad, Y. and Eade, J. 2002. *Community Perceptions of Forced Marriage.* London: Foreign and Commonwealth Office.

Sassen, S. 1996. *Losing Control? Sovereignty in an Age of Globalisation.* New York: Columbia University Press.

Scannell, R. 1987. No Love at First Sight for Indians. *Immigration and Nationality Law and Practice*, 6 April.

Scannell, R. 1989. Recent Developments in Immigration Law. *Legal Action*, 15-16 August.

Scannell, R. 1992a. Primary Purpose: The End of Judicial Sympathy. *Immigration and Nationality Law and Practice*, 6(1), 3-6.

Scannell, R. 1992b. Recent Developments in Immigration Law. *Legal Action*, May.

Scannell, R. 1993a. Recent Developments in Immigration Law. *Legal Action*, February.

Scannell, R. 1993b. Recent Developments in Immigration Law. *Legal Action*, May.

Schmidt, G. 2011. Law and Identity: Transnational Arranged Marriages and the Boundaries of Danishness. *Journal of Ethnic and Migration Studies*, 37(2). 257-75.

Sciortino, G. 1991. Immigration into Europe and Public Policy: Do Stops Really Work? *New Community*, 18(1), 89-99.

Sciortino, G. 2000. Towards a Political Sociology of Entry Policies: Conceptual Problems and Theoretical Proposals. *Journal of Ethnic and Migration Studies*, 26(2), 213-28.

Seaward, P. and Silk, P. 2003. The House of Commons, in *The British Constitution in the Twentieth Century*, edited by V. Bogdanor. Oxford: Oxford University Press, 139-89.

Seddon, D. 2008. Case Comment: *Chikwamba v Secretary of State for Home Department*, *Journal of Immigration Asylum and Nationality Law* 22(4), 366-9.

Select Committee. 1923. *Select Committee Appointed to Join With a Committee of the House of Commons on the Nationality of Married Women – Report.* London: Stationery Office.

Sen, P. 2005. 'Crimes of Honour', Value and Meaning, in *Honour: Crimes, Paradigms and Violence Against Women*, edited by L. Welchman and S. Hossain. London and New York: Zed Books, 42-63.

Shah, P. 2000. *Refugees, Race and the Legal Concept of Asylum in Britain.* London: Cavendish Publishing.

Shah, P. 2003. Attitudes to Polygamy in English law. *International and Comparative Law Quarterly*, 52 (April), 369-400.

Shah, P. 2005. *Legal Pluralism in Conflict: Coping with Cultural Diversity in Law.* London and Portland, Oregon: GlassHouse Press.

Shah, P. 2008. Rituals of Recognition: Ethnic Minority Marriages in British Legal Systems, in *Law and Ethnic Plurality: Socio-Legal Perspectives*, edited by P. Shah. Leiden: Martinus Nijhoff, 177-202.

Shah, P. 2010. Trans-jurisdictional Marriage and Family Reunification for Refugees in the United Kingdom. *Istanbul Kűltűr Űniversitesi Hukuk Fakűltesi Dergisi* 9(2), 93-113.

Shah, P. 2011a. When South Asians Marry Trans-jurisdictionally: Some Reflections on Immigration Cases by an 'Expert', in *Cultural Expertise and Litigation: Patterns, Conflicts, Narratives*, edited by L. Holden. London: Routledge.

Shah, P. 2011b. Transnational Family Relations in Migration Contexts: British Variations on European Themes. http://www.religareproject.eu/content/transnational-family-relations-migration-contexts-british-variations-european-themes (accessed 29 July 2011).

Shah, S. 1979. Asian Marriages: A Case of White Propaganda. *New Society*, 18 October.

Shaw, A. 2001. Kinship, Cultural Preference and Immigration: Consanguineous Marriage amongst British Pakistanis. *Journal of the Royal Anthropological Institute*, 17(2), 315-34.

Shaw, K. 2002. Globalisation, Citizenship and the Role of the State: Can a Consensus Be Reached? *International Politics*, 39 (December), 511-17.

Siddiqui, D. (2005), Of Consent and Contradiction: Forced Marriages in Bangladesh, in *Honour: Crimes, Paradigms and Violence Against Women*, edited by L. Welchman and S. Hossain. London and New York: Zed Books, 282-307.

Siddiqui, H. 2005. 'There is No Honour in Domestic Violence, Only Shame': Womens' Struggles Against 'Honour' Crimes in the UK, in *Honour: Crimes, Paradigms and Violence Against Women*, edited by L. Welchman and S. Hossain. London and New York: Zed Books, 263-81.

Singh, R. 2001. *Report by the Independent Monitor*, London: Joint Entry Clearance Unit.

Smith, D. 2004. An 'Untied' Research Agenda for Family Migration: Loosening the 'Shackles' of the Past. *Journal of Ethnic and Migration Studies*, 30(2), 263-82.

Smith, J. 1984. Divided by the Rules. *New Society*, October, 36-40.

Solomos, J. 1989. *Race and Racism in Contemporary Britain*. London: Macmillan.

Somerville, W. 2007. *Immigration under New Labour*. Bristol: Policy Press.

Sondhi, R. 1987. *Divided Families: British Immigration Control in the Indian Sub-Continent*. London: Runnymede Trust.

Southall Black Sisters 2001. *Forced Marriage: Interim Report*. London: Southall Black Sisters.

Soysal, Y. 1994. *Limits of Citizenship: Migrants and Postnational Membership in Europe*. Chicago and London: University of Chicago Press.

Spencer, I. 1997. *British Immigration Policy Since 1939: The Making of Multi-Racial Britain*. London and New York: Routledge.

Spencer, S. 1995. *Migrants, Refugees and the Boundaries of Citizenship*. Swansea: Institute for Public Policy Research..

Stevens, D. 2001. The Immigration and Asylum Act 1999: A Missed Opportunity. *Modern Law Review*, 64 (May), 413-38.

Stevens, D. 2004. *UK Asylum Law and Policy: Contemporary and Historical Perspectives*. London: Sweet & Maxwell.

Stevens, R. 1999. A loss of Innocence? Judicial Independence and the Separation of Powers. *Oxford Journal of Legal Studies*, 19 (Autumn), 365-402.

Stone Sweet, A. 1999. Judicialization and the Construction of Governance. *Comparative Political Studies*, 32(2), 147-84.

Stone Sweet, A. 2000. *Governing with Judges: Constitutional Politics in Europe*. Oxford: Oxford University Press.

Supperstone, M. and O'Dempsey, D. 1994. *Immigration: The Law and Practice*. London: Longman.

Supperstone, M. and O'Dempsey, D. 1996. *Immigration and Asylum*. London: Pearson.

Tamanaha, B. 2001. *A General Jurisprudence of Law and Society*. Oxford: Oxford University Press.

Temple, B. and Moran, R. 2005. *Learning to Live Together: Developing Communities Containing Dispersed Refugee People Seeking Asylum*. York: Joseph Rowntree Foundation.

Thomas, R. 2003. The Impact of Judicial Review on Asylum. *Public Law*, 479-510.

Thym, D. 2008. Respect for Private and Family Life under Article 8 ECHR in Immigration Cases: A Human Right to Regularize Illegal Stay? *International and Comparative Law Quarterly*, 57(1), 97-112.

Tilly, J. 1999. Moral Arguments for Cultural Relativism. *Netherlands Quarterly of Human Rights.* 17(1), 31-41.

Toner, H. 2006. New Regulations Implementing Directive 2004/38. *Immigration, Asylum and Nationality Law*, 20(3), 158-78.

Travers, M. 1999. *The British Immigration Courts: A Study of Law and Politics.* Bristol: Policy Press.

UK Border Agency. 2008a. *Marriage Visas: The Way Forward.* London: UK Border Agency.

UK Border Agency 2008b. *The Path to Citizenship: Next Steps in Reforming the Immigration System – Government Response to Consultation.* London: UK Border Agency.

UKIAS 1985. *Interviews Conducted by Entry Clearance Officers Overseas.* Paper prepared for submission to the Minister of State. London: UKIAS.

Van Amersfoort, H. 1996. Migration: The Limits of Government Control. *New Community*, 22(2), 243-57.

Van Dyke, V. 1985. *Human Rights, Ethnicity and Discrimination.* Westport, CT and London: Greenwood Press.

Van Walsum, S. 2008. *The Family and the Nation: Dutch Family Migration Policy in the Context of Changing Family Norms.* Newcastle-upon-Tyne: Cambridge Scholars Publishing.

Vertovec, S. 2001. *Transnational Challenges to the New Multiculturalism.* Paper presented to the ASA Conference, University of Sussex, 30 March-2 April 2001.

Vertovec, S. 2007. Super-Diversity and its Implications. *Ethnic and Racial Studies*, 30(6), 1024-54.

Vertovec, S. 2009. *Transnationalism.* London and New York: Routledge.

Vincenzi, C. 1992. Extra-Statutory Ministerial Discretion in Immigration Law. *Public Law*, 300-321.

Vincenzi, C. and Marrington, D. 1992. *Immigration Law: The Rules Explained.* London: Sweet & Maxwell.

Vine, J. 2009a. *Inspection Report of the Visa Section in Abuja.* London: Independent Chief Inspector of the UK Border Agency.

Vine, J. 2009b. *Inspection Report of the Visa Section in Rome.* London: Independent Chief Inspector of the UK Border Agency.

Vine, J. 2010a. *An Inspection of Entry Clearance in Abu Dhabi and Islamabad.* London: Independent Chief Inspector of the UK Border Agency.

Vine, J. 2010b. *Annual Report 2009-10.* London: Independent Chief Inspector of the UK Border Agency.

Walzer, M. 1983. *Spheres of Justice.* Oxford: Martin Robertson.

Webb, D. 1986. Village Enquiries in the Indian Sub-Continent. *Immigration and Nationality Law and Practice*, April, 16-21.

Williams, G. 1947. The Legal Unity of Husband and Wife. *Modern Law Review*, 10, 16-31.

Wilson, G. 2000. The Status of Religious Weddings in English Law. *Family Law*, June, 437-8.

Winder, R. 2004. *Bloody Foreigners*. London: Little, Brown.

Wintermute, R. 2006. The Human Rights Acts First Five Years: Too Strong, Too Weak or Just Right? *Kings Law Journal*, 17, 209-27.

Wolton, S. 2006. Immigration Policy and the 'Crisis of British Values'. *Citizenship Studies*, 10(4), 453-67.

Woodbridge, J. 2005. *Sizing the Unauthorised (Illegal) Migrant Population in the United Kingdom in 2001*. Home Office Online Report 29/05.

Woodfield, K. et al. 2007. *Exploring the Decision-Making of Immigration Officers: A Research Study Examining Non-EEA Passenger Stops and Refusals at UK Ports*. Home Office Online Reports 01/07, London: Home Office.

Wray, H. 2006a. An Ideal Husband? Marriages of Convenience, Moral Gate-Keeping and Immigration to the UK. *European Journal of Migration and Law*, 8(3), 303-20.

Wray, H. 2006b. Guiding the Gatekeepers: Entry Clearance for Settlement on the Indian Sub-Continent. *Journal of Immigration, Asylum and Nationality Law*, 20(2), 112-29.

Wray, H. 2006c. Hidden Purpose: Ethnic Minority Marriages and the Immigration Rules, in *Migrations, Diasporas and Legal Systems in Europe*, edited by P. Shah and W. Menski. London: Routledge-Cavendish, 303-20.

Wray, H. 2006d. The Aliens Act and the Immigration Dilemma. *Journal of Law and Society*, 33(2), 302-23.

Wray, H. 2009a. Moulding the Migrant Family. *Legal Studies*, 29(4), 592-618.

Wray, H. 2009b. The Points Based System: A Blunt Instrument? *Journal of Immigration Asylum and Nationality Law*, 23(3), 231-51.

Wray, H. 2011. *Deprivation of Citizenship and Immigration Control in the UK*. Paper delivered to Workshop on Deprivation of Citizenship, Radboud University, Nijmegen, 18-19 January.

Wray, H. Forthcoming. Any Time, Any Place, Anywhere: Entry Clearance, Marriage Migration and the Border, in *Transnational Marriage: New Perspectives from Europe and Beyond*, edited by K. Charsley. Abingdon: Routledge.

Wray, H. and Quayum, M. 1999. Entry Clearance Applications for Spouses Where Sponsor is on Benefit. *Immigration and Nationality Law and Practice*, 13(4), 133-5.

Yilmaz, I. 2002. The Challenge of Post-Modern Legality and Muslim Legal Pluralism. *Journal of Ethnic and Migration Studies*, 28(2), 343-54.

Young, J. 1987. The Recognition of Extra-Judicial Divorces in the United Kingdom. *Legal Studies*, 7, 78-91.

Yuval-Davis, N. 2006. Belonging and the Politics of Belonging. *Patterns of Prejudice*, 40(3), 197-214.

Yuval-Davis N. and Anthias, F. 1989. Introduction, in *Woman-Nation-State*, edited by N. Yuval-Davis and F. Anthias. London: Macmillan.

Yuval-Davis, N., Floya, A. and Kofman, E. 2005. Secure Borders, Safe Haven and the Gendered Politics of Belonging: Beyond Social Cohesion. *Ethnic and Racial Studies*, 28(3), 513-35.

Zetter, R. Griffiths, D. and Sigona, N. 2006. *Immigration, Social Cohesion and Social Capital: What are the Links?* York: Joseph Rowntree Foundation.

Index

www.ingramcontent.com/pod-product-compliance
Ingram Content Group UK Ltd.
Pitfield, Milton Keynes, MK11 3LW, UK
UKHW010955180926
475701UK00004B/379
9781138255845